Grateful Prey

Grateful Prey

Rock Cree Human-Animal Relationships

Robert A. Brightman

UNIVERSITY OF CALIFORNIA PRESS

Berkeley / Los Angeles / Oxford

University of California Press
Berkeley and Los Angeles, California

University of California Press
Oxford, England

Library of Congress Cataloging-in-Publication Data

Brightman, Robert Alain, 1950–
   Grateful prey: Rock Cree human-animal relationships / Robert A.
Brightman.
      p. cm.
   Includes bibliographical references and index.
   ISBN 0-520-07053-4
   1. Cree Indians—Religion and mythology.   2. Cree Indians—
Hunting.   3. Human-animal relationships—Manitoba.   I. Title.
E99.C88B75   1993
299'.783—dc20   91-39832
                                                                      CIP

Printed in the United States of America

1 2 3 4 5 6 7 8 9

The paper used in this publication meets the minimum requirements
of American National Standard for Information Sciences—
Permanence of Paper for Printed Library Materials, ANSI Z39.48-
1984 ⊗

To Johnny Bighetty, 1934–1980, who once stood up at a table in the Leaf Rapids beer hall and announced publicly, "I like every-body! Cree, Whiteman, Chipewyan . . . even RCMP!"

Contents

Tables

Preface

This first section of the book is for the people about whom it is written, especially for their children. Some white people use the word "civilization" only to talk about their own kind of society and use words like "primitive" or "savage" to talk about people like the Crees who, up until quite recently, were living mostly from hunting, trapping, and fishing. This kind of thinking is, of course, *mīyi*. Every people has their own kind of civilization. So right here I will repeat something that an old friend of mine said about Cree people on another reserve: the Crees were so damn civilized that it was hard for him to go back to New York City in the United States after working with them. Since the time of the earliest contact with whites, the older Cree beliefs about the spiritual world—and many other practices in traditional Cree society as well—have been systematically ridiculed and attacked. The older beliefs have been called "superstition" and even talked about as a form of devil worship. Today, many Cree people are Catholics, and some may think that the older spiritual life that existed before Catholicism is best forgotten and left alone. Some Cree people told me that before the Catholic priests came in the late 1800s, the people had no religion at all. Other people thought that it was a good idea to have a book about the Cree people's traditional spiritual life, and this book contains what they told me about it both in the past and in the present, especially as it concerned the animals and the hunting and trapping life. It was sometimes hard for me to understand, and there are probably many mistakes. I hope a Missinippi Cree will come along and write a better book. What

I especially want to repeat here is what some Cree people told me: the older spiritual beliefs were not "devil worship," and they were not "ignorant superstition." This is a book about the older Cree *religion*. It was not the same kind of religion as Catholicism, but it was a religion all the same, with prayer, ritual, and theology. I believe what people told me, that some men and women who followed this older religion did evil things. I have not tried to make the older way of life look better than it was. But I also believe that there was and maybe still is value in this religion and that such rules of the Cree people as generosity and respect for nature were taught in it. I learned about men and women who used their dreams and powers to help each other through illness, to kill animals to feed their families, and to express their gratitude for the gifts of life.

The book draws on diverse resources. Primary among these are my records of observations and conversations in and around the north-western Manitoba communities of Granville Lake and Pukatawagan between September 1977 and May 1979. The circumstances under which these materials were obtained are considered in chapter 1. The choice of northern Manitoba as a research locale entailed a paradox probably familiar to others. Virtually no ethnographic writing existed (or exists) specifically on the Crees of this area, but the research already possessed a rich context in the writings of Frank Speck (1935a), A. Irving Hallowell (1955, 1976), and, more recently, Richard Preston (1975) and Adrian Tanner (1979) on other Subarctic Algonquian groups. These works influenced the kinds of sense I have attempted to make of what Crees did and said about the subjects addressed in this book. I maintain throughout a disciplined opportunism with respect to these accounts of other Algonquian theologies, identifying resemblance when possible but also registering diversity within and between the conventional groupings of Western Woods Cree, Westmain Cree, Eastern Cree, Montagnais, Naskapi, Saulteaux, and Northern Ojibwa (see Helm 1981).

"Source material," as, James G. E. Smith (1981:270) writes, "on Western Woods Cree is unsatisfactory for most periods of their history." There exists, nonetheless, information in the early chronicles of the fur trade both on and inland from Hudson Bay. All of these sources require, of course, critical evaluation relative to the perspectives and agendas of the authors. The earliest sources from the eighteenth century are the sketchiest in content and the most difficult to evaluate, since many authors, in the fashion of the times, enthusiastically appropriated each other's writing, with and without acknowledgment (Pentland 1976). Of these sources, I have made occasional reference to writings by Bacqueville de La Potherie (1931) and Nicholas Jérémie (1926) which date from the French occupation of York Factory on Hudson Bay between 1694 and 1714. Later English writers such as James Isham (1949 [1743–1749]), Andrew Graham (1969 [1767–1791]), Edward Umfreville (1954 [1790]), Arthur Dobbs (1744), Theodore Swaine Drage (1968 [1748–49]), Henry Ellis (1967 [1748]), Samuel Hearne (1958 [1795]), Alexander Mackenzie (1927 [1801]), and Joseph Robson (1965 [1752]) left descriptions of the Crees trading into the coastal forts or the inland posts during the middle and late 1700s. All these writers address aspects of Cree culture likely to be of interest to European literary consumers as well as subjects directly pertinent to the multiple roles of the Crees in the fur trade.

Of sources that describe populations ancestral to the contemporary Rock Cree inhabitants of the Churchill River, three deserve particular mention. Between 1792 and 1806, David Thompson (1962 [1784–1812]), wintered at posts within present Rock Cree territory in Manitoba and recorded information on conceptions of human-animal relations that persist in many essentials into the present. George Nelson (Brown and Brightman 1988) composed in 1823 at Lac la Ronge, Saskatchewan, an extended manuscript on the spiritual knowledge and practices of the Chippewas, Saulteaux, and Crees with whom he had traded. The Crees of Lac la Ronge belong to the same linguistic and social division as those of Pukatawagan and Granville Lake, and again the continuity between the present and what Nelson observed in the early 1800s is evident. Nelson's intellectual agenda prompted him to produce a document that eclipses in scope, detail, and contextualization any other nonanthropological writing on the subjects addressed here. Finally, the Hudson's Bay Company Archives contain reports, post journals, and account books for the area from the late 1700s to the present century. These records remain a primary and as yet only partially harvested resource for information on subsistence and the social organization of production.

Cree forms are reproduced throughout using H. Christoph Wolfart's (1973:12) modifications of Leonard Bloomfield's (1930:2–6) orthography for Plains Cree: $\bar{e}$ is substituted for a, c for ts, and o for u. Additionally, the orthography includes $\eth$, the voiced dental fricative corresponding to Plains Cree y and Swampy Cree n as the reflex of Proto-Algonquian *l. In modern Woods Cree, $\bar{e}$ and $\bar{\imath}$ have merged; in this text, ē appears only in words from other dialects in which the two are phonemically distinct. Transcriptions of Ojibwa and Saulteaux forms use Bloomfield's (1957) orthography for Walpole Island Ojibwa but with the substitution of macrons to indicate vowel length. The speech of my Cree instructors is usually set off from the text in block quotes. Much of the material reproduced in this way was recorded in English. Cree speech is identified as such in brackets and has been translated by myself or others, with a concern for literalness overriding that for elegance. Certain longer oral narratives told in English have been graphically presented following conventions established by Dennis Tedlock (1983).

Before, during, and after field research, both the book and the author benefited from the expertise and insights of Raymond Fogelson, Eric Hamp, Marshall Sahlins, Michael Silverstein, and Ann Strauss. Ann Strauss gave me the benefit of her knowledge of the Crees' remote collaterals, the Cheyennes, and introduced me on my return to academic currents under way during my sojourn in the north. Michael Silverstein anticipated in his advice to me the concerns with pragmatics and context that emerged in anthropology during the 1980s. Marshall Sahlins convinced me to work with foragers by writing "The Original Affluent Society" (1972) and subsequently shared with me his reflections on the cosmological dimensions of boreal Algonquian economics. From Eric Hamp, I received an invaluable immersion in Algonquian linguistics, punctuated by excursions into Albanian. Most of all, Raymond Fogelson's magisterial knowledge of North American Indian ethnology and relentless skepticism toward the uncomplicated solution (and the detachable conclusion) pushed the book in the direction it finally has taken. I owe a special debt to James G. E. Smith, the foremost non-Indian scholar of the Western Woods Cree, who now rests in the Cree graveyard at Little Buffalo Lake, Alberta, and who first pointed me toward northwestern Manitoba. Others who provided time, assistance, and good ideas are Charles Bishop, Jennifer Brown, Wilson Brown, John Comaroff, Elizabeth Coville, Robert Danforth, Verne Dusenberry, Fred Eggan, Paul Friedrich, David French, Kathrine French, Ives Goddard, Duncan Hamilton, Buddy Hartwig, Gail Kelly, Shepard Krech, David Krupa, Maria Lepowsky, Herbert Lewis, Kitty McClellan, Lou Marano, Manning Nash, John Nichols, Jim Norris, David Pentland, Tim Pettyjohn, Richard Preston, Carol Prindle, Roy Rappaport, Aidan Southall, George Stocking, Sol Tax, Gregory Urban, Tricia Urban, Bonnie Urciuoli, Claude Vaucher, and

H. Christoph Wolfart. David Arthurs of the Hudson's Bay Company Archives and Ann Harper-Fender of Gettysburg College helped me to (begin to) straighten out the mysteries of the Nelson River District. Research in Manitoba was financed with grants from the Canadian Ethnology Service, the Smithsonian Institution, the Melville and Elizabeth Jacobs Research Fund, and the American Philosophical Society. I gratefully acknowledge permission to publish materials contained in the collections of the Hudson's Bay Company Archives, Public Archives of Canada, Winnipeg, Manitoba (cited herein as HBC). Parts of this book were originally prepared while I held a postdoctoral fellowship at the Newberry Library's Darcy McNickle Center for the History of the American Indian. At the Center, then and since, I benefited from the assistance of John Aubrey, David Miller, Kris Jones, Hank Dobyns, Fred Hoxie, Jay Miller, and Calvin Fastwolf.

It would be impossible to enumerate or thank adequately all the individuals in the Cree communities of Pukatawagan, Granville Lake, Burntwood Lake, and Brochet who contributed their time, patience, hospitality, and knowledge. Among many others, I express my gratitude to Antoine Bear, Sarah Bighetty, Dougal Bighetty, Gordon Bighetty, Mary Bighetty, Joe Bighetty, Simon Bighetty, Pascal and Marie Bighetty, Julien and Nancy Bighetty, Sidney Castel, Eli Castel, David Castel, Jeremie and Caroline Caribou, Cornelius Colomb, Eli Caribou, Solomon Colomb, Joe Colomb, Ken Dillon, Luc and Caroline Dumas, Sandy Dumas, Solomon Francois, John Francois, Charlie Hart, Henry and Angelique Linklater, Lawrence Merasty, Jean-Baptise Merasty, Jean-Marie Merasty, Catherine Merasty, Pierre Merasty, Jeremiah Michel, Glenn Monkman, Peter Nateyus, Colin Ross, Matt Sinclair, and Albert and Philomene Umfreville. *Kinonāskomitināwāw.*

Many people helped initiate me into Cree skills, manners, and language, but my most generous preceptor was Johnny Bighetty who nows rests with his wife, Sarah, in the graveyard at Granville Lake. He was one of the most intelligent people I have ever met, combining a disposition for disinterested reflection with a magisterial knowledge of hunting, trapping, fishing, dog teams, and snowmobile mechanics. Exposed intermittently in his youth to Euro-Canadian education and religion, he had necessarily to objectify the culture of the Bush Indians, finding in it values superior to those of "acting like a white man" and reserving a kind of skeptical bewilderment for Crees more implicated than himself in the accelerating changes of the postwar north. His sense of humor was ever-present and sometimes relentlessly strange. On one occasion, when I came up to the house carrying a snared rabbit, he announced loudly, "*ayīkwa, kī-nipahīw paksa!*" [well now, he killed Bugs Bunny!]. Enthusiastic about new tools, he was less committed to the changes accompanying the emerging micro-urban reservations in the 1950s and after. "The Indians," he sometimes observed, "should have stayed with the old ways—with the hunting and the dreaming—and they'd be a hundred percent."

An explanation is necessary regarding the resemblance of language and ideas in this book to those in "Original Ecologists? The Relationship between Yup'ik Eskimos and Animals," a chapter in Ann Fienup-Riordan's recent book *Eskimo Essays* (1990). As a result of editorial accident, both ideas and near-verbatim stretches of text from my doctoral dissertation, *Animal and Human in Rock Cree Religion and Subsistence* (1983), appeared in "Original Ecologists" without acknowledgment. Rutgers University Press issued during summer 1991 a corrected edition of *Eskimo Essays* with appropriate deletions and acknowledgments in this chapter. Some of the ideas and language from my dissertation are retained in *Grateful Prey*, and it is therefore necessary to make clear that they originated in the dissertation and not in Fienup-Riordan's chapter in the uncorrected edition. Thus, for example, the sentence "Overkill operates not on the population of animals but on their accessibility" was retained from the dissertation (Brightman 1983:407) and occurs in chapter 10 of this book; it appears in the uncorrected edition of *Eskimo Essays* as "A hunter did not act on a finite population of animals, only on their accessibility" (Fienup-Riordan 1990:172). Most of the extracts from my dissertation used in Fienup-Riordan's article appear in chapters 6, 9, and 10 of the present book. To the best of my knowledge, the first person to observe in print that Native American ecological concepts might have objectively nonconservationist consequences was Arthur J. Ray (1975:59–60).

1

"You Got to Keep It Holy"

Introduction

The trees around the trapline shack were shrouded with animal remains. Skulls, antlers, and cloth packages of smaller bones hung from the trunk and branches, suspended with twine and leather thongs. The skinned carcasses of otters and martens were ranged along the limbs, frozen and twisted so that their naked heads faced the riverbank. Inside, the owner of the shack, a Cree Indian trapper, explained why he hung animal bones and corpses in trees.

I don't scatter my meat all over the place. Like when I skin an animal I don't just throw it outside. I go and hang it someplace. Well, like beaver meat, if you feed it to the dogs, that's here in the bush. But you don't feed a scrub dog outside in town. Those, y' know, dogs running around in town. You don't feed them. You're going to spoil your luck. The next time you go in the bush you don't kill a beaver. Because you're playing with it, playing with the meat if you scatter it all over the place. You got to keep it holy. I mean not to drop your meat, not get blood all over the house. This way you'll be lucky. *Pīkisitōwin* ['purity'], *ta-pīkisit* ['someone will be pure']. You don't *ī-mītawākīt* ['someone plays with it']. Like if you scatter it, if you don't pay attention what you do with it. Mess around, throw your skins all over the floor, people stepping on them. Animal respect himself, he doesn't want that. You got to try to keep it clean. Away from people. Especially woman. Woman with the rags on, that's terrible if he [woman] starts stepping on your fur. That's bad *maskihkiy* ['medicine'].

In a well-known passage, Max Weber defined action as "social insofar as, by virtue of the subjective meaning attached to it by the acting individual (or individuals), it takes account of the behavior of

1

others and is thereby oriented in its course" (1978,1:4). This book forms in part an extended reflection on the limitations of representing foraging or hunting-gathering ethnographically as a mode of social action implicating exclusively human actors. The foragers themselves may experience their productive project quite differently, with determinate consequences for the practical conduct of their foraging. Writing of the Labrador-Quebec Algonquians, Speck (1935a:72) made this observation long ago and with disarming clarity:

To the Montagnais-Naskapi—hunters on the barest subsistence level—the animals of the forest, the tundra, and the waters of the interior and the coast, exist in a specific relation. They have become the objects of engrossing magico-religious activity, for to them hunting is a holy occupation.

Speck identified here a distinctively Algonquian conception of game animals as reactive social others, alternately collaborating in and obstructing the designs of men and women who kill them with guns and traps. In this conception, society embraces rather than excludes animals, and the events of killing and eating them are experienced and talked about as so many ongoing instances of social interaction.

There is nothing unusual in the claim that American Indian foragers ascribe to their animal quarry intellectual, emotional, and spiritual characteristics paralleling in some respects those constitutive of human selves and persons. More novel in this discussion is the conclusion that these definitions of animals traverse the usual ethnographic partitions between "production" and "religion" as, respectively, technical and symbolic practices. Implicit in the theoretical division of ethnological labor is the ascription to Algonquians and other foragers of distinct and incommensurate conceptions of their quarry. Ecologically oriented analyses of boreal Algonquian foraging strategies represent the hunters' perspective on animals as exclusively instrumental. Conversely, Speck represented hunting as a "holy occupation" but was silent on how this sacredness accrued to the technical conduct of production. Cree conceptions of the social and sacred animal are maximally visible to outsiders when embedded in practices conventionally labeled "religious." Neither the structure of ritual enactments—reverent deposition of animal remains in trees, for example—nor the pragmatic intentions of the ritualists are intelligible apart from this definition of animals as active and reactive social subjects. But the social animal figures also in more technical contexts. Some Rock Crees experience animals as social others not only when they sing and burn offerings to them but also when they search for them, kill them with weapons, butcher their remains, and eat them. Cree discourse itself represents animals concurrently as use values and as social others in all the contexts in which people understand themselves to be interacting with them. Cree *mācīwin* 'hunting' and *manitōkīwin* 'religious practice' are conceptually distinct categories of human practice, but the animal as reactive other figures in both spheres.

In the first section of this book, I attempt to characterize this social animal, to examine the complexities of the Cree human-animal relationship as it is objectified in literature, informal discourse, and ritual enactment. The project thus reconnoiters terrain already traversed by a distinguished community of scholars, pushing the inquiry into an ethnographically little-known corner of northwestern Manitoba and attempting to disclose new perspectives from what people there were kind enough to tell me. This section concludes by suggesting that the Cree representations of the human-animal relationship are profoundly and perhaps necessarily chaotic and disordered. The human and animal categories are themselves continuous rather than discrete, and their interpenetration seems to preclude stable representations of causality or sociality in hunter-prey interactions.

In the second section, I address a different objective, suggesting that aspects of the technical conduct of hunting and trapping cannot be understood or explained without consideration of Cree conceptions of social animals. Both the economic practices of distributing and consuming meat—"social relations of production" in the conventional Marxian idiom—and the technical practice of foraging itself as a "productive force" are irreducibly social (Ingold 1988:274–275). Whether solitary or collective, hunting, like any human labor process, is regulated by social intentionality. Hunting, as the Weberian criterion would suggest, takes careful account of the behavior of others. The social others of whom some Crees take account include not only human foragers but the animals themselves and other beings who regulate hunters' access to them. If we seek a comprehension of Cree decisions about where and when to look for animals, how to hunt and kill them, how many to kill, and how to appropriate them as food, domestic manufactures, and market commodities, the moral commitments and antagonisms that hunters experience with their prey are as pertinent to our understanding as their knowledge of animal habitat and biomass. So much is consistent with the anthropological premise that cultural conceptions taken to be factual are factual in their consequences. Crees have a different understanding than non-Indians of the essential characteristics of the boreal fauna, and they act on this understanding both in ritual and more narrowly technical contexts. In the concluding chapters, I use documentary sources to address three such contexts: the overhunting of big game animals and furbearers, the subsequent inception of management practices, and the priority of immediate over delayed return foraging strategies. In this way, the analysis of three facets of Cree foraging serves as the occasion for extending a semiotic reading to two unfamiliar venues: foraging societies and the labor process itself.

The *Asinīskāwiðiniwak* Cree

The word "Cree" refers today to a continuum of culturally and linguistically related native people inhabiting the subarctic boreal forest from Quebec on the east to British Columbia on the west. The term originated as a contraction of "Kiristinon," a French borrowing of *Kiristinō*, the Ojibwa name for a division of Cree-speaking people living south of James Bay in the mid-seventeenth century (Pentland 1981*a*:227, Bishop 1981*b*:158–159). The shortened form emerged by the late eighteenth century as a generic label for other Cree-speaking groups successively encountered by the French and English traders as they moved north and west. The extension of the name reflected the traders' practical knowledge of linguistic similarities rather than any ethnic or political unity acknowledged by the people so denominated. Documentary sources mention numerous named groups associated with particular regions; these names presumably reflect to some degree ethnic and territorial distinctions recognized by the Crees themselves (Pentland 1981*a*:227–230, 1981*b*:269–270).[1]

Broad ethnic classifications developed by Euro-Canadians and now in common use by academics partially coincide with internal distinctions recognized by Crees. West of Quebec, anthropological usage distinguishes the Plains Crees occupying the southern prairie provinces and adjacent United States from the Western Woods Crees in the boreal forest to the north. The Plains Crees identify themselves as *Paskwāw-iyiniwak* 'prairie people' and speak varieties of the *y*-dialect of Cree. The Western Woods Cree (J. G. E. Smith 1981:256) category is comprised of the Swampy, Thickwoods, and Rock divisions, also groupings recognized by Crees themselves. The Swampy Crees are today *n*-dialect groups inhabiting both the Hudson Bay lowlands and some inland areas of Manitoba, Ontario, and Saskatchewan. They call themselves *Maskēkōwak* 'swamp people', a name attested in 1700 by Bacqueville de La Potherie's reference (1931:258) to the "Mashkegonhyrinis or Savannahs" living on the Nelson River and perhaps by even earlier forms (Pentland 1981*a*:227). Thickwoods Crees are bands who today speak northern varieties of the *y*-dialect and occupy the boreal forest in Saskatchewan, Alberta, and northwestern British Columbia. They call themselves *Sakāw-iyiniwak* 'thick woods people', a name attested in 1749 in the translation "Christinaux du Bois fort" (Margry 1879–1888, 6:616). The Rock or Missinippi Crees, with whom this book is primarily concerned, speak the "Woods Cree" or *ð*-dialect and today occupy the Churchill River drainage in northern Manitoba and Saskatchewan. The people of the Cree communities of Granville Lake and Pukatawagan on the Churchill River in northwestern Manitoba identify themselves in their own language as *Nīhiðawak* 'Crees'. To distinguish themselves from other Cree divisions, they use either *Asinīskāw-iðiniwak* 'people of the country of abundant rock' or *Kīwītinaw-iðiniwak* 'northern people'. When speaking English or French, they identify themselves as "Crees." I refer to them hereafter for brevity as "Rock Crees," a gloss that several individuals suggested for *Asinīskāw-iðiniwak*.

The Swampy, Rock, Thickwoods, and Plains Cree divisions now recognized both by Crees and by anthropologists reflect a complex history of amalgamations and migrations. The project of putting contemporary bands into correspondence with groups noted in early documents is complicated by the fact that group names can refer to three levels of social inclusiveness: broad ethnic divisions, regional bands oriented to particular summer fisheries or trading facilities (later reserves), and hunting groups into which regional bands divided in winter. A Cree of Pukatawagan, Manitoba, might be defined in different contexts as *Nīhiðaw* 'Cree' (as opposed to other Indians or to whites), as *Asinīskāw-iðiniw* 'Rock Cree' (as opposed to Swampy Cree or Plains Cree), as *Pakitawākan-iðiniw* 'Pukatawagan person' (as opposed to other regional bands or reserve groups), and as *Mwākwa-sākahīkan-iðiniw* 'Loon Lake person' or member of a group that hunts and traps at Loon Lake (as opposed to other Pukatawagan trapline groups). It is not always clear to which of these levels of social classification the names given in documentary sources refer. Neither, given the fluidity and mobility of Cree society, is it probable that groups or their names remained stable over time. Contemporary awareness (among non-Indians) of the Rock Crees as a distinct Cree social division derives from Smith's (1975) ethnographic sketch of the Crees of Brochet, Manitoba.[2] The missionary, Marius Rossignol (1938, 1939), served at the Oblate missions at Pelican Narrows and Lac la Ronge and identified the "Assiniskawidiniwok" or "Cree of the Rocks" as a separate group. The only earlier mention of the Rock Crees occurs in a list of what Alanson Skinner (1914*b*) took to be regional band names of the Plains Crees of Saskatchewan. Thompson's (1962 [1784–1812]:71) eighteenth-century description of the Churchill and Nelson River drainages as the "Stony Region" perhaps reflects Cree usage.

In northern Manitoba today, Rock Crees ordinarily use the ð-dialect. No such exact correspondence can be projected into the past, although this dialect was spoken in contemporary Rock Cree territory on the lower Churchill River from at least the late seventeenth century. Henry Kelsey (1929:9) in 1690 used "Nayhaythaways," a nominalized borrowing (with English plural *-s*) of Woods Cree *nēhiðawēw* 's/he is a Cree or speaks Cree' to refer to the people he encountered inland from the coast in northern Manitoba, probably in the Churchill River drainage. This form became an English designation for Crees in northern Manitoba during the eighteenth century (Pentland 1981*b*:268). The ð-dialect was also spoken in the seventeenth and eighteenth centuries along the west coast of Hudson and James bays and inland to the east and south in areas of Ontario, Manitoba, and Sakatchewan where it has since been replaced by the *n*-dialect (Pentland 1978:107–110). During this period, the relationship of dialects to named social divisions is obscure. The single link between the Rock Crees and an earlier named group was provided by Julien Bighetty and Solomon Colomb of Puka-tawagan who identified the *Misinipīy-iðiniwak* as the earliest occupants of the Churchill River. Bighetty represented the Missinippi as making extensive journeys from the source of the Churchill in Alberta to the mouth of the river on Hudson Bay. Following the establishment of the inland trading posts, they settled down at different points along the river in Manitoba and Saskatchewan, merging with other Cree groups to become the Rock Crees. The form is clearly cognate with the "Mis-henipee," "Misshenippe," and "Michinipi" who are noted as trading at York Factory in 1715 and Churchill in 1717 (Ray 1974:53,70; Knight 1932:57). Uncertainty about the early location of this group derives from the varying references of *misinipīy*, literally, great water. Crees today use it to refer to the Churchill River, although Arthur Ray (1974:70) claims that the traders used it in the 1700s both for the western section upstream from its confluence with the Reindeer River in Saskatchewan and for Reindeer Lake. James Knight (1932:161) referred to "ye great Water Lake" as the home of the "Meshinnepee" in 1717. David Pentland (1978:107) suggests plausibly that "ye great Water lake" was Southern Indian Lake and that its Missinippi inhabitants were speakers of the *r*-dialect of Cree, subsequently displaced or absorbed by *ð*-dialect speakers moving west. Southern Indian Lake is today called *Iðiniw-sākahīkan* 'Indian Lake', although this may be a back-translation of the English name. "Missinippi Cree" is emerging in the 1990s as a new social self-designation at Pukatawagan.

Genealogies of members of the Mathias Colomb Band of Pukatawagan and Granville Lake show that they descend primarily from families trading at the Nelson House and Southern Indian Lake posts in the late eighteenth century. Other ancestors came into the area during the later nineteenth century from Churchill, from the area of the second Nelson House post on Three Point Lake, and from Pelican Narrows and Lac la Ronge in Saskatchewan. More broadly, contemporary Rock Crees descend from Woods [*ð*] dialect-speaking people resident there prehistorically and possibly also from *r*-dialect groups long resident on the Churchill and from other Woods dialect groups moving west into the area in the 1700s. They identify the Missinippi Crees of the Churchill River as among their ancestors. Cree presence in the areas west of Lake Winnipeg and the Nelson River has conventionally been regarded as the result of mid-seventeenth-century westward expansion prompted by the military advantage of firearms and the search for new trapping territories (see Jenness 1932:264, Mandelbaum 1940:169–187). Smith (1987) recently demonstrated that Cree-speaking people already occupied their present territory at least as far west as Lac la Biche, Alberta, before European penetration. It was the name "Cree" that initially migrated west as traders successively applied it to the Cree-speaking Indians they encountered. Smith's conclusions are consistent with archaeological findings, although the western limits of prehistoric occupation continue to be debated. Most archaeologists concur that the complexes of materials referred to collectively as the Selkirk composite were manufactured by the ancestors of the groups now recognized as Western Woods Cree. Summarizing the archaeological evidence, David Meyer (1987:196) concludes that "Cree occupation of northern Manitoba began by at least the 1200s." The occupation may, of course, have begun much earlier. The weight of the evidence indicates that the Rock Crees and other Western Woods Cree groups are descendants of populations inhabiting the boreal forest west of the Nelson River and Lake Winnipeg for centuries before the introduction of the fur trade in the late 1600s.

MANITOBA CREES IN THE EARLY FUR TRADE

The Rock Crees' ancestors were hunter-gatherers, sharing with other subarctic and arctic peoples a specialization in meat and only minor utilization of the botanical foods that elsewhere underwrite the reliability of the foraging praxis. Acquisition of European goods and involvement in the trade as fur suppliers to Indian middlemen began in all probability well before the establishment of the Hudson's Bay Company's coastal establishments in the late 1600s. Crees rapidly defined themselves as dependent on such European manufactures as muskets, axes, kettles, metal knives, and ice chisels, and there was also demand for tobacco, tea, rum, and textiles. The introduced technology rapidly displaced indigenous manufactures fabricated from wood, bone, and stone. Men hunted and trapped moose, barren land caribou, woodland caribou, brown bears, beavers, lynxes, porcupines, and waterfowl. In the fur trade, many species such as beavers and lynxes acquired new significance as commodities. Other furbearers of commercial significance were wolves, wolverines, red foxes, arctic foxes, muskrats, skunks, minks, otters, martens, raccoons, fishers, and weasels; some of these were also eaten and used in domestic manufacture of clothing. Women fished, collected berries and other plant foods in summer, and trapped small game such as hares, ptarmigans, and martens. Women also constructed lodges, prepared hides and pelts for clothing, cooked, cared for young children, retrieved game, cut wood, and drew the toboggans during residential movement.

Cree males valued big game hunting over other subsistence pursuits: a verb for "hunt" referred only to pursuit of moose, caribou, and bears (Thompson 1962 [1784–1812]:83). Moose were hunted all year but especially during the rut and when high winds and deep snow made stalking and pursuit more efficient. During deep snow in spring, Crees sometimes chased down moose on foot and killed them with knives (HBC B.91/a/1 [1805–06]). Caribou were hunted most intensively during spring and fall migrations at river crossings; fences and impoundments were also used. Bears were hunted in their dens in winter.

Beavers were shot during times of open water. After freeze-up in winter, hunters chiseled open beaver lodges after blocking the runways. Dogs were used to track and corner animals in many hunting strategies. Smaller animals were killed with deadfalls, springpole snares, and gun traps. Beginning in the 1790s, steel leg hold traps with castoreum or other baits were set for beavers and other animals in both summer and winter. Men were humiliated when it became necessary to fish (HBC B.141/e/1 [1815], Thompson 1962 [1784–1812]:101) but readily resorted to it when necessary: one hunting group was observed angling for northern pike through the ice in December (HBC B.141/a/2 [1808–09]).

In the mid-1700s, Crees assembled in large groups to travel together to the Hudson Bay coastal forts in summer for trade. Most Crees from the lower Churchill River probably traded at Fort Churchill following its establishment in 1717. In that year, Knight was told by Crees from Southern Indian Lake that they could reach Churchill in four days, whereas a trip to York Factory farther south required at least ten (Knight 1932:161–166). Some bands adjusted to the fur trade by spending the winter hunting in the prairie and parklands south of the boreal forest. Here they traded their used European goods for furs produced by Plains Indian groups and brought these down to Hudson Bay in summer (Ray 1974:51–71, Rich 1960). Following the establishment of inland posts and winter outposts by the Hudson's Bay Company and their Canadian competitors in the 1770s, many Crees no longer made the trip down to the bay. The middleman role was eliminated, but Crees provided the inland posts with meat as well as furs. In 1782, the Crees suffered great population losses from a smallpox epidemic. Thompson (1962 [1784–1812]:93, see Ray 1974:105–113) estimated that over half the population died, leaving in the "muskrat country" between the Nelson and Churchill rivers a Cree population of 644 persons or 92 families, each with an average of seven members.

The rivalry between the trading companies intensified after 1783 in the "muskrat country" (Morton 1973:441–446), resulting in construction of numerous posts and outposts.[3] The Hudson's Bay Company's most permanent establishments during this period were Nelson House on either Nelson or Flatrock Lake and its outpost on Southern Indian Lake. The Cree annual cycle was closely articulated with the opening and closing of inland posts in the fall and spring. For Crees, summer was the period of maximal population concentration and sedentism, with the same families usually reuniting seasonally at the same fishing sites. In the aggregate, these families probably composed named regional bands identified with particular rivers or lakes and habitually exploiting the environing territories. Graham (1969 [1767–1791]:171) wrote that the Crees remained around lakes and rivers in the summer subsisting on fish, caribou, and buffalo, "but in winter they move about continually to where provisions are to be had, seldom abiding a fortnight in one place." Thompson (1962 [1784–1812]:79), however, contrasted the Crees who were "scattered by three or four families over a wide extent of forest" with other Indians who sometimes assembled for two or three months, suggesting more mobility and residential dispersal in summer than is usually presumed.

Families assembled at the trading establishments in the fall. George Charles, for example, found ten families waiting for him when he arrived to open Granville House in September 1795. Throughout September, he reported Indians leaving in separate groups for their "winter quarters" (HBC B.83/a [1795]). Before freeze-up, the band divided into multifamily hunting groups that traveled by birchbark canoe to winter hunting areas. Winter residential mobility was frequent, although a large caribou kill sometimes permitted several months of relative sedentism. In winter, hunting groups moved successively from camp to camp on snowshoes, using toboggans to transport equipment and furs. Food storage was minimal, although dried or smoked meat and pemmican products were sometimes prepared and transported. The traders perceived the Crees as usually too indolent to preserve and store food for future use (HBC B.91/a/8 [1822–23]). Both collective and individual hunting strategies were practiced, but meat was always shared among the coresident families, such reciprocity being an irreducible moral axiom. Charles (HBC B.91/a/8 [1822–23]) wrote that "they are a quiet, inoffensive people, and remarkably hospitable, as they seldom or ever fail to offer anything they may possess and generally of the best." In the event of a large kill, the hunting group sometimes moved itself to the kill site.

Crees regarded big game hunting as a more efficient subsistence strategy than fur trapping, although furbearing animals were also eaten. The traders believed that the need or desire to hunt big game for food diverted time from beaver trapping. Men concentrated on trapping during early winter when the furs were prime. Thompson's narrative (1962 [1784–1812]:101–106) of his winter at Reed Lake suggests that Crees scheduled big game and beaver hunting consecutively rather than concurrently. During beaver trapping, the hunting group some-times divided into its component nuclear or polygynous families. For example, "Tapapahtum" trapped beavers in fall and early winter, switching to moose hunting when deep snow accumulated. He was then joined by "Wiskahoo" who had also hunted beavers separately. Similarly, "Apistawahshish" parted from others to hunt beavers. In these cases, the constituent families of hunting groups separated in fall to hunt beavers and then came together again for big game hunting later in the winter. Contact between traders and Crees was frequent throughout the winter: Indians continuously visited the posts to trade, and traders frequently traveled to Indian camps to collect furs. Furs were also cached until the Indians visited posts in summer (HBC B.91/a/1 [1805–06]). Each adult traded his or her own furs. In addi-tion to furs, Crees traded fresh meat, dried meat, fat, and moose and caribou hides. With the breakup of ice in late April or early May, canoes were manufactured or retrieved, and the groups converged toward the summer fishing sites.

Winter hunting groups were flexible in composition, the same fami-lies tending to hunt together each winter but some shifting temporarily or permanently between groups. In 1822, there were six groups trading at Nelson House, the largest with twenty-eight members and the two smallest with eight (HBC B.91/a/8 [1822–23]). These groups were associated with particular regions of the country, but there is no posi-tive evidence for delimited hunting tracts over which individuals held usufructuary or exclusionary rights (see chap. 9). Hunting groups and perhaps some regional bands possessed male leaders whose authority and influence derived from age and foraging expertise. Group decisions were made by consensus, leaders suggesting or initiating courses of ac-tion with which the concurrence of others was voluntary. Most power to control others' decisions and behavior was limited to the authority of men and women over their unmarried junior relatives. Crees viewed with contempt what they conceived as harsh treatment of women by Chipewyan males (Thompson 1962 [1784–1812]:105).

Parents encouraged marriages between first and second cross-cousins, the children and grandchildren of opposite-sex siblings. These unions tended to re-create in successive generations affinal connections among the same hunting groups or the same families within hunting groups, although marriage between previously "unrelated" persons also occurred. Of the Crees trading at York Factory in the 1740s, Drage

wrote, "The consequences of these Marriages are a strict Alliance between the Husband and the Wife's Relations and reciprocally between
the Wife's and the Relations of the Husband, as to their assisting each
other" (1968 [1748–49], 1:208). After marriage, couples lived and
traveled with either spouse's parents and perhaps also with other relatives. A temporary period of residence with the bride's parents was reported by the traders among Crees trading into the coastal forts in the
1700s. Women attempted to space births at three-year intervals to pro-
long lactation and preclude the burden of carrying two infants; botanical medicines and perhaps other means were sometimes used to induce
abortions (Ellis 1967 [1748]:92; Isham 1949 [1743–1749]:104).
Eight of the seventy-six men in Charles's census were married poly-
gynously, seven of these to two wives and one to three. Thompson
(1962 [1784–1812]:82) wrote that polygyny was rare, the number of
co-wives not exceeding three. He associated the practice with widow-
hood, as men married the wives of deceased male relatives and friends.

In late winter and early spring, Crees sometimes moved to the posts
well before open water. In March 1806, John Charles encountered a
number of Crees en route to Nelson House for the spring goose hunt
(HBC B.91/a/1 [1805–06]). He stated that the Indians all came in with
their families to the Indian Lake post in April 1806 (ibid.). The Crees
began building birchbark canoes in late April, including the large
freight canoes commissioned by the traders (HBC B.83/a [1795]).
Crees were inclined to remain in the vicinity of the posts in spring
longer than the traders desired: the need for "getting the Indians away"
is reiterated in April entries from Nelson House (HBC B.141/a/1
[1802–03]). In 1809, the Crees assembled at Nelson House during
April and May, apparently as a response to resource scarcity during
spring (HBC B.141/a/2 [1808–09]).

By 1821, when the competing Hudson's Bay and Northwest companies amalgamated, both furbearing animals and big game were
greatly reduced in numbers in the Churchill and Nelson River drainages. The District Report of Nelson House for 1825–26 states categorically that the furbearing animals were exhausted, the larger game
animals nearly exterminated, and the Crees dependent on the post in
winter for provisions and likely to starve without it (HBC B.141/e/2).
The Indian Lake and Nelson House posts were closed in 1823
and 1827 to allow beaver numbers to increase (Fleming 1940:*lx*),
although posts at Split Lake and Three Points Lake continued to operate in the Nelson River District.

THE LATE EIGHTEENTH AND
NINETEENTH CENTURIES

Crees say that Pukatawagan Lake provides an abundant summer and winter fishery and that it has been a gathering place for their people for time out of mind, a status that probably prompted the construction of Northwest Company and Hudson's Bay Company posts there as early as the 1780s. When the Nelson House and Southern Indian Lake posts closed in the 1820s, trading orientations may have shifted west into Sakatchewan toward Lac la Ronge, southwest to The Pas or Cumberland House, or east to the second Nelson House established on Three Points Lake in 1833. Following the resumption of competition in the area, the Hudson's Bay Company reopened their post at Pelican Narrows, Saskatchewan, in 1874. By 1889, Nelson House maintained outposts at Southern Indian and Burntwood lakes (HBC D.25/6). In 1893 (HBC D.25/17), the Pukatawagan Crees were trading both at Pelican Narrows and at the Burntwood outpost. By 1898, an outpost at Pukatawagan was being supplied from Pelican Narrows and run by Louis Morin (HBC B.158/d/11), and this later became a permanent facility. Rossignol (1939:64) identified Pukatawagan together with Lac la Ronge, Pelican Narrows, Burntwood Lake, and Nelson House as the principal summer gathering sites of the Rock Crees around 1900.

An important trajectory of change began in 1878 with the visit of the Oblate priest Bonald from the mission at Pelican Narrows, Saskatchewan. Bonald visited Pukatawagan during the summer in the expectation of finding Indians there, and he was evidently not disappointed since Oblate tradition states that the entire population gathered to embrace Catholicism. For reasons that remain unclear, the majority of the Crees rapidly converted. Following the construction of a church and the presence of a resident priest after 1913, visits to Pukatawagan at Christmas and Easter became customary. In 1918, Father Émile Desormeaux became the permanent priest and remained in the community until his retirement in 1980. Catholic officiation at baptisms, marriages, and funerals became customary. The church proscribed polygyny and attempted to discourage—seemingly with little success—the preference for marriages between cross-cousins. The acquisition of French and/or biblical names for persons of both sexes began during this period. The mission was also significant as a source of emergency food and of certain Western medical supplies and techniques.

In the late 1800s, the pattern of frequent residential movement during winter began to be modified by the construction of log cabins built in imitation of those used by white trappers; these replaced the conical lodge as the usual winter dwelling. This increasing sedentation was made possible by the introduction of dog traction and thus greater winter mobility, greater commitment to food preservation, and the availability of flour and some other foods from the white traders. Log cabin hamlets contained between two and eight houses, typically occupied by members of one or two winter hunting groups. In winter, men sometimes moved between the hamlet and the bush on extended hunting and trapping trips while women and children remained behind. In other cases, the entire family spent periods of the winter at hunting and trapping camps away from the hamlet. Families often built and occupied two or more cabins at different sites in their territories, one site sometimes being used as a fishing camp in summer.

By 1900, a *de facto* if not *de jure* hunting territory system was in place in the Pukatawagan area (see Rossignol 1939). The log cabin hamlets were positioned on lakes or rivers whose environs were used in recurrent winters by the same multifamily hunting groups. Crees talk about these territories as central places rather than as bounded and continuous tracts of land. The larger winter log cabin communities used by hunting groups who came together at Pukatawagan in summer were at Granville Lake, Burntwood Lake, High Rock Lake, Sisipuk Lake, Hughes Lake, and Russell Lake; Pukatawagan was itself the site of a log cabin community occupied by one or two hunting groups during the winter. These and other winter communities were the sites of trading outposts operated by the Hudson's Bay Company, Revillon Frères, and independent traders.

Administratively, so-called treaty Indians at Pukatawagan and Granville are members of the Mathias Colomb Band, formed in 1911 from a group formerly included in the Peter Ballentyne Band (from 1901) and before that in the James Roberts Band (now the Lac la Ronge Band), which signed adhesion to Treaty Number 6 at Montreal Lake, Saskatchewan, in 1889. References to the James Roberts and Peter Ballentyne bands in government documents suggest that these were administrative labels for Crees occupying Lac la Ronge and points east along the Churchill River who had not yet settled onto reservations; they probably included from the first Crees with a summer fishing and mission orientation to Pukatawagan (Canada 1889:236, 1900:137,

1901:139). Between 1904 and 1907, for instance, the "Ballantine Band" is described as meeting at Pelican Narrows for its annuities, as without any permanent abode, and as scattered across the country as far as Nelson House to the east (Canada 1906:94, 1907:136, 1908:145). In 1911, the 221 Crees trading at Pukatawagan were formally recognized as a separate band with Mathias Colomb as chief. Reservations were surveyed at Pukatawagan and High Rock Lake in 1929; band members' desires for additional reserves at Granville Lake and other log cabin settlements were belatedly addressed in the 1980s and 1990s.

Pukatawagan Crees first encountered Euro-Canadian education when the Guy Hill Indian Residential School was opened in 1926 at Sturgeon Landing, Saskatchewan. In that year, twenty students attended from Pukatawagan, and until a local school was introduced in the 1950s, all students were sent out to either Guy Hill or comparable institutions. It was not possible for me to determine how provincial and federal educational policies were administered and enforced during this period. Some juveniles attended residential schools while others did not, and those who attended did not complete the same number of grades. Assessments of Guy Hill and other residential schools by former students and their parents range from tempered approval through condemnation of the long separations, hard physical work, punishments, and proscription of spoken Cree. The facility was reputedly burned down by an ungrateful student in 1952 and subsequently rebuilt at The Pas. Some students used their acquired knowledge of English and Euro-Canadian culture to exploit opportunities for wage labor that subsequently became available. Until the 1950s, most students returning to Pukatawagan were rapidly resocialized as foragers.

Opportunities for wage labor remained limited through the first half of the present century. Some Crees worked as transporters and in other capacities for the fur trading posts, moving shipments by boat in summer and by tractor train or horses and wagons in winter. Beginning in 1928, construction of the Island Falls hydroelectric dam near the winter settlement of Sandy Bay, Saskatchewan, provided some employment. In the 1930s, improved transportation by plane and tractor train facilitated the extension of commercial fishing into the Pukatawagan area. For some groups, commercial fishing in summer and winter became integrated into the seasonal cycle, alternating with fall and spring trapping. In 1951, mining operations were shifted from Sherridon on the southern margin of the Pukatawagan regional band territory to the present site of Lynn Lake to the north. Extension of the railroad line north from Sherridon to Lynn Lake between 1951 and 1954 provided employment and radically diminished Pukatawagan's isolation.

The early 1950s saw the development of Pukatawagan from a summer fishing–trading post–mission complex to a micro-urban community occupied throughout the year by most families of the Mathias Colomb Band. The influences resulting in the formation of this community were complex and mutually reinforcing, including diminishing economic returns from trapping, the availability of transfer payments and wage labor, and the introduction of a local school. Perhaps because of the activities of white trappers, Cree conservation measures and territorial practices ceased to function in the 1930s, resulting in furbearer and game depletions. As a result, the provincial Department of Mines and Natural Resources closed beaver trapping in 1941, subsequently introducing quotas. A depression in fur prices in 1943 combined with game shortages resulted in extreme economic hardship during the 1940s. Beginning in 1944, members of the band in cooperation with provincial officers divided the total area exploited by the band into bounded traplines registered to individuals or families. Despite trapline registration and the eventual recovery of beavers and other species, income from trapping became increasingly insufficient relative to requirements for food, equipment, clothing, and other commodities obtained from the traders. In 1945, family allowance payments were begun to families with minor children; other federal and provincial payments including old age pensions and emergency rations for the destitute followed. By the late 1940s, many families had shifted their residential orientation toward Pukatawagan, leaving it only for extended periods of trapping in fall and spring. Initially, tents and log cabins were occupied, but the band acquired a tractor and sawmill in the early 1950s, resulting in clusters of occupant-constructed houses linked by a road that was later extended off the reserve to the railroad line. By the mid-1950s, most members of the band were resident in the village throughout most of the year. Perhaps the shrewdest explanations for the "posting" process offered by Crees identify the interaction of family allowance payments with white educational policy. A Department of Indian Affairs grade school staffed by Oblate sisters was established at Pukatawagan in 1952, initially operating between July and April to allow families to disperse to the bush for spring trapping. As several persons noted, families had to send their children to the school if they wanted to continue to receive family allowance checks, and they stayed at Pukatawagan most of the year to be near their children.

The period between the 1950s and the present has been one of increasing community development and movement away from the subsistence foraging and fur trapping economy as full-time occupations. The Department of Indian Affairs provided new houses in the late 1960s, aligning them on the main road to facilitate connections with the hydroelectric generator; this residential pattern replaced an earlier dispersion of house and tent clusters occupied by related families. Telephone service, an airstrip, a permanent nursing station, and a new school building, now with classes through grade twelve, were introduced in the early 1970s. Both men and women have increasingly sought wage labor both within and outside the community: Crees are employed by the Canadian National Railroad, the Hudson's Bay Company, Manitoba Hydroelectric Company, the nursing station, and the school. During the late 1960s, changes in provincial policy made welfare payments widely available to individuals in reserve communities, an innovation whose effects are still debated by the people of Pukatawagan. During the 1970s and 1980s, the community has increasingly assumed control of its own administration and development, resulting in the creation of many additional jobs in the different branches of the band government.

When I came to Pukatawagan in 1977, trapping, hunting, fishing, and collecting edible and medicinal plants continued to be important for many Pukatawagan residents, although people said that commitment to these extractive practices had decreased since the 1950s. Relatively few families perpetuate the older pattern of residing in cabins or log cabin hamlets on their trapline territories throughout the winter. As has been the case since the time of first contact, subsistence activities have been integrated in various ways into the markets of the majority society. Hunting continues to be combined with fur trapping and commercial fishing, and some men combine both with seasonal wage labor. Most trapping and hunting today is undertaken by all-male groups who travel from their homes on the reserve to their trapline cabins, spending variable periods of time in the bush. Mixed sex and age groups still go out to the trapline for extended periods in April for spring trapping. Beavers, muskrats, and lynxes provide both commercially valuable pelts and staple meats. Bears, woodland caribou, and moose continue to provide meat and also hides employed locally in the manufacture of footwear, mitts, and such prestige garments as beaded jackets. It is probably unnecessary to note at this juncture that Pukatawagan and other Indian reserves I have visited remain distinctively "Cree" in language, culture, and self-identification despite the social and environmental transformations they have experienced in the present century. Attitudes toward the bush and the foraging practices strongly identified with Indian culture are variable among all age groups (cf. Brightman 1990). As one Cree elder put it, "The day will come when the Whiteman will not allow you to hunt. The fish and moose will one day disappear. Hunting is no place for modern people" (Bighetty and Senyk 1986:37). In the words of another, Luc Dumas, "The trapline is just like the Whiteman's bank. It's the Indian bank. There should always be one guy in the family covering it. Kids come back here from school, and there are no jobs. No jobs? Well, they can always start up again with the 'bank.'" Behind such reflections is often the deeply felt conviction that whites and their manufactures are only transient presences in the north, perhaps in the cosmos. If the government collapses, if the supply of goods and transfer payments from "up south" is terminated, some Crees believe that they will return to the bush to hunt and fish.

GRANVILLE LAKE

In 1986, seven years after initial work in the area, I returned to Pukatawagan and stayed with a Cree family who in many ways typified successful control of the accelerating changes of the period. The mother held a post in the band office, one daughter was a teacher, another daughter was a band constable. The new house was modern, "comfortable" by contemporary Euro-Canadian criteria. Family members code-switched effortlessly between Cree and English. The food was no different from what I had consumed while staying with white friends a few weeks earlier in Winnipeg. One afternoon, there was a visitor, a middle-aged man from Granville Lake, a relative by marriage who had come to visit the nursing station. He and I were equally surprised to see each other, for I had lived with his brother at Granville Lake, seven years earlier. *Sakāw-iðiniw* is used to refer to *y*-dialect speaking Crees to the west in Sakatchewan and Alberta, but it possesses another narrower and local meaning. Not all the families of the Mathias Colomb Band moved into Pukatawagan during the centrifugal 1950s. A few remained as full-time occupants of the bush hamlets. There were some at High Rock Lake, some at Burntwood Lake, and some at *Okāwīmiðihkānānihk* 'pickerel-oil-rendering-place', a back-water settlement called in English Pickerel Narrows or Granville Lake. The people of these settlements are sometimes called also *Sakāw-iðiniwak* or "Bush Indians," an epithet with mingled connotations of provincialism and authenticity. Such was the visitor. Food must immediately be served when a senior relative visits. Years ago, a meal of white man's food from cans expressed the giver's esteem more lavishly than moose or beaver. But today, at Pukatawagan, where most food comes as groceries from the Bay, it is "Indian food" that honors guests and is uniquely appropriate for a senior relative from "the bush." No wild game had been served in the house for weeks. But a child was dispatched to a neighbor, and a meal of boiled beaver meat was soon served to the "old man" who appreciatively consumed it as his due.

Granville Lake itself was the site between 1794 and 1796 of the Hudson's Bay Company's Granville House and a competing Canadian post. During the winter of 1804–05, George Charles and David Thompson, respectively, represented the competing companies at "Musquawegun Lake" (Thompson 1962 [1784–1812]:xc, 84). *Maskwāwikan Sīpiy* 'Bear-Backbone River' is the Laurie River, and this post was presumably at or near the confluence of the Laurie and Churchill rivers at Granville Lake. By 1900, Granville was among the winter log cabin hamlets occupied by Crees who summered at Pukatawagan and were later included in the Mathias Colomb Band. Revillon Frères operated a post at Granville at this time, and an outpost of the Pukatawagan store was built in 1927. When the Colomb reserves were established in 1929, the band requested that Granville and other hamlets be surveyed as separate parcels. By the 1930s, Granville differed from most log cabin hamlets in that members of at least four hunting groups—two Métis groups and two branches of the extensive Bighetty family— resided there simultaneously. Commercial fishing developed as a supplement to hunting and trapping in the 1940s. In the 1970s, Granville was the biggest of the few persisting bush hamlets whose inhabitants had elected not to "move in" to the Pukatawagan reserve. Approximately sixty-five persons lived there, the number constantly fluctuating as men and families moved in and out from their traplines to the settlement. Residents say the community remained unknown to most government agencies until around 1969, and as late as 1977, Department of Indian Affairs and Northern Development (DIAND) personnel informed me confidently that no village existed there. In 1969, the community was "discovered" in connection with the Manitoba Hydro-

electric Company's proposed Churchill Diversion Project. Manitoba
Hydro's initial plans entailed raising the waters of Granville Lake
thirty-five feet, thereby putting the settlement underwater and forcing
relocation of the residents to the city of Thompson. The Granville
Lake and Southern Indian Lake communities took the case to court,
and Manitoba Hydro was eventually compelled to cut back on its
plans, raising the lake approximately fifteen feet and leaving the settlement intact. During the 1970s, the village belatedly came to the attention of DIAND: a community hall, a tourist lodge, an ice rink, a
garage, an electric generator, one telephone booth, and materials for
new housing were introduced. In 1972, a school with grades one
through six was built; previously some children went out to Guy
Hill residential school at The Pas or lived with relatives and attended
school at Pukatawagan. Nursing supplies were deposited with one
community member who subsequently gained fame by mistakenly
issuing birth control pills to male trappers.

While acquiring some of the facilities of larger reservation communities, Granville remained and remains today relatively isolated. The families resident there are characterized by their commitment to hunting,
trapping, and commercial fishing; intermittent guiding for white sport
fishermen provided the only wage labor in the community. Granville is
inaccessible to commercial travel except by ski- or floatplane and is
effectively isolated during breakup and freeze-up. In 1977, it was ser-
viced twice a month by a scheduled mail and supply flight from Lynn
Lake. The relative autonomy and the resource opportunities afforded
by this isolation were clearly factors in the community's persistence.
Residents said that they preferred Granville because of the low population density, the absence of band council regulations (that prohibiting
drinking, for example), proximity to traplines, better hunting, trapping,
and fishing, distance from the Catholic mission, and, as I was told candidly, the opportunity to interact only minimally with whites. The
community is visited periodically by representatives of the Royal Canadian Mounted Police and the Oblate Mission, but during the period of
study, the only non-Crees resident in the community were the schoolteacher, the free trader, and me.

CONDITIONS OF WORK

Whatever else may be implicated in my decision to work
in the north, I sought a community where indigenous religion was
practiced rather than eulogized and one in which foraging prevailed

over wage labor. I wanted to avoid studying "memory culture." James G. E. Smith had worked with Rock Crees at Brochet and discussed possible field sites in Manitoba with me. I settled on Pukatawagan because no anthropologist had gone there before and because Smith knew that smaller bush settlements such as Granville persisted in the area. I initially wrote to the Mathias Colomb Band Council and to several persons at Granville. No one wrote back, but the letters were useful because some members of both communities appreciated that I had asked to do the research. "We were wondering when you'd show up" was a typical reaction when I finally arrived.

I went first to Pukatawagan, arriving in September 1977. With a population of 1,250 persons, Pukatawagan looked to me like a suburban subdivision dropped into the boreal forest. It had at the time a well-deserved reputation (since dramatically reversed) for social problems and violence, chiefly the consequence of a numerically insignificant but very active group of "problem" families and juveniles. I resided for two months that fall with a white schoolteacher and later with the community development officer and in the home of Luc and Caroline Dumas. I was assimilated into a sector of overlapping Cree-white social life centered around employment by the school. From the outset, I benefited from the interest and support of Paschal Bighetty, then chief of the Mathias Colomb Band, and Sidney Castel of the Manitoba Indian Brotherhood. With Mr. Castel as interpreter, I visited and interviewed a number of older individuals in the community, including Julien and Nancy Bighetty, Selazie Linklater, Solomon Colomb, and Eli Caribou. Mr. Castel was also the first of many individuals from whom I taped the words and phrases that I used to develop some speaking facility in Cree. Initially, I pursued "memory culture" by default, documenting through interviews aspects of the prereserve seasonal round. I was aware from the snowmobile traffic that trappers were continually departing for "the bush," but the people I knew worked at various jobs in town. Those who were in any way visibly "religious" were so in the idioms of Catholicism. During this period, I often inquired about Granville Lake. People were vague or discouraging: "Yeah, there's some people out there." "They're old-fashioned down there." "They don't like white people there."

My offers to bankroll a snowmobile trip downriver to Granville met with no takers. In November, I took the train from Pukatawagan to the mining town of Lynn Lake, timing my arrival to coincide with the scheduled mail flight. I arrived at Granville Lake, Manitoba, encumbered with gear, a minimal speaking knowledge of Cree, and profound uncertainty. Granville looked like my fantasies of a "remote bush settle-ment." Twenty or so houses and log cabins were scattered irregularly around a point jutting out into the lake. Uncertain about what to do with me, the Ukrainian trader, Mike Chuiak, suggested I move into the "lodge," a large and not easily heated structure built some years pre-viously by DIAND in the (unrealized) expectation that visiting sport fishermen would rent it. Over the course of the next few days, while under careful and not always unobtrusive scrutiny by many persons in the hamlet, I struck up a casual friendship with Johnny Bighetty, a Cree trapper about forty-four years old who lived with his wife, Sarah, six of their children, and Jim, a Métis from Winnipeg about my own age (twenty-seven) who was learning the trapping business from him. After further scrutiny and an approving assessment of my willingness to cut wood, haul water, snare rabbits, fish through the ice, drink neat rum, and speak (bad) Cree, Johnny invited me into his household, where began my initiation into taking food and other resources from the bush and acting enough like an Indian to get along. It was progressively an initiation into skills, manners, language, generosity, and ultimately into dreams, an education in which many others played crucial roles but in which Johnny's influence was primary. Independently inventing the doctrine we call participant-observation, he declared that anyone who was "writing a book about the Indians" should live with and like an Indian. My specific motivations for seeking this training involved the conventional objectives of increased rapport, the desire to contribute, however minimally, to the household, and the opportunity to observe and participate in hunting and trapping strategies. It is probably un-necessary to note that the manifest benefits were almost entirely mine and that the training so generously given served more to lessen my liability than to allow a positive contribution of any significance. I be-lieve that the course of instruction recapitulated exactly the sequence employed in training small boys: I began with wood and water, pro-gressed to fishing and rabbit snaring, and finally learned some of the rudiments of trapping.

The representations of Cree beliefs and practices that I attempt here are based on what I observed people doing on various occasions and on what they told me, either informally or in the course of discussions consecrated to the project of increasing my understanding. These latter were sometimes generously undertaken at others' initiatives, out of per-sonal liking for me, or because what I was conceived to be doing was thought important. I was once, for example, summoned out of my sleeping bag at midnight to attend a party at another house where the presiding grandfather had expressed a desire for my presence. More typically, I initiated relationships in which I paid people an hourly wage in exchange for talking to me about particular topics.

These sessions were, at least initially, sometimes bizarre experiences for my Cree preceptors, novel assimilations to the category of "job." No one in Granville Lake or Pukatawagan had ever heard of anthropology. When working with elderly persons, I supplemented the hourly payment with a gift of tobacco, simultaneously establishing a reputation for good manners and obligating them, in their own understanding, to tell me something worthwhile. I rapidly learned certain basic premises of Cree verbal etiquette: that personal questions are impolite, that specific questions are pushy, that long reflective silences should not be interrupted by prompting. The first time I sat down to talk with Jean-Baptiste Merasty, I asked him how the people had divided up the land before the registered trapline system. He gazed into space silently; two minutes became four and then five. I tentatively rephrased the question. Fixing me with a baleful glare, he told me sharply that he was still thinking, and I subsided.

With few exceptions, the discussions were "formal" only in the sense that I arrived with a topical agenda. With some persons and with respect to some topics—genealogy, land tenure, systems of animal classification—I used schedules of prepared questions. Although some valuable information was obtained in this way, most Crees found schedules less to their taste than informal conversation. One long-term benefactor of mine, who after the first few meetings refused to accept anything more than chewing tobacco and rabbits from me in recompense, stated flatly that I would have to pay him a "lot of money" if I wanted to continue plying him with eliciting frames. More usually, because most people disliked batteries of specific questions and because I had doubts about their usefulness, I posed topics in very general terms, and the responses to such questions produced superior material. Depending on the topic, my preceptors would formulate typifications—generalizations about the cultural practices they attributed to their fellow Crees—or, more rarely, refer to their personal experiences. Usually I taped these sessions. Some people did not like the machine; many soon insisted on it. At night, I would review the tapes, identifying the new parameters of uncertainty that each session engendered.

Crees also told me things in less structured circumstances, conversations that developed casually without the use of recording devices in the course of visiting, working, or traveling. These conversations were, in the happiest circumstances, prompted by instances of productive and ritual practice that I observed or participated in. In such circumstances, Cree "culture" first became manifest to me as a factor in whose terms Crees experienced and acted upon animals in the contexts of daily life and as a scheme for interpreting these contexts. After hearing in an interview that Crees "used to believe" that animals regenerate after death, it interested me to hear a man point out details in the coloring of a dead fox and explain to his son that it was the same animal he had killed earlier the same winter. Since many animal carcasses are brought back to the settlement to be skinned out, butchered if relevant, and consumed, some additional rules concerning speech about animals, dietary rules, and disposal of inedible residue were observable off the trapline. Evidence for persisting and very basic disparities between Cree and Western orientations toward animals became apparent. Freshly plucked porcupine quills were identified as "not dead yet" and reverently suspended from the ceiling. A female lynx in a snare was identified as a beautiful woman of whom the trapper had dreamed.

Two obstacles followed me throughout the work. I was interested in people's personal experiences, but on many topics, direct questions of this kind are bad manners of the most palpable kind. Most frequently, I asked for and was given generalizations and typifications. In the fullness of time, some few of my preceptors selectively disclosed themselves. In some cases, I presumed on friendships to ask such questions. Second, I was interested in the human-animal relationship in all its modalities, and aspects of this relationship are inscribed in *manitōkīwin*, the belief and practice of indigenous religion. Of Crees in the 1790s, Thompson wrote that "what[ever] other people may write as the creed of these natives, I have always found it very difficult to learn their real opinion on what may be called religious subjects. Asking them questions on this head is to no purpose, they will give the answer best adapted to avoid other questions, and please the enquirer" (1962 [1784–1812]:74–75). One of Thompson's Cree hunters explained this reticence readily enough: "You White men always laugh and treat with contempt what we have heard and learned from our fathers, and why should we expose ourself to be laughed at?" (ibid.:79). In the 1820s, Nelson (Brown and Brightman 1988:101) noted that "*they* [Lac la Ronge Crees] do not chuse that we become too well-informed of all their ceremonies." Things were much the same in 1977, exacerbated by approximately one hundred years of sustained Catholic condemnation.

The effects of the Oblate missionary enterprise on the indigenous religious complex have been profound. Crees say that most missionaries actively discouraged the indigenous religion. From the earliest times, missionary ire focused on sacred drums. Again and again, I was told that the missionaries forcibly confiscated drums, burning them or throwing them in the lake. Alternatively, Crees desiring baptism were required to renounce their drums and other pagan practices.

That little island there [in Pukatawagan Lake], that's where they were first baptized. Priest come in there, he threw all the drums in the lake. Those people, you know, they used to have drums . . . singing . . .
Question: Why'd he throw them in the lake?
Well, he said . . . there's no more of them [drums]. Well, that's . . . when a guy is drumming like that, that's like he's believing something else. Yeah, it's another god. He's singing against . . . [the scriptural deity].

It is not difficult to understand the reactions of the Rock Cree medicine man who told the Oblate Rossignol (1938:67) that "nothing in the missionary's sermons had surprised him, but that the white man's contempt for the pagan observances had shocked him."

Some Crees were uninterested in the new religion. *Oyāpacikiw* 'Aimer', ancestor of the Cursiteur family at Pukatawagan, reacted to an offer of baptism by threatening to pour water on the minister (ibid.). Most Crees at Pukatawagan accepted Catholicism and "converted" in the late 1800s, reproducing in this context an indigenous receptivity to new forms of spiritual expression. As a result, Catholicism is now Cree "tradition." This new tradition, however, was represented by the priests as incompatible with indigenous spiritual expression. As a result, many persons self-consciously renounced *manitōkīwin*, including the personalized relationship with their dream spirits (cf. Brightman 1989a:162–163, 167–168). Some earlier priests seem never to have doubted the factuality of the beings worshiped by Crees, seeing in them, in fact, manifestations of the scriptural Devil and his minions. Thus was the entire scope of *manitōkīwin* redefined as satanic worship, perhaps with some Crees actively collaborating in the reinterpretation. Some Crees today talk as though they accept this equation. At the same time, there is predictably reluctance even among devout Catholics to identify honored ancestors as devil worshipers.

But I know there were some good guys in the [pre-Christian] past. There were still some good people living. Like my great grandfather there, he was one of them. And he didn't believe in this evil spirit [the *wīhtikōw*, a cannibal monster].

Maybe he did, but he still had enough reason in him that he could oppose these things. There were still some good guys. Even though the Devil was in control of most of them.

In this discourse, the indigenous distinction between good and evil spirit power qualifies the Catholic representation of all indigenous religion as evil.

Some Crees who are practicing Catholics believe that the spirit beings recognized by their pre-Catholic ancestors really exist; they differ as to whether people can still communicate with them. Many Catholics represent indigenous religion itself as something that no longer exists in the present or that exists other places but not at Pukatawagan. I do not know whether any of them really believe this. Some practicing Catholics have experiences and observe rules continuous with the indigenous religion, typically involving aspects of it that do not overtly conflict with Catholic teachings. Some consult Cree medicine specialists and hang up bear skulls, while others do not. Some persons have evolved syntheses equating the superior being Kicimanitōw with the scriptural deity, the *wîhtikōw* and other monstrous beings with devils, and dream spirits with angels. Such syntheses are in unstable equilibrium with the official Catholic position that all pre-Christian beings and practices are evil and that the two religions cannot be concurrently practiced. Christian and indigenous beliefs are in consequence distributed through the communities—and through the discourses of individuals—in an exceptionally varied fashion. I did not observe the compartmentalization of Christian and indigenous practices by the same persons in different contexts (cf. Rousseau 1952, Tanner 1979:108–109). Many persons, especially those in their thirties and younger, have no visible commitment to either tradition.

Virtually everyone born in Pukatawagan or Granville is baptized as a Catholic, and the entire population has long since been nominally converted. Some persons who practice *manitōkīwin* represent themselves as believing Catholics. Others are privately disparaging of the church and skeptical of its teachings. People were usually reluctant initially to acknowledge *manitōkīwin*, apparently anticipating that a white would disapprove on religious grounds or disparage their beliefs as superstition. A man once told me, with a perfectly straight face, that he had never heard of Crees hanging up animal bones in trees and knew nothing about it; every tree around his shack was festooned with skulls and antlers. Some were also concerned that they would provoke ridicule from others or that they would be suspected as sorcerers (see Tanner 1979:108), in whose existence most Rock Crees, I think, continue to believe. As a result, some persons are secretive about their practices. However, at least one man of my acquaintance enjoyed his reputation as a sorcerer. Other factors conditioned what people were willing to tell me, especially about their own experience. Crees expect that misfortune will follow if certain aspects of personal religious experience—a particular song, or a dream, or a part of a dream, for example—should become known to others. Some aspects of such experiences—the identity of a dream spirit, for example—are inferred by others from dietary rules and other details of personal ritual but are seldom verbally communicated. Not least, some of the beings in which I was interested, the *misipisiw* 'underwater panther', for example, are dangerous to speak about. Those who believe are reluctant to talk about them, especially *nōhcimihk*, "in the bush."

The shamanistic prowess of the ancestors is said to have surpassed the decadent practice of the present, and I am sure I would have been told the same thing two hundred years ago. But there has been a reduction not only of power but of belief and practice. Crees talk about *manitōkīwin* in the past tense or as radically attenuated, and there is no reason to question their assertions. Indigenous spirituality has decisively colored at each stage the sense that Crees make of Catholicism and in this sense reproduces itself in new idioms. In another sense, however, I felt that I was presiding over an inquiry into a moribund religion. Crees say that only a minority of people participate in the shaking lodge, the eat-all feast, traditional curing, and prayer with song and drum and that the vision fast at puberty is no longer practiced at all. This coincides with my own impressions, although there was surely more going on than I knew about. Enough is still known and believed of this religion within the community to provide the basis for its reemergence in the future.

Once in Pukatawagan, I attempted to develop some control of spoken Cree, benefiting from the careful instruction of Sidney Castel and Caroline Caribou, among many others. Initially, I was limited to talking to people in English or to using interpreters to talk to non-English-speaking Crees. I eventually began speaking Cree with people in interviews and other contexts, although many of them understandably preferred to use English. The limits on my control of verb inflections and vocabulary made it useful to go over taped interviews with bilinguals. Unless they are identified as Cree, the discourses reproduced here were recorded in English.

As befits the epistemological uncertainty of the 1990s, I identify here certain caveats implicated in this and other anthropological projects. I take my representations of what people said and did as giving some evidence for elements of their inner thought and experience but readily acknowledge that this is a multiply problematic strategy. What they did and said was influenced by my presence and questions, and speech and actions are not, of course, transparent with respect to such inner states. Further, my constructions of what they did and said—both at the time and in subsequent phases of digestion—have been, of course, regimented by my own agenda. Moreover, I have attempted to identify in these representations of other people's acts and discourses characteristics of a socially shared if diversified structural configuration whose design may be in certain respects no more available to the consciousness of its participants than the phonological structure of the Cree language. To accord to the material of my observations the maximum resistance to the potentially outlandish opinions that I or other non-Indians could form about them, I here pursue the course, common enough, although not ubiquitous in such work, of attempting to situate my interpretations in the contexts of Cree discourses that initially suggested them. Throughout, I try to follow Bronislaw Malinowski's (1961:3) old but not unfashionable advice to separate "the results of direct observation and of native statements and interpretation" from my own "inferences," without sharing his optimism that the project is possible.

Animal Signs

In this book, I approach questions about Cree human-animal relations from a perspective that is semiotic in multiple respects. It begins from the premise that both technical and spiritual facets of Cree foraging are organized as sign phenomena. In a use consistent with sociolinguistic and anthropological borrowings from Charles S. Peirce, "semiotic" entails analysis of signs as contextually actualized in the practices and experiences of their users. A semiotic perspective differs in this respect from modes of analysis, seemingly moribund in anthropological discourse in the 1990s, that take such practices only as data from which the formal elements of analytically constructed systems can be abstracted. "Semiotic" thus occurs here in preference to "symbolic," "structuralist," "hermeneutic," and other imaginable substitutes with which it varies freely, often with resonant vagueness, in anthropological usage. I draw, however, on aspects of linguistic and anthropological structuralism, specifically, the definition of linguistic signs— sound images that signify concepts—as arbitrary and oppositive entities. The purpose of the Saussurean (1966 [1915]) argument, convergent in some respects with the findings of a later American relativism, was to explore the consequences of the fact that meanings are not constant across languages and that each language effects a unique classification of conceptual substance or extralinguistic reality. The words and grammatical categories of different languages do not passively and repetitiously encode the same objective discontinuities between external objects, actions, and conditions; they are not different labels for the same independently existing "things." Taking a conventional anthropological example, the meanings of Cree *nistīs* 'my elder brother' and *nisim* 'my younger sibling' derive from the play of contrasts and resemblances within the lexicon of Cree kin terms and not from their denotational relationship to genealogical kin types. Their meanings are not equivalent to those of English "brother" and "sister" or French "frère" and "soeur." Likewise, the meanings of the Cree linguistic signs *pisiskiw* 'animal' and *iðiniw* 'human' or *mācīw* 'he hunts' and *pawāmiw* 'he dreams' are mutually defined in uniquely Cree semiotic environments. To this degree, linguistic signs are oppositive entities, their meanings circumscribed by the meanings of other linguistic signs within semantic environments constituted differently in each language, each social universe. Ferdinand de Saussure's exposition advanced a purely differential concept of meaning on the model of phonemic contrast, the often-cited assertion that "their [signs'] most precise characteristic is in being what the others are not" (Saussure 1966 [1915]:117). As Sergej Karcevskij (1982:51) later observed, "True differentiation presupposes a simultaneous resemblance and difference" (cf. Jakobson 1978:64). Bears, for example, are not significant to Crees only because of their lack of identity with foxes and wolverines. The meaning of "bear" as a linguistic and social sign—and thus the meanings of bears in practical experience—is constituted both by difference and resemblance to other modes of animate being.

Roland Barthes (1972:42) observed of myth that it "has the task of giving an historical intention a natural justification, and making contingency appear eternal." In this respect, ecological explanation in anthropology parallels in certain respects the consciousness people have of their own social practices. Of the linguistic sign, Émile Benveniste (1971:17–18) observed that sound image and concept necessarily evoke one another; their relation is arbitrary "only under the impassive gaze of Sirius" and not in the experience of users. Cultural categories and propositions are understood, probably in most contexts, as more or less transparent representations of reality and experience; put another way, signs are not recognized as such by those who think and act by means of them. Marshall Sahlins (1981:70) observes, "In naive and evidently universal human experience, signs are the names of things 'out there.'" If, as Benveniste shows, the acoustic image and concept united in the linguistic sign are inseparable and thus nonarbitrary in the speaker's consciousness, this perhaps provides the basis for a well-nigh universal folk theory that language is nomenclatural. The mediating effects of the "meaning" are not available to consciousness; people experience words as sounds that name and evoke discrete "things" in the world. In Peirce's terms (1960–1966, 2:157), vocabulary is understood as a diagrammatic icon, a sign whose distinct parts replicate and resemble the distinct parts of its object. As words are felt as names for things, so are cultural propositions felt as factual statements of independently existing states of affairs and social practices represented as realistic and perhaps inevitable accommodations to these. Inedibility is an important aspect of the meaning of "wolverine" for Crees. The social rule does not assert that it is impossible to eat wolverines (starving men are known to do so), but it embodies the "fact" that wolverine meat possesses qualities rendering it undesirable as food. Cree behavior thus enacts and re-creates a claim about wolverine edibility that is not the only one possible "under the impassive gaze of Sirius" but is assumed nonetheless by most Crees to be axiomatic. This naturalization of signs in the consciousness of their users seems to be of very general provenience. Only in privileged contexts—trickster narratives or "reversal" rituals, for example—is the arbitrary character of cultural categorizations and propositions overtly acknowledged or celebrated, and even here the social significance of folly and transgression may be conservative rather than subversive of institutional and cosmic orders (Turner 1982). Like most other people, Crees lack consciousness of external objects and of their experiences with them as the constructs of semiotic mediation by a "culture."

Saussure's exposition took as its object a privileged case of the sign:

that of the word in which a recurrent sound image stands for a recurrent concept. As such, the sign is doubly arbitrary: no necessary bond exists either between the sound image and the concept or between the concept and whatever segment of extralinguistic experience it picks out and categorizes. The second of these relationships has more general implications for the analysis of signs in social life. Any occurrence of a social practice—setting bear traps, for example—implicates multiple constituent objects, actions, processes, and conditions: the trapper's sense of himself as a human agent and as an individual, travel, habitat, weather, bears, trap, bait, setting the traps, and so forth. Some of these elements are lexicalized in Cree, while others are not; all can presumably be referred to at clausal levels of discourse. From the perspective taken here, all of these elements are signs, although they lack the conventionalized referential symbolism of words. Each of them, whether lexicalized or not, is discriminated from semantically related elements by relations of resemblance and contrast. And, like lexical concepts, the elements are arbitrary, not in relation to each other but in their articulation with the coordinates of human biology and the boreal ecosystem. Anthropological writing has overwhelmingly emphasized cultural differences in the classification of tangible objects: colors, animals, plants, and relatives form the usual subject matter. Categories of event and action are equally elements of structure.

I am concerned here with the semiotic structure of Cree animal-human relations at the levels of "structure," of consciously articulated discourses, and of events of practical action in which intentions and dispositions are implicated. In all these modalities, the relations to animals as use-values and social others are organized by socially shared categories, lexicalized or not, of object, action, process, and event which define and circumscribe the world in which Crees understand themselves to be situated. In two of their modalities, cultural signs correspond to the Saussurean distinctions of *langue* and *parole* (Sahlins 1981:68–70). As constituents of structures or systems, the semiotic elements of daily life are abstractions from particular people's discourses and practices, postulated as corresponding to the knowledge, both tacit and conscious, that makes coordinated discourse and practice possible. As a linguistic sign, *maskwa* 'bear' possesses stable meaning as a semantic "type" which it retains from one occasion of its use in speech to the next. And so with more complex cultural signs. As a sign in Cree society, Cree *maskwa* 'bear' is not identical to or a sensory replica of any particular worldly bear that Crees may talk about or interact with. It is, rather, an a priori construct that defines what a bear is and does and to which each worldly experience with bears is oriented and assimilated. Similarly, categories of an event in the world—encountering a bear or setting bear traps or dreaming of a bear—possess recurrent meanings as types of experiences the inform the intentionalities and interpretations of their particular token occurrences as unique events.

In another respect, individual bears and particular events of bear trapping are themselves signs. Crees experience and act both cere-monially and productively on the boreal fauna not as objective qualities but as entities mediated by social meanings. Linguistic signs exist both as types and as tokens in contextualized situations of human speech. On particular occasions of use in speech, "token" occurrences of *maskwa*, by virtue of the stable association of sound image and concept, can refer to a particular bear in the field of vision, or a bear encountered earlier, or a fictional bear, or the entire class of bears, or, metaphorically, a penis or a menstruating woman. The circumstances of the individual utter-ance contribute to each token occurrence of the word a residue of meaning that is never precisely equivalent to the context-independent type. So also with events not only of reference to but of interaction with bears. Bears are understood by many Crees as exceptional animals pos-sessing intelligence equaling or exceeding that of humans. It is said that bears, for example, understand spoken Cree, a competence not conven-tionally generalized to other animals. Consequently, the behavior of bears is likely to be interpreted by Crees as manifesting this intelligence in ways that are not salient to non-Cree observers. Crees are likelier than whites to ascribe a studied deliberateness to the doings of bears. Anything that bears do is likely to be apprehended as a particular token occurrence of a conventional type of ursine acumen. For example,

B. L. cached his clothing and food on a rack for three days before going out to lift his traps. He was worried about bears or wolverines getting into his stuff, so he barked the upright poles on the rack and rubbed them real smooth so no animal could climb up there. When he returned, he was dismayed to find that a bear had been there during his absence. Although the bear couldn't get at the food because it was in the middle of the platform, the bear hooked his claws up over the edge and pulled down all of B.'s clothes. All of his clothes were ripped up into shreds except one new suit of long underwear from the Bay. This suit was spread out on the ground with arms and legs outstretched. It had been carefully arranged. And right on the seat of the underwear, the bear had left a large pile of scats. B. said, "What next?" He said that the bear had gotten mad about the food and gotten even with him on purpose. He said he'd heard about smart bears but he'd never seen one that smart.

This anecdote amused both the Crees and the whites who heard it—but for different reasons. As white humor, the story presents a bear who performs by chance a scatological act suggestive of malicious purpose. The Crees, in contrast, saw nothing accidental in the bear's behavior, the humor deriving precisely from malicious intention. Encounters such as these are interpreted in terms of the conventional expectations about ursine potentialities, and each encounter re-creates the expectations. Each context of interaction contains, however, a residue of emergent significance contributed by the circumstances to which the conventions refer. The fate of B.'s underwear was a novel manifestation of ursine intelligence at the same time that it was a culturally conventional one.

The symbolic character of Cree human-animal interactions, both as types and as occurrences, is not exhausted by the reciprocally defining relations of resemblance and difference that exist within and between the two categories. Or, phrased a different way, the constitution of these categories as separate (or as continuous) has everything to do with propositions about the interactions understood to exist between them. Crees typically explain their own foraging practices, including the most esoteric of them, as instrumental procedures that secure desired objectives by taking realistic account of the objective characteristics of animals (and of the Canadian market). From a Western perspective, the technical procedures for killing bears do exactly this. Crees understand *maskwa* to be a name for something else: bears. Bears themselves and the events of hunting, killing, retrieving, butchering, eating, and ritualizing them, do not as their primary function refer to other things in this way, although bears and interactions with them can, of course, stand for many things. Bears are significant to Crees as omnivorous scavengers, hibernators, fierce fighters, animals whose meat can satisfy the need to eat, owners of marketable hides, and sources of spiritual power, and in many other respects. An event of catching a bear in a trap may stand for the intrinsic value of trapping as a profession, the trapper's technical expertise, the satisfaction of needs for meat and for goods obtained by selling the hide, the opportunity to display generosity by giving away meat, the worldly consequence of a predestining dream, the spiritual "power" of the trapper, and many other possibilities. The categories of animals that Crees understand to exist and the categories of human-animal interaction that they understand themselves to undertake are reciprocally defining and motivating. To trap bears, a man or woman employs different strategies than to trap rabbits;

likewise in more esoteric spheres of interaction where the lavish ritual attention accorded to the bear contrasts with the neglect of the rabbit. The existence of particular modes of interaction is based on the understood character of the animal; reciprocally, the character of the animal is built up in terms of the role it plays in human social life.

As signs in Cree society, humans, animals, and categories of interaction between them are organized by sets of propositions that are themselves complex signs. The existence and meaning of each animal-as-sign is based on overlapping dimensions of resemblance and difference with the others. In an equally basic way, each animal sign is constructed from the aggregate social propositions delineating its instrumental and moral relationships and interactions with the makers and users of the signs. Bears are edible, valuable, powerful, and dangerous. All these attributes encode propositions constitutive of the cultural meaning of "bear," presupposed and re-created in each context of interaction between humans and bears. As Sahlins (1976:64) has shown, cultural propositions about entities may be as arbitrary as the principles of their classification. It is, for example, to some degree arbitrary that Crees distinguish bears from wolverines since societies and languages are imaginable which would not do so. Even more arbitrary is the definition of wolverines—and bears by some Cree individuals—as inedible.

The second part of the book introduces a second sense of "semiotic," one that contrasts not with decontextualized formalism but with the by no means homogeneous congeries of ecological, sociobiological, and Marxian theories that represent social forms as determined by ecosystem variables, human biology, and the labor process. In viewing the labor process and the ecosystem in which Crees themselves participate as semiotic constructs, I suggest that Cree hunting strategies are not now and have never been in the past determined by material forces. The relevant ecosystem is itself a social construction, albeit one with maximal "resistance." The foraging strategies historically attested are only a subset of the possible adjustments that would perpetuate Crees as a biological population in the boreal forest. Other facets of social practice are, in turn, relatively arbitrary with respect to the labor process itself. As the multiple lexical segmentations in different languages demonstrate the arbitrariness of words to external discontinuities, so the multiple possible designs for society in any historical context demonstrate the relative arbitrariness of social forms with respect to their material parameters.

The questioning of such "determination" as a totalizing theory of forager (or other) societies does not, however, exclude consideration of material coordinates. In qualifying Saussure's doctrine of arbitrariness, Paul Friedrich posed the question of "the degree of congruity between the symbolic system and the external one—particularly the degree to which the former makes use of the latter; material reality may be seen as in part a sort of resource for symbolic reality" (1979:23). Social practices must, of course, comply with material constraints as a necessary precondition for the biological reproduction of the practitioners. The Western Woods Crees survived before and after European contact in a boreal ecosystem characterized by extreme fluctuations in animal biomass and limited access to the botanical foods that elsewhere underwrite the (now well-debated) affluence of tropical foragers. References to famine and death by starvation occur in the earliest documentary references to Crees. It is not surprising, therefore, that Crees act upon animals in terms of market principles (e.g., the price of lynx pelts) and characteristics relevant to effective search and capture. Considerations of habitat, density, aggregation, mobility, and biomass enter into Cree animal definitions and classifications, conditioning decisions about hunting. The superiority of a semiotic approach, in contrast to those that would postulate the relevant material properties of resources in advance, derives from its precision in identifying the relevant material parameters of which the foragers take account. Simultaneously, a semiotics of foraging can specify other dimensions of meaning—culturally specific assessments of edibility or availability, for example—that may be of coordinate importance. No foragers forage indiscriminately, none know or act upon all the characteristics of proximal fauna potentially relevant to the provisioning of human populations. Diet breadths and foraging strategies do not passively encode universally recognized material properties. There is always "selection" between alternative possible designs for provisioning society.

The Cree signs *iθiniw* 'human' and *pisiskiw* 'animal' and the many signs discriminating modes of interaction between them cannot readily be arrayed as discretely bounded categories in sets of logically interrelated propositions. Neither would such an exposition exhaust the interest of the subject. Much anthropological writing identified as "symbolic" or "structuralist" has been characterized with some justification as unrealistic in its formalism, antisemiotic in its inattention to practice, power, context, history, emotion, contradiction, and human purpose (cf. Ortner 1984). In seeking to make sense of how Crees both talk about and enact human-animal relationships, I proceed by assuming a dialectic, unstable both synchronically and in short and long *durées*, between a "structure" of reciprocally defining signs and their predicated interrelations, enactments of these signs in social practices, and the actors' articulated consciousness of their own knowledge and practices. None of these three facets is internally systemic; none is autonomous from or a replication of any of the others. The Cree human-animal relationship is disordered both in the instability of the two categories and in the irreconcilable propositions about their interactions. This is not, I think, a historically engendered chaos arising from the confrontation of the magic animals of Cree *manitōkīwin* with their mute and soulless counterparts in Western biology and scripture. It is probably prehistoric and echoed in the consciousness of other foragers. The animals are endlessly regenerated, and yet they are finite. I am more powerful than the animal because I kill and eat it. The animal is more powerful than I because it can elude me and cause me to starve. The animal is my benefactor and friend. The animal is my victim and adversary. The animal is different from me, and yet it is like me, as much like me as its ancestors were in the earliest time of the world.

2

"There Was Just Animals Before"

Animals and Temporality

So
it happens
in the time
when people start to . . .
before there was no people.
Well anyway people start to . . .
Well, there happen to be people in these times.
There was just animals before.
Way back there was no people, just animals.
Well, I guess the people move into our country, this side of the country.
So they notice there was people.

In Rock Cree cosmogonic thought, animals existed before human beings in the first condition of the Earth, the age of the narratives called *ācaðōhkīwin*. Some Crees say that the superior being Kicimanitōw made the Earth and the animals. Others speculate that the Earth and its animal inhabitants are without beginning, that they have always existed. Human beings were created and moved into the Churchill River country after the animals. Beyond this, there exists little unanimity or interest regarding the temporal ordering of such primordial events as the flood, human creation, or the differentiation of humans and animals.

"*Ācaðōhkīwin*" refers to a narrative recounting events that occurred in the early period of the world, a past both continuous with and detached from the present. During this era, animals talked and behaved in other respects like *iðiniwak* 'human beings', and this, in fact, is the char-

37

acteristic that Crees emphasize when describing it. The early world is also talked about in terms of the activities of the trickster-transformer character, Wīsahkīcāhk, whose exploits transformed the social and biophysical environments. A blurring of human and animal categories and a changeful plasticity differentiate this epoch from the ensuing period that extends into the present. No event of abrupt transition between the two periods is identified. *Ācimōwin* refers to a narrative of events transpiring in this more recent condition of the universe. These incorporate spiritual events and presences, nonfactual from a Western perspective, as well as more prosaic stories of battles, trapping, hunting, marriage, and travel. The category is not limited to formal narratives but also includes gossip, reports of recent events, jokes, and humorous stories understood as fabrications. Whereas *ācimōwina* may be either true or false, *ācoðōhkīwina* are usually regarded as true accounts of factual events. The stories are said to have been passed down by word of mouth from the time of the events they describe or to have been dreamed long ago. The characters of *ācimōwina* are human beings, tied to geographic, genealogical, and other social contexts with which tellers and hearers are familiar. The characters of *ācaðōhkīwina* are not contextualized in this way: they include both animal and human (or humanoid) characters, but these are never identified as persons with whom the tellers have genealogical ties or immediate personal knowledge from waking experience.

The *ācaðōhkīwina* include stories of two distinguishable types from the point of view of their dramatis personae. The first type is exclusively concerned with animal characters, imaged in part theriomorphically but possessing also such characteristics as speech, fire, social organization, technology, and clothing. The second type focuses on what appear to be human characters who interact with each other and also with animals. The Wīsahkīcāhk stories, for example, focus on the trickster-transformer, variously identified as a Cree Indian or as an *ahcāk* 'spirit', and his encounters with both human and animal characters. Some Crees speculate that the "human" characters in these myths were not beings of the same kind as modern Indians. Representations of animals in these latter stories are variable. Some animal characters converse and otherwise participate in culture while retaining animal attributes. In the myth of Ayās, for example, the hero successively encounters a frog and a mouse who live in three-pole lodges and provide food and sewing services for their human "grandchild." Each repairs the hero's damaged moccasins but does so in a fashion consistent with her species' characteristics. The frog woman sews the moccasins in the way that she jumps, such that the stitches are too far apart. The mouse woman sews with the stitches close together, like mouse tracks in the snow (Brightman 1989b). Other animal characters seem not to differ from their modern counterparts. Crees say that stories with exclusively animal characters describe events that occurred earlier than those in stories of the trickster and other humanoid heroes.

Animal Origins

When asked about animal "origins," Crees usually say that each modern species is the transformation or descendant of an individual animal being (or a class of such beings) who existed in the mythological age. The origins of these individual or multiple proto-animals, the characters of the first class of ācaðōhkīwin, are not themselves the subject of mythological elaboration: they are presupposed rather than explained. There is no myth describing the origin of these protoanimals. The closest approximation to a Rock Cree account of animal origins that I obtained was Johnny Bighetty's recollection of what his father had related on the subject:

I don't know any stories about how the animals were first made. They say they were here before the first people. But my father told me something that the old people learned in their dreams long ago. The animals came into the Churchill River country flying from the four directions. Some kinds came from the south and some from the north and east and west. All the dangerous animals came from the north. That happened before the time that Wīsahkīcāhk [the transformer] was alive.

Johnny added that bears, wolverines, snakes, frogs, and *misipisiwak* 'water panthers' were the harmful animals associated with the north. The association of animals with the four cardinal points here evokes the complex directional symbolism in a Swampy Cree cosmogonic myth recorded by Cree Anglican clergyman James Settee in 1823 (Brown 1977), but the latter narrative lacks an account of animal origins. Myths describing single generalized creations of the modern animal species exist among Plains Cree groups, but these suggest the effects of Assiniboine or other infuences since they are without known parallel in the literature of Western Woods Crees. In the Plains Cree stories, the modern animal species are transformed by hero characters from humanoid beings (Bloomfield 1930:82, 120, 295) or from the *cimiskwanak*, anthropophagous animals who ate the early humans (Ahenakew 1929:323).

The Rock Cree conception that modern animals derive by descent from the timeless protoanimals of the first condition of the world is supplemented by certain myths that identify some individual modern species as the transformation of humanoid characters. Claude Lévi-Strauss (1988:6–7) has recently drawn attention in the mythologies of South America to doctrines that animal species are derived from human or protohuman ancestors, a conception noted long ago by Speck (1935*a*:49) as characteristic of Eastern Cree evolutionary thought. For example, the hero character, Ayās, after bringing about an epic conflagration, voluntarily transforms himself into the first crow and his mother into the first woodpecker (Brightman 1989*a*:111); a Swampy Cree version (Skinner 1911:95) substitutes the gray jay and robin, respectively. The macabre rolling head that pursues Wīsahkīcāhk and his younger brother becomes in Rock Cree myth the first sturgeon (Brightman 1989*b*:12–13; cf. Russell 1898:203, Vandersteene 1969:47) when it falls from the back of the aquatic animal carrying it across a river. Wīsahkīcāhk's adversarial father-in-law, Wīmisōs, becomes after his defeat the first northern pike in one account and the first tamarack tree in another (Brightman 1989*a*:26). The conception of human characters as the ancestors of animals is not, however, consistently elaborated or even very frequent in Rock Cree and other Western Woods Cree myth and is focused on fish and birds rather than on mammals.

Since Crees say that bears and beavers are closer in their attributes to human beings than other species, it might be expected that some myths would assign these animals human or humanoid ancestry. Johnny Bighetty speculated humorously on one occasion that bears might once have been human beings who stayed out in the bush too long, a conjecture based on the Cree custom of addressing bears as *nimosōm* 'my grandfather'. The Crees' Saulteaux neighbors to the south related to Nelson in 1811 a myth identifying beavers as descendants of an Indian family, this ancestry then accounting for the sociality and architectural proclivities of the species (Brown and Brightman 1988:121–122). Some idea of the variability of these conceptions is afforded by the account obtained by Thompson from Saulteaux or Crees fourteen years earlier: "The Beavers had been an ancient people, and then in the remote past lived on the dry land; they were always Beavers, not Men"

(Thompson 1962 [1784–1812]:155). The idea that animals derive from transformed humans is intermittently explored in boreal Algonquian thought; the reverse conception is absent.

The protoanimals possessed social and linguistic attributes today exhibited by human beings but possessed also the physical and behavioral traits of animals and are spoken of as *pisiskiwak* 'animals'. It is significant that the indigenous cosmogony figures modern humans as the descendants of images fashioned out of earth while tracing the animal species to beings who may always have existed or whose origin is beyond the scope of knowledge. Animals, unlike humans, have no specified beginning; they are of broader cosmic provenience. It is also significant that the cultural accomplishments of humans—speech, fire, food preservation, clothing—are represented as originally the possessions of animals, long before human beings existed in the world.

The World of the Animals

The first *ācaðōhkīwin* category represents social animals inhabiting a world devoid of human beings where they interact with members of their own and other species. When I asked people what the animals in these stories looked like, their reactions sometimes suggested that the question had not previously been entertained. Some said that they looked like animals but with such hominid attributes as upright carriage and clothing. Others said only that they looked like contemporary animals. The stories about *Omiðāhcīs* 'Wolverine', for example, make pointed reference to his tail, which he used to chisel beaver lodges. The way of life of the animal characters is overtly cultural. Animals are represented as talking, making fires, arranging marriages, living in lodges, exchanging food, making dry meat, practicing sorcery, and using such manufactures as toboggans. Since human beings were not yet in the world, these myths implicitly suggest that Cree designs for living are to some degree carried over from the animals who originated them. At the same time, the myths are strongly etiological: features of the appearance and behavior of modern animals are explained as resulting from the experiences of the prototypes. Representations of animals in this first category of myth need to be distinguished from images in the transformer cycle and other hero narratives in which the animals interact with humanoid characters. In these latter stories, the animals are often physically more theriomorphic and less overtly cultural, although they continue to be shown as possessing speech. Like the protoanimals, they are subject to transformations.

Most protoanimals possessed as their proper names the nouns that refer today to members of the same species: *Omiðāhcīs* 'Wolverine', *Māhīhkan* 'Wolf', *Sākwīsiw* 'Mink'. Other animal characters possessed different names: *Cīcīhkwāðōs* 'Narrowtail', the ancestor of dogs; *Misiskānātōs* 'Great Skunk', the monstrous prototype of modern skunks; and *Apiscisākwīsis* 'Small Mink', the weasel. The animals that figure as primary characters are carnivores: there are no individuated caribou, moose, hare, or beaver personalities, although prototypes of these species are talked about as having been present. The bear, otherwise eminent in Cree religious thought, is conspicuously absent. Aside from Wolverine, it is not always clear whether Crees imagine the individual animal characters in different stories as the same person. The speech styles of animal characters possess distinctive characteristics: Dog, for example, interjects a growly "*wanam*" in utterances otherwise delivered in a polite and formal style. Wolverine interjects "*cin-cin-cin-cin*" when pleased or excited.

Wolverine is the most complex of the protoanimal personalities. Stories describe Wolverine's temporary residence with a band of Wolves, his misuse of the Wolves' gift of fire, his heroic triumph over Great Skunk, and finally his death at the hands of his Wolf affines. A collection of these myths has been published in the language of the narrator's English translations (Brightman 1989*a*:97–100, 133–134, 143–149). In these stories, Wolverine's character takes on different values: he is variously buffoon, trickster, hero, and villain. These Rock Cree stories are paralleled by a larger cycle of Wolverine trickster narratives known to the Eastern Cree (Savard 1974). In all these respects, Wolverine emerges as the animal counterpart to the humanoid trickster, Wīsahkīcāhk, a parallelism epitomized in an unusual Plains Cree version of the trickster cycle (Skinner 1916) that identifies the two characters as the same. The literary eminence and morally ambiguous persona of Wolverine perhaps reflect the status of his worldly descendants as the respected antagonists of Cree fur trappers. Crees say that the wolverine follows the trapline like the human trapper, plundering sets that contain animals, consuming the carcasses or concealing them under lichen or snow, urinating on trap sets and on caches of fresh or dried meat. As one Cree put it, "When a trapper sees those tracks crossing back and forth on his trapline, he thinks that he might as well turn around [and go home]. He gets a bad feeling. He knows what's happened already." Because of its skill as a robber of trap sets, the wolverine is regarded as intelligent and enterprising. Also respected as a fighter and traveler, the wolverine is said to be able to cover a fifty-mile area in a day; Johnny Bighetty named his snowmobile Omiθāhcīs because "it goes all over just like wolverine." Mingled with the respect is genuine hostility. Today the wolverine's depredations cost the trapper time and cash; in the past, families sometimes starved when trap sets and caches were plundered.

Representations in myth of interspecific relations between animal characters are exceedingly varied. In some stories, animals of different species live and travel together, sharing a common language and cooperating in common projects. According to one Cree narrator, "Animals used to travel in bunches like humans . . . all mixed animals: squirrels, rabbits, foxes, coyotes, all the animals." Just as these proto-animals differed less from humans (who did not yet exist) than do their modern counterparts, so did the species differ less from each other. In a Swampy Cree myth from Manitoba (Clay 1938:34–37), the animals live in fraternal solidarity, lacking modern predator-prey relationships and freely conversing with each other. Initially uniform in coloration, they solicit different kinds of skin covering from the transformer and thereafter become physically distinct, losing in consequence the ability to communicate.

Other myths represent interspecific relations between animals as hostile, working imaginative variations and embellishments on modern predator-prey relationships. Thus, one myth posits a motley band of animals—Wolverine, Mink, Weasel, and others—united in flight and defense against the monstrous and predatory Great Skunk. Seeking to learn how closely behind them their adversary is following, Mink and Weasel successively stay behind on the trail and play dead. The scenes in which Great Skunk discovers, examines, and discards the "corpses" suggests the surreal quality of some events in these stories; it was sometimes difficult for me to understand why characters thought and behaved as they did. Turning the "corpses" over in his giant claws, Great Skunk notices their anuses and identifies them as lethal arrow wounds. It turns out that Great Skunk, big as he is, is unaware of his own anus and thus that other animals also have them. When Weasel reports to the other animals that Great Skunk is close behind them, Wolverine volunteers to face him down at a beaver lodge. He tricks Great Skunk into discharging all his "medicine" and then immobilizes him while the other animals tear him apart; the fragments become the ancestors of modern skunks. Wolverine, however, is blinded by a last spray of Great Skunk "medicine" and must travel down to Hudson Bay to wash; thereafter, the Bay water is salty and unfit to drink.

Other stories focus on the incompatibility between Wolverine in his antisocial mode and the Wolves with whom he interacts. In each of these stories, the socially acceptable conduct of Wolves is opposed to the objectionable behavior of Wolverine. In one myth, Wolves generously share their magical fire with Wolverine, who proceeds to waste the gift by making fires for his own diversion. Another myth describes Wolverine's temporary residence with a band of Wolves, contrasting the Wolves' solicitous hospitality with Wolverine's greed, ingratitude, and overall social defectiveness. The Wolves are pursuing a moose and courteously invite Wolverine and Dog to follow behind at a leisurely pace in the company of the younger Wolves. The party successively encounters objects on the trail which Wolverine sees as refuse but which Wolves and Dog see as manufactures. By the time Wolverine straggles into the Wolves' camp that night, the moose they have killed has been butchered and buried in the snow. Thinking the Wolves have eaten the whole moose, Wolverine hungrily gobbles up blood spots on the snow, muttering about their bad manners. When they bring out the meat to divide it, Wolverine rejects the delicacies they offer him and insists on receiving meat from the rump. Wolverine eats most of his portion rather than sharing it, urinating on the remainder and burying it in the snow. Wolves dry and pound their meat, boiling the bones for marrow fat. Wolverine sleeps through most of this activity, awaking only in time to dry a few chunks of his remaining meat. At the next camp, he discourteously takes leave of the Wolves, complaining that they are too hard to get along with. Throughout, Wolverine represents the egocentric individual as conceived in opposition to the well-socialized person. As a solitary animal, Wolverine is a natural symbol of such individualism, opposed to the sociality of the Wolves against whom he was, in all probability, didactically held up as bad example in pedagogical recitations of the myth. It is also likely that the myth is "totemic" in Lévi-Strauss's particular sense, using natural discontinuities—in this case, differences between animal species—as a metalanguage to represent differences between Crees and other Indians and perhaps between Crees and Euro-Canadians.

The opening scenes in which Wolverine and Wolves have different perceptual experiences of the same objects foreground a theme that reappears in Cree reflections on the modern human-animal relationship. The party encounters an object lying on the path.

There is dung on the ground.
"Well, well, *wanam*.
A fur coat, big brother, pick it up." [Dog addresses Wolverine]
"I'm not dirtying my hands on wolf dung!" [Wolverine]
"Hey, what's this big brother of ours saying?" [Wolves]
A Wolf vigorously shakes it [dung] free of debris . . . a fur coat.
"Well, a fur coat. I didn't know it." [Wolverine]

They subsequently encounter another object.

Somebody's tooth is sticking there in a tree, a wolf tooth.
"Well, big brother, take it, *wanam*." [Dog to Wolverine]
They [Wolves] detach that bone arrow they see sticking there from where
   someone shot and missed.
Well, he [Wolverine] sees it.
"Get out, I'm not bothering with this little wolf tooth!" [Wolverine]
"Hey, what's this big brother of ours saying?" [Wolves]
He [Wolf] pulls it out.
It's a bone arrow that he pulls out. [Cree]

The narrator's English translation contains an element missing in the
Cree version: Wolverine once again acknowledges he was wrong, explaining, "Oh, I didn't know it was a bow and arrow. I thought it was a
wolf tooth."

The two scenes are closely parallel in organization, and in each, the
narrator uses the same strategy to signal to the listener the events of
discrepant perception. First, the objects are reported by the narrator
and identified as wolf dung and a wolf tooth. Next, the narrator signals
that Dog and Wolves experience the object as something else, in the
first scene by quoting Dog's identification of it as a fur coat and in the
second by reporting that the Wolves (and Dog) see an arrow. In each
case, Dog instructs Wolverine to retrieve the object and Wolverine
haughtily refuses, identifying it as something not worth bothering
with: the dung and tooth initially reported by the narrator. The Wolves
are confused by Wolverine's apparent hallucination. In each scene, a
Wolf retrieves the object and the narrator then reports the object as
being what Dog and Wolves perceive. Wolverine's perception then
seemingly changes, and he acknowledges that his initial identification
was mistaken. The language chosen by Cornelius Colomb, the narrator,
to report these events of discrepant perception is ultimately noncom-
mittal concerning the differential validity of the two points of view.

Possibly the act of shaking magically converts wolf excrement into a
fur garment, and the act of extraction changes the tooth to an arrow.
The text itself suggests not a physical change of one object into another

but a change in Wolverine's perception of a single object. The narrative states that Dog and Wolves initially identify the objects as a coat and an arrow, perceiving them as such all along. Shaking and extraction, therefore, seemingly allow Wolverine to perceive the objects in the same way they do. The verb used is *kā-pahpawitāt* 'he shakes it free of debris', a metaphoric likening of Wolverine's changing perception to the process by which intervening material is cleared away to disclose the identity of a concealed object. The narrator's identification of the object as a fur coat after it is shaken is thus a report of Wolverine's new perception; the listener is invited to share Wolverine's surprise at this unexpected turn of events. This seems to be suggested by Wolverine's chagrined reaction: beginning with perceptual disparity, each episode concludes with perceptual consensus.

The members of each of the two pairs of objects whose identity Wolverine disputes with the wolves are commutable in certain respects. The metaphoric relationship between a wolf tooth and an arrow is straightforward: both are pointed weapons used in killing animals. The connection between wolf dung and fur coats is more obscure. Wolves excrete rather than digest much of the fur of their prey, as their scats visibly attest (Leslie Saxon, personal communication). Crees also say wolves roll in their own excrement to keep warm. There exists, therefore, a resemblance between these two objects as well, suggesting that in each case, Wolverine and Wolves are perceiving differently the identical external entity. Metaphorically, scats and teeth are the coats and arrows of wolves. The Wolves see the two objects as useful goods, the salvageable result of deliberate cultural artifice. Wolverine initially sees the same objects as worthless physiological residue, the antithesis of manufacture. It is only after they are physically appropriated—picked up off the trail or pulled out of a tree—that Wolverine acquiesces and shares in the knowledge of the others, agreeing that they are manufactures. The developmental trajectory of Wolverine's knowledge of these objects in the myth thus parallels the transformation in modern Cree experience of such raw materials as animal skins and bones—useless on the face of them—into clothing, weapons, and other valuable and useful goods.

These scenes typify epistemological themes that resonate in other myths, in dreams, and in Cree reflections on the quality of their waking perceptions. Beings or selves of two different species or kind may have radically different perceptions and understandings of the same events in which both participate. More specifically, individuals or selves of one species or kind experience individuals of other species as different from themselves in appearance and practices. The experience that each "self" has of the "other" may be, however, radically different from the experience that that "other" has of its own appearance and practices. Further, selves of different species or kind may each experience *themselves* in similar or identical terms: as users of fire, speech, and manufactured objects. In the age of the *ācaðōhkīwin*, the animals possessed cultural attributes. In the present, it is human beings who possess these attributes and the animals manifestly lack them. The contrast seemingly intimates a "historical" transition in the condition of animals: sometime in the past, they lost the cultural characteristics that the myths assert they once possessed and became as they now appear to men and women in the present. At least today, Cree religious thought postulates no objective transition. Crees speculate that modern animals, whatever they may look like to humans, experience themselves as participating in the same appearances and behaviors that Crees understand themselves to possess. In the myth, Wolverine represents, from this point of view, the human perspective on an animal "other," displaced, in this case, from the animal itself and onto its manufactures. Wolverine sees as worthless detached body parts what the Wolves see as valuable manufactured artifacts. He comes, however, to participate in the experience the Wolves have of themselves.

Wolverine's difficulties with the wolves culminate ultimately in his death.

Once then and long ago, the animals lived like human beings. Once then this Wolverine and he intends to marry the daughter from a family of Wolves. So he goes to where they stay and he asks the mother of that Wolf-girl for permission. Really, she thinks badly of it, but she consents. Then that Wolf-girl goes to stay with Wolverine as his wife. They have several children. All of them resemble Wolverine, except one only, which resembles a Wolf.

Shortly after he marries her, this Wolverine curses the Wolves so that they cannot hunt successfully. Really, he intends that they all should starve. Soon they are close to starving. Wolverine tells them that he is crying for them. "I cry because I have no meat to relieve my mother-in-law," he tells her. But he has beaver meat, that Wolverine. That one boy, Wolverine's son, he takes beaver meat and gives it to the Wolves. He doesn't tell his father that he gives them meat. That old woman knows that Wolverine is cursing them. She sends her sons out to hunt moose. Finally they succeed in killing one and bring it back at evening. The old woman cooks that moose; she knows that Wolverine comes to spy on their camp and she wants him to know that they are cooking and eating moose. They have a large feast. Later on that night, they move their camp some distance away.

In the morning, Wolverine comes to spy on the Wolf camp. Well! No one is to be seen there. He returns to his camp. He wakes his wife. "I fear for the welfare of your relatives," he says to her. "Perhaps for some reason they are not successful in hunting." And to those two boys, he says, "Go find where they [Wolves] have made their camp." He sends those Wolverine-boys to look for the Wolf family. They find the new camp, and see that the Wolf family has plenty of moose meat. They find scraps of moose meat on the trail and really they fight over them, those boys.

The Wolverine-boys return to their father. "Our grandmother is cooking moose meat," they say. The Wolverine has a little beaver meat. He intends to trade the beaver with the old woman for some moose meat. He travels on ahead to the Wolves' camp and offers the Wolves the beaver meat. One of the Wolves says, "Our brother-in-law is hungry, we should give him some moose meat." The old woman says, "Why should we feed him? He tried to starve us." Finally she agrees to feed him. "Sit down, my son-in-law," she says. "When we Wolves eat moose meat, we must shut our eyes." "Well, then, I will shut my eyes," he says. Then the old woman strikes him on the head with a stone and kills him. They bury Wolverine in the snow by the trail with just his tail sticking up. Later, the Wolf-girl and those children arrive there, pulling their toboggan through the snow. They see the tail protruding from the snow and begin to cry. The old woman tells her daughter, "Stop crying! We had to kill your husband because he tried to starve us. These children of his, they will behave like their father when they grow older." Then that old woman kills all of the children, except the boy who looks like a Wolf. He has a Wolf nature, that one who brought meat to the old woman [Cree].

This meditation on affinity and miscegenation, by turns comical and somber, is particularly detailed with respect to the cultural practices of the protoanimals. It concludes a cycle of myths that juxtapose Wolverine to the Wolves as foolish to wise, wicked to moral, egoistic individual to socialized person.

Human Origins

—————————————————————————

While in Europe during World War II, Albert Umfreville took the Cree story of human creation as an occasion for verbal dueling with a white officer who remarked on his complexion.

Now I'm going to tell it again in English.
When I was overseas the time of the war, there was a bunch of officers laying
    out on the lawn
and I happened to be passing by there with just my shorts.

And I had my shirt off and one of the officers called to me
and he said, "Umfreville, what do you want to get a tan for?
You're black enough."
So I turned around and I told him. I says, "I don't burn like you guys, I'm
   natural."
And I says,

"You know, when God made the world,
he made men.
He made a man.
The first one he made of his image, he put in the oven.
And while he was working, he forgot all about it. When he did think about it,
   when he opened his oven and pulled his image out, it was burned black.
Well, that was the Negro.

So the next image of himself he made, he put it in the oven.
And he didn't leave it in long enough. So when he pulled it out it was all pale
   and that was the white man.

So when he made the third image of himself, he put it in the oven. And went to
   work for awhile.
He waited for awhile before he opened his oven.
And when he did,
it was just nicely browned.

So that was me," I told my officer,
"just nice and brown.
I'm an Indian."

This is an old story. During the 1770s, W. Wales (Cooper 1934:56) obtained the same polygenetic account from Crees trading into York Factory. The superior being Okimāw 'leader', evidently another name for the deity, Kicimanitōw, molds three pairs of male and female figures from differently pigmented clays. The excessively dark and light coloring of the first two pairs causes the creator to discard them contemptuously and they become the progenitors of blacks and whites. The creator retains the aesthetically satisfying "brown" figures, which become the first Indians. By at least the late 1700s, Crees were familiar enough with black Hudson's Bay Company employees to have invented a noun for them (Graham 1969 [1767–1791]:207). Other polygenetic versions date from the present century. An Albany (Westmain Swampy) Cree version collected by Skinner (1911:112) describes the "Great Spirit's" creation of three male clay figures ancestral to the Indian, white, and black races. The pigmentation of the latter two resulted from under- and overcooking, respectively. When Oblate missionary Rossignol (1938:68) queried Rock Crees regarding their ideas of human origins, he was told that the creator deity had fashioned Crees and Europeans of brown and white earth, respectively. He was also told didactically that Europeans and Crees had been given distinct religions to follow.

In 1823, Nelson (Brown and Brightman 1988:48–49) recorded another polygenetic account that differs from those discussed in identifying Wīsahkīcāhk, the trickster-transformer, as the sculptor and situating the creation as a postfluvial innovation. The stories of the transformer's many exploits may be narrated singly or concatenated in longer narratives. Although great variability is evident in composition, three of these stories—the flight from the rolling head, the contest with the sorcerer, Wīmisōs, and the re-creation of the flooded earth—are understood to describe consecutive events, and they occur sequentially in composite narrations recorded in widely separated Cree communities (Brightman 1989a). It is after Wīsahkīcāhk has remade the world from mud brought from under the water by the muskrat that he turns his attention to human beings, creating Indian and white males from earth. The Moon creates their female counterparts, fashioning the white female from the rib of the male; Crees were seemingly integrating scriptural ideas into their formulations of where the Europeans came from. Such humanoid characters as Wīsahkīcāhk's parents, wives, and murderous father-in-law figure in events that Crees say preceded the flood, seeming to suggest that these beings were of a different order from the fabricated ancestors of the modern humans.

Although addressing the question of how different "races" originated and also clearly subject to some mediated scriptural influences, these historical fragments presumably represent indigenous Cree concepts of human creation. The details of the different versions indicate obvious connections with the Earth and with baking and pottery, but the Earth, to my knowledge, possesses no female or maternal associations. Nelson's version preserves another aboriginal motif: the creator's initial intention to create humans from stone and his contemplative substitution of earth.

Whilst at this work it struck him that by forming them of so hard and strong a substance that in time when they would become to know their nature, they would grow insolent and rebellious and be a great annoyance to each other and of course also would never die. "This will not do, I must make them of a more weak and fragile substance, so that they may live a reasonable time and behave as becomes human beings." (Brown and Brightman 1988:49, cf. Simms 1906:338–339)

The rejection of stone is here consistent with a rationally formulated cosmogonic design, first of all, one implementing a "reasonable" demographic management of the new beings relative to the space and resources of the Earth; a comparative analysis of myths explaining the innovation of death would provide a further basis for elucidation of Malthusian themes in Native American demographic thought. Second, the creator desires to cultivate conduct as "becomes human beings." The association of stone and its physical qualities of hardness and sharpness with antisocial conduct figures also in the character of the culture hero's flint twin in Ojibwa-Saulteaux and Iroquoian literature. John M. Cooper's (1934) claim that Westmain Swampy Crees regarded spirit beings as unconcerned with the moral character of human conduct needs to be examined in the context of other evidence for ethical dimensions in Algonquian religion. The possibility of mediated scriptural influence needs to be considered, but there exist, of course, difficulties with ascribing all moral content to borrowing. With specific reference to Western Woods Crees, Thompson (1962 [1784–1812]: 74) was told in the late 1700s that the creator, Kicimanitōw, had such compassion for human beings that it hated to see human blood on the ground and sent the rains to wash it away. Thompson was also told a version of the flood myth in which the creator caused the deluge as a punishment for quarreling and bloodshed (ibid.:78, cf. Vandersteene 1969). Nelson recorded in the early 1800s accounts of dreams, visions, and shaking lodge performances in which spirit beings exhorted humans to refrain from violence and sorcery (Brown and Brightman 1988:43, 57).

Animal Transformations

Insofar as Crees "explain" the origin of contemporary animal species, it is by identifying them as the genealogical descendants of the protoanimals. Diverse aspects of modern species—diet, habitat, appearance, antipathies—are further explained as the result of transformation experiences undergone by these prototypes. Rock Cree myths of the all-animal and mixed-human/animal character types are rich in such etiological themes. Such themes have been consistently and curiously ignored in British, French, and American anthropologies throughout the present century, presumably in reaction to the different nineteenth-century schools of "nature mythology." In any event, the consensus among anthropological scholars of myth is that such themes express no aesthetic or intellectual orientation to the nonhuman ecosystem. Franz Boas (1940:468–469) regarded explanatory elements in North American Indian mythology as peripheral stylistic devices, not expressions of "a rationalizing faculty in primitive man." T. T. Waterman's (1914) distributional study was a detailed exploration of the Boasian thesis that the explanations are maximally detachable from the plots in which they figure, playing no part in the composition of myths. Things were no better among the Trobriand Islanders. "As to any explanatory function of these myths," wrote Malinowski, "there is no problem which they cover, no curiosity which they satisfy, no theory which they contain" (1954:110). Likewise devoid of etiological significance were the myths of the Andamaners of whom A. R. Radcliffe-Brown (1933:342) asked rhetorically, "Why should the Andaman Islanders want to explain the markings of animals?" Lévi-Strauss (1966a:95) wrote that myths do not explain "nature" as an object but employ its categories as a reservoir of symbols for representing oppositive logical categories (in both social and biophysical orders) and their mediations. Myths from all over the world contain these etiological themes, and the arguments for their nonsignificance are both equivocal and tenuous. Boas (1940:468–470), for example, acknowledged that some etiological myths exist, and Radcliffe-Brown's claim that Andamanese myths express only the "social vaue" of natural entities—their status as symbols of sociality—seems today excessively tortuous. No one denies that etiological themes exist in myths; everyone denies that they exist for their own sake. The analyses of Lévi-Strauss are illustrative. His most recent writing on myth (1988) addresses the symbolic equivalence of potters' clay, marital jealousy, and goatsucker bird in a Jívaro etiological myth, but the etiological themes themselves are interpreted as symbolic metacommentaries or restatements of sociological "anomaly, contradiction, or scandal" (ibid.: 171). Since the volumes of *Mythologiques* demonstrate a complex articulation of etiological themes with oppositional and mediatory "structure," the relationship between what people take their myths to explain and what structuralists take them to explain remains an important desideratum.

As Boas argued cogently, the distal origins of myths are irretrievable and the proximal origins manifestly the product of diffusional combinatorics. It is impossible to prove that particular myths "originated" in a desire to explain natural facts (or, for that matter, that they did not). This impasse neither exhausts the interest of etiological themes nor explains their neglect in successive distributional, functional, psychoanalytic, and structuralist phases of interpretation. My experiences with Cree narrators indicate that these etiological elements continue to engage people's interests, that they are central to what Crees find most compelling in the *ācaðōhkīwin* literature: the constructive effect of primordial events on the design of their contemporary social and biophysical environments. The etiological themes themselves are symbolically complex, often integral rather than peripheral to the plots that are their contexts.

I was fortunate enough to be present at the probable birth of an etiological element. In the winter of 1978, I recorded in the trapline cabin of Henry and Angelique Linklater the latter's recitation of the hero myth, *Mistacayawāsis* (Brightman 1989a:117–124). The story culminates with the death of the villain, Macikaðawis, who has taken the form of a caribou. The caribou corpse spontaneously transforms into a *wīskacānis*, the gray jay, "whiskey-jack" or "camp-robber" (*Perisoreus canadensis*). The gray jay is a garrulous and personable bird that steals food from camps and is thus imagined by Crees as existing in a condition of perpetual and insatiable voraciousness. Henry found it interesting that the villain, who displays greedy behavior and suffers famine and emaciation in the course of the story, should become a gray jay. He observed that the gray jay eats all day, often by stealing food from camp, but never gets fat. With a tentative air, he speculated that perhaps the myth event explained the hunger and greediness of contemporary gray jays. I asked him whether gray jays existed in the world before the posthumous transformation. He said that they did but that their hunger perhaps derived from the event described. I later noted that "*macikaðawis*" figures in many people's vocabularies as a humorous synonym of "*wīskacānis*."

This etiological theme exemplifies most of the characteristics of others I have recorded. The events narrated in *ācaðōhkīwina* are temporally situated in a primordial past within which the biophysical and social environments are not yet entirely in their modern condition. Each etiological passage embodies a paradox that characterizes conceptions of the mythological age throughout North America. The myth time is profoundly impressible in that potential for the inception of new social and cosmological arrangements is always present. It is in this respect that the age is formative: prior states of affairs in the myth age are modified and changed, giving rise to new configurations. At the same time, the mythic period is infused with immutability and conservatism: the new order, once innovated, becomes fixed and perpetual. Only in the earliest time could the transformation of a starving man's corpse into a single Canada jay synecdochally transfer voraciousness to the whole species, and again only in this age would voraciousness thereafter become an eternal attribute of jays, endlessly reiterated into the present. Some Crees are much engaged with this reciprocal interplay between a past that is an imagined transformation of the present and simultaneously its template and crucible.

Every etiological theme necessarily encompasses four components. The first of these is the worldly "object," the contemporary entity or state of affairs whose innovation the myth accounts for. By tabulating etiological themes in Rock Cree myths with others in published collections of Cree literature, it was possible to compile an inventory of two hundred fifty such passages. Of these, 66 percent address animal origins, attributes, and human-animal relations. This figure includes varying explanations of the same object in different myths or versions of the same myth but excludes recurrent instances of the same explanation. In this sample, the animal accorded most attention in Cree mythology is the humble snowshoe hare, followed by the beaver, the bear, the muskrat, the gray jay, and the common nighthawk. Neither the species nor the attributes that figure as etiological objects in Cree myth are readily assimilable to utilitarian explanation: mythological explanations encompass objects both external and internal to the Crees' foraging praxis. Forty-one percent of the animal explanations concern species not eaten, marketed, or used in domestic manufacture. Typical objects are the blindness of moles, the aquatic habitat of frogs, the red eyes of the American coot, and the wide mouth of the common nighthawk. In the case of species that do figure in Cree production, explanations are divided between attributes relevant to capture or utilization and those that are not. For instance, both the amphibiousness of the beaver and the brown coloration of its incisors are accounted for. The myths scan, as it were, between productively relevant and irrelevant animals and characteristics. Of the other explanatory elements, 21 percent concern topographical, meteorological, and astronomical phenomena, 9 percent concern human beings and social practices, and 4 percent concern trees and other botanicals. Explanations pertaining to humans range from the cosmological questions of the origins of human "races" and of fire through the custom of polygyny to such esoterica as the differences between human and frog anuses. Cree mythological explanations are engaged less with the human than with the nonhuman world and, with respect to the latter, not exclusively or even primarily with those elements that are materially appropriated.

The remaining three components are textual and internal to mythological narratives. Minimally, such passages entail an "antecedent" subject to a "transformation" that produces a "result." It is from the result, an entity described in the myth, that Crees say the contemporary object derives. The representation of the antecedents necessarily involves creative inversions and rearrangements of the characteristics of contemporary experience: entities do not exist, or exist in alternate conditions or in different distributions or in different relations to other entities. The authority and authenticity of the mythical age in Cree experience is attested in its capacity to engender its own explanations. Every etiological passage accounts simultaneously for the structure of contemporary existence and for the *nonexistence* of alternative structures, the antecedents whose prior existence is presupposed by and well known to those who listen to myths. In some instances, this nonexistence is foregrounded explicitly as the focus of explanation. Rock Cree narratives describe, for example, anthropophagous monsters that preyed on the early humans. One narrator concluded his account of the destruction of one such race—the *wīhcikōsisak* 'small cannibals'—with the following remarks:

So that's how this man, he wiped them out. He was hunting them all the time. There was none of them left. He was a smart man. He kept on hunting them. That's how there are no more of these now. He cleans them out. (Brightman 1989a:137)

The object here is the contemporary absence of the monsters. In this respect, etiological passages possess a marked duplex structure, since they account not only for what exists but also for the nonexistence of imaginable alternatives. Myths are thus vehicles of a discourse that questions why contemporary social and cosmological arrangements—from among all the possible ones—should prevail. The transformations to which the antecedents are subjected are exceedingly diverse. In the discussion below, "transformation" is deliberately broad in compass, subsuming the sometimes multiple aspects of events represented as transformative. The change may be directly physical, as when Wīsahkī-cāhk widens the mouth of the nighthawk. Or it may come about as the result of an experience that imparts to the antecedent a new habitat or disposition. Transformations may be deliberate or seemingly accidental; they may implement a rational cosmic design or transpire through momentary spite.

Analysis of Cree etiological themes requires consideration both of the relationships among the narrated characters and events and the modes in which these latter are represented as connected to the modern objects. Peirce's (1960–1966, 2:134–173) writing on semiosis and the classification of sign types has provided sets and subsets of distinctions applied in a diverse array of anthropological and linguistic research contexts (cf. Mertz and Parmentier 1985; Silverstein 1976; Singer 1984; Boon 1982; Jakobson 1980). These distinctions permit a certain precision in the exposition and description of Cree transformation themes, particularly in the elucidation of Cree conceptions of the relations between elements. Peirce's three principal trichotomies of sign types are defined by contrasting relations existing between the representamen, or sign vehicle, the interpretant, or mental representation, created by it, and the object for which it stands.

A sign, or representamen, is something which stands to somebody for something in some respect or capacity. It addresses somebody, that is, creates in the mind of that person an equivalent sign, or perhaps a more developed sign. That sign which it creates I call the *interpretant* of the first sign. The sign stands for something, its *object*. It stands for that object, not in all respects, but in reference to a sort of an idea, which I have sometimes called the *ground* of the representamen. (Peirce 1960–1966, 2:135)

The trichotomy with which I will be most concerned here—the celebrated triad of icon, index, and symbol—is based on the "ground," the relationship of the sign to the object for which it stands. Icons resemble their objects: "Anything whatever, be it quality, existent individual or law, is an Icon of anything, insofar as it is like that thing and is used as a sign of it" (ibid.:143). Diagrammatic icons, a subclass, resemble their objects only in the relations of their respective parts (ibid.:159), as with, for example, an architectural blueprint. Symbols stand for their objects "by virtue of a law, usually an association of general ideas" (ibid.:143), as with the conventional relationship existing between the sounds and meanings of words in natural languages. Indexes are signs spatially or temporally connected to their objects, the shine of an animal's eyes in a flashlight, for example, indexing its presence. Modern animals and attributes are, in the terms of Peirce's semiotic, indexical icons of the narrated protoanimals and their experiences. They are not, I think, for many Crees, conventional representations of them. I once inadvertently gave offense when I asked Henry Linklater how the stories had first begun, meaning how it was that humans first became aware of them. He understood me to be asking him if the stories were imaginative fabrications, and, usually a jocular man, he became grave and earnest. "No, no," he said, "nobody made them up. These stories really happened. They come down to us from when they happened."

In a basic sense, myths as narratives are experienced by their tellers as icons of the characters and events that are represented in the narration. Mythological events innovated the stories that report them: the stories are understood to have originated as discourse about actual occurrences, either related by eyewitnesses and handed down through the generations or learned about in dreams. The stories are in this sense iconic since it is said to be possible to tell them incorrectly, and the incorrect versions are disparaged because they distort or fail to resemble adequately in their content the real occurrences that gave rise to them, including such details as event sequences and the identity of characters. In these respects, the narrations and the persons and events they describe are alternately signs of one another. Below I will be concerned with more specific relations existing among characters and events in narration and between these and modern animals.

A Cree myth explains the origin of a luminescent fungus by identifying it as the transformation of a vain and beautiful woman who lived in the time of the *ācaðōhkīwin*. Within the narrative, the woman is the antecedent, and the fungus is the result; the object is the class of luminescent fungi in the contemporary environment. From one point of view, the narrative itself and the explanatory element are built up from an iconic relationship present to contemporary experience. Beautiful, vain women and luminescent fungi—or vain beauty and luminosity—imaginably resemble one another, and the resemblance is reproduced in the narrative as an identity of a particular beautiful woman with the first luminous fungus. Each of the two narrated terms is an icon of the other. Each is also an icon of its worldly counterpart: the vain heroine of all conceited women and the fungus of its modern descendants. It is necessarily also the case that the narrated botanical is an icon of modern vain women just as the narrated vain heroine is an icon of modern luminescent fungi. As with these two, so with modern and ancient animals, more specifically with the latter as they become results in transformation events. Crees experience contemporary animal species as icons of the protoanimal characters in myth, resembling them in name and in defining aspects of behavior and appearance.

Crees sometimes talk about the relationship between the protoanimal and the modern species that derive from it in terms that suggest the relationship of a sign type to its tokens or, in Peirce's idiom, of a "legisign" to its "sinsigns." The legisign is "not a single object, but a general type which, it has been agreed, shall be significant. . . . Thus the word 'the' will usually occur from fifteen to twenty-five times on a page. It is in all these occurrences [sinsigns] one and the same word, the same legisign" (Peirce 1960–1966, 2:143). It follows that each occurrence of a sinsign is an icon of the generalized legisign. Crees represent the specimens of each recognized modern species as though they were so many individuated sinsign-occurrences of a primordial legisign constituted by the protoanimal. Each modern animal is one instance of a class whose intensional properties are imagined as originating in the attributes of the mythical protoanimal. Phrased another way, the relationship is synecdochic: each modern animal is a *part* of the proto-animal, simultaneously its icon and an individual manifestation. We have here a notion of species and individual or legisign and sinsign played out chronologically between the time of the *ācaðōhkīwin* and the present. In the same way, each individual instance of an animal attribute may be the token and icon of a transformed characteristic of the protoanimal.

The conception of the protoanimal/modern animal relationship as one to many, legisign to sinsign, and whole to part is given literal expression in the story of Great Skunk. After Great Skunk is immobilized, the other animals tear it into small pieces and scatter them about:

So they [animals] all came down and said, "Cut him into all small pieces and throw them all over the place so he wouldn't be that big." That's how you see a small skunk now. They tear him up in small pieces and scatter him. Until there was just little pieces. He was too dangerous being the size of a moose. (Brightman 1989a:45)

The result of the disarticulation is a plurality of small skunks, each a miniaturized replica of the prototype. No other Cree myth establishes so directly the connection between the contemporary species and its protoanimal. More typically, narrators presuppose or report the relationship without additional elaboration, as with the assertion that wolves are descended from the lupine brother of the transformer Wīsahkīcāhk.

The iconic resemblance between protoanimal and modern species is further communicated in prophetic dialogues in myth where the quotative first- and second-person pronouns signal the iconic relation of modern animals to their protoanimal objects. In a passage from a

Swampy Cree myth, for example, the first snowshoe hare announces the role of future hares in Cree subsistence and manufacture: "*I* will provide food and raiment to keep the young families warm. *My* service will be welcomed by the whole human [race]" (Brown 1977:47, emphasis added). The pronoun "I" expands in the future tense to denote not only the speaker in the narrative context but the plurality of his descendants or replicas in the contemporary world. Similarly, in the Rock Cree myth explaining the enmity between wolves and dogs, Wolf informs Dog that they will be enemies in the future because Wolf envies Dog's protected status as human servant. Wolf says to Dog, *ati-nīkan, kā-wāpamitāni ka-nipahitin*, 'in the coming future, when I see you I'll kill you'. The person references in the verb denote not only speaker and addressee but all subsequent wolves and dogs that are part of and derived from these two and whose enmity endlessly and iconically recreates their primordial dispute.

In etiological themes, the worldly object is invariably an icon of the narrative result. Iconic relations among the three component narrative elements are more complex. In the example of the vain woman and the luminescent fungus, antecedent and result are icons. Only a very few Western Woods Cree myths describe the creation of a protoanimal from a being of another kind. In the vast majority of etiological themes, the protoanimal is postulated as already existent, and the transformation imbues it with a new attribute. Antecedent and result are, in one sense, the identical character. In these themes, the focus is on the attribute; thus, in a myth in which Wīsahkīcāhk lengthens the legs of Frog, the antecedent is a short-legged frog and the result is a long-legged one. In such cases of substitution or accretion, the antecedent and resulting features are not readily identifiable as icons. It is, however, often the case that elements of the transformation event are icons of the result they produce, as, for example, when differential ingestion of fatty meat results in differentially fatty animals (see below).

If iconic similitude characterizes relations of narrated results to worldly objects, it is the specifically indexical relationships postulated between these that are most significant to Crees. Peirce (1960–1966, 2:135) defined indexical signs as spatially and temporally connected to their objects, as with effect to cause: "An Index is a sign which refers to the object it denotes by virtue of being really affected by that object." In Cree thought, modern objects and states of affairs are the indexes of the results postulated in the narrative. For example, in the conclusion of the

Wolf-Wolverine marriage myth cited earlier (in a different version), Wolverine and two of his three children are killed, leaving only a single wolverine in the world.

The old lady wolf got mad. Took an axe and went down. Killed the little ones. Except that one—the little one, the one that always feed them, you know. Saved that one. So he [she] said, "From now on," he said, "there'd be too many wolverines." That's why he [she] killed all the rest of the young ones. And their dad. Left just one. *That's why you usually see one wolverine. You never see two wolverines in a pack. There's always one travelling alone. Funny, eh? That's how it started.* Yeah, he killed the rest of them. They only had one so there wouldn't be too many wolverines. You never see two wolverines travelling together. But if you have a moose cached, one might get there and there'll be another one coming in. But after, they split again. There's always one wolverine, never two. Well, maybe when they're mating. That's the only time. (Brightman 1989*b*, emphasis added)

An antecedent condition of plural and social wolverines is transformed by an event of killing into a result: a single surviving wolverine. Today, there are again not one but many wolverines in the world (the myth does not explain how this transpired), and all the modern animals iconically resemble the solitary prototype. More specifically, this theme embodies a duplex iconicity: of wolverine cub to modern wolverines and of the singularity of this survivor to the solitude of modern wolverines. Cree etiological thought predicates this iconic relationship on a more fundamental indexical connection. Modern wolverines are icons of and resemble the myth prototype—their object, in Peirce's terms—only because they are thought to derive from it in some physical modality conceived as continuous through space and time. Wolverines exist today with definite characteristics only because the surviving wolverine cub once existed and possessed the same characteristics. This derivation is often but not invariably identified as genealogical; as later chapters will show, reproduction is only one of multiple ways in which Crees conceive animals to appear in the world. The indexical connection of worldly animals to narrated prototype is the basis for the multiple secondary indexical relations between the attributes of the former and the transformative experiences of the latter, the Lamarckian transmission of acquired characteristics from the prototype to its modern replicas. It is because all wolverines derive from the solitary cub—whether through descent or some unspecified emanation—that they reiterate in their solitary behavior its acquired singularity.

The discussion thus far has proposed that Crees experience modern animals as signs of, among many other things, protoanimal objects, specifically, as indexical-iconic signs that simultaneously resemble their objects and are spatiotemporally contiguous to them. The complex of indigenous literature and its etiological themes itself constitutes a complex sign that reproduces this mode of apprehending animals in recurrent contexts of recitation. Peirce (1960–1966, 2:144) proposed another semiotic trichotomy that classified signs in terms of the relationship postulated by their users to exist between the sign and its object. For Peirce, the "interpretant" of a sign is a corresponding sign that it creates in the mind of the person for whom it stands for something. One component of the interpretant is a representation of how the sign is connected to its object, a representation potentially quite distinct from what semiotic analysis might ultimately disclose the sign/object relation to be. The distinctions in this trichotomy parallel those between symbol, icon, and index. In Peirce's arcane nomenclature, an "argument" is a sign conceived to stand for its object by a conventional agreement. A "rheme" is a sign conceived as resembling its object, and a "dicent sign" or "dicisign" "is a Sign which, for its interpretant, is a Sign of actual existence," that is, one whose interpretant represents the sign/object relationship as indexical. Etiological themes are themselves complex signs that include as one facet of their interpretant representations of how the protoanimals of narrative are related to the modern animals encountered in the bush. From this point of view, if we seek to characterize the Cree conception, worldly animals and their characteristics are "rhematic dicisigns" of their protoanimal objects.

From perspectives institutionalized in Western canons of myth interpretation—and these perspectives are potentially objectionable to Crees who construe the ācaðōhkīwin as a narrative of factual events—the etiological themes are fictions, constructed discourses of the cumulative social imagination. The protoanimals now become literary icons, imaginatively embellished, of real animal objects, simultaneously their symbols in the Peircian idiom because they are identified with them only through the conventions of a literary genre and the indigenous theology of a culture. Cree myths, from this point of view, embody iconic representations of worldly objects and states of affairs. Once the themes are categorized as fictions, they exhibit two typifying characteristics. The first is the utilization within the theme of diverse indexical and iconic relations suggested by experience. The etiological themes are themselves iconic representations of iconic or indexical relations among external objects and states of affairs. A narrative passage, for example, that identifies luminescent fungi [result] as the transformation of a beautiful woman [antecedent] is itself a diagrammatic icon of the iconic resemblance between vain beauty and luminosity in the world. Their juxtaposition in the narrative is an icon of an existing or emergent trope likening luminescence to vain beauty. Similarly, the relation of the sur-viving wolverine cub [result] to the solitary habits of modern wolver-ines object is built on the iconic resemblance of singularity to solitude. The second characteristic is the postulation of iconic-indexical rela-tionships between the theme's characters and the worldly objects of explanation. The interpretant of the themes represents modern animals as indexical icons of the narratized protoanimals, and the themes them-selves are therefore rhematic dicisigns in Peirce's idiom. There exist ob-vious analogies with the logic of non-Western magics as these have been expounded by James Frazer and his successors and also with the principles of sixteenth-century epistemology explored by Michel Foucault. If, for example, aconite is good for ocular diseases, this can be known by marking the resemblance of its seeds to the human eye (Foucault 1972:27). Etiological themes concern themselves less with applications than with the satisfactions attending knowledge of the be-ginning of things.

Etiological themes can be conceived as originating in two ways. The myth may be conceived as building up an account of the origin of some object by postulating that it became what it is through the agency of things perceptibly resembling or connected to it in the present. Alterna-tively, the resemblance may be identified as one between the events in an existing narrative and a worldly object whose origin these events may serve opportunistically to explain. Crees explain that the aversive-ness of wolves to deep water began when the transformer's Wolf brother pursued a moose into a lake and was killed there by *misipisiwak*, underwater panthers. Wīsahkīcāhk has premonitions of his brother's death and warns him to avoid water.

Wīsahkīcāhk said, "That's good. But remember, never run—never chase a moose over the lake, in the water." You know, water . . . a wolf wouldn't chase a—a moose to the lake. It's not true [that a wolf won't enter water at all], but as soon as a wolf—I mean this much water [two feet]. If a moose gets down in the lake about this much water, he'll—he'll turn around on the wolf. A wolf, he's got a hard time to move around in the water so he [moose] starts pounding him. That's why you never see a wolf do something to a moose in a lake 'cause they kill 'em right there, the moose'll kill him.

The narrated event in which the protowolf pursues prey into water and dies (result) is an icon of the modern wolves' aversion to water (object). Possibly, the etiological passage is an embellishment on an existing text in which a wolf dies in water. Alternatively, the "selection," in the first instance, of a wolf character who drowns in water may have been conditioned by awareness of the species' antipathy to water, the myth therefore embodying the object it serves to explain. The latter interpretation assigns to etiological themes a more decisive influence on the narrative content of myths.

Full semiotic consideration of etiological themes would necessarily comprise consideration of the iconic and indexical relations among the elements of antecedent, transformation, and result and between all of these and the worldly object of explanation. The examples already discussed suggest that the selection and composition of these terms are conditioned by indexical and iconic relations conceived to exist between the object and other entities and agencies in the world. The skeins of metaphor and metonymy in some etiological themes are quite complex. The Swampy Crees tell a story that accounts for the varying fat content of the different animal species. In a version told at Grand Rapids, Manitoba, the hero kills a bear and prepares the meat and grease for a solitary feast. Carnivorous animals and birds steal the meat, and the hero subsequently loses the grease when the muskrat he deputizes to cool it in the water gnaws a hole in the bladder container and allows it to escape:

Wisagatchak, unable to save it, called all the animals of the forest about him. Taking the rabbit, he threw it into the stream but withdrew it as soon as a little fat had adhered to its neck and breast where it remains to this day. All the animals were dipped in the river; the bear, being allowed to remain longest, secured the most fat. (Russell 1898:208–209)

In a different version, the muskrat successfully cools the grease, but the transformer again loses his feast. While trees imprison him, animals come and devour both the grease and the meat: "Of all the animals, Seal got the most grease and Rabbit the least. That is why Seal is so fat and Rabbit is so lean" (Skinner 1911:87 [Fort Albany]). A Fisher River version (Clay 1938:85–88) explains only the fatty necks of snowshoe hares: the hero petulantly throws the hare into the water where the grease adheres to its neck.

The object of the myth is the differential fat content of the boreal fauna, a matter of both practical and culinary interest. The abbreviated version focused on the hare reflects the northern saying that "you can starve on rabbit" (because of their relative lack of fat), as well as the anatomical locus of the species' meager fat deposits. The antecedent condition is a community of species with uniform fat content, or perhaps no fat content. The transformation is effected by the animals' ingestion of or immersal in the liquid bear fat. The result is animals that have acquired different quantities of fat, a distribution thereafter perpetuated among modern animals descended from the prototypes. The antecedents are homogeneous with respect to fat content, while the results are differentially fatty and are not readily analyzable as icons, unless the oppositive values of sameness and difference or presence and absence are assimilated to iconicity. The transformation event is, however, itself an icon of the narrative result and of the worldly object: each represents a proportional distribution. More specifically, the etiological transformation and result are diagrammatic icons of the object since the relations between the parts of each element are replicated. The theme specifically identifies *bear* fat as the medium of transformation, employing a mode of synecdoche that represents one part of the object as its source. Crees say that bears have more fat than other animals, a fact the Grand Rapids myth makes clear in circular fashion by stating that the bear became the fattest animal by remaining longest in the pool of bear grease. The fat of all other animals is thus represented as an indexical icon of that of the fattest of animals.

Etiological themes sometimes aggregate explanations of mutiple objects whose semiotic relations cross-reference one another. Rock Crees share with boreal Algonquians to the east a cycle of stories about the hero, Cahkāpīs (cf. Brightman 1989a:140–142), the innovator of solar periodicity. Originally, the sun passed continually overhead and there was no night. Cahkāpīs sets out with a snare made from his sister's pubic hair and hangs it over a large trail. Subsequently darkness falls over the world. Investigating his snare set, Cahkāpīs discovers that he has snared the sun and enlists the aid of Boreal Red-Backed Vole to release it.

So he come into the place and he see he couldn't go close to the sun. Too hot. Couldn't do nothing. So he hired this little mouse. This one mouse that we see in the winter time. Stupid mouse. On the trail, if he comes into the trail—well, the snow stiffens [forms crust] right away. He doesn't have no idea to punch a hole in the side to get into the warm [soft] snow. He stays in the bottom. Once he gets on the road, he got no idea to get off the road. So he freezes. You see lots in wintertime. It's brown as if its burned. But that's the only one. The rest of them, you don't see these mice like the ones that stick around the house. Big ears. Kind of brown, light colored ones. And the ones with long tails. The ones with long noses. You don't see those freeze in the road. But this special one, it looks like it's burned. Brownish color in the back. It's got a small tail. That's the one. That's the one that went and cut that rope.

Cahkāpīs said, "Don't worry. I'll pull you through. See if you can cut the rope [snare holding the sun]." So he [mouse] went and cut the rope but he was burned on the back. So he put him back to life. "But every time," Cahkāpīs said, "after this, every time you run into a trail, you'll die." So every time you see that mouse, he comes into the road and you'll see him laying there dead, frozen. That's the story of the mouse and the sun. That's why it's dark at night now. Before it used to be straight daylight. After Cahkāpīs snare the sun, that's how it comes to—the sun is weaker. It stops now and then because it's—not enough energy to make it. He's got to stop to rest every twelve hours. Every twelve hours he stops to rest. That's why you see dark. Because Cahkāpīs wanted to have it that way. (Brightman 1989a:139)

This myth addresses three objects: the alternation of day and night, the vole's coloration, and the clearly more engaging question of its immobilization on frozen paths. Beginning with an antecedent condition of perpetual daylight, the story leads to the result of contemporary solar periodicity by means of two medial transformations: the imprisonment of the sun by a pubic hair trap and its release—in a weakened condition—by the vole. Each of these two transformation elements is an icon of the result. The myth contrasts an antecedent condition of continuous daylight with the modern alternation of day and night. The significance of the pubic hair snare is its indexical contiguity to menstruation, and menstruation is, in turn, an icon of solar periodicity (cf. Lévi-Strauss 1978:390, 395). The narrative juxtaposition of solar periodicity (result) to pubic hair (transformation) as effect to cause is itself the icon both of the iconic relationship of menstrual to solar periodicity and of the indexical relationship of menstruation to pubic hair. Additionally, the narrative opposes the "strength" of the aperiodic solar antecedent to the "weakness" of the periodic result, an icon of the postulated antagonism between menstrual blood and other powerful agencies in the world (chap. 4).

The narrative "selection" of the boreal red-backed vole as the animal that effects the sun's transformation is an icon of multiple relationships. First, most trivially, it is an icon of the vole's "burned" coloration, which, in turn, indexes prior contact with fire. Second, the vole's proclivity for spatial confinement on frozen trails is a terrestrial icon of the sun's temporal and spatial confinement to a solar path that it now traverses at periodic intervals. The vole's fate is also iconically connected to periodicity since it is seen in winter. The etiological theme represents all these relationships as index to object or cause to effect. The vole's periodic confinement indexes the confinement of the sun that engendered it, just as its coloration indexes the sun's heat.

The Language of Transformation

Cree narrators employ a standardized repertoire of devices to signal that an event is to be understood as a transformation, that is, as the first instance of a condition that will endure into the present. In many cases, the transformation is indicated in the quoted speech of the transformer character. These discourses typically refer to the future with the verb *ati-nīkan*, the preverbal element *ati* indicating progression and giving the construction the sense of 'as the future unfolds'. The transformer also refers with verbs in subjunctive mode to the ascendant humans who will populate the future and utters a proposition about the future state of affairs. Most of these devices are employed in an etiological passage in which a bear-woman's drowning brother announces that he will become a place-name (Brightman 1989a).

"otī ati-nīkan   wī-itātwāwi   iðiniwak tay-itwīwak ʿiyako
here in the future when they speak of him people   they will say just this

awa   osīmimaw   nāpīw,' ʿiyako   nīða"
this one her younger sibling male,'   just this myself

The association of naming with the innovation of new species poses the question of how Crees understand the transformer's utterances to be related to his creative acts. Consider the following utterance that Wīsahkīcāhk addresses to the severed head of his mother.

"otī ati-nīkan   iðiniwak pī-yātwāwi   'namīw' ki-t-īsiðīhkātikwak"
here in the future people   when they dwell here sturgeon they will call you

"Here in the future, when people dwell here, they will call you 'sturgeon.'" This utterance is in indicative rather than imperative mode and appears superficially to express a proposition, perhaps prophetic, concerning an independently engendered state of affairs. These discourses do not contain such performative verbs as "command" or "name" which in some constructions simultaneously refer to and effect the speech acts of commanding or naming. Crees, nonetheless, understand these utterances to be performative in the sense that they are thought constructively to have innovated the states of affairs they describe. In Cree ideology, they are "declarations," John Searle's (1976) term for a speech act that introduces changes in the nonlinguistic context of the utterance. Superficially, Wīsahkīcāhk simply utters a proposition about what human beings will call the head in the future. However, Crees say that the utterance possessed two perlocutionary effects, both innovating *namīw* as the Cree name for "sturgeon" and physically transforming the head into the first sturgeon.

The same conception informs a passage from a Plains Cree myth (Bloomfield 1930:75–76, 82) in which the hero, Snow Dart, transforms his wife's brother into the first lynx:

"kīya nistēsē   *ayisiyiniwak nīhtāwikitwāwi*   *ohpikitwāwi*
you   my brother-in-law humans   when they are born when they grow

'pahkwacōw' ki-k-ēsiyīhkātikwak nīkan.   *kīya sakahk*   *ki-kōh-pimācihon"*
'lynx'   they will call you in the future.   you in the bush you will subsist

"As for you, my brother-in-law, in the future when humans are born and grow up, they will call you 'lynx.' You will subsist in the woods." Here again, the ascribed perlocutionary effects are equivalent to those of English "I ordain that humans will call you 'lynx,'" "I ordain that you will become the first lynx," and "I ordain that you will dwell in the woods." The event of naming is conceived to have effected the physical transformation. This is made clear in a passage from a similar myth whose narrator, after quotatively reciting the hero's acts of naming, adds summarily, "Thus he made all the animals" (Bloomfield 1930: 120). Plains Cree myths describe generalized creations of the modern animal species by these means. The Rock Cree literature, as discussed earlier, treats the existence of most of the protoanimals as given but describes the creation of some individual fish and bird species, as with the severed head/sturgeon transformation above. An Eastern Cree version of the Ayās hero myth likewise associates naming with the transformation of the protoanimals into their modern forms (Skinner 1911:

108), as does a Plains Cree myth (Ahenakew 1929:320). To characterize these transformation events first in Cree terms, they are creations of
objects effected by uttering the names of objects. The narratives represent the connection between names (and perhaps other lexical forms)
and their worldly denotata as grounded in innate resemblance and contiguity rather than in convention.

In this sense, modern animals—or certain of them—are indexes of
their names because it was originally through the utterance of the name
that the animal was innovated. The indexical juxtaposition of naming
and transformation in the etiological theme is therefore itself the icon of
a postulated indexical-iconic relationship between words and things in
Cree linguistic ideology. The significance of names in etiological
themes is further embedded in the postulated indexical-iconic connection between propositions uttered by the transformer and states of
affairs that then come into being in the contemporary world. When
asked how Wīsahkīcāhk could make things happen by saying them, one
Cree said that he was an *ahcāk*, spirit, implying such was the way of
these beings: "He use his mind to do things. So when he say it, it come
to be like that." There exist obvious parallels between this ideology
and Cree conceptions of "magical" speech as it occurs in the present
(chap. 4).

Ecological Design

Certain transformations of animals and other entities are
represented as implementations of a cosmogonic design already envisioned by Wīsahkīcāhk or the deity, Kicimanitōw. This design is
sometimes signaled the heroes' references to themselves as cosmogonic
architects. For example, the Plains Cree hero, Snow Dart, explains his
transformations by stating "*ntaw-oyasowēh e-kīy-itikawiyān*" 'I was instructed to go and introduce order' (Bloomfield 1930:82). Not all
etiological passages exemplify this conception of design: Cahkāpīs, for
example, snares the sun unwittingly, and solar periodicity is seemingly
innovated as an unintended consequence, although it is interesting that
one narrator (see above) assimilated the event to the concept of design.
But in many etiological themes, it appears as if the transformer acts
upon an axiomatic conception of how animals should exist in the
future, declaring without rational justification that an alternative state

of affairs to the existing condition is preordained. *"Mōða kōwi-tiðimikōwisin,"* Wīsahkīcāhk explains to Bear in a Rock Cree myth as he cuts his long tail off: 'You are not shaped that way'. In the same myth, he imprisons Frog, and the latter lengthens its legs in trying to escape. Later, he announces:

"īyako nitatoskīwin.   mōða kīða ta-kī-papāmōhtin   Aðīkis,
just so my employment. Not   you you will walk around frog,

ta-kī-papāmikwāskwāskohtin. īyako   ohci   ka-kinōkatitān"
you will hop around   just so from this I will lengthen your legs

"Such is my employment. You will not be able to walk around, Frog, you will be able to hop around. So just for this reason, I will lengthen your legs."

Often, the transformers' motivations are broadly "ecological" in the sense that they concern predator-prey relationships, adaptations of species to niches, and the possibility of species extermination. A Swampy Cree myth relates how the transformer rewards the mouse who has sewn his clothing.

And when Wesukechak saw Appekoosees, the Mouse, come out he stooped down and took it up in his hands, and he made its nose long and soft. "That will help you to ferret out your food," said Wesukechak. Then he brushed the hair on the Mouse's body, and made it sleek and smooth. "That will help you to run through your little holes in the earth," said Wesukechak. (Clay 1938:66–67)

Concern with predator-prey relations are expressed in other myths where the transformer rewards the weasel by replacing his bright colors with alternating brown and white coats "so that your enemies cannot see you" (Russell 1898:212) or prevents the rabbit from drinking fattening grease so as to reduce its attractiveness to predators (Dusenberry 1962:240). The monstrous Great Skunk is cut into small pieces—the origin of modern skunks—because "he was too dangerous being the size of a moose" (Brightman 1989a:45). The myths also address demography. In the Wolverine-Wolf marriage myth, the old Wolf-woman kills two of the three Wolverine children because "from now on there'd be too many wolverines." Similarly, in a version of the myth of human creation, Wīsahkīcāhk makes humans from earth rather than rock so that "they will live a reasonable time" (Brown and Brightman 1988:49).

A version of the hero myth of Ayās contains an especially elaborated account of design and ecological transformation. After destroying the existing world with fire, the hero sets about transforming the surviving animals.

After the fire was over, there were lots and lots of animals on the patch of ground. The man named some of them. He put the beaver to live in the water. The rabbit wanted to be a beaver, but he wouldn't allow it. The rabbit even jumped into the water, but the man pulled him out and drained the water off of him. He said his legs were too long and even if he did eat willow like a beaver, he couldn't go about in the water properly. The squirrel wished to be a bear. He did all he could to be a bear. The man said he wouldn't do, he was too noisy. He said, "If you were a bear, when people got numerous again, you will get thinned down too much. The bear must be a very canny animal and keep quiet; he has too many enemies." The squirrel began to weep. He wept a great deal until his eyes were white. If you take a notice the next time you see a squirrel you will notice that his eyes are bright and swollen from weeping. The man made the bear then because he was nice and quiet and canny. Somebody else wanted to be a deer [caribou] but I don't remember who it was, but the deer was put in too. The real deer was appointed because he was swift and could run from his enemies. (Skinner 1911:108 [Eastern Cree])

The story exhibits with unusual clarity the imaginative deconstruction of the modern world that enters into the representation of antecedents. It addresses the contemporary structure of the world but also the question, often implicit in etiological themes, of why this from among all the imaginable alternative structures should prevail. The transformer operates on an existing set of animals, each of whom already possesses individuating attributes and will become the prototype of a modern species. The hero has in mind a set of correspondences between their existing traits and the envisioned characteristics, habitats, and predator-prey relations of the modern species he intends to innovate. But individual protoanimals possess aspirations to become the prototypes of newly established species for which their existing traits make them pathetically unsuitable. Thus, the animal that becomes the squirrel— and that already possesses the garrulousness of modern squirrels—is prevented from becoming the modern bear because the transformer intends the bear to have characteristics that will give it "too many enemies," an implicit reference to humans, who are the bear's only predator. He reasons that the squirrel's chattering is incompatible with these characteristics and would result in the species being "thinned out"; he appoints instead a protoanimal already possessing the wariness appropriate to bears. Similarly, an already swift proto-animal becomes the first caribou, and Crees are spared the spectacle of an amphibious rabbit-beaver.

Humans and Animals in the Early World

Some Cree myths address aspects of the human-animal relationship, and without exception, they anticipate a world in which animals will be the prey of human hunters. Transformations bearing on this relationship occur in stories with both all-animal and mixed human and animal characters. As should now be clear, the social animals of the earliest mythological period are in no respects less cultured than modern humans. Like the myth discussed above, the Rock Cree myth that explains why humans and not animals possess fire poses the question as an ecological problem of potential species extermination.

Well, that's this Wolverine, the guy with the . . .
Him and the
Wolves, they were out hunting one day.
Only the Wolves had the matches,
they make a magic fire.
They just jump over the dry wood and that thing explodes.

And the Wolverine never had that kind of . . .
He didn't have that kind of—
power.
So he asked the Wolves to have some of the power. So Wolves said, "We'll try
    it, brother." Because of course he was the brother of the animals.
So he tried it
and that damn thing exploded.
And they said, "Alright, brother, long as you don't play with it."
And he said, "No, oh shit no! I wouldn't do no such a thing!
I *need* a fire!"

So as he was monkeying around always on the shoreline.
Sometimes old beaver houses, that's where you see lots of dry wood.
Everytime he sees dry wood, he wants to make fire.
Pretend that he's cold.
Throw a few sticks together and jump over them and it explodes.
Few minutes with the fire and away he goes again.
So every morning, everywhere he goes you see about five or six fires.
That's Wolverine
making fires all morning for nothing.

So the Wolves got mad at him:
"I guess our brother is making fun of our match.
Every time we seen him going, he always fires all the way
here and there."
So they say, "We gotta cut off the match."
So, it so happens

the next fire, he couldn't start a fire.
Tried it again, no.

So one cool morning he went up on the hill and seen lots of fires.
All kinds of animals, you know.
All different kinds of smoke.
One animal's got a different kind of smoke than the other.
And him, he had nothing. It was cold.
So he hollered, "Oh, my little kid brothers, sisters.
Best if we don't have any lights, no match, no way of making fire.
There'll be people years ahead.
They're going to clean us up if they seen our fire.
All they'll do is start hunting us when they seen our fires, yeah.
Best if we don't have any fire. This way
we'll make it.
But if we have fires, they'll clean us up."

Oh, all the animals agree with him.
"Oh, I think it will be true.
If there's going to be any people, they're going to clean us out
because they're going to see our fires."
So they holler at him, "OKAY, BROTHER, NO MORE FIRES!"

So that's how come there's no fire. Otherwise
it would have been lots . . .
Now people would be making lots of money.
Fire fighters, you know, these days make money.
Animals would be putting on forest fires [laughs].
Okay, that's the end of it.

Although Wolverine's prophecy is probably motivated more by jealousy than ecological wisdom, this myth again dwells on the themes of predation and extermination and contains intimations of antagonism in the hunter-prey relationship.

Hunters and Prey

The relationship of the trickster-transformer Wīsahkī-cāhk to animals encapsulates the ambivalence characterizing hunting and human-animal relations in the contemporary world. Several stories (Brightman 1989a) describing Wīsahkīcāhk's volitional transformation into a fly, a goose, and a moose may express both speculation and envy. Although he is selectively benevolent to individual animals who assist him, most Wīsahkīcāhk stories detail his attempts to kill and eat animals by tricking them. Predictably, the animals' responses are antagonistic, and the trickster is himself sometimes represented as a victim. If human and animal relations are understood in some contexts as adversarial, Wīsahkīcāhk is clearly aligned with the interests of human beings. His sponsorship of human hegemony is consistent both with his own predatory conduct and with his role in the myth of the flood (Brightman 1989a). Wīsahkīcāhk's younger brother and hunting partner is a wolf. The hero experiences a dream prompting him to warn his brother not to pursue moose into the water. Disregarding this premonition, the wolf is killed by the aquatic *misipisiwak*, underwater panthers, feline beings with horns and long tails. To avenge his brother, Wīsahkīcāhk kills their chief, an event unleashing a flood that inundates the Earth. Wīsahkīcāhk survives by constructing a raft on which, in some versions, he installs animals to repopulate the world. He re-creates the Earth by magically expanding a bit of mud brought from the bottom of the waters by the muskrat. After the flood, in a version obtained in the 1820s,

Weesuck then blessed the others [animals] and sent them away telling them to multiply "and be good, not vicious or ill-inclined, nor secret or hide themselves too much from my little brothers (the human beings which he was about to create) when they might want to eat." (Brown and Brightman 1988:48)

In other Cree versions of the flood myth, *mistamiskwak* 'great beavers' and *misikinīpikwak* 'great horned snakes' join or replace the panthers as the hero's aquatic antagonists. In Cree and Algonquian cosmology more widely, these underwater and subterranean monsters are represented as the antagonists of the *piθīsiwak* 'thunderbirds', signaling a vertical opposition between the sky and the spaces below the surface of earth and water. The flood myth introduces two further oppositions situated on the horizontal rather than vertical plane. First, the water monsters are opposed to terrestrial beings and spaces: they kill Wīsahkī-cāhk's wolf brother, an animal that today does not enter water, and unleash from their bodies a flood that inundates the Earth with water. A second level of significance is expressed only obliquely in some versions of the myth and turns on the motivation of the underwater panthers for destroying the lupine brother. Christopher Vecsey (1983:94–96) has argued cogently that the parallel myth in the Ojibwa cycle is implicitly concerned with hunting: certain versions state that the underwater panthers kill the lupine brother because his excessive predation threatens to exterminate game animals. Most versions of the myth state that the lupine brother is a successful hunter, and he is aligned as a metaphoric human with Wīsahkīcāhk in oppositions of predators to prey and humans to animals. The killing of the wolf is thus an act of stewardship by the underwater panthers on behalf of terrestrial animals, suggesting an archaic association of all animals with water (chap. 4). The same theme occurs in at least one Western Woods Cree version of the flood myth (Clay 1938:16). This theme of antagonism between predators and animals is not consistently maintained throughout the myth since it is Wīsahkīcāhk who saves the animals (as a resource population?) on his raft, and it is amphibious animals who collaborate with him in restoring the world after the flood.

Rock Cree myths represent the early humans as themselves the victims of carnivorous predators, both the primitive mimiθitīhīsiwak 'hairy heart people' and the wīhcikōsisak, small witikos or cannibals (Brightman 1990). Images of a prehistoric period in which all animals were carnivorous, and perhaps anthropophagous, are shared by Thickwoods Crees (Vandersteene 1969:43) and Severn Ojibwa (Stevens 1971:25). The Plains Crees specifically identify animals themselves as the original predator-aggressors and humans as the prey species. One Plains Cree myth explains both the origins of modern animals and the innovation of the modern hunter-prey relationship (Ahenakew 1929:320). In an earlier condition of the cosmos, the protohumans are eaten by anthropophagous animals called cimiskwanak, short-nose beings. The transformer accomplishes their destruction by instructing the protohumans in the use of bows and arrows and then creates modern animals from their corpses. Picking up each in turn, he pronounces its name, and the moose, deer, skunk, mouse, and other species are created and flee into the bush. The myth exhibits a threatening image of the ascendancy of anthropophagous animals over humans, which is "displayed" to demonstrate the relative excellence of the contemporary human-animal relationship that is the iconic opposite of its antecedent. Animals that prey on humans are changed into animals of which humans themselves thereafter become predators, and the transformation is catalyzed by the use of bows and arrows. The Short Noses, terrestrial in the myth just described, appear elsewhere in both Plains and Rock Cree versions of the flood myth as the transformer's aquatic antagonists (Brightman 1989a, Ahenakew and Hardlotte 1977), replacing the underwater panthers who usually occupy this role. The substitutability of the Short Noses with the panthers appears strongly motivated: both question the inevitability of human hunting, either by punishing or inverting it.

Rock Crees today have no account of a transition in which the anthropomorphic animals of ācaðōhkīwin assume the characteristics of modern animals. Other subarctic Algonquian traditions relating to this question were, however, recorded by fur traders in the eighteenth century. These do not explicitly represent animals as anthropophagous but foreground themes of competition, suspicion, and hostility; the animals lose speech and other cultural attributes as punishments for aggression against humans (Henry 1969 [1809]:204–206, Thompson 1962 [1784–1812]:155). But an alternative design was also envisioned in Cree mythological thought and expressed in the version of the flood myth told to Thompson (ibid: 76–78) in the late 1700s. The myth represents the superior being, Kicimanitōw, as a benign and rational entity who deputizes Wīsahkīcāhk to instruct humans and animals how to live peacefully. The latter instead incites humans and animals to quarrel and shed blood on the ground, and the creator tells him that he will take everything from him unless he keeps the ground free of blood. Wīsahkīcāhk ignores these instructions and continues to incite men and animals to quarrel, whereupon the creator makes good his threat and raises the waters to wash the ground clean of blood. In another context, Thompson observes that the creator being felt kindly disposed toward human beings, hated to see human blood on the ground, and sent rain to Earth to wash it away. The scriptural parallels suggest that this conception of the flood as a divinely willed punishment was borrowed into Cree cosmogony from Western sources; it is also found in a version told by Thickwoods Crees in Alberta (Vandersteene 1969:47). The significance of bloodstained earth as a tangible sign of conflict between humans or between human and animal beings appears to be a distinctively Algonquian rather than European element. The creator being here appears to desire a bloodless world in which human beings and animals live in harmony without discord and perhaps without the predator-prey relations presently indispensable in the world.

3

"Dreaming All the Bottom of the Water"

Introduction

Many Crees talk of success and failure in foraging as influenced both by technical expertise and by beings that make deliberate decisions that facilitate or obstruct the foragers' objectives. Animals themselves are commonly said to exert such influences. Both human beings and animals possess a *-yaw* 'body' and an *ahcāk*, soul, which survives after the death of the body. Some Crees say that animals do not "really" die when hunters kill them: the soul continues after death and returns to the world either as a fetal animal or a regenerated adult. Animals are talked about as being capable in both embodied and disembodied conditions of observing human conduct (or misconduct) and reacting to it by rewarding or punishing the hunter. Diverse other entities may in addition affect the ability to locate and kill animals. The noun *ahcāk* also refers to beings that Crees call "angels" or "spirits" in English, including the deity, Kicimanitōw, thunderbirds, the spirits of the four cardinal points, rulers of the major game species, underwater panthers, and many others. A man or woman may also conceive their hunting prospects to be influenced by an entity called *pawākan*. The *pawākan*, literally, dream image, is an individuated *ahcāk* being with whom persons understand themselves to experience recurrent communication in dreams. The *pawākan* may be a being categorized as an *ahcāk*, or it may be identified as an individual animal, bird, tool, or specimen of virtually any class of objects. Crees say that dreams are often the source of knowledge used in hunting, and it is the *pawākan* that appears in dreams or that brings a hunter dream experiences with animals.

The Pawākan

Whether or not it is identified as an animal, the *pawākan* may be talked about as essential to foraging success, communicating with its human dependent in dreams, facilitating dreams about individual animals, serving as a conduit for information about animal numbers and movements, and imparting "power" deployed in hunting.[1] Explaining the concept of the *pawākan*, Johnny Bighetty said, "If you're in any kind of trouble, you dream. You dream things, all kinds of things . . . animals, trees, stones, ice. If you love. . . if you do everything it says to do, it'll help you."

Jérémie (1926) provided an early oblique reference to the *pawākan* concept on Hudson Bay in the 1700s: "They [Crees] have no kind of religion; each makes a god after his own fashion, and to him they have recourse in their need, and especially when they are sick." Umfreville (1954 [1790]:21) gave a more detailed account:

His good or bad success in hunting, the welfare of his friends and family, his duration in this mortal state, &c. all depend upon the capricious will and pleasure of some invisible agent, whom he supposes to preside over all his undertakings: for instance, one man will invoke a conspicuous star, another a wolf, one a bear, and another a particular tree; which he imagines influences his good or ill fortune in this life.

Crees ascribe animateness, self-awareness, intelligence, and sometimes covert humanoid characteristics to many nonhuman beings and objects. They reiterate that "anything" can be a *pawākan*:

Any kind of thing can be a *pawākan*. Animals, fish, worms in water, water, ice, rock, wind. When people see them, they would look like a person.

They call them *pawākan*. It's something like . . . like when you were a kid there, you dream something when you were a kid. They're your boss. Anything . . . like a little animal. You'd say, that's your hired man. Anything you want, he'll do it for you. Like a dog, mouse, bird, anything.[2]

Animals are numerically the most common entities with which Crees experience *pawākan* relationships, the first that people mention when trying to explain the concept extensionally. The bear, wolf, and wolverine—all predators—are said to be the most powerful. The question of how the animal *pawākan* corresponds with individual animals of the same species encountered in waking states is complex. Rock Crees do not identify the *pawākan* with a distinct class of "spirit animals" separate from the animals in the bush that might be hunted or trapped. The statement that a man possesses a bear as a *pawākan* means that he dreams of an individual bear dwelling somewhere in the bush. I was told that a man might encounter his individual animal benefactor in the bush and that the latter might offer itself to be killed if the hunter were in need of food. Such an event would not interrupt the relationship, since the soul of the animal would later resume its tangible form.[3] People do not talk about having an entire species as a *pawākan*, only an individual. At the same time, a measure of substitutability exists in Cree religious thought between individual animals of the same species, including the individual *pawākan*. A man may be told by his animal *pawākan* in a dream to observe certain dietary rules (see chap. 4) that typically apply to all animals of the relevant species. Similarly, a man with an animal *pawākan* enjoys success in hunting animals of the like species. Adam Ballentyne, a Rock Cree *opawāmiw* 'dreamer' from Pelican Narrows, Saskatchewan, stated that animals themselves possessed a *pawākan*.

A man would always obey his puagan. If he wished to kill the animal which was his puagan, the animal through its puagan would tell the man if it wished to be killed or not. He would not kill that animal unless it wished to be killed and told him so. (Cockburn 1984:41)

Rock Crees today do not talk about animals as possessing their own *pawākan*, or at least I did not encounter the idea. Possibly Ballentyne possessed more esoteric conceptions than those general in the region or was speaking of the *ahcāk*, or soul, of the animal. The phrase "the animal which was his puagan" may indicate an individual or all members of the species to which the puagan belongs.

Parents formerly encouraged children to fast for the *pawākan* at around age fourteen. Crees refer to this event as *pawāmiwin* 'dreaming' or with the construction *ī-nitī-wī-pawāmit* 'someone will dream there'.[4] At this time, most males and some females fasted at an isolated camp in the bush. In some cases, women's visionary experience occurred during their seclusion at first menstruation (see chap. 4), and they did not undertake a distinct fast. This seems to be the import of Adam

Ballentyne's observation (ibid.) that "girls sought their puagan at the time when they first became women." Attawapiskat Swampy Cree women seemingly fasted just as men did at puberty, although the (male) informant stated that the power of their visions never exceeded those of men (Honigmann 1956:71). Rock Cree men say that women were likely to dream of botanical medicines. In some cases, a boy's father sponsored the "eat-all" feast prior to the fast.[5]

The condition Crees call *pīkisitōwin* ideally characterized both the dreamer and the vision site: *pīkisiw* 'someone is clean', *pīkan* 'something is clean'. The word refers to physical cleanliness and also to states of purity that Crees translate as "holy." The opposite condition is *wīðipisiwin*, which means "dirty" but possesses also meanings of impurity and pollution: *wīðipaw* 'something is impure', *wīðipisiw* 'someone is impure'. These verbs predicate of such agencies as dogs, excrement, and menstrual blood and also of intrinsically "clean" things such as drums or animal remains that have been brought into physical contact with them. *Ahcāk* beings are averse to these entities and to the human settlements that contain them. For example, poles for the shaking lodge should be kept "clean"; if dogs urinate on them, they are "dirty." The dreamers bathed before leaving and dressed in new clothing. Tom Boulanger (1971:50), a Manitoba Swampy Cree, wrote of dreamers that "their clothes have to be real clean and their life clean too." The distinction between *ōtīnahk* 'town/settlement' and *nōhcimihk* 'bush' is relevant to the spatial organization of the vision fast and of the shaking lodge (see chap. 6), both of which occurred at a remove from the sites of human occupation. The bush is considered "clean" in contrast to human habitations, which are talked about as relatively "dirty" or impure (cf. Tanner 1979:11). *Ahcāk* beings are said to avoid persons and locations in an impure condition.

Both sexes were admonished by their relatives to avoid sexual experience before the fast. Seemingly, sexual encounters create impurity in the context of the initial contact with the *pawākan*.

Nowadays, especially now, all these kids not being in the bush. All on welfare. I guess there's not much of that *pawākan* now. Everybody's fucking soon as he's five years old. Before, you can't fuck a woman if you're a young man. That's against your . . . you got to stay away from a woman until you're married. Otherwise you wouldn't be any good later. That's what my old grandfather used to tell me. "Don't fuck around with a woman. Not before you dreamed of the guy." And then he'd turn around and tell stories of women when he was young [laughs].

Crees sometimes used black face paint during the fast, a practice noted in the earliest reference to the institution in the late 1600s (Bacqueville de La Potherie 1931:232). Black face painting occurred in other contexts involving interaction with spirit beings. Children's faces were painted as a protective measure at the time of death in the family, and some men painted themselves during self-induced waking trance states or before operating the shaking lodge. Black face paint symbolized separation from human society and from conventional states of consciousness, and possibly the likening of this separation to death. The visionary was instructed to make no use of fire, perhaps because it would alienate spirit visitors. Although two brothers sometimes fasted together at this time, Crees regard the vision fast as a solitary undertaking.[6]

Well, since people are baptized they can't do it. If a guy's not baptized, a kid— if he's not baptized, he's got to keep—well, he's got to keep people—[he stays] away from people. Well, if you want to have a holy man, you don't let him to monkey around with other people. Stay away from people. So this way he'll be holy. Something like holy guy. Then he start dreaming.

The requirements for solitude and chastity are consistent with other Cree pollution concepts (see Chap. 4). The relationship with the *pawā-kan* resembles in certain respects an intimate relation with another human being and seemingly must be established separately in time and space.

The fast usually lasted three or four days and sometimes extended for longer periods if the dreamer was either unsuccessful or exceptionally ambitious.[7] The vision was protracted or interrupted and successively resumed until the faster experienced the desired visions. Some famous men allegedly undertook fasts that lasted through entire seasons or years. The number and relative power of the beings dreamed of might increase with the period spent in the bush. An obvious factor setting an upper limit on the duration of the fast was the novice's ability to endure short rations or fasting and also isolation. People say that the novices might turn into animals or forget that they were human beings and "go crazy" if they remained out too long.[8]

Dreamers might fast outright, although they were permitted to take small quantities of dried meat or fish with them to eat (cf. Honigmann 1956:71, Boulanger 1971:50). The conventional ethnological reading of the North American Indian vision complex assumes that fasting— like self-torture, drugs, and other techniques—produces nonordinary perceptual states that are then interpreted in terms of the novices' pre-suppositions as events of contact with spirit beings (Lowie 1954:157–161). Crees say that fasting (kōwahkatahōw 'someone fasts') makes it "easy" to dream, enhancing human receptivity to communication from spirit beings. Conversely, alcohol is said to impede such contact (cf. Speck 1935a:43 for a contrary Eastern Cree doctrine). In more social terms, the act of fasting evokes the "pity" of potential guardians, conveying to them the seriousness of the novice's intentions. Boulanger's (1971:49) statement that it was easier for orphans to have powerful dreams than for others suggests that pity is an important component in the orientation of the pawākan toward the young visionary. Rock Crees rejected the idea that persons mutilated themselves or practiced self-torture to secure pity and were amused and sometimes incredulous when I described Plains Indian behavior in this regard.

The spatial orientations expressed in the Cree vision fast were continuous with those of other sacred practices in which contiguity with ahcāk beings was sought. These entities are talked about as observing human conduct in camp and town and sometimes as being physically present, although invisible, in domestic space. At the same time, they are typically represented as inhabiting four categories of space far removed from direct human access: the upper air, underwater, underground, and remote terrestrial distances.[9] As noted in the previous chapter, the oppositivity of these spaces is an elemental theme in Algonquian cosmology. Crees use or create spaces that are imagined as conduits traversing the boundaries between these domains and human space: sacrifices are burned in stoves and lofted upward as smoke, left in rock fissures, placed underwater, eaten in lodges sealed from the outside world. In the vision fast, dreamers oriented themselves to these spaces. The narrative below recounts the successive fasting experiences of Michel Dumas, one of the most powerful dreamers known on the lower Churchill.

People used to sleep in the water. You wouldn't believe it. They make a coffin. In wintertime, they put them . . . like first freeze-up, early freeze-up, they put them in the bogs. Kind of bogs. Just trees tied up together. Doesn't have to be real sealed. Cover the guy and put him in the water. About March, about this time of year, they go and take the guy out. They stay there in the water all winter. They say they don't eat and they don't . . . if the guy pull through, then he's all right. That means he's dreaming all the bottom of the water. He's dreaming all the animals, they gotta come to him. This way he's alive all winter. He's not alive . . . he's not breathing or nothing.

Then he sleeps in the top of the tree. Then in the spring they make like a nest for him. Put him in there. And he sleeps there all summer. They take him down again in the fall. That's the birds. He's dreaming about the top of the earth.

Or they take him on the reef. If they don't want him to sleep in the tree, they take him to the reef. But nobody goes there. Just him. Then they go back in the fall to get the guy. There's one at Granville Lake. At Granville Lake, you might see a sand reef out in the lake there. This guy was laying there all summer. His dad left him there in the spring. And he woke up in the fall, two days ahead of when the old man came back. You can see where he was laying all summer. No grass left. I don't know how in hell he pull through. In Granville Lake, that's the same place where they put him in the water, the same guy. He stay there all winter. Right by the village. That's where he was all winter. In the bogs. Trees tied up together. All winter. They took him out in April. And he come to life.

This narrative incorporates multiple "legendary" elements: the seasonal duration of the dream, protracted immersion in a bog in winter, and the statement that the dreamer died during the vision and later returned to life. Crees insist that immersion in bogs was sometimes practiced, and such vision sites were, perhaps, utilized in summer. There is no question but that riparian and arboreal sites were and are occupied and that these were selected because they induced contiguity with particular classes of *ahcāk* beings. The successive utilization of these different sites by Dumas bespeaks an ambitious attempt to dream the entire world.

Considering first "the top of the earth," the Dumas text mentions birds, but Crees also dreamed of such sky beings as *piðīsiwak* 'thunderbirds', *Kōna* 'Snow', *Pīsim* 'Sun', *Tipiskāwipīsim* 'Moon', *waskōwak* 'clouds', and individual *acāhkosak* 'stars'. In Cree narratives (Brightman 1989*b*), the dream guardians are sometimes represented generically as birdlike beings that fly to their owner's aid and sometimes move him through the air from place to place. Like other divisions of Western Woods Cree, Rock Crees used wooden platforms, scaffolds erected between trees, or trees themselves as the sites of the vigil.[10] The platforms were built ten feet or more off the ground and might be used successively by different dreamers. A boy's senior male relatives erected his stage for him, if a new site was selected. Crees say that the platform was made with four living trees to provide the vertical supports. Four horizontal poles were secured to the trees, and then smaller poles were laid across the resulting frame to form the stage. If it was desired to situate the platform at a higher level than could be reached from the ground, the first platform served as scaffolding for the construction of another at a higher elevation. Attawapiskat Crees correlated the height of the vision platform with the relative "power" of the being dreamed of.

Kiiookii pointed out that the higher one went, the more powerful the dream. A week on a scaffold six feet high enabled one to see "deer, moose, not much." At eleven feet more powerful visitants appeared while two weeks on the highest level brought "anybody, cloud every one kind." (Honigmann 1956:71)

The platforms were usually built on bluffs overlooking lakes or rivers. The missionary John Semmens (1884:109–110) described such platforms as "huge nests," and Crees indeed refer to the platform as *waciston* 'bird's nest'. Brush was sometimes attached to the platform so that it would resemble a bird's nest; both the lexical and physical metaphors suggest the dependent condition of infant birds. The use of hills as vision sites (Merasty 1974:17) functioned like the stages to elevate the dreamer into empyrean space.

The reference to "dreaming all the bottom of the water" on reefs or in submerged wooden boxes indicates a second spatial orientation of the vision fast to underwater environments. Among beings explicitly associated with the underwater sphere are varieties of fish, leeches, *Misinamīw* 'Giant Sturgeon', which lives in Granville Lake, and *Atāmipīkōw-iskwīw* 'Underwater Woman'. The water is also the domain of beings with whom Crees are concerned to avoid communication. *Maskwamiy* 'Ice' lives below Granville Lake, appearing in dreams, perhaps in disguised form, and, in the past, predestining the dreamer who accepted it to witiko illness (chap. 5). The *misipisiwak* 'underwater panthers' are malignant feline beings with horns and long tails. They dwell near rapids and are associated with drowning and mysterious disappearances. Motivated by jealousy, they may cause the deaths of their human "lover's" spouses and children. The aquatic *misikinīpikwak* 'great horned snakes' have similar inauspicious associations, although they appear in a more positive light in some myths. The narrator stated of Michel Dumas's watery immersion that "he's dreaming all the bottom of the water. He's dreaming all the animals. They got to come to him." This seems to suggest a general association of all mammals, both terrestrial and amphibious, with underwater spaces, although no Cree explicitly stated as much. Ojibwa versions of the flood myth—which have the underwater panthers slay the hero's lupine brother to prevent the extermination of game—suggest a parallel although diachronically remote Algonquian association, since the panthers assume the role of game guardians. Additionally, water is significant in animal mortuary practices. Bones and carcasses of both terrestrial and aquatic animals are usually hung on the *mistikōhkān*, a tree or pole, in mortuary deposition, but they are also deposited in open water or holes in the ice during winter. The trees and poles used for hanging bones are themselves typically on the shores of lakes and rivers, and in many cases, skulls or carcasses are positioned to face out to the water. Perhaps underwater space is or was once the domain of animal souls.

Subterranean spaces are also identified with spirit beings and animals in Cree and other Algonquian contexts. Panthers and great horned serpents are talked about as living both underwater and underground, suggesting that the two categories of space may be assimilated or conceptually interchangeable. Certain Cree myths refer to subterranean worlds. In the Maskōkosān hero myth (Brightman 1989*a*), an Algonquianized transformation of "The Brave Tailor," the hero descends a rope to enter a subterranean world populated by witiko monsters. The *mīmīkwīsiwak*, diminutive and hirsute creatures who appear in dreams, live in caves or less accessible underground spaces along the shores of lakes and rivers. These beings are also represented as subterranean by Plains Cree groups, although the latter locate them under sand hills rather than in riparian caves (Brightman 1990). Eastern Cree, Montagnais, and Naskapi groups of Quebec-Labrador represent the caribou as occupying a subterranean realm inside a remote mountain during summer (Speck 1935*a*:82–83).

Finally, remote terrestrial spaces are identified with *ahcāk* beings. In a Swampy Cree cosmogonic myth (Brown 1977), each of the four wind brothers introduces different biophysical phenomena and cultural institutions, effecting a convergence in the center of the terrestrial plane from the distant cardinal points. In Rock Cree tradition, the animals came into the Churchill River country from the extremities of the four directions, with the harmful animals coming from the north. The terrestrial dead country of indigenous tradition is understood to be situated in the remote west. Crees seeking a directionally oriented *pawākan* slept during the fast with their head to the appropriate cardinal point.

The significance of tree platforms in fasts and of trees in mortuary ritual is not exhausted by the opportunity they offer for separation from the terrestrial plane. Crees usually selected riparian sites for the platforms. Semmens (1884:109) observed a group of these stages on the Burntwood River, and such a site existed on the Laurie River, some miles upriver from its confluence with the Churchill at Granville Lake. The *manitōhkanak*, wooden statues representing the *pawākan* or other beings, were formerly carved in groups, also facing water. Like mortuary trees for animal remains, the effigies and the vision platforms were positioned simultaneously in the air and at the edge of water, inviting communication with both spheres. The single platform that I observed in 1978 was a rudimentary affair attached to three birch trees at an elevation of eight feet. It was used periodically during the summer months by an elderly man. The "nest" was located at the terminus of a short ten-yard portage between two lakes and aligned so that its user could sleep with his head toward either lake. Trees facing water simultaneously traverse the boundaries between terrestrial, celestial, underwater, and underground spaces. This instrumental juxtaposition is mentioned in other sources on Cree fasting. Albany and Moose Factory Crees seeking the blessings appropriate to a doctor constructed a stage on a tree hanging *over* the water to induce the appropriate vision (Skinner 1911:61). Both metaphorically and literally, the tree is represented as an *iskwāhtīm* 'doorway'. In a discourse on fasting, Jeremiah Michel remarked that the tree was "just like a door." He then said that at a certain stage of the vision dream, an aperture might appear in the trunk supporting the platform. By passing through the door, the dreamer entered a different world "inside the tree" populated by *ahcāk* beings. My interpreter, a science fiction aficionado, spontaneously likened this space to "another dimension."

I was successful in obtaining only two firsthand accounts of experiences during the visionary fast at puberty, and neither individual wanted his narrative included in a book. Crees provided typified reports, however, that were, I believe, influenced by their own experiences. The accounts are remarkably consistent in their details. The visionary is instructed by a senior relative to concentrate strongly while awake on the entities with which he desired a *pawākan* relationship. At the time of the event of contact, the faster might be either asleep or awake. He is conscious of himself, either on the platform or walking in the bush, and is approached by someone who resembles a human being and who converses with him in Cree. The visitor asks the dreamer if he recognizes him, has ever seen him before, or can guess his identity; it derives satisfaction from an admission of ignorance. The visitor instructs the dreamer to follow it to its abode. In or near the dream visitor's dwelling, the dreamer is subjected to experiences that will predestine later events in his life and will determine the willingness of the spirit to provide knowledge and aid. An individual may be instructed, for example, to go out hunting and, regardless of his hunger, kill only the fourth animal that he encounters. On complying with this directive, he is told that he may experience hunger in the future but that his benefactor will always assure that he does not starve. The visitor stipulates certain offerings that the dreamer must subsequently make to it, teaches medicines that can be used in hunting or curing, instructs the dreamer in a song with which it can be summoned in the future, and sometimes imposes certain dietary rules specifying parts of animals that the dreamer is obliged either to eat regularly or forgo. The dreamer may be told that the visitor will leave him if he regularly attends the Catholic church. If its "identity" is still unclear to the dreamer, the being metamorphoses repeatedly between human shape and another form that reveals its worldly appearance in waking consciousness. Alternatively, the faster may look behind him as he leaves and thus divine the identity of his visitor.

The continuities in discourses about these experiences, at least in the Churchill River region, are demonstrated by a composite description from Lac la Ronge around 1823:

Everything in nature appears unto them, but in the Shape of a human being. They dream they meet a man who asks them (after some preliminary conversation of course) "Dost thou know me? (who or what I am?)"—"No." "Follow me then," replies this stranger. The Indian follows—the other leads him to his abode and again makes the inquiry—the answer is perhaps as before. Then the stranger assumes his proper form, which is perhaps that of a Tree, a Stone, a fish, &c. &c., and after rechanging several times in this manner, till such time as the second comes perfectly to know him, then this stranger gives him to smoke, learns him his Song &c., thus addressing him: "Now don't you remember my song? . . . Whenever you will wish to call upon me, sing this Song and I shall not be far—I will come and do for you what you require." They know many of these spirits as soon as they see them (in their dreams) by the descriptions other Indians have given of them—some however they know from their nature. (Brown and Brightman 1988:35)

After awakening from the dream, the faster returned to camp or village and resumed ordinary occupations. Thereafter, he or she seldom verbally revealed the identity of the *pawākan* or the content of the vision. An exception occurred in cases when the dreamer felt unsure of the identity of the being and confided the experience to a senior relative who helped to interpret it. The identity of the *pawākan* could often be inferred by others from dietary rules and other observances of the dreamer. It is said that formerly nearly all males and many females secured *pawākan* relationships in the past. Semmens (1884:110) wrote that Crees who were unsuccessful in their attempts to secure a *pawākan* were the object of ridicule. Rock Crees say that such persons were unsuccessful in their objectives and did not live long. Some individuals later established relationships with additional beings, either during repeated isolated fasting or in dreams that occurred without this inducement. Men who cured or operated the shaking lodge cultivated many of these beings, but most people possessed only one.

Differences in the degree and character of a person's skills and powers derive both from the number and the identity of the dream guardians they possess. This implies a more or less systematic hierarchy of animate beings in terms of their relative "power" (Black 1977). Bears, the game ruler entities, thunderbirds, clouds, the sun, the moon, the morning star, and the beings associated with the four winds and directions are today identified as especially powerful agencies. The *pawākan* is represented as polyfunctional and aiding its human dependent in many spheres of endeavor, but individual beings or classes of beings confer specific gifts. There is little consensus about this division of labor, but people agree that men and women who become doctors dream of Sāwanis, the spirit of the south wind and cardinal direction, or of a bear. Dreams of carnivorous animals give power in hunting and trapping, and, paradoxically, the *pākahkwak*, skeleton beings associated with starvation, confer the same gifts. A person who dreams of an animal may conceive himself as especially fortunate in killing members of the same species.

Crees use "dream" to describe any event of communication with *ahcāk* beings. Usually, the *pawākan* appears in dreams during sleep, but some Crees also induce waking trance states, an act called *pawākwamiw* 'someone trances', by concentrating, drumming, or singing. These states are represented in narrative as a means for physically summoning the *pawākan* to the dreamer's aid. The *pawākan* is understood to assist its human dependent by providing "power." When these abilities manifest themselves in events of curing, sorcery, prophecy, operation of the shaking lodge, and exceptional foraging success they are termed *mamāhtāwisiwin*; their enactment or use by a human or spirit agent is signaled by the verb *mamāhtāwisiw* 'someone uses power'. Other abilities that merit this appellation are ascribed to ancestors in narratives: flying, igniting wet firewood, slaying witiko monsters, making musket balls from snow, living underwater, and leaping across the Burntwood River. The *pawākan* is represented in narratives as physically appearing to its owner and intervening on his behalf: "Suppose he gets into trouble with something, it will take his place and kill that thing." The influence of the *pawākan* overlaps into other less spectacular indexes such as canoeing skills and longevity.

To others, and perhaps subjectively, the individual's ability to survive accidents and disease, enjoy long life, forage successfully, cure others, know and influence future events, and do anything with exceptional skill can be tangible signs of the strength and devotion of the *pawākan*. Today, as in the past, the *pawākan* is strongly associated with the ability to prevail in adversarial situations and thus is represented as a factor in the destruction of monsters and in aggressive or retaliatory sorcery. Crees gloss the verb *pawākanowīw* as 'curse someone' or 'put bad medicine on someone'. During the 1700s, the *pawākan* was associated also with success in war against the Eskimo; images of the dream spirit were painted on hide shields prior to raids (Umfreville 1954 [1790]:48).

If he dreams of a bear, he will be able to overcome dangerous beings like the witiko. If someone is trying to harm him, the *pawākan* will act in his stead and kill that one [Cree].

You use it if someone is trying to hurt you, make you sick. Yeah. You just . . . *īyako, nimosōm!* ['let's go, my grandfather!']. Yeah, you say that: "Go get him!"

There'll be a day when you need help and the guy . . . you gotta ask the guy to do it for you. Or he'll tell you what's going to happen to you. Things like that. Or somebody might try to kill you and the guy will pull you through. That's the way it was. Otherwise witiko ['cannibal monster'] would have killed everybody.

"Powers" transmitted by the *pawākan* may be represented as persisting capacities to be exercised at will or as transient blessings, as when *Kōna* 'Snow' allows a starving man to fabricate cartridges out of that substance. The "power" is seemingly immaterial, although it may be embodied in plants, stones, and other objects whose possession or manipulation is necessary for its exercise. The success of these techniques in individual deployments is said to depend on the concurrent assistance of the *pawākan*, although the traffic in love and hunting medicines suggests that more impersonal processes are also postulated. Crees say that "the person isn't strong but the *pawākan* is." Nelson was told the same by Lac la Ronge Crees in the 1820s.

"But how is it possible that such things can be? Do you really think that an insignificant root of no apparent power or virtue whatsoever can effect such things?" Thus I would frequently question them, and their answers with little variation universally the same: "Yes, most certainly; it is not the root alone but with the assistance of that one of his dreamed [*pawākan*] that is most powerful and most fond of him." (Brown and Brightman 1988:66)

The *pawākan* gives information in dreams which may be communicated directly or shrouded in a symbolic medium. Thus, men and women dream the location of animals, the imminence of successful kills, the welfare of absent relatives, and the diagnosis and appropriate treatment of particular health disorders. The *pawākan* also transmits information through physical sensations that the human subject learns to interpret:

Like if you want to hunt moose. You go to bed at night. Then you'll know what kind of moose. I had that kind of feeling when I was about twenty-five year old, twenty year old. Lots of times I go to bed at night—I was traveling with my brother. About nine o'clock, I tell him what kind of moose we're going to track next day. I was a good hunter. Nineteen moose one winter. You want a moose, there'll be a moose tomorrow. I tell him what kind of moose we'll get tomorrow. I know it right away. A cow or a young bull. You get different feeling. You feel it. Same as a guy stretching [?] . . . left is my bull. It gets me harder. On your side. A young bull, just tight and a little touch. On my right, that's a cow. Soft touch, that's a cow moose. Before I go to bed at night. About nine o'clock, that's when I notice. If we're going to track a wolf, I know it right away, too. That was given to us Indians. You know what's going to happen tomorrow. You just about can tell. If anything's going to happen, you know ahead of time.

The verb *sākihīw* 'love someone' subsumes a variety of types of positive affect including emotions existing between relatives, spouses, lovers, and partners or friends. The *pawākan* is sometimes talked about as "loving" its human dependent and concerned to promote his or her welfare. The human subject may reciprocally "love" the dream spirit. The relationship grows more solidary with age. Crees say that the *pawākan* "does more" as its dependent ages and that "the more he uses it, the more it does." Others viewed their dream spirit more instrumentally:

Q: Do people say that [*ī-sākihāt* 'love'] about the *pawākan*?
A: I don't think . . . No you don't love it. You don't like it. It's just there like something waiting for you. Like I got my guns over there, see. Well, of course I like them, eh? I depend on them. If I wanna kill something I just grab whatever one I want. Well, people use *pawākan* like that. He takes what he wants to get what he wants. Almost a tool. A lot of people like that. That's what people live on. For a long time they depend on the *pawākan*. If you don't have one, you're

helpless. *ī-y-āpacāt opawākana*, he's using him. Using his *pawākan*. That's his tool. That what people use . . . that was their tools.

Crees say that the *pawākan* is desirous of sacrifices that it is thought literally to consume and enjoy. The dream spirit is the beneficiary of offerings—tobacco, knives, clothing, food—that may be rendered as a matter of course or accompanied by a prayer for assistance. Dreamers may experience the *pawākan* as jealous, motivated by a mercenary desire for human offerings of food and material goods, and readily angered by unintentional insult or neglect. Nelson wrote in 1823,

Indeed, from what I can learn, there are few of these *familiars* but do evil to their votaries if they (the votary, i.e., the Indian) neglect performing the regular annual, or perhaps more distant periodical sacrifice; and this sacrifice, their *familiar* tells them what it is he expects. (Brown and Brightman 1988:51)

The Cumberland House Crees of the 1820s likewise understood spirit beings as anxious for human products since their petitions to a being called "Kepoochikawn" included threats that gifts would be withheld if it failed to supply them with game animals (Franklin 1823: 115). The relationship is here negotiated in the exchange of tobacco, cooked food, and other cultural largesse for the "power" endowments that human beings lack. But these nonhuman agencies may esteem offerings more as signs of respect and belief than as material satisfactions. Following the introduction of Catholicism into the Churchill River region in the late nineteenth century, many Crees regretfully severed relationships with their *pawākan*, often through a terminal offering. Reciprocally, the dream guardians abandoned those of their human dependents who underwent baptism.

I suspect that only a small minority of Crees today define themselves as having a *pawākan*, although many more probably have dreams to which they ascribe spiritual significance. Crees talk about the formal vision fast at puberty as an institution that is either moribund or long vanished, and there is no reason to question their conclusions. The last men to undertake such fasts did so in the 1930s. Thereafter, the initial *pawākan* experience, when it occurred, came in dreams experienced while sleeping in camp or settlement. The few modern instances of protracted visionary fasting of which I learned involve middle-aged or elderly men who thus cultivate existing relations with their *pawākan*. One man explained, "Even the very oldest people here, most of them don't have the *pawākan*. Plenty of them *used* to have it. You can have it your whole life until you die as long as you believe in it."

The Game Rulers

Crees say that species of animals are under the direction and control of individual spirit agencies who may regulate their movements, distribution, and numbers. There is no specific term for this class of beings. The term *okimāw*, which refers to leaders or people occupying offices, is used, as are the English terms "boss" and "chief." The "bosses" are conceived as protecting the animals and advancing their interests. Crees seemingly have no parallel to the Lele idea that the game ruler may send an animal to hunters to punish it for some transgression (Douglas 1963:37).

In theory, each recognized species of animal possesses a distinct ruler, but the doctrine is not systematically extended to nonresources, or even to all creatures of economic importance. The ruler is understood to appear as a giant exemplar of the species it controls and is referred to by prefixing the particles *mis-*, *misi-* 'big' or 'great' to the species name.

For every kind of animal, they say that there's one big one. That's the one that can tell the others where they should go.
Q: Where do they stay?
A: [hesitates] They stay out amongst the animals. But in a particular place. They tell an animal to help a hunter. Then that animal tells the hunter where he can find him. I hear from my dad of *mistamisk* ['great beaver'], *mistamōswa* ['great moose'], *misimahīhkan* ['great wolf']. They even say there's *mistītakōm* ['great beetle']. You ask PB about *mistomiðāhcīs* ['great wolverine'] some time. That's why PB won't go to sleep in the bush without rifle right next to him.

Crees today do not recognize any entity with an encompassing control over all species of animals or groupings of them. Some say, however, that bears are the "boss" of other animals and sometimes exert influence over them. In consequence, hunters address wishes for hunting success to bears and define as auspicious dreams in which bears figure. Bears themselves conspicuously lack a game ruler entity, paralleling Swampy Cree belief in which "each bear is a chief by himself" (Skinner 1911:95).

Concepts of more generalized rulers were held in the past in some areas. Crees of Cumberland House in the 1820s appear to have possessed the idea of a single ruler of large game animals.

As most of their petitions are for plenty of food, they do not trust entirely to the favor of Kepoochikawn [a spirit being], but endeavor at the same time to propitiate the *animal*, an imaginary representative of the whole race of larger quadrupeds that are objects of the chase. (Franklin 1823:115)

Thompson (1962 [1784–1812]:26, 72–88) wrote of the game ruler beliefs of the Rock Crees' ancestors in the late 1700s. He described the rulers as occupying a node within the cosmogonic design of the deity Kicimanitōw who granted human beings autonomy but placed all other kinds of living things under the guardianship of "manitos" over which it in turn exercised control. Of the functions of the rulers in relation to their species, Thompson's clients emphasized control of migration. Caribou, they said, are quiet when left to themselves and migrate only at the directive of their game ruler. Similarly, a "manito of aquatic fowl" directed the seasonal migrations of geese and ducks.

Some Crees today agree that the rulers influence caribou migrations and also that they are responsible for the distribution of nonmigratory animals in the bush. The ruler may "space" animals throughout an area such that they have plenty to eat and prompt the departure of two-year-old beavers from the colony. The game ruler is also said to regulate the regeneration or rebirth of animals slain by hunters. The number of animals born each year is said to be decided by the game ruler. The same control over fertility is ascribed to the "master of the moose" by the Eastern Cree of Waswanipi (Feit 1973a:118).

Thompson (1962 [1784–1812]:75–76) wrote that the game rulers regulated human access to the animals. Consequently, hunters thanked them for successful kills and performed rites to avoid offending them. When a moose was killed, the hunter suspended a strip of hide from the throat to a tree as an offering. In another instance (ibid.:22–23), Crees shot a polar bear on the mud flats of Hudson Bay near Churchill but were able only to sever and retrieve the head before the tide came in. Onshore, they painted the nose with ocher, oriented the head to the water, and petitioned the "manito of the bears," asserting that they had treated the head properly and asking that the skin be floated ashore. Bones from the heads of bears and other animals were deposited in water. On another occasion, Cree women, who specialized in trapping martens, danced at night to the "Manitoo of the Martens" for a successful catch. The Crees believed that if they neglected these rites, the rulers would "drive the animals from the hunter."

Although the "bosses" today are conventionally understood to punish only the ritually delinquent hunter, Thompson learned of a game ruler who seemingly disapproved categorically of hunting. Crees objected when he measured a variety of woodland caribou: "We do not like to see you measure the Deer for fear their Manito would be angry, he is soon displeased, and does not like his Deer to be killed, and has not many of them" (ibid.:88). This suggests the idea, one refractory to the dominant ideology, that hunters can kill animals despite the game rulers' disapproval. The modern idea that the rulers resent "waste" of animals, as when a beaver colony is deliberately trapped out or when more animals are killed than can be used, suggest the continuity of the caribou ruler's proprietary attitude (chap. 10).

Thompson's writing suggests that ritual observances were addressed exclusively or primarily to the game ruler and not to the slain animals themselves. It is the game ruler who exacts correct ritual observances, rewards their practice, and punishes their omission. By implication, the animals were conceived as objects, their availability negotiated between the hunters (and their personal *pawākanak*) and game rulers. Such may have been the prevalent conception of the times, perhaps influenced by the increased effectiveness of the introduced technology. More probably, Thompson oversimplified a more complex and less orderly relationship. Today, Crees understand ritual practice as satisfying both the "bosses" and the individual animals killed. The bear ceremonies of Ontario Saulteaux similarly honored both the slain bear and the "bear manito" (Skinner 1911:75). The wishes of the animals and the rulers are imagined as convergent. When asked to whom hunting rituals are addressed, Crees typically identified the animal or the hunter's *pawākan*, introducing the concept of the "boss" only after reflection. It is my impression that the "bosses" of the game are presently peripheral to the practice of indigenous religion by Crees in northern Manitoba.

Hunting Sorcery

Other humans also influence the outcomes of foraging prospects. In positive terms, men may benefit from dream events of their wives which prefigure successful hunts. More typically, men sometimes express fear that others are using spiritual techniques to give them bad luck. *Maci-maskihkiwīðiniw* 'bad medicine person' (or sorcerer) refers to any individual who employs "power" to harm others. Sorcery is an imaginable correlate of any adversarial relationship, but Crees also say that sorcerers may be motivated by envy, the desire to coerce the victim, revenge for imagined insults, or an involuntary wickedness to which their *pawākan* predisposes them. *Nānipōmīw* refers to the event of one person cursing another, or "throwing bad medicine at him" in Cree-English vernacular. *Māsakwamāw* designates the type of sorcery here at issue, that in which one person starves another by impeding their access to game. Such sorcery is represented as a contest between human beings, its outcome a consequence of their relative power and that of their *pawākanak*. The animals are understood as objects whose location or accessibility the sorcerer and the *pawākan* manipulate, and the sorcery seemingly proceeds independently of their decisions.

The circumstances prompting such a curse sometimes relate directly to subsistence activities. Curses befall persons who deny food to others, or originate from a jealous elder who envies a younger man's hunting prowess. Curses are said to be preceded by unsubtle verbal threats of which "*namwāc ka-papíwān*" 'you won't be lucky' is representative. Crees say the sorcerer may send his or her *pawākan* to frighten animals away from the victim and/or his traps, a procedure described by Nelson in 1923.

With this also, principally, they succeed in bewitching anyone they are averse to and prevent them from killing such animals as they please. They draw the likeness of the animal or animals, they do not choose the others to kill, put of this medicine . . . upon the hearts and desire that they may become shy and fly off upon any the least appearance or approach of them. Or, they will *conjure* and desire some one of their *familiars*, one, or several, *to haunt such a one* in all his motions and scare and frighten off, and *render wise* any *such* and *such* animals; and let the distance be hundreds of miles off—their familiars that are spirits residing in the air, and transport themselves in an instant to any place they please, and see all that is going on *below*, keep *all* away accordingly. (Brown and Brightman 1988:71)

The text "The Youth Who Was a Bony Spectre" (Bloomfield 1934:218–54) provides a detailed narrative example of how Plains Crees understood this sorcery to proceed among their Thickwoods Cree neighbors to the north.

Considered in the aggregate, the conceptions discussed here express multiple representations of relationships between hunters and animals.

Crees talk about ritual practice as obligations addressed to individual slain animals whose souls are reactive subjects. The game ruler being exists as a mediating figure who may order or influence animals to surrender themselves to the hunter. The *pawākan* of the hunter, whether or not it is identified as an animal or a game ruler, also exerts influence over the hunt. In these latter cases, the animals are represented as objects to which the hunter's access is regulated by relationships with other more individuated beings. Finally, sorcerers can suspend contact between men and animals.

Animal Dreams

Crees say that animals are sometimes killed twice, first in a dream and subsequently in waking life. The noun *pawāmiwin* can refer either to a single dream or to dreaming as a category of human experience. The noun readily occurs with the locative suffix *-ihk*: *nipawāmiwinihk* 'in my dream', *opawāmiwinihk* 'in his/her dream'. Reference to dreams and dreaming is typically with the verbs *pawāmiw* 'someone dreams', *pawātīw* 'dream of someone', and *pawātam* 'dream of something'. The noun *opawāmiw* refers to a spiritually powerful individual blessed with such skills as curing, operating the shaking lodge, or metamorphosis. Crees explain the content of many dreams as influenced by what we call "day residues": the fears, desires, and other mental events of waking life. Some dreams are apparently viewed as private psychological experiences with no practical significance for waking life. One man's dream, for example, of sex with a particular woman, was interpreted rather prosaically as expressing only his desire for sex with that woman; for Crees, dreams about sex may be only dreams about sex. Cree dream theory, however, exhibits commitment neither to a Cartesian dualism of spirit and matter nor to the boundary between an external objective reality and a subjective psychic reality to which dreams are assigned. Crees say that many dreams are perceptions of actually occurring events that the dreaming self witnesses or in which it constructively participates. Such dreams are conceived to be as real as the data of waking consciousness, although the two domains are, of course, distinguished, and reality may exhibit itself differently to waking and dreaming selves. The manifest content of these dreams is varied. The dreamer himself may be a passive onlooker or an active character in dream events. He or she may converse with others in the dream or interact silently with them. It is not clear to me how Crees assign individual dreams to these categories; they say that people sometimes err in their identification.

To the question of who dreams, Crees answer variously that it is the person himself or the person's *ahcāk*, or personal soul. The *ahcāk* is an animating and individuating force present in the human fetus at conception, and its prolonged absence from the body results in death. It remains unclear to me whether the reflexive, named, and individuated self—the self of autobiography that thinks, perceives, and acts in waking life—is identified by Crees with the soul; the two are thought, in any case, to be closely related. A person's soul can be abducted by a sorcerer, and the body is then said to become inert or berserk, deprived of rational consciousness and identity. In a nineteenth-century narration of such an experience, the victim evidently used the pronoun "I" to refer alternately to his body and to his detached soul, which had been summoned into a sorcerer's shaking lodge (Brown and Brightman 1988:63). Crees today use first-person pronouns to refer to the activities of their souls in dreams. The fact that the waking self sometimes possesses only imperfect memory of dream events suggests, however, that it is implicitly distinguished from the sleeping self. The possessed construction *nitahcāk* 'my soul' also suggests that the soul is a possession or component of the self, not its equivalent. To the best of my knowledge, Rock Crees do not define dreams as expressing, either literally or symbolically, desires of the soul that must be satisfied to maintain health, an Iroquoian doctrine (Wallace 1958) shared with the Eastern Crees (Speck 1935a:35–36).

Crees recognize multiple factors that influence the occurrence and content of particular dreams. The fact that people dream at all is attributed both to their own initiative and to the cooperation of beings that appear in or cause dream experiences. Crees talk about dreaming as a capacity with which they as a people were deliberately endowed by Kicimanitōw. Indian dreaming is compensatory in this respect for the technological knowledge and money with which whites were divinely endowed. Individual dreams are talked about as being catalyzed by spirit beings, most typically the dreamer's *pawākan*. The *pawākan* causes its owner to dream, by means that are not identified, and, like other spirit beings, it may additionally elect to appear in individual dreams and interact with the dreamer's soul. Crees themselves attempt to induce dreams by observing dietary rules or by using the drum. They seek to influence the content of particular dreams by a variety of strategies, for example, concentrating on an object of desire with the intention of dreaming about it.

While Crees enjoy telling dreams and clearly find them interesting, their interest is motivated pragmatically by the postulate that dreams are multiply relevant to experiences of waking life in the present or future. Dream events are first of all understood representationally as literal or metaphoric sources of information relevant to the dreamers' practical interests. Crees talk about dreams as containing solutions to such questions as where to locate animal traps and how to deal with health disorders. They may also believe that others are capable of dreaming solutions to their problems. Thompson, during his winter sojourn at Reed Lake, became the unwilling object of this doctrine. One of his Cree clients, deeply distraught by his failure to kill moose, became convinced that Thompson was capable of remedying the problem. Thompson remonstrated that only the "Great Spirit" could produce the optimal weather conditions needed to stalk moose.

Ah, that is always your way of talking to us, when you will not hear us, then you talk to us of the Great Spirit. I want a Wind, I must have it, now think on it, and dream, how I am to get it. (Thompson 1962 [1784–1812]:101–102)

Dream images may be understood as prophetic, as literal or symbolically disguised representations of future states of affairs. Memories of the dream are then retained by the waking self, providing foreknowledge of future occurrences. For example, a man dreamed that his brother's pregnant dog gave birth to four puppies. When, some days later, the dog obligingly gave birth to four puppies, the prophet's friends humorously began calling him "*opawāmiw*," dreamer, a term connoting great spiritual power, and suggested that he set about trying to dream about more important things. Representations of the future in prophetic dreams may be literal. A dream, for example, about trapping an otter, may prophesy a subsequent event of successful otter trapping. Similarly, one woman told me that she dreamed of *Atāmipīkōw-iskwīw* 'Underwater Woman', who spoke to her, assuring her that she would save her children from drowning in the event of an accident.

Crees also say that entities and events perceived by the dreaming soul may be disguised forms of corresponding entities and events in waking experience. Persons, actions, and discourses in dreams may all refer to something other than what they appear to be, and, in such cases, the dream requires interpretation. Some dream events possess conventional meanings, whereas the significance of others can only be guessed at. Cree men and women often interpret entities and events in dreams as having disguised reference to events of hunting and trapping that will occur in the future. Metaphoric symbolism is quite frequent in such dreams, and some dream events possess conventional meanings. To dream of a bear usually prefigures successful hunting or trapping that may or may not involve a bear: "I respect that. . . I know I'm going to have good trapping when I dream about a bear. Yeah, I respect that. . . [hence I am a] good trapper." Dreams of sexual encounters, visits from friends or relatives, and chance meetings are also said to prefigure successful foraging. In these cases, the symbolism is duplex, since the human dream characters correspond to worldly animals and the dream events of sex and visiting correspond to worldly events of hunting. Animals and other entities frequently but not invariably are perceived in human form in dreams. Reciprocally, dreams of animals may be interpreted as prophesying future events of interaction with humans. Events transpiring in the dream itself may or may not reveal that a humanoid dream character is an animal of a particular kind.

I am walking across the muskeg along the shores of the Laurie River. Far ahead of me a woman is walking, wearing an old-time Cree dress. She keeps pace with me, this woman, maintaining the same distance between us. I try to catch up to her but am not able to succeed. She walks rapidly and maintains an invariable distance between us. Finally I am almost able to approach her closely. I walk toward her. Just there she begins removing all her clothing [laughs]. She stands there naked. Then she disappears, I can't see her anywhere. Only her dress remains on the ground. I walk up and I retrieve her dress. Of course, I am watching her closely as she disrobes [laughs]. Later, in the spring, I kill a cow moose on the Laurie River. So I know that it is the one whom I dreamed of there. This dreaming was given to us, we Crees. [Cree]

In subsequent worldly experience, woman becomes cow moose, clothing becomes body, disrobing becomes death, and the retrieval of the dress becomes the retrieval of the carcass. The dreamer interpreted the disrobing event as prefiguring the separation of the moose's soul from its body at the moment of death, and in other dreams, clothing often represents the animal's body (cf. Tanner 1979:137). While the animal in this dream appears anthropomorphically "disguised," its gender and the location of the encounter replicate the ensuing events in waking life. Here and in other dreams, the gender of entities in dreams often corresponds to the gender of the worldly beings with which the dream is concerned.

Although dreams are representations of existing or impending states of affairs. Cree dream theory is often more actively constructivist in its assumptions. The narrator of the dream just discussed understood the worldly outcome of his caribou hunt not simply as prophesied in but as caused by the events in his dream. Crees say that dream events may *determine* the occurrence of like events—their worldly simulacra—that have not yet happened but that will transpire in waking life only as a result of their having initially been dreamed. The dream experience as a whole predestines its worldly simulacrum, and, within the dream, multiple courses of action are possible for the dreaming self just as multiple resolutions of the worldly event are possible. That dream resolution that occurs from among the possible ones is talked about as influenced by the intentional or unwitting actions of the human dreamer in the dream. The dreamer, therefore, conceives him or herself as capable of influencing worldly outcomes by choosing certain courses of action in the anticipatory dream. The performative conception coexists with but is distinct from the doctrine that dreams simply provide foreknowledge of events independently underway and not themselves originating in dreams.

This performative theory of dreaming fosters the cultivation of deliberate action in dreams. Specifically, Crees say that they attempt to dream about specific objects of desire, maintain consciousness during the transition into sleep, recognize when they are dreaming, and act volitionally within dreams, whether or not the dream is one that they understand themselves deliberately to have cultivated. They say that they try to act purposefully in their dreams. The studied deliberateness with which Crees approached their dreams was noted in the late 1700s by Thompson (1962 [1784–1812]:81):

At times they know how to dream for their own interest or convenience; and when one of them told me he had been dreaming it was for what he wished to have, or to do, for some favor, or as some excuse for not performing his promises, for so far as their interests are concerned they do not want policy.

Or, as I was told didactically in the 1980s, "You got to know how to do things in your dream. Make things happen then." Individual dreams thus possess for their dreamers a dual temporal orientation, to the antecedent desire that may play a part in their occurrence and to the worldly consequence that they predestine. Not all dream events, of course, are thought about as being susceptible to the dreamer's deliberate intention, but this is often the expressed ideal. These equivalents to the phenomenon Western psychology calls "lucid dreaming" seemingly remain very much a part of modern Cree experience, but I know virtually nothing of the modes of instruction and discipline that impart and cultivate them. Parents encourage children to remember and relate their dreams, but I do not know whether more specific instruction occurs or, indeed, whether any Crees succeed in lucid dreaming to the degree that some say they do.

Events prophesied or predestined in dreams may occur anywhere from a few hours to decades after the dream itself. It was a characteristic of events in the induced visionary dream at puberty that they predestined events that were to occur much later in the dreamer's life. It is my impression that Crees concurrently remember multiple dreams and causally assimilate particular worldly events to them, after the fact. Crees say that they sometimes do not know the meaning of a particular dream until the consummation occurs in waking life and is retrospectively attributed to the dream experience. Thus, a dream about an otter may refer to and create a successful harvest of fish, but this interpretation does not occur until the dreamer hauls in his net and makes the retrospective connection.

Dreams of hostile encounters are also talked about as requiring deliberate action by the dream self. Given these cultural assumptions, bad dreams or nightmares can assume a particularly threatening significance for Crees. Events in such dreams are described as instigated by sorcerers or malignant spirit beings, and they predestine worldly misfortunes: injury, mental disorder, illness, or death. It is said that the realization in waking life of events in "bad dreams" can be averted if the dreaming self acts appropriately in confronting the aggressor. Alternatively, such dreams may be interpreted in waking life, the instigator identified, and countermeasures taken. Some Crees travel extensively and pay sizable sums to obtain such treatment. As one Cree described this,

Even my brother-in-law here, he don't eat a she-beaver. Me, I eat anything. I never had a bad dream about anything like that. I could have but I usually fight like hell in a bad dream. That's the only way you'll pull through [prevail], they say. If you fight like hell. Nobody get the best of you. If you back out, that's when people get bad dreams. Scared. Can't go alone. Lot of people like that who can't go alone. Scared. They can't sleep alone. Lot of people can't even go two hours in the bush. Otherwise they go crazy. Scared. Get lost.
Q: How do you fight in a dream?
A: Like something is chasing you, like that one in the rapids [*misipisiw* 'underwater panther']. You double around and you go after it. I never dream that. Or

if some guy is trying to make you sick you knock him out. Punch him out [in the dream]. That way he won't be able to do nothing to you.

Some Crees understand the control they exert over their worldly goals as significantly conditioned by the control they can exert over their own actions in dreams.

Such control can be complicated by the opacity of dream symbolism. Entities, actions, and events perceived in dreams correspond to entities, actions, and events that exist or will later exist in waking life. But events seemingly possess a dual aspect within the dream itself. The dual character of the dream image may result in a situation where the dreaming self understands itself to be encountering entities or performing actions quite different from those it is actually encountering or performing in the dream. Such misperception of the "real" nature of these entities and actions may cause the dreaming self to behave in ways that predestine undesired results in subsequent waking life.

The misrecognition of objects and actions in dreams is sometimes said to result from intentional deception practiced by malevolent spirits. The paradigm case of such misrepresentation is said to have occurred in the visionary dream at puberty. Evil beings would approach the dreamer and misrepresent their identity. If the visionary accepted their songs and subsequently sacrificed to them, he or she unknowingly established a *pawākan* or dream spirit relationship that would predestine misfortune. For example, a man or woman who unwittingly established such a bond with an opposite-sexed *misipisiw*, or underwater panther, thereby jeopardized the lives of their human spouse and children. Crees seemingly were concerned with events in dreams which predestine degeneration into a witiko, or cannibal monster. The spirit being *Maskwamiy*, Ice, might appear to a visionary and identify itself as a game animal. The unwitting visionary would accept what he perceived as an animal *pawākan* and observe the dietary rules it imposed. When, in subsequent waking experience, the visionary ate the flesh of an animal of the same species, he would become a witiko. Similar concerns are expressed in a dream related to Nelson in the 1820s in which the evil being *Kīwītin* 'North' tempts the dreamer with delicacies that are actually human body parts (Brown and Brightman 1988:90–91). A woman related to me a somewhat similar dream experience in which, after her temporary "death," she misheard the crying of her children as wolves howling and determined to return to life only after correcting the misperception. The dreamer's ability to act appropriately relative to subsequent events depends on the ability to see beyond illusory appearances. Wolves howling may be children crying, or animal flesh may be human flesh. In each case, it is the "real" phenomenon rather than the illusory appearance which is the simulacrum of the worldly result waiting to be predestined in waking life.

The dreams in which hunters conceive themselves initially to encounter the animals they later kill are intersections of diverse presences and influences. So also are the waking practices with which the dreamer prepares for the hunt and with which the animal is carefully shown the extremes of hospitality and respect as it is killed, brought into domestic space, and transformed into food.

4

"The Same Respect You Give Yourself"

Introduction

Crees talk about the complex of religious observances surrounding animals as expressing a respect born of necessity. The conventional rationalization for these practices is that they materially affect the efficiency of hunting and trapping in an environment where animals consciously regulate hunters' access to them. If these acts are performed correctly, it is said that slain animals will be reborn and voluntarily offer themselves to hunters by entering traps and allowing themselves to be killed with guns. Crees sometimes say that hunters can only kill animals when this voluntary self-sacrifice occurs. If the practices are omitted or performed incorrectly, it is said that animals will fail to be reborn or will withhold themselves from hunters by frustrating attempts to kill them. These offenses are the type case of *pāstāhōwin* (noun), the process through which people antagonize spirit beings (or other humans) by diverse acts of commission or omission and thus reflexively provoke misfortune: *pāstāhōw* (verb) 'someone brings retribution on himself'. Crees find worldly confirmation of these doctrines in what they perceive as the ineffective foraging of younger and more secular hunters. The observances possess for some men and women an inherent appropriateness transcending their practical advantages. Some Crees who participate intensively in foraging are socialized to experience feelings of thankfulness when they kill animals, and they say that they find in the enactment of these practices a satisfying medium for the expression of these feelings.

Singing to Animals

Nikamon 'song' is a genre with many subtypes, of which love and hunting songs are most common. Singing to animals or other beings, sometimes with accompanying percussion from rattles or drums, may occur before or after foraging events. The drum, *pakamā-hīskikwan* or *mistikwaskihk*, was symbolically important to the Catholic missionaries who are said to have burned them, thrown them into the water, or insisted that their owners do so as a prerequisite for baptism. Perhaps as a result of Catholic hostility, few people today make and possess drums or, in any event, are willing to talk about making and possessing them. I have only seen five Cree drums, although I suspect many more people own them. Drums are carefully stored under owners' beds, where they are talked about as "sleeping" and removed only before use. Drums are taken out and played at the conclusion of some eat-all feasts. They are played by their owners at trapline cabins at the beginning of trapping season or before going moose hunting. People say that playing the drum and singing is a way of praying or asking animals and other nonhuman agencies for gifts of food. Singing is also an expression of gratitude and respect, and the idea is widely shared that animals derive aesthetic pleasure from the performances: "Yeah, they like to hear that . . . like to hear people singing." I was also told that the songs exert a positive influence over the hunter's luck, and there are obvious parallels with the ideology of verbal magic.

Cree hunting songs are one subset of a more inclusive group of songs whose performance is associated with communication with spirit beings and typically also with positive influence on some objective desired by the singer. Gambling songs, curing songs, traveling songs, and some love songs also fall into this class. There also exist "secular" songs that are not expected to exert such influences. Crees say that both the music and the lyrics of sacred or magical songs originate in dreams, the singer either learning them in a dream experience or composing them to commemorate one. Songs are taught to others, sometimes for monetary or other payment. Both magical and secular song lyrics can be ranged along a continuum between the relatively literal and the relatively allusive. The text below is an example of a relatively literal magical song expressing the singer's heartfelt desire that his homebrew will soon come to successful fruition.

āsay   at-icākamisin   niminikwīwinis, māskōc apoh ta-ti-ispakwan
already it changes color my little batch maybe so   it will taste good

ati-pī-tāpākī
in the morning

"My little batch is changing color already so maybe it will taste good in the morning." Magical song texts are more usually indirect, allusive, and characterized by metonymic and metaphoric tropes. The song below is sung before hunting big game animals.

ni-ta-y-ōōōtīn   askiy   wa-mīcisōwāni
I will howl to it the earth when I intend to eat

The reference to howling metonymically evokes the wolf who is the song's subject and, quotatively, its singer. The lyrics are unusual in drawing on the resemblance of wolves and humans as predators to create a metaphoric likeness of the human singer-hunter to the quotative wolf-predator he momentarily impersonates. The song's owner explained it as expressing his hope that he would be, like a wolf, a good and successful hunter. Other hunting song lyrics are similarly indirect, as in this bear-hunting song.

ītātōw   piskwacak   nikiskīðitīn
all the mounds the ground is uneven I know it

Here, the mounded snow over a den metonymically references a hibernating bear, and the song, as one expects, is intended to prefigure the singer's discovery of a bear den in winter. In these three cases, the song lyrics refer, however elliptically, to a desired outcome. Other songs are associated with wishes in a more diffuse fashion:

askiy ka-kiskīðimikon askiy nōsisim
earth will know you earth my grandchild

The singer's English gloss was, "Wherever you go, grandchild, the earth'll know you." The lyrics were further explained as meaning that the bear is at home in whatever terrain or surroundings it finds itself. More generally, the earth's knowledge of the bear metaphorically expresses that animal's worldly preeminence. I suspect also that the singer, in performing the song and becoming the "I" of "my grandchild," hopes to partake in the earth's omniscience about the bear, particularly given the reference to movement and location in the gloss. The bear is nowhere overtly signaled as the song's subject; the lyrics could be praising another entity. Preston (1975:198–220) has published a valuable series of Eastern Cree song lyrics in English together with the singers' interpretations and his own analysis; these lyrics exhibit metonymic and metaphoric figures similar to those above (cf. Speck 1935a:182–186).

Verbal Petition

Like songs, certain utterances are understood to exert influence over the outcomes of foraging and other activities, or, in any case, Crees say that they hope these utterances will do so. They occur when sacrifices are offered, when traps are set, and when *maskihkiy* 'medicine' is applied to traps and trap bait. Most are continuous in surface form with a variety of expressions that signal speakers' wishes or desires to human interlocutors. The particle *mãhti* resists ready translation; it occurs in conversation to preface directives or proposals for joint activity: "*mãhti anima mītawītān maskokācōsīwin*" 'mãhti let's play that bear hunt game'. In magical speech, "*mãhti*" occurs with verbs in future tense to indicate a projective state of affairs desired by the speaker. In a textual example taken from Plains Cree (Bloomfield 1934:196–197), a moose hunter addresses his dream guardian:

maht ōki   nama ni-ka-mōsihikwak   ōki   mōswak
maht these not   they will perceive me these moose

Similar constructions occur today in the worldly discourse of Crees in Manitoba. An acquaintance of mine repeated the utterance below twice after rubbing "medicine" over the branches to which a snare set for a lynx was attached.

mãht ōta   ka-pī-ōtihtam
mãhti here he will come to it

A similar invocation was repeated several times at a beaver lodge after snares were set.

mãht īkwa mwāc n-ka-tapasīkwak
mãhti then not   they will flee from me

In these contexts, *māhti* is best glossed as "let it be that x." Another device for communicating desire in everyday affairs concatenates the preverbs *ta* and *wī* with a verb expressing the desired future state of affairs. *Ta* is a future tense preverb, according to Wolfart (1973:77), a reduced variant of the future preverb *kita*. For Swampy Cree, Plains Cree, and Woods Cree speakers, *ta* may connote the speaker's confidence regarding the occurrence of a future event. As one of Voorhis's Swampy Cree colleagues put it, "Only God could say "*ta-mispon*" ['it will snow']" (Voorhis 1977:4.3). *Wī* is also a future tense preverb, usually connoting the agent's intentionality. The sequence of *ta* + *wī* would thus seemingly communicate either redundancy—a doubled futurity—or a future intention, as in English "he *will* want to go hunting" (but does not now want to do so). The combination of definiteness with intentionality signals, however, something quite different: the speaker's fervent desire for the occurrence of the predication. The *ta* +*wī* construction is thus a covertly modal indexical category that references the speaker's attitude. As with "*māhti*," the construction can be glossed as "let it be that x," and it occurs in magical speech. The words below were uttered while burning an offering of cigarettes in the stove.

īkosi nimosōm,   *ta-wī-misi-ðōtīn*
so   my grandfather let it be very windy

The speaker wanted strong winds for hunting moose. The addressee could be any number of entities but was most probably one of the four wind beings. The *ta* + *wī* construction occurs also in magical speech in Plains Cree narratives (Bloomfield 1934:272–273).

Cree magical language in the 1820s was evidently similar. Nelson used English constructions similar to "let it be that x" to translate Cree utterances used in sorcery. A man burning a leather effigy of his enemy

generally utters words like these, "Let the Heart of *such a one* become like this Leather, let it shrivel and die within him!" If it is a leg, an arm, the head, or any other particular part, or parts, or even the whole body, it is the same and the words also; unless he doth not wish for the death; then he will say, "Let *such a part* become lame, useless, ulcerous," &c. (Brown and Brightman 1988:65)

Presumably, the Cree discourse Nelson originally heard used *māhti*, the *ta* + *wī* construction, or similar devices to express these uncharitable desires. It remains to be ascertained whether Cree magical expressions of desire for particular events have an invariant linguistic form like the "spells" familiar from Melanesian and Southeast Asian ethnography. My impression is that Cree magical utterances are composed more or less ad hoc in each occurrence of their use.

Anthropological writing on magical speech has proposed three principal explanations for the globally common postulate that utterances can, under some circumstances, produce effects on external states of affairs in the future, independently of human interlocutors and technical procedures. These theories seek to identify aspects of language use that would engender intuitions or deductions constitutive of this postulate. Malinowski's (1923,1961,1965) foundation texts on Trobriand magical speech proposed both performative and indexical theories. The "performative theory" derives the ideology of magical speech from speakers' mistaken generalization of the perlocutionary effectiveness of speech acts, especially as these are experienced in infancy. By crying for an object, the infant causes it to appear. As a result, speakers acquire an intuition of the "indexical" connectedness (or resemblance) of word to object in space and time: naming the desired state of affairs causes it to come into existence. An alternative phrasing of the indexical theory might derive it from the copresence of sounds and meanings in the native speaker's consciousness (cf. Benveniste 1971:43–46), a psychological affinity exteriorized as the postulate that linguistic signs can influence worldly denotata. More recently, a "tropological theory" has grounded the ideology of magical speech in metaphor and metonymy, identifying the transposition of meaning between the linguistic elements of tropes as a model for the intuition that desired attributes can be transferred between worldly objects (Tambiah 1968). All such theories need to be contextualized in broader ethnographic studies of how the members of societies in which magical speech is practiced understand words to be related to objects. Little is known of Algonquian folk semantics, but there is evidence that each of the three theories may be pertinent. Tambiah's claim that the indexical and performative theories are incompatible with tropological interpretation is not persuasively argued. And the latter approach is, in any case, local rather than global in its provenience, since there exist in Cree, and in other languages, varieties of magical speech that do not employ tropes.

The Cree genres relevant to this problem include the "let it be that x" forms discussed above, the lyrics of song texts, the performative utterances of transformer characters in myth, and, finally, a set of linguistic "taboos," words and utterances that should not be spoken, either generally or in certain circumstances. The tropological theory is clearly relevant to song texts that may employ metaphoric and metonymic likenesses between elements in the lyrics and between these and both the singer and the desired worldly objective. While the behavioristic components of Malinowski's performative theory have been justifiably criticized (Tambiah 1968), Cree magical speech is clearly performative in the sense that some speakers understand songs and other utterances as prayers that they hope nonhuman interlocutors will hear, understand, and respond to, much as would a well-disposed human addressee. The "magical" effectiveness is not, from this point of view, in the words themselves but in their effect on beings conceived to exert control over foraging or other outcomes.

The converse of such prayers are utterances that, if spoken, are believed to bring about harmful worldly outcomes. I noted above that the noun *pāstāhōwin* refers to misfortune provoked by incorrect actions or omissions. Graham (1988:83) discusses the Swampy Cree cognate, *pāstāhōwin*, noting that one of its meanings is "that by saying something, it may happen to you." Rock Crees use the related noun *pāstāmōwin* to refer to misfortune provoked specifically by speech: *pāstāmōw* (verb) 'someone brings misfortune on himself by speech'. Similarly, Eastern Cree *pāštāmōw* "refers to what someone said which led to something undesirable happening" (Craik 1979:70). "*Pāstāmōwin*" paradigmatically includes both verbal ridicule of *ahcāk* beings or large game animals (see below) and any references to misfortune in the future. The instance of *pāstāmōwin* I remember most vividly occurred when a woman, during the course of a violent argument, uttered the wish that a fatal accident would befall her boyfriend while he was on his trapline. Her mother and sister immediately remonstrated with her for saying such a thing. After her friend's departure for the bush, she became frantic with anxiety, repeatedly claiming that she would kill herself if her wish came true. In events of this kind, it is not always clear whether *ahcāk* beings are the mediating agents or whether the words themselves are felt to acquire a transitive force that compels their external realization. In the latter case, there exist intuitions or postulates of indexical relations not only between nouns and their denotata—as evident in the "naming" transformations in myth—but between whole propositions and external states of affairs in the future.

I was often not comfortable asking Crees to whom their verbal prayers for hunting luck were addressed. Some petitions contain the vocative *nimosōm* 'my grandfather', which may refer to any respected nonhuman personage. The examples given above all refer to the desired animals in the third person, and it is probable that they address the speaker's *pawākan* or other spirit beings with control over animals. One man told me that he did not know who might be listening. It is by no means clear that all such utterances are understood by their speakers as having well-defined interlocutors. Some of the *māhti* and *ta + wī* forms may be conceived by the speakers as exerting an unmediated effect on future events. The same forms possess such effects when spirits utter them in narrative, as, for example, when Wīsahkīcāhk verbally produces a magical fire (Bloomfield 1930:9). With respect to the animals themselves, then, magical speech may be conceived as coercion rather than supplication.

Quick Killing

Kill them quickly! You can't let them suffer! Kill 'em quick! You got to give them the same respect you give yourself. That's why a lot of these young trappers don't kill hardly nothing.

Humans can cause pain or perhaps objectionable levels of pain to animals through certain exploitative techniques, and they have the obligation to minimize this suffering. Some Crees express guilt about particular productive episodes that they perceive as inflicting excessive pain. One man returned from his line with a lynx that had been caught in a leg-hold trap and starved to death with a broken leg during the interval between capture and retrieval. The "correct" procedure when leg-hold traps are used in terrestrial sets is to visit the line frequently and dispatch the animals quickly with a club or gun. The trapper was visibly depressed (and perhaps worried) about what had happened, observing, "That lynx must really have suffered . . . starved. That's no good." He stated that snare sets were better for lynxes because they strangled the animals quickly. People say that meat from animals that have suffered acquires an unpleasant taste. For example, we retrieved on one occasion a rabbit that had been caught and constricted around midbody by the snare wire. Later, the meat was pronounced inedible: "He suffered for hours and hours. All that goes into the body and makes the meat bad." Implicit in these statements is recognition that hunters and trappers capture animals against their will rather than exclusively through the animals' voluntary self-sacrifice.

Unnecessary cruelty is said to diminish trapping success. The wolverine's habit of plundering trap sets sometimes provokes hostile reactions from trappers. Even in such cases, physical cruelty may be understood as inappropriate.

It's no good to make animals suffer. One time me and my partners were being bothered . . . wolverine is taking all our fur. We had sets for fox all up and down our lines. Every time we lift traps, the wolverine takes our foxes. So we try to kill this wolverine. Otherwise we don't get nothing. So we put up [vertical] posts and bait them and put [leg-hold] traps around the ground. Next time we come, we catch that wolverine. My two partners got there ahead of me. When I get there, they're tormenting that wolverine. I said, "Don't, man, that's no good!" I take ax and hit it in the head. Kill it quick. After that I get no more trouble with wolverine, but my partners [are] still getting cleaned out. Finally they have to move away from there. Nothing happens to my traps . . . one time wolverine takes mink out of my trap but he just puts it down nearby. Don't bother it. I told those guys, "Don't do that." Maybe he'll try to get back at them somehow.

The implication is that the same or another wolverine takes revenge on the offenders by attacking their sets with special intensity while exempting the narrator in acknowledgment of his humane conduct.

The issue of humane trapping was already becoming politicized during the 1970s with agitation by animal rights groups and anticipation of legislation that would outlaw leg-hold traps or trapping altogether. During this period, the Manitoba Trappers Association responded by promoting research on humane trapping. The focus became the "quick kill" conibear trap that ideally breaks the animal's neck or back when it takes the bait trigger. Cree reactions to conibear traps are predictably diverse; some trappers had already begun experimenting with them long before their promotion. Some persons appreciate the quick kill effect because it is consistent with the religious values discussed above. Some conclude that the conibear is technically more efficient in its own right, preventing animals from escaping, for example. Others prefer the older leg-hold trap because they are "used to it" and it is lighter and less difficult and dangerous to set. Some resistance to the conibear results from its association with animal rights activists, outsiders who know nothing of trapping and clearly care more about animals than trappers' livelihoods. As a result, people remark that the conibear is not necessarily humane: if improperly set or otherwise incorrectly triggered, it may close on the animal's body without killing it. Similarly, the "humane" qualities of the leg-hold trap may be extolled: when set underwater, they drown the animal caught in them, and on land, the animal may be said to "go into shock" when trapped, experiencing little pain. Since many Crees are concerned with animal suffering from pragmatic and moral points of view but resent external interference in their trapping techniques, the humane trapping issue continues to be a controversial one. As one Nelson House Cree stated in the course of a trapper education seminar, "We don't want to make animals suffer. Indian people were taught to respect animals."

Crees say that animals resent restraint in the same way that they resent unnecessary suffering (cf. Nelson 1983:23–24). It is said that white researchers who tagged members of the caribou herd north of Brochet offended the animals in such a way as to "break their hearts." Tagged animals were allegedly found starving and in a state of shock. Whatever the factuality of these stories, they are widely disseminated and believed. Some Rock Crees at Brochet expressed the opinion that the herd no longer comes south into their territory because the animals resented the tagging and the researchers. These remarks echo those of the Crees who objected when Thompson measured a slain caribou (Thompson 1962 [1784–1812]:88). Modes of appropriate human-animal interaction are narrowly circumscribed, restricted to killing, transport, butchering, eating, utilization of skins and bones, and reverent disposal of the residue. Other modes of contact are regarded as inauspicious.

Butchering

I was traveling across McKnight Lake during a cold January day in the company of two young trappers—cousins to each other—and their grandfather. I was in the towed toboggan with the grandfather while the two cousins each drove snowmobiles. An otter raced across the snow in front of us. We stopped, grabbed heavy sticks, and eventually cornered the animal and killed it with several blows to the head. The grandfather watched with keen interest, shouting encouragement and disparaging remarks whenever the otter succeeded in breaking away from our circle. The otter was carried trimphantly back to the toboggan. The grandfather, by now in a position to observe the kill site, angrily ordered us back to cover over the blood from the otter's head wounds which stained the snow. Without saying anything, we went back and kicked up the snow to cover the blood. The prescribed condition for the killing and butchering of animals is *pīkisitōwin*, which means both a sanctified condition of purity and, more prosaically, cleanliness or the absence of dirt. Undisturbed snow is *pīkisiw*, pure, while snow with bloodstains scattered over it is *wīðipisiw*, impure or dirty.

Concern with keeping animals "clean" persists throughout their entry into village or camp and their transformation into food, skins, and other residues. Animals the size of beaver or smaller are placed in bags or boxes to be transported. Today, this is usually done by lashing such containers to a toboggan, which is pulled by a snowmobile or dog team. An animal may be dragged over the snow but not over the exposed ground. The animal should not be left temporarily at the side of a trail and should not brush against the doorway when brought into a dwelling. It is not to be thrown down but gently laid in the area where it will be butchered or stored. All these rules apply also to the meat of large game animals that may be butchered or cut into segments at the kill site. Butchering should take place on a clean surface: cardboard on a floor or table is appropriate indoors, and clean snow or a bed of spruce boughs is used outside. After butchering, the bloody boughs or cardboard should be burned. Dogs, adolescent females, and menstruating women should avoid the butchering site. Meat, hides, bones, and other residue are ideally stored in an elevated position on a shelf or stage, safe from dogs and from women who may accidentally step over them.

Address and Reference

Any discourse that ridicules wild animals' appearance or behavior is said to result in impaired hunting. Considerations of this kind presuppose the ability of the animal's soul to monitor what is said about it. "Just like goddamn RCMP," as one younger trapper phrased it. Such utterances are *pāstāmōwin*, blasphemous or dangerous speech thought to bring misfortune to the speaker. Additionally, reference to large game animals is either avoided or effected with circumlocutions before and after hunting or when the remains are present. Animals just introduced into camp or town should not be spoken of with animal-referring nouns; indeed, they are ideally not spoken of at all. Boasting of one's success is *pāstāmōwin*. The hunter does not announce the kind or number of the animals he has killed, and others, as I quickly learned, should not attempt to elicit this information. Others learn what has been killed by observing as the animals are unpacked and stored or processed. Since the identity and number of animals brought in from the bush are of great interest, the atmosphere surrounding the return is often one of poorly concealed excitement among those at home together with studied casualness on the part of hunters. It was and is still sometimes customary for a man's wife or other relative to travel to the kill site and bring back the carcass on a toboggan, today usually with dog traction or snowmobile. In such circumstances, the hunter brings with him a part of the animal—typically a paw or hoof—and gives this to his wife, verbally identifying the location but not the species killed.

It is the bear on which rules of address and reference focus. Members of the family with whom I was most familiar typically avoided direct reference to all recently slain animals, except hares and fish. The stratification of these deference behaviors suggests that the bear occupies one extreme of a continuum bounded at the other end by the minimally respected hare and fish. One individual, for example, repeatedly joked about hares. On one occasion, he referred to a complex of hare snares we had set as *wāpos-ōtīnaw* 'rabbit village'. On another occasion, when I arrived at the house after a successful visit to my rabbit snares, he announced loudly to his wife, "*Ay īkwa, kī-nipahīw paksa!*" "Well now, he killed Bugs Bunny!" I do not believe he would have made jocular reference to a bear, lynx, caribou, moose, or beaver in the presence of the carcass. The same person made joking reference on another occasion to lynx herds; lynxes do not herd, but the high price of lynx pelts that winter would have made such aggregation desirable. It is not that joking reference to animals never occurs, but I believe that some Crees consider it dangerous when animals have recently been killed or when they are going to be hunted. In this family, these observances applied to both Cree and English animal-referring nouns, suggesting an implicit postulate that the omniscient animals are multilingual.

Circumlocutions replace the noun *maskwa* in contexts where bears are addressed or referred to in such contexts. Of these, I heard: *wākisoy* 'crooked tail', *pimic* 'galloping along' [?], and *wākayōs*, which is said to refer to the shape of the bear's body. Downes (Cockburn 1984:70) noted the circumlocutions "black one" and "old man" in use by Rock

Crees at Pelican Narrows. The kin term *nimosōm* 'my grandfather' is used to address and refer to bears and other spiritually powerful non-humans. The substitute forms are characteristically explained as objectifications of "respect" and suggest an analogy between animal-referring nouns such as *maskwa* and the personal names of humans. Older and/or more "traditional" Crees avoid addressing others of approximately the same age or older by their Cree or English names and also avoid referential use of names in the presence of their owners. For such speakers, personal names are used politely only in reference to absent persons. It is also improper to utter the name of a recently deceased person. Since the souls of animals are talked about as being proximal to their remains, they are effectively present in the speech situation, as well as being "deceased," and the animal and human name avoidances are in these respects parallel. Kin terms like *nimosōm* are freely used in address and reference to humans, but I know of no parallels to the circumlocutions used for bears.

Crees say that it is appropriate to address a bear when it is being hunted in its den in winter. I observed one den hunt in early spring during which the animal was provoked with a long stick to emerge from its den. Prior to rousting the bear, the oldest man present sang for several minutes in Cree and repeated the phrase, "Come out, my grandfather." The bear did not come out, and the men enlarged the cavity with chisels and shovels until the animal could be shot. The men silently smoked cigarettes and blew smoke over the carcass. Typified discourses are more elaborate.

You're supposed to say to him that you don't. . . You don't wake him up for a [without] good reason. But he's your guest, eh? So you tell him he'll be treated good when he comes to stay with people. He's visiting them [after being killed]. So you say that you're going to treat him good. That you don't. . . make him die for nothing. Kind of like you're thanking him.

Downes (Cockburn 1984:70) recorded from the Pelican Narrows Cree Adam Ballentyne an idealized version of how the ritual address was supposed to proceed long ago:

When hunting bears before breakup, when they were in their houses (and this was not often done), it was the custom, before the bear came out, to talk to it, calling him "grandfather" and asking his forgiveness. Then the men would wait and wait until the bear gave his answer, and he would say, if all was done correctly, "It is all right, my children, for I will come back again (into this world as another bear) after I am dead."

Burnt Offerings

The verb *pakitinamowīw* refers to acts of sacrifice or offering; the object or objects offered are *pakitinikīwin*. As in other modes of Cree religious practice, actions focused on animals parallel those oriented to the *pawākan*, deceased ancestors, and other *ahcāk* beings. At meals in the trapline camps and cabins, small amounts of meat and other foods are sometimes burned with tobacco either in the stove or in an outside fire. In most families today, the offerings occur only before meals with some special social or religious significance. These offerings are sometimes said to be intended for the souls of the animals being eaten, although other recipients are readily identified, and it may be that multiple beneficiaries are imagined. In addition to meat and grease, I observed the following commodities being sacrificed: tobacco and cigarettes, the smoke of burning tobacco from pipes and cigarettes, tea, whiskey, colored cloth, a knife, and unopened cans of stew from the Hudson's Bay Company.

You might throw tobacco in the fire to . . . ask for luck. Or you put it in the water to ask for good hunting. If you go along the [Laurie] River, there are steep cliffs up over the water. People when they travel by there, they put tobacco . . . deep into those cracks. You're asking for luck that way. If there's an old man [relative] who had lots of those *pawākanak* . . . if he died, you could ask him . . . you make tea in a pot and spill tea in the fireplace. You ask your relative for a moose.

Offerings are sometimes left at portages or at other sites associated with the beings petitioned. Some Crees associate the practice of sacrifice most strongly with the *manitōhkān*, the wood statue carved to represent the head and sometimes the upper body of a humanoid figure. The *manitōhkān* is usually a representation of the *pawākan*, carved and sometimes clothed and ornamented by the dreamer. Semmens (1884:109) observed in the 1870s on the shore of the Nelson River a group of ornamented *manitōhkān* sculpted from trees cut off three feet above the ground. The four Cree images I observed had been sculpted from three- or four-foot lengths of wood and erected singly near trapline cabins. One image was ornamented with the ubiquitous billed cap of older Cree men, a neck handkerchief, a pipe affixed to the mouth cavity, and (without irony) sunglasses. The area in front of the images was strewn with cigarettes, unopened canned goods, dishes and utensils, and, in one case, a knife.

Waste

The verb *wīsakīhīw* refers to acts of wasting animal meat and other products; it refers also to wasting other kinds of commodities. To avoid waste, the hunter or trapper makes appropriate use of all the conventionally employed parts of the animal. Today, these parts are limited primarily to meats, hides, and pelts, although some persons make skinning tools from bear, moose, and caribou bones. It is not waste to suspend the carcass of a marten in a tree, because martens are not defined as edible. However, it is waste to throw away edible meat or allow a moose hide to go unused by not tanning it. Logistical difficulties sometimes dictate that meat or hides from large mammal kills are wasted, but practice follows the precept rather closely. Large surpluses of meat or fish are preserved with different techniques rather than being allowed to rot before they can be consumed. Opportunities to convert meat and skins into prestige and moral capital by distributing them also motivate foragers to retrieve all that they kill, even if domestic supplies are ample. The paradigm case of waste involves killing animals for sport without retrieving or making any use of the meat or hides. This is an extreme case of what is expressed as *mītawākīw pisiskiwa* 'he plays with an animal/animals'. One of the primary meanings of the *wīhkōhtōwin*, or eat-all feast, is the ceremonial negation of waste in a collective act of complete consumption.

The idea of avoiding waste extends in at least some instances to decisions to limit kills to what is needed by the hunter and his dependents in the short term. For example, one individual refrained from shooting a woodland caribou that he could have dispatched and retrieved with relative ease, explaining that he already had plenty of caribou meat. Trappers may also use the term "waste" to refer to what they define as excessive exploitation of beavers and muskrats, even if the animals are properly utilized.

Mortuary Deposition

The most visible signs of persisting indigenous religion in the Churchill River drainage are animal bones and carcasses that hunters and trappers suspend on trees facing lakes or rivers. The parts most frequently hung up by Crees are moose and caribou antlers; the head skin of the moose; the skulls of any animal, bird, or fish but especially bears, beavers, moose, and caribou; the bills of ducks and geese; the skinned carcasses of otters, martens, fishers, weasels, and foxes; and bundles of bones from beavers, bears, and other large animals that are wrapped in cloth, paper, or birch bark. Bones that have been crushed to make soups and broths are dropped into the water or burned in the stove; deposition in water is an appropriate way to deal with animal bones when time does not permit hanging them up. Bear skulls are sometimes painted with horizontal stripes across the forehead. Bones are sometimes hung not on a living tree but on a pollarded trunk, usually about twelve feet high. The pole is then erected vertically with the bones attached to it. Such a pole is called "*mistikōkān*." One specimen I observed had the bark removed in a three-inch circular band at three points equidistant between bottom and top; the bands were then colored bright red with a magic market.

My initial questions about these hangings were met with reticence, both because many Crees expect ridicule from whites about such practices and because the questions were probably uncomfortably direct. One elderly man, for example, categorically denied any knowledge of such things, although every tree around his cabin was festooned with animal remains. The response of another was polite and masterful evasion.

Q: Why do they put those bones in the tree?
A: The skull of the animal. . . I don't know. Well, I usually hang up a skull whenever I . . . like a bear skull or . . . I don't know for what reason, but for me I just hang it up for nothing, so it . . . stay that way for a long time. I dunno.
Q: Just to get it out of the way, eh?
A: Yeah, just to remind you of when he was . . . you might see a skull someplace and you look at it. "Jesus, I dunno how long it's been there," you know? It's just a reminder, you know? [changes subject]

As far as it goes, this is an informative answer. Some weeks later, the same individual reintroduced the subject.

Yeah, it's the way you put it up after you eat the animals. They tie up the bone and hang them, and they say the animals turn back again after they're gone. They turn back to life and start scattering again. They go back to life.

Rock Crees say that animals, like human beings, possess an *ahcāk*, or soul, which is the seat of identity, perception, and intelligence. In traditional understanding, the souls of human beings travel to a country in the west after the death of the body. The souls of animals, however, are spoken of as renewable: *pimātisiwak kākīhtwām* 'they live over and over'. Crees say that the soul may be reborn in fetal form or that it may mysteriously regenerate a short time after it has been killed as an animal of the same sex, age, and physical characteristics. This latter process of regeneration is spoken of as *akwanaham otoskana* 's/he covers their bones'. Some Crees take interest in this process, especially when they successively kill in the same season what they identify as the "same animal." Others regard it with a casualness and indifference disconcerting to the outsider. I was told on three occasions that an animal just removed from a trap—a lynx and two foxes—was the "same one" that had been killed in the area the same or a preceding winter. Jenness (1935:25) identified the same idea in the religious thought of the Ojibwa-Potawatomi of Parry Island and described two men debating whether bears use the same or different bones in successive reincarnations.

Both reincarnation and regeneration are usually defined as resulting from the decisions of the game ruler being responsible for the species. It is also said that rebirth or regeneration may not occur unless the remains of game animals are treated correctly. Humans thus intervene both negatively and positively in animal life cycles, killing them but also contributing to their regeneration. Crees say that animals eventually become very old and "really die," their souls perhaps traveling to the dead country in the west. The typical explanation of bone disposal practices is that they objectify "respect" and promote good hunting. Putting animal bones in trees or in other elevated places also precludes the danger that women may step over them or dogs may gnaw them. Seemingly, the bones also stood for the family's foraging prowess and industry. Following the introduction of canned goods in the early 1900s, Crees readily identified empty cans with animal bones, hanging them in the same or adjoining trees. Caroline Caribou interpreted this as "conspicuous consumption," a way of representing to others that the inhabitants were successful trappers capable of buying store food.

The association of bones with reproduction and re-creation is evident in a version of the cosmogonic myth (Thompson 1962 [1784–1812]:78) in which the transformer re-creates the different animal species from their bones after the flood. Both animal and human fetuses are sometimes said to be formed from the blood of the mother (flesh and blood) and from the semen of the father (bone). Given these associations, mortuary trees and the *mistikōkān* may possess phallic significance, but there is no evidence that Crees attach such meanings to them. Like bone, animal blood is associated with reproduction, imaginably through analogy to menstrual blood. Blood from a kill or butchering site is covered with moss or snow, and animals are skinned out and butchered on cloth, cardboard, or pine boughs that are later burned without allowing blood to drip on the floor or ground. In the myth of Ayās (Brightman 1989a), blood is given the same ritual treatment as bone. While carrying the hero across a lake, a great serpent is attacked by thunder and blown into fragments. The hero collects the serpent's blood from the ground in a birch-bark vessel and deposits it in a tree. The next day, he discovers a miniature snake swimming in the blood, immerses it in water, and restores its earlier dimensions and identity.

Not only bone disposal but procedures for butchering, cooking, and eating animals are talked about as influencing animal renewal. Among Eastern Crees (Preston 1975:97, cf. Tanner 1979:169), the practice of roasting a whole porcupine is associated with the renewal of the animal and the recovering of its bones. When applied to the first member of a species caught in the fall, the Eastern Cree "cook whole" method appears to suggest that disarticulation interferes with regeneration. The practice of leaving the first carcass inviolate thus seemingly transfers its regenerative influences to its successors, which are subjected to conventional butchering.

The "Medicine Piece"

In the late 1600s, York Factory Cree men selected after their visionary fast a particular part of "each kind of deer," like the tongue or nose, which thereafter became sacred to them (Bacqueville de La Potherie 1931:232). The noun *ouetchitigan* 'the piece reserved' referred to the cut that no one within the household touched except the "owner" and his guests. Kelsey's (1929 [1683–1722]:22) remarks on the same subject say nothing about the appropriation of particular cuts by individual males but suggest that such portions were selected from an existing subset of animal body parts identified as men's food and forbidden to women.

But now no Beast they kill but some part or other is alloted for man's meat wch ye women are not to taste of upon no accot, but more especially at this time [menstruation] than others by reason they think it will be a hindrance to ther [sic] killing anymore Beast nay if a woman should eat any of this mans meat wch is called in their Language crett**tgh cuttawatchetaugun & fall sick in a year or 2 afterwards & dye they will not stick to say it was yt kill'd her for all it was so long ago she eat it.

Of the Crees trading at York Factory and Churchill, Robson (1965 [1752]:51) wrote that each family head possessed a particular part of an animal—the "appropriated part"—that he cooked at feasts and then served to guests, the order of serving reflecting the esteem in which he held the recipients. Women could not be present at these feasts or eat the special portion. Cameron wrote of the Nipigon Cree:

Every Indian has what he calls his "medecine piece" of all the game he kills such as the snout of the moose, the tongue and heart of the deer, the paws of the bear, and so on; this piece is always cooked by itself and no female, young or old, ever dare taste it, if she did, she would either die or turn as black as jet and lose all their nails. They sometimes pay us the great compliment of bringing us such a piece, but they will then inform us of its sacred quality, and tell us not to allow any women to touch it, as they would immediately die. I need not say that I have often seen several women living with the White men eat of those forbidden morsels without the least inconvenience. (Masson 1889–90, 2:262)

These remarks describe three intersecting dietary structures. First, meats were separated into male, female, and perhaps unmarked (male-female) categories. Second, within the first category, meats were sub-categorized by age and other prestige distinctions among men. Finally, within the first category, male family heads dreamed individual meats sacred to them. The foods forbidden to women were precisely those conferring honor when served to men, and it was from among these that the "medicine piece" was selected.

Crees at Granville Lake do not today recognize "ouetchitigan" or Kelsey's "crett**tgh cuttawatchetaugun" as Cree words, but the three classifications persist. Male family heads do not exclusively appropriate particular meats, but both men and women dream meats whose ingestion has religious meaning. The scope of these rules is variable: they may concern an entire species, males or females of a species, or—most typically—particular meats from one of these. Some people dream that they should eat species like mink or marten which are not conventionally defined as edible. In one case, a man conceived of his observance as temporary and observed it only for the duration of the winter trapping season. Crees say that the *pawākan* teaches which foods to select or avoid.

So he [lynx *pawākan*] says to the guy, "You take this . . . you always eat this . . . meat of mine. So that way, you'll always be able to know me." It's like he's saying he can always get in touch with the guy [lynx] that way.

Eating animal flesh effects communion between human and animal *pawākan*, and Crees presumably encountered nothing novel when the ritual of communion was first introduced among them by the Oblates. When one eats in compliance with one's dreams, Crees say that the meat imparts health and that the *pawākan* is pleased and helps the man with further blessings. Synechdochic and substitutive relationships exist between the species of the *pawākan* (if it is an animal) and individual specimens of the same species. If a man's *pawākan* is a lynx, he achieves communion with it and exchanges with it by eating the prescribed parts of any lynx. Some food dreams concern meats from species other than that with which the *pawākan* is identified. One man suggested a sacrificial interpretation not inconsistent with the ideology of communion. "Every time you eat that meat, it's going to the guy you dream of. He can take it." Of comparable significance are meats that people conclude they should *not* eat as a result of dream directives. Such proscriptions were in one context associated with "bad dreams": "Oh yeah. Even my brother-in-law here, he doesn't eat a she-beaver. Me, I eat anything. I never have a bad dream about anything like that."

Some Crees thus dream their own diets but do so within existing parameters fixed by age and gender. I was often told—and also frequently observed—that people no longer "pay attention" to these rules, but they persist today in some households. As in the past, classes of meat and other animal foods are divided into male, female, and unmarked categories, although not everyone agrees on the constituencies of these. Within the male series, different meats are said to be appropriate for elders, adults, younger unmarried men, and boys. Female foods are not, to my knowledge, similarly subcategorized. Hosts can express the esteem or disesteem in which they hold a particular guest both by what they serve them and by the order of serving. In some households, older men are served before younger and adult men as a group before women and preadolescents, sometimes at successive seatings.

Male and Female Meats

As noted, the particular meats that connote honor in their apportionment to men are precisely the foods women are forbidden to eat. These rules apply with particular emphasis to bears. Men and women agreed that women should not eat the head, heart, front legs, and front paws of the bear; one woman added also the intestines and deposits of fat around the heart. Additionally, the heads, hearts, and front legs of moose, caribou, and beavers, heads of large northern pike and sturgeon, moose nose, porcupine testicles, and possibly caribou tongues are male foods. Seemingly, the posterior part of the animal is women's food, and the anterior part is men's food. Men eat the heads and front legs of major species and the front legs of the bear. The rear legs and rump of the bear are eaten by women. When beavers are eaten, meat from the front half of the animal is often served to men while women eat from the posterior. With the exceptions noted above, all parts of rabbits, porcupine, and fish are eaten interchangeably by both sexes. Menstruating and pregnant women should ideally abstain from all bear meat. Rules applying to postmenopausal women require additional inquiry.

The earlier documentary references suggest great stability in these dietary rules over time. According to Graham (1969 [1767–1791]: 188), writing of York Factory in the 1700s,

there are several things the women never meddle with, custom or superstition having appropriated them to the men, as the head of a porcupine, the hearts of most animals, and many other parts. The tongue of the deer, buffalo etc. is a god-bit with the great warrior, hunter, doctor, and conjuror.

The entire head of the moose was proscribed at Cumberland House in the 1800s, according to Richardson (Franklin 1823:111). Ethnographic sources from the present century are similar in content. The Attawapiskat Swampy Cree proscribed the heads and hearts of bears, caribou, moose, beavers, martens, and otters as well as caribou tongues and fetal caribou and rabbit (Honigmann 1956:69). According to Downes (1943:70), Cree women at Pelican Narrows did not eat the head, paws, and heart of bears.

Concepts of sacredness intersect with sexual and other politics in distinctions between male and female meats and differentially prestigious male portions. The heads, hearts, and forelegs of animals are honored portions inappropriate for women. Posterior and anterior portions imaginably connote lesser and greater modes of prestige, as the serving rules for men indicate, and it is surely no accident that such valued delicacies as tongues and moose nose are appropriated by men. Cameron's remarks, cited above, show that Indian women married to white fur traders possessed no ideological commitment to the scheme, since they readily ate the forbidden portions.

Animals and Women

Women's dietary rules are part of a larger series of practices proscribing certain contacts between women and slain animals. Violation of these rules is a paradigm case of *pāstāhōwin* or misfortune evoked by offending the *ahcāk* beings. The dietary rules are indexes of male power but are also continuous with others from which men derive no material advantage (from a non-Indian perspective) and which express religious postulates pertaining to meat, eating, hunting, and human reproduction. It is primarily men who forage for large animals and thus incur the greatest benefit from the communion-sacrifice effected by eating special meats in which the powers of animals are most concentrated. But the separation of women and animals that the dietary rules effect is also consistent with a more pervasive antagonism between animals and female fertility. These can be stated as a set of propositions representing a consensus about what Crees say they believe or used to believe. Many persons represent these rules as vanished or obsolescent superstition; others continue to observe them.

1. Animals resent physical contact between certain of their remains and women, especially adolescent, menstruating, or pregnant women. The interdicted modes of contact are physical contiguity, especially with the vagina, and ingestion. Butchering and cooking meat and preparing hides and furs are conventional female occupations that must be shifted to other women during menstruation and pregnancy or to men.

2. Such contact results in "a hindrance to ther [sic] killing anymore Beast," as Kelsey phrased it in the 1690s. In 1977, I watched a man skin out an otter on a piece of canvas in front of his house. His adolescent granddaughter came running up to him with several friends, eager to

see what was going on. Visibly disturbed, he ordered the girls away, berating them for not knowing better than to approach.

And like a young woman. That's one of the dirtiest things you can do . . . dirtiest thing that happens is a woman stepping over your furs [grimaces with distaste]. Or over bones or meat. That's bad luck for the hunter. Hunter have . . . no luck if they do that.

The rule that meat and furs should not be left on the ground or floor is often expressed as a strategy to prevent accidents in which women might step over them. The disposition of animal remains is such as to avoid even their momentary positioning immediately below the female genital area. The gender of the slain animal is irrelevant.

Oh yeah, like young girl. Never throw a beaver or any kind of animal on the roadside. Like hitting the door side [doorway]. Never throw nothing [on the floor]. Especially if there's a young woman inside. If she steps on your fur, you're kaput! You can't kill nothing. Bad luck. It brings you bad luck.

Similar rules pertain to male clothing, guns, traps, fishnets, ice chisels, and, in one case, snowmobile parts. Women should avoid walking across the trail of an animal since this would prevent hunters from capturing it. Men who are shooting beavers at night avoid looking at the moon because this also will give them bad luck.

3. Women are themselves vulnerable to contact with animal remains. Crees told the traders that women who ate the portions reserved for male family heads would die, turn black, and lose their nails. Crees today say that women might become ill or have difficulties conceiving. These afflictions suggest acceleration through the life cycle and infertility, rather as though women's reproductive capacities are endangered by contact with powerful meats. Since it is known that many (or most?) Cree women violate these rules with seeming impunity, the negative consequences are sometimes phrased very vaguely.

4. Pubescent women can endanger the health of males, especially adolescent boys. They may do this by looking at them, addressing them, and touching their food. These hazards are the typical explanation given for the initial menstrual seclusion and menstrual observances thereafter. Attention to these practices is exceptionally variable between households. One adolescent girl casually disposed of used tampons in the family slop bucket with no one exhibiting any concern, whereas, across the bay, her counterpart underwent a four-day isolation. In mid-

April, the girl moved to a small cabin several yards from the house. A barrel stove was rigged up to heat the shack, and other amenities such as a Coleman lantern and a cassette player were provided. She slept in the shack for five nights, receiving visits from her mother during the day and from girlfriends both day and night. Her mother brought cooked food out to the shack; she was given fish, eggs, corned beef hash, tea, and bannocks. She used the same dishes, cups, and utensils each day and continued with these after moving back into the cabin, where she shared a room with her siblings as before. Today, as in the past, the seclusion is not repeated thereafter every month, but some women cook and eat separately, use separate utensils, and sleep apart from others on a different mattress or floor space. The practices show that women are most dangerous to others at and immediately following menarche and thereafter, to a much diminished degree, whenever they menstruate. In some houses where I stayed, people were concerned with isolating the food and utensils used by menstruating women, measures preventing the penetration of menstrual blood or its influences into others' bodies via involuntary ingestion. The traders' accounts differ with respect to periodic seclusion after menarche but are otherwise consistent in suggesting the volatility of pubescent girls.[1]

5. Sexual encounters interfere with adolescent males' quest for the *pawākan*, which may or may not be an animal. Crees intimate that compliance with such celibacy was not always taken seriously.

6. Sexual encounters do not, however, interfere with a man's foraging prospects, unless his partner is menstruating. Crees denied that men abstained from sex before or during foraging trips. Eastern Crees told Speck (1935a) that it was auspicious for wives to accompany husbands on hunting trips.

7. Although women must avoid contact with certain animal *remains*, especially when menstruating or pregnant, no rules forbid them from killing animals. Women routinely snare small game, trap furbearers, and assist in fishing. Some women hunt moose, caribou, and even the maximally respected bear in partnership with their husbands or alone. A man who would be outraged if his wife stepped over a beaver pelt will boast to other men of her accomplishments in trapping the same animal. Women also serve as the transporters of animals from the bush into camp, as butchers, and as cooks. Crees of both sexes say that women are especially lucky as trappers of martens. Thompson (1962 [1784–1812]:76) recalled with nostalgic pleasure among the Rock

Crees' eighteenth-century ancestors a religious dance by women—instigated by their husbands—to the "Manitoo of the martens" for successful trapping. Whether women hunt when menstruating is not known.

Cree practices, in summary, express a primordial antagonism between female fertility and animals and between female sexuality and the male-*pawākan* relationship but not between sexuality and hunting. Neither are Cree women ineligible for hunting big game. Most Crees cannot or do not explain these avoidances beyond saying that bad luck follows their violation, and it is possible that the logic of the scheme is not available to conscious reflection.

These facts suggest that it is specifically female fertility that is incompatible with animals and men's access to them. Although some dietary rules were theoretically observed by women at all times, they applied with particular force, perhaps with augmentation, during menstruation. Concern with women stepping over animal remains exists at all times. It is as if the vagina is a conduit from which female essences emanate and through which external animal essences can enter women's bodies. Adolescent girls and women presently menstruating are those who are the most threatening to the success of male hunters if they touch animal remains or hunting equipment. Women in their aspects as sexual partners or foragers do not pose such hazards. Cree metaphors represent human male-female relationships as homologous with hunter-prey relationships and with sexual contact between animals, an insight first established by Preston (1975) and Tanner (1979) in work with the Eastern Crees. From the point of view of male hunters, sex is a metaphor for hunting, and women are metaphors for animals. Similar tropes figuring male-animal resemblances probably exist in women's discourse. When I was working out a translation of a text, my young male interpreter provided the translation "let's go chase girls" for the verb *nāciskwītan*, a bewildering gloss in the narrative context. I later learned that *nāciskw-* is 'hunt bears'; the transferred meaning had become conventional among younger nonforagers. Likewise, compare Ahenakew's Plains Cree forms *noo'chechikao* 'he works at fur hunting'; *noocheneki'kwao* 'he hunts otters'; *noo'chehao* 'he hunts him' or 'he follows her' (as a dog follows the female); *noochehi'toowuk* 'they are mating' (as animals); *noochehi'toowin* 'courting, mating, cohabitation'; *noochena'pawao* 'she is fond of men'; among others (Faries 1938:367). The interchangeability of human women with game animals is objectified in Cree dream experiences. In dream events, animals elect to interact with men in the form of human women, and sexual or other encounters with these "women" predestine events of successful foraging. The techniques and ideology of hunting and love magic also exhibit close parallels.

Given these correspondences, it is to be expected that bestiality might possess ritual significance. The Crees of Lac la Ronge in the 1820s ascribed such practices to the Athapaskan-speaking Beavers:

There is a tribe of Athabaska that go by the name of Beaver Indians. From the tenets of their religion I am told that when they are laying under any malediction, bewitchisms, &c., or conceive themselves so; they make a vow that the first animal they shall kill, they will do *so* [bestiality]—they do not fail but immediately proceed in quest of another which by this diabolical action they think they will soon find and kill. They do not touch the animal afterwards as those beasts among the Cree and Sauteux do, but leave it lay as a sacrifice: they consider it a duty imposed upon them, but the others do it from mere bestiality. "Such a one did so, brot home part of the meat, and we all of us eat it—Oh! the dog!" said an Indian not long ago to me. (Brown and Brightman 1988:99)

Here, sexual relations *with* animals are represented as hunting ritual. As an account by Crees of the practices of former enemies, the report has limited ethnographic credibility, but it exemplifies further associations of sex with hunting in Cree thought. Nelson's Cree informant ascribed a secular penchant for bestiality to some in his own band, but the passage is explicit about how the practices—if they occurred—and the polluted meat were regarded.

All these observances suggest that the two metonymic series— killing-hunting-eating and menstruation-sex-conception-birth—are the constituents of a fundamental metaphor likening the provisioning of society to its reproduction. The explicit sex [women] and hunting [animals] likenesses in dreams and verbal polysemy are the patent expressions of this metaphor. Menstrual blood possesses multiple values in this scheme. A symbol of female fertility because coextensive with it in the life cycle, menstrual blood is simultaneously the material cause of fertility as the substance out of which fetal flesh is formed. Some Cree men say that menstruating women are especially likely to conceive. Women biologically reproduce the human community, their ability to do so evidenced by the flow of blood that, however, in the event of conception, they begin to retain within their bodies. Human life is also visibly reproduced by killing and eating animals. Hunting and trapping are paradigmatically male occupations through which men enact a reproductive role complementing that of women. The animal blood spilled at kill sites and trap sets corresponds to menstrual blood, which is the precondition of female fertility. These series subsume the opposition between male life-taking (in war and hunting) and female life-giving (cf. Rosaldo and Atkinson 1975), because hunting and female fertility both create life. There may also exist analogies between the fixed periodicity of human reproduction and the irregular but cyclical rhythms of foraging: search, pursuit, capture, retrieval, preparation, and ingestion. In both conception and hunting, human life is reproduced through the flow of blood, but in the second case, the reproducers are male, and the flow simultaneously entails the death of animals. This metaphor explains the seeming paradox that women in their reproductive aspect are verbally likened to the animals with whose remains their contact is interdicted. *Maskwōwiwak* 'they are bears' predicates metaphorically of girls at menarche and during menstruation. I obtained no Cree narrative explaining the origin of menstruation, but the Menominees, Algonquians of Wisconsin, derive it from a clot of blood thrown at the transformer's grandmother by a bear. Bears are the most spiritually empowered of animals, the marked case of the whole class of creatures with which the menstrual condition is antagonistic, and the species on which menstrual avoidances are most elaborately focused.

Menstruation is conceived as antagonistic to other beings and processes associated with the shedding of blood. Contact with menstruating women threatens male health, which may be equivalent to the proposition that female fertility ruins hunting not only by angering the acquiescent prey but by enfeebling the predator. Crees do not retain knowledge of earlier practices associated with war, but it is probable that menstrual blood was thought to threaten the success of raids against Eskimoan and Athapaskan enemies. Finally, it is significant that menstrual blood is thought to drive away the witiko, the anthropophagous monster that hunts and eats human beings. Crees conceptualize power relationships in terms of food chains, and the witiko is said to be very strong because it can overcome human prey. In the course of listening to witiko stories in a trapline cabin one evening, someone half-jokingly suggested that it would be best to stop talking about the creature to forestall a visitation. A teenage girl confidently remarked that the witiko would be frightened to approach the cabin because there were several "young (i.e., recently pubescent) girls" including herself staying there. The inference is that such girls and the reproductive principle in their menstrual blood are exceptionally powerful if they are capable of impeding such formidable adversaries (cf. Fogelson 1980). Like the witiko, game animals may be imagined as fearing menstrual blood, although the conventional idiom has it that they are offended. The parallel with conventional hunting is also clear: menstrual blood forestalls in advance the shedding of human blood by the witiko just as it forestalls the shedding of animal blood by humans.

While the menstruation-sex-conception-birth and hunting-killing-eating series are clearly the two constituents of a metaphor, the question remains why each series exerts deleterious rather than positive influences over the other. One can readily imagine alternate practices in which the life-giving influences of women are transferred to the life-giving project of hunting. In some foraging societies, the female-fertility/male-hunting metaphor is the basis of beliefs that women can exert a beneficial effect on hunting by taking novel roles in ritual or the foraging process. In North America, the most famous example is the consecration of Mandan eagle traps by menstruating women (Lévi-Strauss 1966a:52). Comparable practices are absent on the Churchill River: in Cree thought, fertility is always antagonistic to hunting. Women, of course, may themselves trap and hunt, but there is no evidence that their fertility is thought to exert positive influences. Crees entertain the possibility that female fertility may transfer life-giving effects to the labor process, but it does so to the detriment of human interests. In virtually the only exegesis on women's avoidances I obtained, a Cree stated that pregnant women should not eat animal hearts because animals of the species eaten would thereafter become impossible to kill. The life-giving principle seemingly is transferred to the animals, allowing them to escape death at the hands of hunters.

The exposition thus far has considered menstrual blood as a metonym of female fertility and has examined its incompatibility with hunting exclusively in these terms. The blood may concurrently embody in Cree thought meanings and influences antithetical both to fertility and successful hunting. As "wasted" or putrified material expelled from the womb rather than material effecting an event of conception there, the blood may symbolize infertility and death, imparting inauspicious influences on hunting, war, and other processes metaphorically likened to successful reproduction. Cree practices patently suggest that menstrual blood when "diverted" in this way from its generative function remains powerful but becomes exceptionally volatile. Inside the body, it is the material source of human life; outside, it is a poison, threatening illness and starvation. Parallels between avoidances practiced by pregnant and menstruating women suggest, however, that menstrual rules concern fertility more fundamentally than putrifaction.

In Mandan eagle trapping, the birds' blood must not be spilled, and it is only in this bloodless hunt that menstruating women are auspicious. When applied to Cree practices, this alternation suggests that the two kinds of blood epitomize the two constituent series of the hunting-fertility metaphor and that these are so irreducibly antagonistic that they cannot be reconciled or exist within the same spatial and temporal coordinates: each drives away the other. Menstrual avoidances thus appear as human responses to an axiological antipathy: if society is to produce and reproduce successfully, women must avoid contact with certain meats, other animal remains, and taking devices. The reciprocally polluting contiguity causes women to become infertile and, in the extreme antithesis to reproduction, to die, while simultaneously preventing future events of hunting in which animal blood will be spilled. Parallel antagonisms characterize the effects of female fertility on human-witiko relations and perhaps formerly on relations with human enemies in war. In these cases, female fertility is incompatible with three other spheres of human experience that Cree thought identifies as similar to it. It is not known whether hunting and warfare were similarly opposed to each other and separated by avoidance practices. If this were so, one could characterize the Cree concept of "*wiðipisiwin*," dirt or pollution, in one of its aspects as a condition produced by contiguity between distinct processes whose fundamental similitude results in reciprocal negative influences and thus requires their physical and temporal separation.

The antagonism between fertility and animal regeneration exemplifies further this incompatibility of the similar. The regeneration of animal souls is the terminal stage of the hunting-killing-eating series. As noted earlier, the treatment of animal remains is held to influence this cycling, positively or negatively. Although Crees talk about menstrual avoidances as influencing decisions by animals to allow their own capture, the practices suggest also that the interdicted contact interrupts the cyclical regeneration of animal souls in fetal or mature forms. Women's avoidances focus above all not on *living* animals but on the physical remains within which the animals' potential for rebirth is concentrated. It is not polluting for female hunters and trappers to transform a live animal into a dead one, but the reverse transformation is vulnerable to female fertility.

Hunting parallels female fertility as a mode of life-giving enacted by males. Crees talk about successful events of hunting as resulting from decisions by animals to allow themselves to be captured. From this perspective, it is ultimately animals themselves who enact a female role and reproduce human life by voluntarily shedding their own blood. As noted earlier, animals are said to resent the scattering of their blood at kill and butchering sites, and this is one meaning of the practice of covering bloodstains and burning boughs or other butchering surfaces. Crees also talk about the human-animal relationship as adversarial, in which case, the blood they shed is not a voluntary gift but a sign of exploitation. The Rock Crees' ancestors in the 1700s associated human blood on the ground with violent conflict, saying that the superior being Kicimanitōw disapproved of it and sent rain to wash it away (Thompson 1962 [1784–1812]:75). Imaginably, blood at kill sites has similar significance. Animals resent the blood as a mnemonic of the violence done to them, suggesting that covering it has meanings of concealment as well as pacification. Perhaps the women-animal avoidances express the fundamental paradox that the reproduction of human life through hunting is only effected through the destruction of animal life. Spilled animal blood, like menstrual blood, concurrently indexes both life and death. There exists, perhaps, a moral appropriateness to the separation of the blood that reproduces the lives of human predators from the animals whose blood the predators spill. This at least is consistent with the threats of sterility and death that follow from violations of the dietary rules. The antagonism between women and animals resonates with the more primordial hostility between human hunters and animal victims.

Dogs

The possibility that dogs will gnaw or eat animal bones and certain meats provokes anxiety similar to that associated with menstrual contact, and the practice of hanging up bones is a strategy for preventing this sacrilege. Certain meats should not be fed to dogs. This applies most explicitly to bear, moose, and caribou meat. Some trappers will give their dogs the carcasses of martens, weasels, otters, and other furbearers classified as inedible by humans; others say that this insults those animals. Fish are the most appropriate dog food, and hare may also be used. Beaver meat is sometimes given to dogs. When this is done, men will sometimes feed each tied dog separately so that they don't "scatter" the meat around. Others say that it is all right to feed beaver meat to dogs in the bush but not "in town" at Granville or Pukatawagan. The residues of any food eaten at an eat-all feast must be kept from dogs, and they are excluded from the cabins or tents where it is enacted. When I asked what would happen if a dog did get at the food eaten in such feasts, I was told that the animal might be killed and burned. The Montagnais described by McKenzie used a different procedure when a dog invaded a bear feast.

Should a dog, amidst all this religious mummery, be sacrilegious enough to pass any of the fat or flesh between his unhallowed jaws, in order to appease the wrath of the angry deity, the vile animal is instantly slaughtered, the flesh is devoured and each guest must eat a teaspoonful of his excrements, and then the bones are hung to a tree. (Masson 1889–90, 2:416)

In the early 1800s at Cumberland House, Richardson (Franklin 1823:111) reported that the Crees avoided giving moose heads to the white traders because they feared they would give the bones to dogs.

Dogs occupy a multiply ambiguous position in the Cree social universe, possessing neither the sanctity of the wild animal nor the privileges of the house pet. Although some families make pets of dogs and keep them inside their houses, they are regarded as eccentric and may be disparaged as *atimiðiniwak* 'dog people'. As servants in hunting and transportation, dogs, especially talented dogs, are owed and receive a measure of respect. At the same time, dogs are regarded as "dirty," the habit of eating excrement being their most salient attribute. Dogs are today axiomatically inedible. In relating to me a story about a man who ate his dogs during a starvation crisis, Johnny Bighetty reiterated several times that the story was true, seemingly convinced that I would be unlikely to believe such extremities. The antagonism between dogs and animals is rationalized by statements that dogs are dirty and that it would insult animals to be eaten by dirty creatures. At the same time, there are connotations of conflict based on the idea that dogs help human hunters and trappers kill animals. Fish are said to be appropriate dog food precisely because dogs play no part in killing them. The same may be true of beavers and the smaller furbearers, although Crees at one time used beaver trapping strategies that employed dogs. The pollution concept is developed most strongly with respect to caribou, moose, and bears, all of which may be hunted with dogs.

The incorporation of the dog into human society was symbolized linguistically in the *kosāpahcikan*, or shaking tent ceremonies, of the 1820s at Lac la Ronge. In the performance, the voices of spirit beings can be heard emanating from a barrel-shaped tent into which they have been summoned. According to Nelson, "The Dog entered and spoke perfectly plain and distinct, and with a more elegant and harmonious voice than I ever heard in my life" (Brown and Brightman 1988:104). The Rock Cree myth explaining the incorporation of dogs into human society emphasizes the conflict that results between Dog and the animal it most resembles, Wolf. Here, the condition of domesticated animal is represented somewhat idealistically as one to which Wolf jealously aspires.

There was just wolves and the dog was . . .
Oh, he was bigger than the wolf.
But they used to call him . . .
They didn't call him a dog like *atim* ['dog'] in them days.
They used to call him
Narrowtail.
That was his name because his tail was narrow.
Not bushy tail like a wolf.
Cīcīkwāðōs, that was his name.
At that time, he was bigger than a wolf.
His name was *Cīcīkwāðōs* then.
So they had a race.
The winner
is going to be the one to go stay with the people.

Well, of course, the dog win the race because he was a lot bigger, slimmer.
After the race
the wolf got mad.
He was left behind.
Said, "You're too big to stay with the people.
You're gonna eat twice
as much as me."
"Oh," he [Dog] said, "I wouldn't be this size.
I'll be way smaller than your size.
So this way I won't eat that much."
So he [Wolf] says, "Good!
But remember," Wolf said,
"Every time I see you I'm going to kill you.
Cause you beat me in the race."
That's why you hear . . .
If you're camping and there's wolves close by they'll holler
as if they're crying.
They're crying because a dog is there and not working for himself,
not hunting.

He's just fed without
worrying when he's going to eat next.
Indians . . . trappers, they look after their dogs so . . .
That's why
a wolf, every time he get a chance to get ahold of a dog he kill it right away.
That's his punishment.
And you hear
wolves howling, they're crying because they got to hunt for their feed.

5

"And Some Guys Dream Bad Things"

Introduction

Crees conceive themselves simultaneously as hunters of animals and as the prey of monsters who are the hunters of humans. For Rock Crees and other boreal forest Algonquians, the noun *wīhtikōw* and its cognates refer either to an anthropophagous monster or to a human individual exhibiting symptoms of transformation into such a monster. Rock Crees say that all witikos were formerly human beings, although a subclass without human origins is recognized by the Ojibwas and Swampy Crees. Humans are said to have become witikos through dream predestination, possession, freezing, and commission of famine cannibalism. Crees say that an event of such cannibalism sometimes transformed its practitioner into a witiko who thereafter ate humans gratuitously; they also say that others became witikos through dreaming or possession without the prior occurrence of cannibalism. Witiko dispositions sometimes manifested themselves during times of famine, but Crees also say that incipient witikos sought human flesh even when acceptable food was abundant. The noun also refers metaphorically to historically known famine cannibals and also to gluttons and insane or violent individuals without ascribed cannibal impulses. In the remote age of the *ācaðōhkīwin*, the early humans were stalked by two "races" of witiko-like beings, the *wīhcikōsisak*, small witikos, and the *mīmīðītīhisiwak*, hairy heart beings. These races are not ancestral or otherwise etiologically related to the witikos said to exist in the present but share many of their characteristics.

For some Crees, the witiko continues to constitute a thing of this world whose presence may condition decisions about bush-related activities and whose appearance in dreams prompts recourse to Indian medicine. For white academics, the witiko or "windigo" (from Ojibwa *wīndigō*) has been of perennial interest, the subject of an expanding anthropological literature including descriptive, folkloristic, historical, ecological, psychoanalytic, and structural readings (cf. Marano 1982). The symbolism of witiko has figured in many of these studies, but the most engrossing facet of the topic has been the so-called windigo psychosis of preceding centuries whose Algonquian sufferers exhibited symptoms of anxiety and depression and expressed the desire to eat human flesh. In at least one documented instance, and in many others if the Indian testimony is accepted, the nominal "psychotic" gratified these desires, killing and eating human beings rather than seeking conventional food (Brightman 1988). The windigo psychosis has been anthropologically rendered as a culture-specific psychiatric syndrome unique to Great Lakes and boreal forest Algonquians. Persons suffering from it are understood to have subjectively experienced the symptoms of their disorder as signs of incipient witiko transformation. Such persons were, in turn, defined by their relatives and friends as witikos; variously, they have been ostracized, cured, or executed by their relatives or Euro-Canadian authorities.

In discussing the relationship of the Algonquian windigo figure to the Iroquoian "Stonecoat" and related beings, Fogelson (1980:147–148) remarked on the cross-cultural generality of oppositive relations between monstrous and human categories.

On a more general level, it should be pointed out that monsters cannot exist except in classificatory relation to others. Thus a universal function of monsters is to define what is human through contrast and opposition.

From this point of view, humanity monstrously distorted throws into relief the defining characteristics of the human condition. Following the lines of interpretation outlined here, it may be expected that a comparative ethnoteratology would disclose considerable variation, each society distorting its distinctive conception of the human. Witiko traits comprise a systematic oppositional inversion of traits Crees understand as constitutive of the human state, or, more specifically, of the state of *nīhiðawīwin* 'Cree-ness'. It is as if the image of the witiko has been constructed on the basis of successively more inclusive reflections on defining human attributes.

The Domestication of the Hairy Hearts

A narrative told by Mrs. Selazie Linklater of Pukatawa-gan provides a suitable point of departure as it formulates and reiterates the contrasts between human and witiko conditions in a particularly direct fashion. The story describes the conflict of a human family with two Hairy Hearts, myth-age counterparts of the witiko. As will be seen, these differ from contemporary images of witiko in certain respects, being capable of speech and sociality.

Once then and very long ago this happened. There were then in this country Hairy Hearts. They say of these that they are without hearts or goodness. Then at this time there are two of these Hairy Hearts: a male and his son. They travel between the camps of the people, and they kill and eat the people. At one camp there is an old man, a "dreamer" himself, who has spiritual power. He can know before it happens that those Hairy Hearts are coming to his camp. He tells this to the others, his relatives and the people who stay with him. Really, very quickly then they break their camp and travel to a place there where the old man intends to hide. They have with them a moose hide. They use this hide by filling it with grass, and then just there they hang it on wooden poles. It looks like a living moose. Then I suppose just there they dig a hole under the snow. Over the hole they position this "moose." The head of the moose faces north from there. "Truly they will not look for us here," that old man says. "Those ones who are coming are not interested in moose. Only people they intend to eat." A long time they will stay in that hole so that the Hairy Hearts will not find them.

This Hairy Heart old man owns a staff. Straight up and down he aligns this staff, placing one end in the snow so it stands upright. Then, when he sings, this staff is able to incline toward that place where people are hiding. He sings to his staff, this Hairy Heart. But the human old man, he who hides in the snow, exerts his power. Then really that staff inclines in the opposite direction. For a long time they hunt the human beings, those Hairy Hearts, and the old man [Hairy Heart] always uses his staff. Always that old man in the snow uses his power to overcome them. Finally, then, those Hairy Hearts leave that place there and travel to another lake. When they are gone, those [human] people come out of their dwelling in the snow. They intend to warn the other people around that lake that these Hairy Hearts are going around.

Those Hairy Hearts are truly almost starved to death now. "Near us there are people in a camp," that Hairy Heart old man says to his son. "Go and hunt for us. Bring from that camp two children. Run rawhide cordage through them so I can roast them." Then he catches them, two children who are playing outside of that camp. Those two children scream with fear. He brings them to the old man. Then really that old man roasts those two boys. The people at that camp hear those children screaming. Really, they are frightened. Then they break their camp and move from there, towards where the others stay at the lake.

That old man warns the people that they should stay together in a large camp. "We should not be in small groups," he says to them. They all travel together to a bay just there. Just there they will be able to see what might come towards them from across the lake. That old man is able to know that the Hairy Hearts will again hunt them, that the Hairy Hearts will transform into trees. In this way, they will stalk them [the people], those Hairy Hearts. He [old man] says to the children, "Always watch the ice on the lake. Maybe soon you will see something coming towards us from there. You will see trees. They will be closer to us each time you see them. When you see them, those trees, say loudly, 'Trees are on the ice!'"

Soon those children see trees on the ice. Each time that they look, they are a little closer to the camp. Those children are very frightened. Very close to the camp those trees approached. And then: "Trees on the ice!" they say. Just then, right there those Hairy Hearts stopped.

That old [human] man does not act frightened. He tells those Hairy Hearts to come inside the lodge. Inside the lodge, they are eating beaver meat. And then really when they come into the lodge, they become human beings. They lose all their powers and the ice in their bodies melts. And then they eat beaver meat with the others. Really, those Hairy Hearts would be frightened of fires and heat because it melts the ice in their bodies and they lose their strength.

They stay there then with the people in that camp. They always eat animal meat like the others. That old man and his son both marry women in that group of families just there. In the winter, the young man goes out hunting with his brothers-in-law. He brings back to the camp every kind of meat. But he stays a long time outside the lodge; seldom does he go in and stay by the fire. Really, he is still wicked, that young man. By staying out in the cold, he is getting stronger. Again there begins to be ice in his body. He stays out in the bush because he doesn't want to be warm.

It becomes spring there. Still that young man goes hunting with his brothers-in-law. Then really: "When I hunt with your younger brothers, they resemble animals to me," that young man says to his wife. In the morning, he will go out hunting again with his brothers-in-law. They are preparing, outside the lodge. Then she hides the snowshoes of her brother, that woman. He comes inside the lodge to look for them. "There is something wrong again with my husband," she tells her brother. "Be careful when you hunt with him. Watch out for the welfare of our younger sibling."

They leave and go to hunt animals. That Hairy Heart young man doesn't walk with his brothers-in-law. He follows behind them, looking at their snow-shoe tracks. He sees their snowshow trail as the trail of a moose. He walks ahead of them through the bush. Then just there, he jumps out and grabs him. Then just there, the other one [older brother] chops off his head.

At the camp, those two old men are sitting in the lodge. Immediately, that old Hairy Heart knows it, that his son has been killed. He says to all of them there: "You killed my son. Now, if you don't kill me I will destroy all of you." They take sticks and try to kill that old man. He is too powerful for them, always he overcomes them. One woman stabs him in his arm with a sharp roasting stick. There is bone marrow on the stick, and he eats his own marrow. "How does it taste to you?" that woman says to him. "It is fat, good-tasting marrow," he says. Then right there, he seizes her with his other arm and kills her. Now the others are frightened that they cannot prevail over him. They run from the lodge. Just then those two men return to the camp. They enter the lodge and see that old Hairy Heart sitting by the fire. With their clubs, they strike him until he is dead. Those men are able to kill him only because he is near the fire. [Cree]

There are a great many specific attributes ascribed both to developed witiko beings and to incipient ones. The discussion below groups these characteristics into four dimensions defined by the themes of cannibalism, acultural practices, power, and frozenness.

Anthropophagy

"'Truly they will not look for us here,' that old man says. 'Those ones who are coming are not interested in moose.'" The most salient trait of the windigo is clearly anthropophagy, which contrasts with human zoophagy. The term "cannibalism" is imprecise, since Crees emphasize that the witiko, although formerly human, no longer is so. The very fact of eating or desiring to eat human flesh results in the loss of human identity, paradoxically resulting in a diet that is thereafter not technically cannibalistic. Crees say that practitioners of famine cannibalism in the past became witikos and sometimes represent the condition as the automatic consequence of such cannibalism: "From the moment he began to eat human flesh, he was a true Wetigo" (Merasty 1974:1). Similarly, the Plains Cree, Waypast, told Ahenakew that "the person kills and soon he (or she) is eating. He has passed from being a human being to beastliness" (Preston 1978:62).

In a passage of the Hairy Heart myth that listeners find especially gruesome, the older cannibal sucks his own marrow from a stick and avows that it pleases him. This propensity for autocannibalism is generalized in the conventional image of developed witikos who eat the flesh from their fingers, hands, and lips, leaving their teeth and gums exposed in a terrifying grimace (see also Vandersteene 1969:53, Merasty 1974:3). In addition to eating themselves, witiko beings are thought to prey on each other.

Witikos are imagined as existing in a state of chronic ravenousness, evocative of the famine tragedies said to induce the condition. One man said that persons who greedily ate acceptable food in great quantities were thought likely to be incipient witikos. In the absence of human victims, or as a supplement, developed witikos eat other objectionable foods. In a tale recounting the adventures of a solitary family on the tundra, the victims barricade themselves in their cabin while the sensed but unseen witiko hovers outside; periodically, there are squeals as the monster eats the sled dogs staked out around the camp (Brightman 1989a:169–170). In another tale, a female witiko enters a small bush settlement, seats itself in the center of the cabins, and announces that it intends to eat all the resident dogs before beginning on the people (ibid.:173). The idea of eating dogs disgusts contemporary Rock Crees, although dogs were an esteemed food among some Cree populations in the nineteenth century (Harmon 1905 [1821]:281, 325). In another Rock Cree narrative, a witiko is encountered while roasting a worn-out rawhide mitt over a fire; at this point, the narrator, seemingly finding it anomalous that a windigo would have a mitt, paused and then remarked, "It must have found that old rawhide mitt somewhere" (Brightman 1989a:155). Dog meat and hide clothing were among the emergency foods to which isolated families might resort in extreme famine conditions, suggesting a network of associations between the witiko, ravenousness, and starvation. In this connection, it is interesting to note that the Southwestern Ojibwa word for rock tripe (*Actinogyra muhlenberggi*), another starvation food, is "windigo-egg" (Kohl 1985:365). Witikos are said to become especially active in the spring, as the activities of the imperfectly domesticated Hairy Hearts suggest. The period immediately prior to and during spring breakup in April is identified by Crees as the season during which food crises were formerly likeliest to occur.

The contrast between the witiko and the human diet is foregrounded by the monsters' antipathy to esteemed foods such as grease and meat. As one Cree stated tersely, "If you try to feed it [witiko] good food, it won't take it. Never mind if you put good food out, it won't take it. It just wants to eat people. That's what it's hungry for." The witiko's indifference to animal meat is dramatized in the Hairy Heart myth by the old man's ruse with the makeshift "moose" in which he knows the cannibals will take no interest. At the same time, the story associates the transient human condition of the cannibals with their acceptance of beaver meat. Anorexia is identified by Crees as one symptom of an incipient windigo condition. It was reportedly present also in the cases of the Oak Bay Ojibwa cannibal (Henry 1969 [1809]:199–201) and the Cree Moostoos (Teicher 1960:95). Witikos are represented as averse to animal meat, an antipathy that functions as a plot device in narratives where the monster, in an attempt to conceal its condition, pretends to eat meat but actually conceals it (Merasty 1974:6). In an incident reported to Nelson (Brown and Brightman 1988:89) at Lac la Ronge, an old woman suspected of being a witiko was experimentally offered marrow fat and grease to determine her condition; witikos were thought incapable of eating these foods.

RAW MEAT AND UNGROOMED HAIR

The eating of human flesh is itself sufficient to produce the nonhuman condition into which the witiko degenerates and is thus directly associated with the loss of cultural characteristics. From a moral point of view, the cruelty and exploitation of such a diet—dramatized forcibly by the passage in which the Hairy Hearts abduct and eat children—is itself a sign of a noncultural condition. The Hairy Hearts, who use language and possess family relationships, are relatively socialized in contrast to typical witiko images but nonetheless run true to type by lacking dwellings and fire. The myth juxtaposes their frozen and monstrous state outside with the transient condition of domestication effected by their entrance into a human dwelling, exposure to fire, and ingestion of beaver meat. The typical witiko is represented by Cree as dirty, naked or dressed in rags, solitary, ungroomed, unhoused, lacking fire, and eating flesh raw or half-roasted. I have grouped these features as an anticultural dimension.

Cree narratives devote attention to how witikos ingest human flesh. The usual image is that the witiko consumes human victims as *askīwiyās* 'raw meat'. In Cree reports of witiko disorders, the sufferer's consumption of raw animal flesh or blood is interpreted by others as a symptom of the condition (Masson 1889–90:249–250, Cooper 1933:22, Brown and Brightman 1988:92). I was told the story of a Cree who had to be executed because he turned witiko after incurring the enmity of a sorcerer. The early stage of the disorder was both symbolized and caused by the victim's consumption of raw bear meat. The narrator clearly saw this as materially effecting the disorder: "He (sorcerer) sent that. . . The guy'd eat that bear so he turn crazy. He eat the head-part raw. He turned sick, wouldn't eat. Ah shit, [he'd] turn to *wīhtikōw* then" (Brightman 1989a:179–180).

Another man stated with evident disgust that, not content with eating human flesh, witikos ate it raw in the same way that Eskimos eat caribou meat. Crees familiar with Eskimo dietary habits expressed dismay at this practice, and Crees say that "Eskimo" derives from a Cree word meaning 'raw meat eater'. This translation is of some interest since Crees in the eighteenth century are said to have practiced on Eskimos a form of war-related ritual exocannibalism, eating small pieces of the raw flesh of slain enemies (Drage 1968 [1748–49], 2:45–46; Umfreville 1954 [1790]:48; Graham 1969 [1767–1791]:174; Skinner 1911:79). The only other example known to me of Crees using raw meat foods is the practice of drinking moose and caribou blood from the neck of a freshly slain animal. Evidently, the cooking process blocks acquisition by the eater of desired immaterial properties contained in the raw food. The Hairy Hearts exemplify the other typical witiko culinary practice: roasting over an open fire. Roasting is a conventional cooking technique, and some of the shock value of these narratives derives precisely from its juxtaposition with human flesh. In the story in which Wīsahkīcāhk becomes involved with a witiko (Brightman 1989a:40), he is ordered to go and himself cut the pronged roasting sticks on which he will be spitted and cooked. In the hero myth of Mistacayawāsis, the witiko villainess only half-roasts her child victims, a compromise between the raw and cooked (ibid.:117–119).

In his celebrated exposition of the culinary triangle, Lévi-Strauss (1966b, 1978:471–495) outlined a continuum of symbolic values concerning the relatively "natural" and "cultural" character of foods and cooking methods. The terms "nature" and "culture" are represented in Lévi-Strauss's comparativist structuralism and in writing influenced by it as universally recognized and opposed social constructs (cf. Ortner 1984). Strathern (1980) has since argued that Western conceptions of "nature" and "culture" cannot be regarded as universal and that non-Western societies may lack equivalent concepts or construct them differently. Without, at present, engaging the question of whether or how Crees make these distinctions, I use "cultural" in what follows as a predicate of attributes associated with human beings and "natural" as a predicate of contrasting attributes exhibited by animals and witikos. Beginning with the postulate that all cooking is a mediatory relation between "natural" or raw food and "cultural" or cooked food, Lévi-Strauss proposed that both the methods of cooking and the foods that result can be further partitioned between relatively more or less natural conditions. This results in a proportion of the type $A:B:B_1:B_2$, with the contrast between raw and cooked foods paralleling that between roasted and boiled foods. Lévi-Strauss defines roasting as a relatively natural cooking method insofar as neither manufactured cooking vessels nor water are interposed between the meat and the fire. The affinity of roast meat itself with the natural rests on the fact that it may be incompletely cooked, either on one of two surfaces or on the inside, preserving thereby aspects of rawness. Roast meat is thus relatively natural in relation to boiled meat and is a transitional term between raw and boiled foods strongly marked as "natural" and "cultural," respectively.

In narratives, the witiko—a being that has lost its cultural identity— eats human flesh raw, half-roasted, or roasted but never boiled. Witiko dietary habits are thus opposed to those of human beings by a threefold contrast between human and animal flesh, raw and cooked flesh, and roasted (or half-roasted) and boiled flesh. Crees roast, fry, and boil meat; boiling, however, was and is the commonly preferred method, and the witiko is seemingly never represented as employing it. Since Lévi-Strauss suggests that the relatively natural character of roast meat derives from the absence of manufactures in its preparation, it is interesting to note that a comparable idea influences Cree eating practices at the *wīhkōhtōwin*, or eat-all feast (chap. 8). Certain cuts of meat, typically bear meat, may be eaten without using knives or other utensils and sometimes without using the hands. Eating food raw—as with moose blood or with Eskimo flesh in the 1700s—and eating it without utensils—as in the eat-all feast—appear as parallel strategies for ingesting spiritual qualities of foods that would be neutralized by cooking or by manufactures. With specific reference to cannibalism, Lévi-Strauss has further argued (1966b:589) that since human flesh is a cultural kind of food, cannibals would ordinarily employ boiling, the most cultural of techniques. Since, however, enemies may be categorized as noncultural or nonhuman, he predicts associations of roasting with exocannibalism and boiling with reverent endocannibalism, in which deceased relatives are the fare. Cree exocannibalism was even more radically natural, since the flesh was eaten raw. The idea that roasting correlates with distance between eater and eaten, however, is consistent with the use of roasting by the witiko, since the latter, from the Cree perspective, is no longer a human being.

If raw or roasted human flesh induces witiko transformation, hot liquid animal grease is described as a remedy for the witiko condition if administered at an early stage. Rohrl (1970) suggested that fats may have possessed therapeutic benefit with respect to posited nutritional components of windigo disorder. Brown (1971) subsequently questioned the premise that grease possessed other than symbolic significance. The idea that grease may effect a cure for the witiko condition is widely distributed among Algonquians (Cooper 1933, Bloomfield 1934:55) and affirmed by Crees at Granville Lake. They explain the effectiveness of grease and other liquid cures as resulting from the hot temperature at which they are ingested. Below, I discuss these cures in terms of the witiko's frozen condition but suggest here that the identification of grease, especially bear grease, as the exemplary witiko remedy is motivated by its symbolic value as the prototype of human foods. Fatty meat and its by-products are esteemed foods in the Cree diet. Grease is drunk as a warm liquid, eaten when congealed, used as a condiment for meat and bread, and mixed with dried meat and berries to make pemmicanlike foods. Cree cooking methods maximize the collection of grease. When meat is roasted, a vessel may be positioned to collect the drippings that collect at the bottom. Boiled fatty meat and crushed metapodial bones of moose and caribou yield grease that is skimmed from the surface of the kettle when the contents cool.

The witiko feeds on human flesh eaten either raw or in a roasted or partially roasted condition. In contrast, human beings feed on cooked animal flesh. Since fire and cooking convert raw meat products into cooked meals, they possess marked human associations. Conversely, a person defined as witiko converts itself from a human to a nonhuman condition by eating human flesh. The significance of grease derives from the fact that it is a precipitate of the cooking process, typically of boiling, and thereby strongly marked as a human food since it epitomizes cooking. Rock Crees say that grease from the bear, the fattest of the big game animals, was the ideal witiko cure. From at least three points of view, bear grease might be understood as precisely the wrong food to give to an incipient witiko whose human identity is endangered. First, bears are defined as the most spiritually powerful animal, their power attributes concentrated in certain body parts, including the intestinal fat. Second, the bear is alone among the boreal fauna in its capacity to hunt, kill, and eat Indians. Although such attacks are rare, Crees are well aware that the animal is potentially capable of reversing the hunter-prey relationship in this way. The fact that bears eat human beings explains the association of the species with witiko, as in narratives where bears haunt the graves of executed witikos (Brightman 1989a:18, Bloomfield 1934:155). Finally, Crees say bears resemble humans more closely than other species, an affinity expressed by the

honorific name *āpitawiðiniw* 'half-human'. Eating bears therefore possesses for some Crees connotations of cannibalism. In all these respects,
bear grease might be expected to exacerbate rather than reverse a
witiko condition. That it does not do so suggests that bear grease, as
a product of the most powerful game animal and a precipitate of
cooking, metonymically evokes the entire process through which animals are overcome and eaten. To be human is to eat cooked animal
meat, and grease, the by-product of cooking, represents the human
condition from which the witiko has deviated but to which it may be
restored.

The raw or half-raw diet of the witiko is paralleled by other features
that define it as acultural. The witiko is usually solitary, traveling by
itself and possessing neither relatives nor friends. In some narratives,
incipient witikos conceal their condition and continue to reside with
their families, but this is prompted by predation rather than sociality.
Second, in its fully developed condition, the witiko loses the ability to
speak. One person explained this muteness by speculating that witikos
ravenously eat their own tongues; others say that the witiko aphasically
"forgets" language. When it encounters humans, the monster usually
remains mute but sometimes emits grotesque and incomprehensible
sounds. In one narrative describing an encounter with a witiko near
Nelson House, the human survivor is struck dumb by the fright he
experiences. Possibly related to the impaired speech of witikos are
stories (cf. Merasty 1974:13–14) in which they are defeated by losing
a shouting match with a human opponent. Unusual speech behavior is
also ascribed to persons who in the past were identified as incipient
witikos. Both silence and incomprehensible raving were reported by a
firsthand observer in 1823.

I look upon this as a sort of mania, or fever, a distemper of the brain. Their eyes
(for I have seen people who are thus perplexed) are wild and uncommonly
clear—they seem as if they glistened. It [the disorder] seems to me to lodge in
the Head. They are generally rational, except at short, sudden intervals when
the paroxysms cease [seize] them: their motions then are various and diametrically contrary at one time to what they are at the next moment—Sullen,
thoughtful wild look and perfectly mute: staring, in sudden convulsions, wild,
incoherent, and extravagant language. (Brown and Brightman 1988:91)

Crees say that incipient witikos are *kīskwīw* 'crazy' or 'insane' and
may use "witiko" to refer metaphorically to persons so categorized (cf.
Landes 1938:30, Marano 1982:389). I did not systematically examine
Cree definitions of insanity, but witikos exemplify three characteristics

probably assimilable to this condition. First, they lose control over their own behavior, a condition associated with the loss of autonomy produced by possession or dream predestination: "Some spirit goes into Chipewyans or Eskimos up in the Northwest Territories and they go crazy." As another Cree put it, "It's that evil spirit controlling his mind." Second, the witiko's cannibal acts were so monstrous that Crees say only an insane person would commit them. Narratives foreground this theme by describing lucid periods during which witikos express guilt and horror over past or potential crimes against relatives and request their own execution (Bloomfield 1934:155, Brightman 1989a: 92); persons who defined themselves as witiko sometimes made the same requests (Brightman 1988). Third, in the Hairy Heart myth, the younger monster perceives his affines as game animals and their snowshoe tracks as an animal trail. This parallels an attribute generally ascribed to witikos: hallucinations in which it perceives humans as game animals. Such impaired perceptions parallel other ascribed disturbances with regard to self, place, and memory. A fully developed witiko is said not to recall its human identity.

The developed witiko being is represented as lacking characteristic human artifacts and techniques. The witiko is imagined as sleeping in the open and as ignorant of the use of fire. Similarly, it does not use canoes and enters water only as a swimmer. The appearance of the witiko, already distinctive, is made more grotesque by its indifference to hygiene and dress. The following image is a composite of several Rock Cree accounts (cf. Merasty 1974:3, Vandersteene 1969:53). The witiko is naked or dressed in dirty and ragged clothing, lacks moccasins, and may wear only a loincloth. Its body is unwashed and its hair long, ungroomed, and dirty. These characteristics suggest a loss of concern with the conventions of appearance: the witiko no longer cares what it looks like to others.

Power and Domination

The feature of *mamāhtāwisiwin*, power, is continuous rather than discrete: the witiko possesses greater spiritual abilities than most humans, manifested in such attributes as physical strength, hypnotic control of victims, invulnerability, and resurrection after death. On another dimension, the destructive power of the witiko, and of the sorcerers with whom it is associated, contrasts with beneficial uses of power.

Crees emphasize the control the witiko exerts over its human victims, suggesting a comprehension of the food chain as a series of dominance/subordination relationships. Power is concretely manifested by killing and eating others, and he who kills and eats is most powerful. Just as the power of the witiko is pragmatically identified by its ability to kill human prey, so is the human flesh itself identified as a source of the witiko's power. Crees say that the strength, endurance, and other less material powers of animals are concentrated in certain body parts; humans can acquire these traits by eating these body parts as cooked food (chap. 4). The same concept presumably explained the practices of martial cannibalism discussed above. Crees say that once a witiko has succeeded in eating human flesh, it grows excessively powerful, presumably by ingesting the power attributes of its victim (cf. Speck 1935a:37).

Cree narratives dwell on the measures used by the witiko to stalk and overcome in advance their human victims. The witiko produces by means of its frightful appearance or by exerting its will a condition of melancholy, acute fear, or hypnotic control over its victims which prevents them from taking effective action. As Savage (Merasty 1974:14) puts it, "Staying alive was made less difficult for a Wetiko by the fact that most people were rendered helpless just by sighting it." Said Ahenakew's Plains Cree instructor, Waypast,

The rest of the family realizes that they have a Wetikoo to cope with. All that they have heard about such monsters comes into their minds. A great dread overwhelms them, the *marrow* inside the bones seems to melt and they have no power to move or fight. While they might have met ordinary dangers bravely, they were as frightened children in the presence of a powerful inhuman monster. They give in and very soon share the fate of the first victim. (Preston 1978:62)

The older Hairy Heart's oracular staff parallels other extraordinary techniques used by the witiko to locate and immobilize its victims.

According to legend, a Wetiko would sometimes sit through the night among the pines a short distance from a tipi. The spirits of the people within the tipi would fly out in the form of fireballs and whirl about the Wetiko. If it were able to catch the fireballs, all those within would die. Otherwise, the fireballs flew back into the tipi and the people were spared. (Merasty 1974:11)

Crees described to me a similar practice by an incipient witiko still residing with others. At night, the witiko sat by the fire or stove, snatching and devouring the sparks that flew up. The sparks represented souls of potential victims, each spark captured prefiguring a victim that the monster would later kill and eat. These techniques closely parallel the kinds of preparatory control over hunting that Crees say they exert in dreams and in performances of the shaking lodge.

The witiko possesses extraordinary physical strength, and some Crees say they can fly (see Mason 1967:58), a capacity not mentioned in nineteenth-century sources. This ability is associated with the appearance of powerful winds in late winter and early spring, and there are stories of witiko tracks that lead into a clearing and then disappear. The giant size of the witiko, in certain Ojibwa (Landes 1968:12–13), Eastern Cree (Speck 1935a:67–68), and Swampy Cree (Honigmann 1956:68) images, is absent from Rock Cree conceptions. The idea that the witiko is about the same size as a human being appears to be general among Rock Cree (Smith 1976), Thickwoods Cree (Vandersteene 1969:53), and Plains Cree (Preston 1978:60) divisions.

The witiko is represented as invulnerable to certain forms of attack or as capable of returning to an animated condition after a nominal "death" at the hands of human executioners. Both of these capacities are related to the idea that the heart or other internal organs turn to ice and that the monster cannot be killed unless the ice is chopped apart or melted. Whatever the method used to kill the witiko, narratives express concern with preventing reanimation of the corpse. Decapitation, cremation, and pouring hot liquids into the chest cavity are the methods noted, all of them paralleled by the treatment afforded corpses in historical cases of witiko execution (Brightman 1988). Axes are often used to kill witikos; in a sample of twenty-one narratives, axes figure as the weapon of execution in eleven (see Hallowell 1976:421). The younger Hairy Heart is killed and decapitated with an axe, and the hero in a narrative discussed below prepares for a witiko encounter by cleaning an ax handle and sharpening an ax head. In 1815, the Nelson House Post Journal states of famine cannibals that "they seldom if ever escape the punishment they so richly deserve of being burnt by their countrymen after they have killed them with hatchets, as they consider them unworthy of being killed with the gun" (HBC B.141/e/1).

The reference to cremation strongly suggests that the persons described here were identified by Crees as incipient witikos and thus as likely to become reanimated in a witiko condition. The use of the ax suggests less the stigma of a dishonorable death than the conviction that shooting was a chancy solution. In a story told to Nelson in 1823, a woman threatens her incipient witiko husband: "'Keep quiet, for

thou dog if a Gun hath no effect on thee, my axe shall—I shall chop
thee up into slices: thou hadst then better be quiet.' This indeed kept
him quiet for some time" (Brown and Brightman 1988:94).

The belief that a nominally "dead" human witiko can become reanimated is attested in an early reference to a man identified as one at Fort
Severn in 1774 (Bishop 1975:243). Additionally, Brown (1982:399)
described a case in which a human being without obvious witiko characteristics was thought likely to return as a witiko after death. Both
decapitation and cremation were intended to prevent such resurrection.
Decapitation figures in the Hairy Heart narrative, in two other Rock
Cree witiko stories (Merasty 1974:10–11, 23), in the death of the
Beaver Indian "Moostoos" executed as an incipient witiko by his
Thickwoods Cree relatives (Teicher 1960:95), and in another such execution by a Plains Cree band (Cameron 1926:46). Cremation is noted
in the 1815 Nelson House report cited above, in three historical windigo executions, and in five Cree narratives. In two such stories collected
by the author, the melting icy heart adds an element of suspense as the
thawed water extinguishes the crematory fire and the "corpse" begins
to revive before additional wood is piled on (cf. Merasty 1974:6,14).

Crees say that only very powerful men could prevail over the superior spiritual strength of the witiko, and narratives of the battles between
witiko beings and known persons identified as strong *opawāmiwak*
'dreamers' comprise a popular Cree literary genre. Vandersteene
(1969:54) wrote of the Thickwoods Cree, "To overpower a Witigo, an
austere preparation is necessary." Rock Cree narratives describing such
encounters emphasize this preparation, the dependence of the "dreamer" on his spirit guardians, and the exhaustion entailed by exertion of
spiritual resources. The account below paraphrases Johnny Bighetty's
account of the experiences of his great-grandfather.

Long ago, each bunch of Indians during the winter had to have an old man
with them who could beat witiko. If they had no one like that there, then witiko
might come and eat everyone in the camp. These old men could tell ahead of
time when witiko was coming. I told you about my great-grandfather. He was
one of those old men with powers. If a witiko is coming he would suddenly
start to dream. He won't talk or move; it's like he doesn't know anything that's
happening around him [Question: "How do you say that in Cree?" "ī-
pawākwamit. He's dreaming, but he's not really asleep. His mind is far away
from there, going around someplace else."] Then he wakes up, and he tells the
people there, all the people that are staying with him, that a witiko is coming
toward them, that it's forty miles away. Right away, he starts telling everyone
what to do. He tells them to give him an ax handle and an ax blade. He cleans

the ax handle, and then he sharpens that ax blade till it's sharp. Next, he tells them to get charcoal and mix it up with water to make that black paint, and he takes off his clothes and paints himself all over until he's black. Then he puts on an animal hide shirt. He tells his son: "When I come back from where I'm going, I'm going to be just about dead. When I come back, you have to rub me all over with bear grease." Then he starts dreaming again. He's dreaming for about an hour. All that time, he's talking to his spirits and calling them. Then he wakes up again. He tells all the people that those spirits are going to come and pick him up and carry him through the air to where the witiko was. Then he goes outside in the snow. The people could hear the spirits flying through the air. They can't see them, but they can hear them. These things that are coming are animals or anything that he dreams of. And they're all talking at once. You know what a radio sounds like when reception is bad and four channels are coming in at once? That's what they sound like. They came and picked him up and he was gone for four hours. Then they bring him back to the camp, but they land him about a quarter of a mile out on the lake. Just like an airplane coming in the winter. Or when a ptarmigan lands in the snow, it shows this trail of messed up snow? It looked like that. All the people went there and saw the snow where he landed. He walks back to camp from the lake. When he comes inside, he slumps over and passes out. Looks like he's dead. Then his friends did what he told them, they rubbed him all over with bear grease, and he came to and told them what happened. That witiko was forty miles away from them but coming closer. His spirits put him up at the top of a tree, right above witiko. The witiko had made a fire and was roasting an old rawhide moose mitt in it. Then he sent his spirits down there to tell the witiko to go off in the opposite direction. So he scared that witiko away from there.

It is probable that the departure and return of raiding parties that fought human enemies in the eighteenth century were similarly ritualized. Here, the encounter with the witiko requires preliminary trance, preparation of weapons (which remain unused), an animal hide garment, and the black paints associated with the shaking lodge, the vision fast at puberty, and, among some Cree groups (cf. Mackenzie 1927 [1801]:ciii), funerary rites. Bear grease, the witiko cure, occurs here as a restorative. The idea that such encounters physically exhaust those who undertake them occurs in another narrative whose hero must be restored with a sweat bath before he can dispose of the bodies of slain witikos (Brightman 1989a:162–163).

The witiko's use of its power to kill and devour human prey is the antithesis both of appropriate moral conduct and the ideal circumstances under which personal power is exerted. The idealized Cree conception is expressed in what Crees told Nelson of the instructions given by a spirit while revealing both the beneficial and harmful uses of plant medicines.

He explains every *circumstance* &c., relating to them; but with a most strict injunction never to employ them at his *Peril*: "unless you wish to die: I teach you all these things because I love you and know your heart to be compassionate: but *mind my words*, if ever you employ them with an ill or evil view thou shalt die. Other *Indians*, as well as thyself, love life—it is sweet to everybody; render it therefore not a burden or a *disgrace*; and I *hate* those who thus abuse my confident affection" &c., &c. (Brown and Brightman 1988:57)

In a detailed exposition of the Ojibwa category of "bad medicine," Black (1977) argued that the practices so characterized are conceptually unified not simply because they may impose physical harm, although this is often entailed, but because they interfere with the autonomy and independence of others. This is consistent with the ethical precepts expounded by Nelson's consultant. Power is legitimately exerted only to help the self and others; the witiko is the extreme case of power used to harm and exploit others. In similar terms, a Rock Cree distinguished between the "good" dream spirits that helped him in hunting and their "evil" counterparts that aided him in disposing of enemies (Rossignol 1938:69–70). In this respect, the relationship of the witiko to its prey parallels that of the *maci-maskihkiwīðiniw*, sorcerer, to his or her victim, and Crees indeed identify sorcery as a cause of both witiko attacks and witiko transformations.

Witiko doesn't exist.
No? I thought they had that thing here. Long time ago.
Well, they do . . . they do exist, alright. Some bad people, you know, one like that. If you make them mad, they'll send you witiko. He'll kill you or give you a good chase anyway. That's how they used to do. If you'd make them mad, well, they'd give . . . they'd send you a witiko. Or you'd turn to witiko.

The human reaction to witiko aggression in one Cree narrative suggests that that destructive power is only legitimate against others when it is used defensively. A "dreamer" uses a magically charged caribou antler knife to kill the witiko that has attacked him and his family, all the while carefully and didactically explaining to the monster that his actions are motivated only by the need for self-defense. He adds, before dismembering the witiko with his knife, that he has been angered by the threats to his family members' lives and that the witiko has brought its fate on itself. The tone of emotional self-control and the elaborate justification of hostile action in this narrative are characteristically Algonquian (Brightman 1989a:156–157, see Hallowell 1976:410–420). The hero concludes by telling the witiko that it simply should have left his family alone.

Dreams of Ice

The myth of the Hairy Heart beings associates their monstrous condition and power with the ice inside their bodies. Their transitions between monstrous and human states and between more and less powerful conditions correlate with the contrast between cold temperatures outside and the warmth inside the lodge. Ice exists in their bodies outside but melts inside. Residence in the lodge "humanizes" both monsters transiently, but the younger reverts as a result of staying outside. When the ice melts, their power is proportionately diminished, allowing, finally, the elder monster to be defeated after he stays too long by the fire. The monsters are also associated with the northern direction from which they approach their victims. As all these aspects of the story suggest, the witiko is surrounded by associations with frozenness: the northern and eastern directions from which the coldest winds blow, winter, and ice. The witiko is adapted to cold and embodies it, whereas humans survive in it by using a technology—clothing, shelter, and fire—that the witiko lacks.

The witiko condition may be directly produced by freezing:

It's not in its right mind. It was froze in winter time, and it gets cold air in its mind. That cold air goes in its head. They stay frozen all winter, but their brains are still working. In spring, they thaw out and begin moving around. When they thaw out, they go crazy.

Rock Crees say that the heart and other viscera of any incipient witiko gradually turn to ice. This condition is simultaneously represented as cause, consequence, and correlate of the disorder. Of the Crees of Lac la Ronge in the 1820s, Nelson wrote, "They also think that firearms are absolutely unable to injure them—'a ball cannot injure *Ice*: to destroy *Ice*, it must be *chopped up*: and *the heart then* [in the witiko condition] *is all Ice*'" (Brown and Brightman 1988:94). Nelson also related a Cree account of a witiko exececution in which the self-diagnosed witiko begs his brothers during a lucid period to execute him before he commits murder. Accordingly, the brothers lay an ambush for him after moving their camp, but the witiko perceives the one who is waiting to shoot him and addresses him as follows:

"Thou thinkest thyself well hid from me, my brother; but I see thee; it is well thou undertakest it. It had been better for thee however hadst thou begun sooner. Remember what I told you all—it is my *heart*; my *heart*, that is terrible, and however you may injure my body if you do not completely annihilate my *heart* nothing is done,". . . accordingly he shot, straight for the heart—he [witiko] dropped, but rose immediately and continued toward the camp that was within sight, laughing at their undertaking. "The ball went through and through, but not a drop of blood was seen—*his heart was already formed into Ice.*" Here they seized and bound him and with ice chisels and axes set to work to dispatch him. According to his desire they had collected a large pile of dry wood, and laid him upon it. The body was soon consumed, but the heart remained perfect and entire: it rolled several times off the Pile—they replaced it as often: fear ceased [sic] them—then with their (Ice) chisels they cut and hacked it into small bits, but yet with difficulty was it consumed!!! (Brown and Brightman 1988:93)

These ideas were not limited to narrative but were acted on in the contexts of witiko accusations and executions. Self-defined witikos stated that they felt their internal organs freezing (Brightman 1988). The depositions given in the case of Moostoos, a Beaver Indian resident with a Thickwoods Cree band near Little Slave Lake in 1899, provide detailed descriptions of postmortem measures and the motivations of the executioners (Teicher 1960). Moostoos was executed by his Cree companions as a witiko after an unsuccessful attempt at curing. The body was subsequently shackled with trap chains, staked to the ground through the chest, and decapitated. Hot tea was poured into the chest wound in an attempt to melt the internal ice, a measure reported also in a Cree witiko execution at Sturgeon Lake, Saskatchewan, in 1889 (Duchaussois 1923:293). The accounts of the executioners show that the corpse continued to be an object of fear even after mortal injuries were inflicted:

All the day before I thought there must be ice in him to make him sick that way. I thought that if the ice was allowed to stay there, that the evil spirit could not be killed out, and I suggested the hot tea. (Teicher 1960:96)

We stuck the stick in so that he could not get up. We believed he had an evil spirit in his body. We thought he had ice in his breast, therefore we poured tea into the body. We were going to melt the ice so we got the hot tea. We poured the tea in the same hole where the stick was driven in. . . . The man was dead while this was done. I was afraid he would rise again. I do not believe another man could rise, but that man could. (ibid.:101)

These observations relate the possibility of resurrection to the persistence of the frozen viscera inside the nominal corpse.

The aversion of the witiko to cooked food and its propensity for raw flesh are further indexes of the incompatibility between the monstrous condition and warmth. The significance of liquid grease as a witiko cure relates in part to the hot temperature at which it is served. Warmth also reverses the witiko condition in other contexts: the grease is part of a series including fire, noted in the Hairy Heart myth, fortified wines, sunlight and hot weather (Brown and Brightman 1988:93), hot water (Duchaussois 1923:293–294), and hot tea (Teicher 1960:101), which are used either as cures or postmortem measures to prevent resurrection. Eastern Crees imagined the witiko to alternate between monstrous and human conditions in winter and summer (Speck 1935a:69). More positively, an incipient witiko might be cured permanently during the warmth of summer, as a Cree told Nelson, "for the sun then *animates* all nature" (Brown and Brightman 1988:94). Some Crees today say that people who freeze to death in winter become witiko; they "thaw" in spring and then are active until summer, when the warmth kills them.

Witikos are closely associated with the northern direction and, like the Hairy Hearts, characteristically approach their victims from that direction. Associations with the north occur also among Ojibwas, who identify the "North Pole" as the home of cannibal giants (Brown and Brightman 1988:88). Some Crees today say that witikos originate among non-Algonquian groups living to the north. An alternative directional classification is indicated in a Cree cosmogonic myth from York Factory in 1823 (Brown 1977:46) in which the witiko is introduced into the world by East Wind, a being associated with cold winds and weather. The witiko condition is said to be caused by possession or predestining dreams. In Cree thought, beneficial and harmful power attributes derive from the characteristics of the spirit agencies who bestow them. The disposition to use power in harmful or evil ways may then be understood as ultimately exogenous: the individual is shaped by the character of his or her dream spirit. This parallels conceptions of human witikos who have the condition thrust on them through possession or dream predetermination. As one Cree expressed this,

Then he start dreaming. And some guys dream bad things. That's the guys that turn witiko. Most of the people turn witiko cause they dream bad things. Even now there's people like that. After all, they're baptized, but still there's things in bad dreams. They got to hire an older guy to try and kill it for you. That's the only way that thing don't happen to you.

The Crees of Lac la Ronge in the 1820s associated the windigo condition with dreams of Kīwītin, the North Wind spirit, and Maskwamiy, the spirit of Ice. Those who accepted such beings as their dream spirit at puberty or encountered them in dreams later in life were said to be predestined to witiko degeneration. Nelson recorded a complex dream whose narrator narrowly escaped this fate by refusing to eat (in the dream) what he initially perceived as animal meat but later learned to be human flesh (Brown and Brightman 1988:90). Granville Lake Crees associate witiko dreams with Maskwamiy, as do the Rock Crees of Pelican Narrows, Saskatchewan: "Sometimes a man who had left to get his puagan [dream spirit] would come back a weetigo because his dream had brought him the puagan of ice. He would go crazy, and if this happened, if he had this ice puagan, he would become a weetigo" (Cockburn 1984:41). I was told that Maskwamiy might appear to the dreamer as an animal. If the dreamer unwittingly accepted its blessings, he or she was predestined to become a witiko after eating an animal of the same species that the ice being had used as a disguise. Of similar import is the idea that ingestion of ice by children predestines their or their parents' degeneration into a witiko (Brown and Brightman 1988:91, Cooper 1933).

Winter and spring, the north and east, ice, cold, starvation, famine, cannibalism, and the witiko together comprise a metonymic series. More fundamentally, the witiko complex is a complex metaphor likening the most obscene expression of human violence to the climatic conditions most inimical to human survival. With negligible exceptions, summer appears to have been a season of reliable foraging throughout the Algonquian subarctic. Winter provided the hazards of isolation, freezing, famine, and, correlatively, emergency cannibalism. Famine cannibalism and the spirits of the cold create the witiko.

Witiko and Human

When speaking English, Crees usually refer pronominally to the witiko as "it," an index of the impersonality of the condition. The fascination of the witiko turns in large part on the belief that it was once a human being but is no longer. The contrasts between *nīhiðawīwin*, Cree-ness, and *wīhtikōwātisiwin* 'witiko-ness' (a Plains Cree form) are formulable in terms of attributes that the witiko has lost, and it is these that the witiko image represents as constitutive of the human state.

Humans are defined by what they eat: animal flesh, the product of beings other than the self. The witiko is defined by its diet of human flesh, the product of beings with which it was initially identical in kind. Cree exegesis makes clear that diet is a fundamental constituent of one's self and kind: the witiko stops being human when it stops eating animal meat. Humans distinguish between humans and animals; the witiko is sometimes represented as confusing them and perceiving humans as moose and beavers.

Humans are defined also by how they eat, by their use of cooking techniques that transform raw meat into food. The witiko contrastively eats either raw, half-cooked, or roasted meat, the latter perhaps the least "cultural" of cooked foods. The use of hot grease, a precipitate of cooking, as a witiko remedy signals the incompatibility of the witiko condition with culinary techniques.

Humans are warm-bodied and perishable beings, vulnerable to the climatic hazards of winter. They interpose between themselves and these extremes manufactures—dwellings, clothing, and fires—on which their ability to survive depends. The witiko, in contrast, takes the external cold inside its own body, literally freezing internally. This physical transformation is engendered by freezing or by dream experiences with the *ahcāk* beings who rule the winter. As a result, the witiko "forgets" and survives in the cold without human technical artifices; it goes about during winter naked or in rags, without dwellings, ignorant of fire. Contact with the cold produces witikos; warmth sometimes restores their humanity.

Humans live and travel together in social groups; the witiko is solitary. As Thompson (1962 [1784–1812]:174) wrote in the 1790s, the witiko "no longer keeps company with his relations and friends, but roams all alone through the forests." Humans communicate by speaking Cree and other languages; the witiko is aphasic and mute. Humans are concerned with their appearance to others. Clothing with its fur, bead, quill, and thread ornamentation, cosmetics, hairstyles, ornamented hats and hoods, bracelets, necklaces, earrings, cleanliness, depilation, face painting, and tattoos all serve or served to express the wearer's gender, attractiveness, and self-esteem. The witiko is dirty, naked, ungroomed, unornamented. Humans consciously regulate their actions, a capacity linked with the ability to recognize objects correctly. The witiko is deprived of its own will and of control over its actions, its faculties usurped by an evil spirit or sorcerer. In narratives, transiently lucid witikos beg for execution. With respect to power endowments, the witiko exhibits certain abilities not conventionally ascribed to human beings but equaled or exceeded by some powerful dreamers: imperviousness to bullets, immortality or resurrection, the ability to withstand winter cold, and a paralyzing control of human victims.

Finally, the noun *kisiwātisīwin* and related verbs refer to the quality of disposition and conduct that the Crees translate as "goodness" or "kindness." Predictably, a wide range of actions merit this term, typical of which are adopting orphans and caring for the elderly or ill. The defining and axiomatic criterion of "goodness," however, is the sharing of food within and beyond the domestic group. Cree converges with English in associating moral dispositions with the heart: one who is *miðotīhīw*, or "good-hearted," distributes meat and fish; only a *macitī-hīw*, or "bad-hearted," person hoards it. The witiko is a being with a heart of ice, and the eponymous significance of the name "Hairy Hearts" is clear: "They say of these that they are without hearts or goodness." The conduct of the witiko is, of course, the obscene and antisocial extreme of reciprocity: instead of giving food, it steals life, murdering and converting its victims into food and thus continued life for itself. Identifying famine cannibalism as a cause of witiko disorder, Crees say that this exploitative treatment of fellow humans as food changes men and women into beings themselves no longer human, lacking speech, sociality, and culture.

6

"They Come to Be Like Human"

Introduction

North American Indians are said to conceptualize animals in their own image, ascribing to them anthropomorphic social and cognitive characteristics. Indians, for example, believe that "the animals reside in lodges, gather in council, and act according to the norms and regulations of kinship" (Wax and Wax 1962:181). Specifically of boreal forest Algonquians, Skinner (1911:76) wrote, "The Indians think that all animals are speaking and thinking beings, in many ways not one whit less intelligent than human beings." According to Speck (1935a:72),

The animals (*awa'cats*) pursue an existence corresponding to that of man as regards emotions and purpose in life. The difference between man and animals, they believe, lies chiefly in outward form. In the beginning of the world, before humans were formed, all animals existed grouped under "tribes" of their kinds who could talk like men, and were even covered with the same protection.

Likewise, the Eastern Crees of Mistassini believe that "the game animal is gifted with a soul similar to that of man; its reactions and social organization are imagined as similar to those of its human brethren" (Lips 1947:6). There exist obvious problems with these generalizations, not the least of which is how Indians could believe them to be true. Differences between humans and animals must be as significant to hunters as resemblances.

It was in the primordial era of the *ācaðōhkīwin* that differences be-

159

tween human beings and animals were least in evidence. In the stories of the very earliest times, animal characters speak, marry, use fire, live in camps, and cooperate in joint undertakings. These protoanimals possess both human and theriomorphic physical characteristics. Animals with speech and other social traits appear also in the narratives with protohuman heroes and heroines, although in these they are more obviously theriomorphic. Sometime in the remote past, the descendants of these animals seemingly assumed the characteristics of modern species, changing their mode of life, abandoning or losing involuntarily the anthropomorphic physical and social characteristics they once possessed. No single narrative accounts for this transition, and there is no evidence that Crees imagine it to have been a single epochal event. Stories explain how the animals lost fire and how individual protoanimals acquired particular traits perpetuated by their descendants. The overall Cree perspective on human-animal relations opposes a primordial similitude between the protoanimals and humans (who did not yet exist) to modern differentiation between the emergent humans and modified animals. Through time, animals also progressively lose interspecific sociality among themselves. This conception parallels Ojibwa traditions recorded in the 1700s which relate how beavers and other animals were deprived of speech and other powers by the transformer heroes (Henry 1969:204–206, Thompson 1962 [1784–1812]:155).

Patent physical and behavioral difference between humans and the animal species is, of course, the stuff of conventional perception, as readily apparent to Cree *opawāmiwak*, dreamers, as to non-Indians. As foragers, Crees were and are in business to locate and kill animals, a vocation requiring detailed knowledge of the characteristics of each species. When asked how animals differed from humans, Crees noted a variety of physical, behavioral, and spiritual differences, of both discrete and continuous types.

Dwelling/technology "Don't live in houses" (except muskrats and
     beavers).
     "Some live in the water and under the ground."
     "Don't make fires; don't need to."
     "Don't need clothing. Don't get cold in
     winter."
     "Live in the bush. People live in camp or
     town."

Physical traits	"Hairy coats."
	"Can't walk around on two legs" (except bears).
	"Stronger than people" (bears, wolverines, moose).
	"Faster than people" (wolves, wolverines, dogs).
	"Don't get tired as easy as people."
	"Don't get cold like people."
Spiritual traits	"Souls are stronger than people's. They say if you kill an animal it gets its body back and goes back in the bush."
	"Cleaner than human beings. Like to be clean all the time. Dogs are dirty because they live in town."
Speech	"Can't talk" (bears may understand Cree).
	"They say that they *used* to talk like people."
	"Maybe they talk to each other when there are no people there."
	"Talk among themselves but not like people."
Intelligence	"Not as smart as people."
	"Smarter than people about some things: never get lost in bush, always know where their food is."
	"Smart just like people" (bears, beavers, wolves).

The responses exhibit an expected diversity of opinion as well as consideration of individual species rather than the "animal" category as a whole. Most reflect conceptions of animals as they are experienced in waking life. The response regarding reincarnation, however, concerns qualities not accessible to ordinary observation.

People point out that the transformer Wīsahkīcāhk could converse with animals, as though this was a singular and desirable state of affairs, lamentably absent in the present. In conventional waking experience, animals are usually seen as mute, noncultural, and unreactive socially with human beings. There is a Cree commonsense view that these visible differences separate animals from humans as qualitatively distinct life forms, whatever their similarities. Cree discourse on beavers is especially relevant because, as one would expect, they compare the architectural activities and sociality of these animals to their own. It needs to be emphasized in a book of this kind that while Crees talk often of animals, the topic is more usually the technical rather than the spiritual facets of foraging. I cite here from my field notes a composite account of beaver behavior obtained from Johnny Bighetty and Henry Linklater.

The length of time beavers occupy a house determined by quantity of available food; given abundant food, might stay in same house for as long as three years. Beavers eat birch, willow, poplar, and *oskatamōw*, a round "applelike" botanical found in bottom mud. Rejects jackpine but uses it as weight to hold down buoyant willows in feed pile. Main predators are wolf and wolverine, which wait for beavers to come up on land to get food/building material. Usually only one family (male and female pair, young) in a lodge around Brochet; bigger multifamily lodges sometimes found around Granville.
   Male and female are monogamous and stay together for life. Might be brother and sister to each other. If one dies, other will find a mate. Have young in spring or early summer; usually in May. Young move away from the "old people" after the first or second winter and build their own house nearby. Will sometimes build lodges on lake far removed from other water source; travel far overland to find these; know that they're there from hearing loons calling from them. Stay at home most of the time like old (human) people.
   Beavers real smart—just like human beings—like engineers or carpenters— work hard all the time. Looks inside of beaver lodge and admires appearance: sticks used as flooring for feeding and sleeping platform are smooth as though they were split by a carpenter. Sleeping platforms are like beds: "beaver furniture." Differ regarding source of architectural knowledge: instructed by older beaver re lodge building vs. "born to them, they know it."
   Re vertical snare sets under ice: Beavers move a lot so can never be sure when one will be caught. Easier to catch young than older beaver. Former stay around lodge and runways; adults found "all over" in lodge, runways, feed pile, and away from complex. Set away from runway and lodge if want older beaver. Beaver not scared by dead beaver in snare on runway—proof of this is that three might be caught on same snare pole—if one is caught, the others have less space in which to swim and get snared more easily.

This is a sample of what Crees talk about when invited to instruct a novice about the characteristics of beavers. References occur here to characteristics that are *similar* to those of human beings—monogamy, engineering skill, and the purposeful arrangement of the dwelling space. It is my impression that most Crees ascribe greater self-awareness, rationality, and intelligence to animals than do non-Indians. Both of the contributors to this composite sketch had looked inside beaver lodges and admired the ingenuity exemplified there, but they made no reference in this context to beavers conversing in human languages, wearing clothing, using fires, constructing dwellings like those used by humans, or exhibiting other behaviors ascribed to the proto-animals in the early period of the world.

Animal Marriages

Crees share with other boreal Algonquians and Athapaskans a genre of narratives describing marriages between human and animal characters. The marriage stories, although situated like other *ācaðōhkīwina* in the remote past, presuppose that the modern differences between humans and animals have already been innovated, and the marriages are thus represented as singular and anomalous events. Three of the marriage myths involving bear, beaver, and caribou spouses have been recorded in a number of variants from different Algonquian and Athapaskan groups in the subarctic.[1]

These myths provide a perspective on what can be termed the "infrahuman" animal, "infra" here possessing the sense of "beneath" or "within." My introduction to the image occurred when Angelique Linklater, after narrating the story of a man who married a beaver woman, remarked casually that the man saw the beaver woman as human and the beaver house as a three-pole lodge built on dry land. I begin by examining a text of a similar myth from the Nett Lake Chippewa of Minnesota, in which the human character is a woman and the animal spouse a male. This story explores in more detailed fashion than available Cree variants the theme of the human spouse's perceptions.

A woman fasting in the bush is approached by a man and accompanies him to his lodge which is well provisioned with food and clothing. Initially concerned that her relatives will miss her, she agrees to marry him and forgets her parents. She lives happily with the man who provides her with beautiful clothing, abundant fish and game, and firewood. She gives birth to four children, makes reed mats and baskets, and keeps the lodge orderly. When they are visited by human beings who do not enter but walk around outside, she realizes she is married to a beaver and is resident in a beaver lodge. Periodically, her husband and children "visit" human beings when they are slain by hunters, but always return to her bringing kettles, bowls, knives, tobacco and other objects and offerings used at beaver feasts.

When her beaver husband grows old and departs, he advises her to return to her family. When a hunter comes to the lodge, she calls to him from inside, asking him to open the lodge. When he does so, she emerges and returns to her people. Thereafter, she does not eat beaver meat and instructs her family always to speak respectfully of beaver if they expect to be lucky in killing them. (paraphrased from Jones 1919:251–257)

The narrator who dictated this text to Jones began his story from the perspective of the heroine: she sees her suitor as human, his dwelling as a human habitation, and their marriage as typical of Chippewa practices. The narrator, however, suggests that matters are more complex than the woman initially surmises. He refers, for example, to the husband as "he who was in the form of a human being" and notes that "four was the number" of children to whom the heroine gave birth simultaneously. The listener is apprised in this way that the marriage is a novel one, finally learning the identity of the husband only when the heroine herself discovers it. Although she learns that her husband is a beaver, her perceptions of him, herself, their children, and their surroundings continue to be in human and not animal terms. The narrator throughout contrasts these perceptions with conventional human perceptions of beavers. Her husband and children appear to her as physically human. The beavers converse with the heroine and among themselves in a language functionally equivalent to Chippewa, if not identical to it. She perceives the beaver house as an Ojibwa lodge by a lake. The firewood outside the dwelling is presumably a reference to what humans ordinarily perceive as the beaver feed pile. Beaver material culture parallels that used by humans beings: dwellings, fire, mats, kettles, clothing, ornamentation. They subsist on fish and small game. The sexual division of labor parallels Chippewa practice: he hunts while she weaves mats and baskets and keeps the lodge "in a very beautiful order."

The heroine loses the ability to distinguish between humans and animals, since she experiences as human the same entities whom the human trappers experience as beavers. One explanation for the woman's inability to perceive her husband as a beaver is that she is "enchanted," the beaver having changed his form so as to appear to her as human. The heroine's perspective, however, does not change after she becomes aware of her unusual circumstances: the narrator continues to describe her beaver companions in human terms. The narrator does not, in fact, state that the woman was physically transformed into a beaver, and when she emerges from the beaver lodge at the end, she is elegantly garbed in beaded clothing and jewelry. The premise of the story is that the degree of human-animal difference is a question of perspective or of surface appearances. The story represents the heroine's perceptions not as delusional but as appropriate with respect to a covert reality. As a result of her marriage, she sees through appearances to the infrahuman identity in whose terms beavers experience themselves. Her perceptions, enlarged by her vision or by her incorporation into beaver society, include facts about beavers that are known to human beings by tradition but not conventionally available to their direct observation.

With respect to productive relations between humans and animals, the myth provides a beaver's perspective on the religiously postulated events of sacrifice and regeneration. The beavers "visit" human beings and then return to the beaver house with lavish gifts.

From time to time with the human person that had come to where they were, would the children [beavers] go back home; frequently, too, would the man [husband] return home with the person. And back home would they always return again. All sorts of things would they fetch—kettles and bowls, knives, tobacco, and all the things that are used when a beaver is eaten; such was what they brought. Continually were they adding to their great wealth. (Jones 1919:253)

Subsequently, the narrator makes clear that he is describing the killing and eating of the husband and children by humans.

Now and then by a person were they visited; then they would go to where the person lived, whereupon the people would then slay the beavers, yet they did not really kill them; but back home would they come again. . . . That was the time when very numerous were the beavers, and the beavers were very fond of the people; in the same way as people are when visiting one another, so were (the beavers) in their mental attitude toward the people. Even though they were slain (by the people), yet they really were not dead. (Ibid.:255)

Here, the narrator juxtaposes human perceptions of trapping—"the people would then slay the beavers"—with beaver perceptions of trapping as visiting and hospitality. Like Crees, Chippewas represent events of killing and eating as moments in an endless cycle of reciprocities between humans and animals. This process, in which animals voluntarily trade their infinitely renewable bodies for offerings, is portrayed in the myth as it might be perceived by the beavers among themselves. Animals are said to appropriate immaterial counterparts of the utensils used and tobacco smoked at sacred meals, as well as other sacrifices burned or otherwise directly conveyed to them. The myth dramatically represents from the animal's point of view events that are theologically postulated but not visible to humans: the survival of animals after death, their return to their dwellings, the renewal of their bodies, and their enjoyment of sacrifices. It also makes clear not the least significant of the beavers' "infrahuman" attributes, their moral character. "And the beavers were very fond of the people; in the same way as people are when visiting one another, so were (the beavers) in their mental attitude toward the people." The animals of the myth, and of the modern world, are moral beings who share food with human beneficiaries.

Other Algonquian beaver marriage myths refer to the altered perceptions of the in-married human. In a version collected from the Ungava Naskapis (Turner 1894:339–340), the human hero is approached by a female beaver whom he perceives as such. She asks him to be her husband, but he raises practical objections, saying that he cannot live in water or eat willow bark and that he will not like living in a beaver house. The beaver responds that he will like the lodge and that he will not be aware that he is living in water or eating bark. He enters the water and joins the beaver, and her predictions are proven true: he finds the lodge comfortable, is unaware of immersion in water, and does not recognize as such the meal of willow bark that she serves him. As in the Ojibwa myth, the human character loses the ability to differentiate between human and animal modes of living, in this case, between terrestrial and aquatic habitats and carnivorous and vegetable diets. The story again implies that these are only surface distinctions that disappear when closer and more intimate knowledge of beavers is acquired. Turner's translation states that the hero does "not feel the water touching him," which can be taken to mean that his experience of the new aquatic medium is no different from that of his former terrestrial habitat. Like the heroine of the Ojibwa myth, he begins to participate in the experiences beavers themselves have of their own lives.

Human and animal perceptions are similarly juxtaposed in the Naskapi caribou wife myth from Northwest River, Labrador (Tanner 1979:136–137). Here, the in-married human husband observes a caribou hunt. While the human hunters see caribou being shot and falling to their deaths, the hero observes human figures removing capes and then running away unharmed. As Tanner has aptly written, in myths "game animals participate simultaneously in two levels of reality, one 'natural' and the other 'cultural,' in the sense that it is modeled on conventional Cree patterns of social and cultural organization" (ibid.:137).

There is, throughout these myths, no identification of human and animal categories: the two are lexically distinguished by the narrators. The Chippewa myth, in fact, foregrounds human-beaver differences that persist even at the "infrahuman" level: the simultaneous birth of four children, the dispersal of young beavers "two by two" from the parental lodge, and the father's instructions to establish new lodges and multiply so that the numbers of beavers may be increased. The story also identifies more esoteric differences: unlike humans, beavers survive death. The story may also suggest that most of the material culture used by the beavers is not manufactured by them but received as sacrifices from their hunters. The beaver remains nonhuman but less so than ordinary experience discloses.

All these marriage myths represent physical and behavioral differences between humans and animals as appearances masking an underlying resemblance. The obvious question concerns the connection of these "infrahuman" images of animals in myths to Cree experiences with modern animals. The narrative events in which these images figure are said to have occurred in the remote past beyond living memory. The participation of animals in "two levels of reality" may be imagined to have existed in the past but no longer in the present. As discussed above, Rock Crees today say that modern animals lack speech, clothing, fire, and the other cultural attributes that their human spouses observe among them in the marriage myths. Such is consistent with Rock Cree statements that modern animals are the transformed descendants of more humanoid protoanimals.

On this question in the thought of the Eastern Cree of Mistassini, Tanner (1979:137) wrote,

To the extent that the myths constitute a form of belief, they indicate the state of affairs that existed in the remote past. But the myths also explain the origins of the hunting rituals that are used today. Ritual action is primarily symbolic in nature. We may say that the hunting rites are believed to constitute an effective form of magical action, and that they depend to some extent on reconstituting the world 'as if' the conditions of mythical time were in place.

Tanner goes on to note that the premises of hunting ritual presuppose the presence of the animals as figured in myths, social persons with whom the Crees can enter into relations of friendship and material exchange. Tanner's remarks on "reconstituting the world" are insightful, pointing to aspects of the Cree understanding of time and the effectiveness of ritual action that remain to be elucidated and that may prove to resemble in some respects Australian conceptions of the "dreamtime."

Possibly, Crees believe that modern animals ordinarily lack the overt or covert human qualities of their myth-age predecessors. If this is the case, rituals such as the shaking lodge and the eat-all feast may be imagined to create contiguity between the present and this remote past, which continues to exist separately from but concurrently with the present. In simulating and thus recovering this past, Crees interact with the humanized animals who inhabit it, exchanging with them their prayers and gifts for control over the hunt of their modern descendents. In such a case, the present assumes the character of the past—and modern animals, the character of the prototypes—but only for the duration of ritual time.

There is evidence, however, that some Crees believe the infrahuman identity of animals to exist continuously within the present. Some conjecture that the modern differences between human and animal are delusions induced purposely on humans by animals. As one man phrased this problem,

Really they resemble human beings, they differ only a little. They talk and eat and live like human beings. But you can only know this if you dream of them. It is excessively difficult to know these things. The animal doesn't want us to see it. Maybe we see a "small piece" of animals only. Only a "small piece" is what they show the people. In this way they appear to us. [Cree]

The speaker was discussing modern animals in the contemporary world. It should also be pointed out that that the marriage myths bracket the infrahuman image of animals with such spiritual processes as sacrifice and physical regeneration of slain animals after death, and for some Crees, these remain factual but not directly observable events in the 1990s. From this point of view, the "real" forms and behaviors of animals are perhaps anthropomorphic but hidden. Their ordinarily perceptible forms are transient facades, edible and marketable, which they assume when interacting with human beings.

Insofar as boreal Algonquians are sometimes skeptical about the adequacy of their conventional perceptions of animals, their skepticism aligns with certain facets of Western philosophical dualism. Common to both is the conviction that there may exist discontinuities between the properties of external object and the sensory experiences that people have of them. The (Western philosophical) argument from perceptual relativity presupposes that discrete sensible qualities—say, the pelt of a beaver and the hairless skin of an Indian—cannot simultaneously occupy the same surface of a material object. Discrepant sensory experiences of different percipients with the same object cannot then be attributed to qualities of the object but are the result of mediate influences not identifiable with it. The perceptible properties of some object thus may vary in relation to some characteristic of the percipient or other mediate influence to which the latter is subject. One can consider also the argument that one of the multiple discrepant sensory experiences of the object may effectively represent it while the others do not. This argument may be the epistemological message of Cree images of infrahuman animals. In the myths, the human affines and the animals themselves experience animals as possessing humanoid forms and practices. Possibly the sensible theriomorphic qualities of animals ordinarily perceived by humans are hallucinatory and the human affines' perceptions in myth superior rather than delusional.

The Animals of the Dream

From this perspective, both the protoanimals of the prehuman age and the animal spouses in marriage myths are continuous or interchangeable with contemporary animals. The "historical" differentiation of human beings and animals is a differentiation of surface features only. In two sets of contemporary contexts, the conventional image of the mute and nonhuman animal interchanges with infrahuman images. In their dreams of animal *pawākanak* or of animals they will later kill, some Crees today experience the humanized and social animals of myth. As noted in chapter 3, Crees say that some dreams are events during which the dreamer's soul interacts with other animate agencies in temporal and spatial coordinates detached from those of the sleeping body. Events in dreams are prototypes that determine the occurrence or nonoccurrence of corresponding events in subsequent waking life. Dreams can be sources of knowledge about and influence on beings and events not directly accessible to waking observation or inquiry—those in the future or in the past or at a distance or beyond barriers set by such substances as water or rock. In these aspects, dreams complement waking observations and are integrated with them in making decisions. In two senses, dreams provide knowledge superior to that of waking perception since they extend the spatiotemporal boundaries to which the latter is subject and because dream events are causes of which worldly happenings are effects. However, dream knowledge can be defective and is not accepted uncritically: the beings who appear in dreams are capable of duplicity, and there exists the possibility of failure in human interpretation of the dream.

Although theriomorphic animals appear in dreams, Crees say that animals also appear to the dreamer in human form, often in the role of a visitor or sexual partner (cf. Speck 1935a:189, Tanner 1979:125). In addition to appearing human physically, animals in such dreams may speak Cree, wear clothing, smoke tobacco, and live in houses. Some Crees identify their *pawākan*, or dream guardian, as an individual animal. A recurring element in typified accounts of the initial dream is the appearance of the *pawākan* in human form and its query to the dreamer: "Do you know who I am?" or "Have you seen me before?" Typically, the dreamer is ignorant of the being's identity, whereupon it changes repeatedly between the human form and another with which the dreamer is familiar. Crees say that the *pawākan* is an animal in the bush and that they might encounter it while awake. One naturally desires to know whether Crees take the humanized animal of the dream or the theriomorphic animal of waking perception to be the more "innate." Both can be regarded as disguises behind which animals elect to retreat.

The Animals of the Shaking Lodge

The operation of the *kosāpahcikan*, or shaking lodge, provides persons in the audience and certainly the operator with a waking experience of infrahuman animals. I was never fortunate enough to observe the *kosāpahcikan* in northern Manitoba, but eyewitness accounts and other sources (Brown and Brightman 1988) suggest the part that animals play in it. In the course of the shaking lodge, the *okosāpahcikiw* or 'operator' enters at twilight a small five-foot-high barrel-shaped tent that conceals him from the audience seated around it. The tent itself is constructed during the previous daylight hours, the operator specifying the types of trees from which the poles are taken. After seating himself within the lodge, the operator drums and sings, summoning multiple *ahcāk* beings to join him within. These beings are invisible as they fly through the air and enter the lodge through the top but may assume some tangible form once inside. The shaking of the lodge back and forth visibly and audibly signals the entry, exit, and presence of the spirits. During the course of the performance, they converse among themselves, with the operator, and with members of the audience outside, responding to questions either in known languages or in unintelligible speech requiring translation by other spirits or by the operator. Crees say that the operator is awake throughout the performance and that the spirits speak independently of him. They readily suggest that the operator himself might impersonate voices or shake the lodge but emphasize that only a fraud would do this.

So they make that kind of a thing, a *kosāpahcikan*. Like a barrel. But they use three poles [horizontal around circumference] so that thing can hang on. Covered it with a tarp. Before they had the tarp, I guess they had moose hide or anything. And the guy went inside. And those guys [audience] were sitting close by. Well, you hear a guy [spirit] hitting that—it's like someone hitting the wigwam [lodge]. Somebody come in through the top. And you hear him talking. You can hear the old man [operator] talking. So's [talking] the other guy [spirit] who come in. They'd be talking to this guy [operator]. They talk Cree all right. But some they couldn't understand. Some are hard to understand, but the old man [operator] understands them.

Members of the audience addressed requests for information or assistance to particular beings in the lodge or to all of them collectively. Questions concerned the numbers and location of game animals, when they would be killed, the causes and remedies of health disorders, life expectancy, the welfare of absent relatives, and the location of missing objects. The spirits provide material assistance as well as advice and prophecy, traveling vast distances on behalf of their petitioners and dispensing lost objects or medicines via the operator.

With few exceptions, the *ahcāk* beings are never visible to the audience and the forms they assume in the lodge—purportedly they appear as small birds or points of light—would not, in any event, allow the audience to identify them. As a result, *kosāpahcikan* is a performance in which the personae of individual spirits exist vocally, constructed and experienced almost exclusively through the medium of spoken languages. Animals in the shaking lodge, like animals in dreams, use human speech. We unfortunately lack Cree texts of shaking lodge performances, although Preston (1975) published a careful English translation of an Eastern Cree performance at Rupert's House. In the absence of Cree texts, the various metalingual descriptions of the shaking lodge as a speech event provide some insight into how characters are vocally constructed. The shaking lodge features a recurring stock of characters, variable to some degree among different operators and different performances by the same operator. Many characters possess individuating speech characteristics, familiar to the audience from hearsay and from other performances. Four aspects of the characters' speech identify them: songs, choice of linguistic code, paralinguistic effects, and typified genres, taking the latter to refer to particular topics and styles of discourse. Some of these characters figure also in myths, exhibiting there the same vocal attributes. All these features are indexical in that they obligatorily signal a variable in the speech situation—the identity of the speaker—much as "accent" may signal a speaker's ethnicity or geographic background. These features are also iconic: they resemble in socially agreed on ways the character of spirits who exhibit them.

The association of particular spirits with particular vocal features is quite strong in the Granville Lake area today, as it was at Lac la Ronge in the 1820s (Brown and Brightman 1988:152–156). With respect to the feature of code, particular spirits are associated with the Cree language, with other known human languages, or with an unknown "spirit" language or languages intelligible only to the operator. Different spirits speak known languages in more or less intelligible fashion. Since members of an audience exhibit different degrees of multilingualism, some spirits are thus intelligible to some listeners but not to others. Today, most spirits speak in Cree, and others use English, French, Saulteaux, and Chipewyan, or unknown spirit languages. At Oxford House (Mason 1967), evidently a less cosmopolitan community, only Cree, Saulteaux, and English were heard in the 1930s. In the Lac la Ronge performances observed by Nelson, Cree was spoken by the transformer Wīsahkīcāhk, the evil being Macimanitōw, Turtle, the Hairy Heart beings, Flying Squirrel, Dog, a being called "Strong Neck," and the souls of absent living Crees. That Turtle should speak fluent Cree is consistent with its role at Lac la Ronge as the patron spirit of the shaking lodge. The Sun and the Moon, beings who repaired Euro-Canadian guns, spoke English, a facility suggesting both power and, as Preston (personal communication) suggests, the likening of social and spatial distance. Jackfish (northern pike) spoke French.

The Buffalo, three species of Bears, the Horse, the Moose, the *pākahk* or skeleton, and the spirits of the human dead spoke unintelligible languages. As Henry (1969 [1809]:161–162) wrote of an Ojibwa performance in 1763, "Articulate speech was also uttered as if from human lips, but in a tongue unknown to any of the audience." That the Horse and Buffalo, "foreign" animals associated with the parklands to the south of Lac la Ronge, should speak unintelligible languages is consistent with their marginality to the boreal forest. The other animal codes are less readily interpretable: Flying Squirrel, an omen of bad hunting, speaks Cree while three species of Bear and the Moose, all game animals, speak unknown languages.

Comparable diversity characterizes modern Rock Cree associations.

It's got to be a guy [operator] that's willing to do it. People got to collect the man that they want, who they figure can do it. Amongst the people, they pick one. Maybe they might want to know...like from Pelican Narrows. They want to know if this guy [a relative at Pelican Narrows to the west] is alive. Someone here, you know, he want to know if the guy is still alive. He tell the guy [operator], "I want to know if the guy is still alive. I want to talk to him." Give him so much and he make one like that [lodge]. And he goes in there. And he send for the guy. And he hear the guy talking inside the tent. He's talking to the guy. He bring him in alive like that. That's what happens when you dream you're talking to a friend, you know? [i.e., "you" have been summoned into the lodge while sleeping]. But you can't talk to him [the person summoned into the lodge] because you're not that much...you haven't got enough...not well equipped. But this guy [operator] can do it. He bring the guy over there. He talk to him inside the little tent. Like if he's [the one who commissioned the rite] sitting outside, he hear, "This guy wants to know how you're doing?" Oh, he'll hear, "I'm okay, I'm doing good." After he finish, you hear that thing moving. Gone. And the guy come out and say, "Did you hear him? I ask him and he's alright." That's how they find things out. It's like a telephone. But the trouble is, the guy can't talk [directly] to you. The guy in the tent relates the message to you. That's how it is.

Question: When the animals come in, how do they talk?

They talk Cree. That *mīmīðītīhīsiw* [Hairy Heart] that's the one that sound like they sound in the story. You can understand him talking. My old man [father] says he can understand *mīmīðītīhīsiw*. That's the one he says you can understand the way...old people tell stories about *mīmīðītīhīsiw*. He says, "I understand him." The animals talk mostly like ordinary person. But some you can't understand. Could be a Frog or somebody who's hard to understand. Jackfish has a big mouth, you know?

Here, the souls of living persons speak an unintelligible language, but animals are represented as speaking Cree. Another individual confirmed to me the association between Jackfish and the French language, evidently a connection of some extent and antiquity. Possibly, the "big mouth" of Jackfish is an icon of perceived French speech behaviors. The discourse cited above suggests that the Frog and Jackfish are unintelligible not because they lack competence in Cree but because their vocal apparatus interferes with lucid speech.

The songs sung by animals and other beings after they enter the lodge also index their identity. As Nelson wrote, "The Stone was the first one known to us, by his song; for every one almost that entered sang *his* song, to which those (the Indians) on the outside would keep chorus" (Brown and Brightman 1988:104). I did not obtain examples of these shaking lodge songs, but it is likely that the lyrics referred directly or obliquely to the spirit's identity. Individual spirits were further identified by the characteristic genre features of their utterances. In Nelson's description, as in Manitoba today, the *mimiõītīhīsiwak* or Hairy Hearts are distinguished by their boastfulness and their demands for burnt offerings. The Turtle was popular for his jokes and humorous impersonations of drunks. Flying Squirrel answered questions contrarily, requiring the audience to deduce the opposite of his responses. Wīsahkīcāhk was distinguished by his professed benevolence toward the audience, just as Macimanitōw was characterized by his abusiveness and threats. These oppositive moral characteristics were theatrically developed in the performances Nelson observed, taking the form of a verbal and physical contest in which the hero thwarted the demon's malignant intentions, cowed him into silence, and climactically expelled him from the lodge. In reading Nelson, one can sense, as if from very far away, the engagement of the audience's emotions in this enactment of the victory of creative over destructive force.

Animal beings are today distinguished by paralinguistic features. First, such vocalisms as the heavy breathing and growling of the bear, the hissing of the lynx, the mating call of the moose, and the call of the loon are heard from the tent. In some cases, animals utterances are preceded by a formulaic vocalism: thus, the Crow in Oxford House (Swampy Cree) performances prefaced a signature of "Caw Caw" to messages otherwise spoken in Cree (Mason 1967). Similarly, at Granville Lake, "When the bear speaks from there, we hear first his growling and breathing. The loon calls also" [Cree]. These vocalisms are not translated by the operator and are typically intermingled with intelligible speech. The animals' identities are signaled not only by characteristic calls but by the interference of the latter in the Cree they speak. Rock Crees say that animal voices are distinguished by predictable intonations: bears speak in a low and rumbling voice, lynxes in a hissing voice, and fish with a gurgling intonation as if from underwater. Similarly, Nelson wrote that "the Ice entered—he made a noise extremely resembling that made by a person shivering with cold, loud and hoarse and *liquid*" (Brown and Brightman 1988:104). Nelson also noted that Dog "spoke perfectly plain and distinct, and with a more elegant and harmonious voice than I ever heard in my life" (ibid.:156). This elegance also characterizes Dog's quoted speech in myths today, perhaps reflecting his status as domesticated animal. According to one Rock Cree woman, the animals brought into the lodge begin by producing animal vocalisms that become gradually and progressively intelligible as spoken Cree. A similar pattern of gradually improving intelligibility was observed by Nelson, who wrote that the Sun "speaks very bad English at the offset but by degrees becomes to speak it very easily and fluently" (ibid.:41). With respect to animals and humans, this pattern of increasing lucidity perhaps mirrors the gradual attenuation of boundaries between them which the performance progressively effects. The aggregate significance of the animal voices in *kosāpahcikan* is not that animals are human but that they can converse like humans using varieties of Cree and other languages inflected by their individual natures.

Crees addressed questions about hunting to animals in the shaking lodge, and the latter, if favorably disposed, responded with information and instructions to be followed for a successful hunt. An Eastern Cree decribed animal messages in similar terms.

Every animal and human being could speak the same language in the old days. There were no special words for the starting of a shaking tent. They just mentioned they wanted to know about deer (caribou) or whatever else they wanted to know. They heard these animals talking in the shaking tent. They could, for example, hear a deer talking. "My brother," it might say, "is 250 miles to the northeast of you. There's a group of us in a special place. Brother, you go there if you want to kill us." This is only for hunting purposes. At no other time did they hear animal voices in the tent. There were no special words like "This is the Canadian Broadcasting Company." (Bauer 1971:24)

The question arises whether Crees identify the pseudoanthropomorphic animals of dream and shaking lodge with the animals of waking life. If they are spirit "personifications" or otherwise different from conventional animals, this would explain the paradox raised by the mute animals of the trapline and the voluble animals of the ceremony. The Rock Cree answers, however, were always the same.

Question: Is that like the same animal [i.e., in dreams and the shaking lodge] you'd find in the bush?
Oh, yeah, yeah! Beaver, mouse, eagle, anything. Trees. Root. *Everything is different*. Something you dream about. You know, like a spoon. Hammer, spear, chisel, *osihcikan* ['inanimate thing']. Any kind of thing. *They come to be . . . like human*. You can use them anytime you want it [emphasis added].

Clearly, not only animals participate in a covert humanoid identity. But these modern experiences of infrahuman animals in dreams and in the shaking lodge articulate with the premises motivating the animal ceremonialism practiced by some Crees. The detailed inventory of respect behaviors owed to the animal carcass presupposes the existence of an intelligent, self-aware, and reciprocally reactive presence with whom moral relationships can be established. Animal images in dreams and in the shaking lodge suggest that the animal bodies men and women kill and eat are merely transient forms of beings whose continuing and unseen essence more closely approximates *nīhiðawīwin*, Cree-ness.

In Quest of the Anthropomorphic Animal

Cree narratives imply that the ancestors of modern animals lost their humanlike attributes in the remote past and that their descendants consequently lack them. At the same time, they readily ascribe humanlike attributes to the animals who appear in dreams and shaking lodge performances in the twentieth century.

Initially, it struck me that Crees behave as though animals are successively and cyclically nonhuman and infrahuman. In the bush, they assume theriomorphic form and lose cultural attributes. When "killed," their disembodied spirits "come to be like human," and the perishable carcass is the medium through which human hunters seek to exchange with them. Thereafter, they are reborn or regenerate, lose their cultural attributes, and the cycle begins anew. The seeming paradox would thus be dispelled by temporal alternation. To the two images would correspond two exclusive orientations to animals, one spiritual that anticipates and commemorates the hunt and one technical that dominates the hunt itself.

There exist numerous difficulties with aligning in this way the two images in complementary distribution. First, as noted earlier, the "infrahuman" animals of myth, dream, and shaking lodge are not identical to human beings but possess also their individuating species characteristics. Likewise, the nonhuman image does not entail a Western measure of the intellectual or spiritual distance between men and animals. Crees may say that modern animals lack speech, fire, and manufactures, but many of them credit animals nonetheless with cognitive and spiritual capacities close to those of humans. More specifically, the infrahuman image suffuses the practical conduct of the hunt. The very fact of a successful kill is sometimes ascribed to the animal's voluntary surrender, and this presupposes a reciprocally reactive "other" whose deliberate decisions may be influenced by gifts of tobacco, songs, drumming, and other cultural commodities. Finally, aspects of animal behavior perceptible in foraging contexts may be interpreted as objective signs of the hidden infrahuman qualities. The practice of addressing living bears in Cree provides examples. Thompson (1962 [1784–1812]:96) observed a bear hunt in which a Cree reproached the cornered animal for hostility toward humans, and was moved to ask whether the Cree really thought the bear understood his reprimand:

When a bear thus killed was hauled out of it's [sic] den, I inquired of the Indian who made the speech, whether he really thought the Bear understood him. He replied, "how can you doubt it, did you not see how ashamed I made him, and how he held down his head."

The infrahuman animal thus overlaps into the nominally secular context of waking perception and productive technique.

These concurrent nonhuman and infrahuman images, from the perspective of Cree mythological history, could correspond to two developmental sequences, both beginning from the premise that animals originally possessed forms and behaviors similar to those of human beings. One sequence, corresponding to the nonhuman image, postulates events in which animals "lost" these forms and behaviors, a conclusion consistent with the sensible differences between humans and animals in the modern world. The second sequence, corresponding to the infrahuman image, premises the same "loss" but restricts it to only one level of human experience, that of perception of the animals' "outward form" in waking life. At another level, accessible only in dreams and the shaking lodge, animals continue in the present to possess speech, culture, and human bodies. Crees never expressed these solutions to me and spoke rather of the limits of human knowledge when, on rare occasions, I attempted to resolve the two images.

Animals as Selves and Others

The animal as other is probably everywhere significant as refraction, reflection, distortion, and counterpoint of the socially constructed categories of human self and person. It might be anticipated that animals will become especially saturated with these values in foraging societies. Wagner (1977) has identified the tension between difference and continuity—between discrete categories and the relationships that exist among categories and thus confound their boundaries—as a potentially universal epistemological paradox. He seemingly suggests that the integrity of the distinctions between categories is inversely related to the precision with which the relationships between them are identified; this paradox is solved differently by different cultural traditions. Wagner goes on to suggest that most (Western) scientific practice represents the distinctions—the bounded categories of analysis—as innate or "given" and the relationships among them as the artificial constructs of its own activity. The Tsembaga and Daribi of New Guinea, and also the ecosystem perspective in Western biology, conversely identify the relationships and continuities as innate and the categorical distinctions as human constructs. The resemblances Wagner identifies between Western conceptions of ecosystems and the "cognized environments" of New Guinea consist first in the inclusion of humans among other units comprising the "whole system" and second in the parallel between ecological flows of energy and nutrients and unconstrained flows of sociality between men, women, and nonhuman entities.

Wagner's distinctions between the innate and the constructed are of considerable relevance in Cree society, where religious thought recurrently problematizes categorial distinctions not only between humans and animals but between humans and perhaps all other entities in the universe. Wolverine initially sees a wolf tooth but then comes to see it like the Wolves do as an arrow. The beaver's human wife experiences beavers as human beings. In the shaking lodge, mute animals speak. In dreams, animals manifest themselves in humanoid forms. All these examples identify categorial distinctions between the "given" kinds of animate and inanimate being if not precisely as artificial constructions, then as limited in their provenience. The distinctions are seemingly encompassed by a fundamental (and usually invisible) similitude. It is the resemblances and relationships among beings that are, in Wagner's terms, the most innate, intimating a shared "humanoid" appearance and cultural way of life in which all entities participate. It is not surprising that animals partake in this similitude because, as the myths make clear, it was the animals who originally owned the forms and practices now possessed by human beings. The boundaries of the categories *iθiniw*, human, and *pisiskiw*, animal, at least as these are given by waking perception and common sense, are called into question. The Cree verb *itātisiw* predicates of the essential or the habitual qualities of animate entities, as individuals or as kinds, corresponding in this respect to one meaning of English "nature." The corresponding noun

itātisiwin [means] the way a guy lives. The way you behave, the way you live. Either you live as a bad person or a good person. The way he lives. *miðwātisiw*, that means he's a good person. *ī-miðwātisit*. Or a bad actor. *ī-macātisit*. Like a guy who say talk all roughly all the time, swearing, all that. That means "bad person."

Each kind of animal is spoken of as possessing its own *itātisiwin* 'nature': it is *itātisiwak* that caribou migrate, that beavers build lodges, and so forth. In the shaking lodge and in dreams, animals share human *itātisiwin*: "They come to be . . . like human."

But the differentiation of animal from human is also fundamentally important, constitutive of and endlessly objectified in the human practice of killing and eating animals. Further, the categorial differences that beings recognize between own kind and other kind are represented as themselves the product of difference: it is by virtue of being a wolverine and not a wolf that Wolverine sees objects differently than Wolves see them. It is unclear what logical criteria could be employed to determine whether resemblance or difference are taken as more "innate" by Crees. The Cree categories "human"and "animal" represent, in any event, a particularly rich case of the instability inherent in all cultural categorization.

In the wake of functionalist and structuralist concerns with integration and order, multiple perspectives on the relatively chaotic and entropic properties of social forms have emerged or been resurrected, threatening, as Sherry Ortner (1984:157) notes, to displace entirely questions of consensus and cohesion. The modes of cultural disorder have proliferated, augmenting persisting anthropological concerns with the antisocial potentials of the egoistic individual and the disparities between norm and practice. Structuralism itself, with its focus on antinomian contradictions and oppositions in society and nature, hardly neglected the problem of disorder, but more recent structural writing has abandoned formal systems and emphasized instead the contrapuntal and unarticulated relations between the institutional sectors of society—the different machineries of status ranking, for example, in James Boon's (1986) analysis of Bali. The extensive literature inspired by Victor Turner (1982) on the symbolism of liminal conditions and persons is also ancestral to current preoccupations with disorder and folly, although, as in Turner's earlier writing, liminal symbolism is sometimes represented as creating the orderly social reproduction imagined in the functionalist tradition. An exceptionally important dimension of sociocultural chaos concerns ecological maladaptation, contexts in which the enactment of cultural routines subjects the actors and the ecosystems in which they participate to biological stress (Rappaport 1984:422–431). Such contexts are instances of a more general disorderly condition, one in which actors define the properties of the external world in terms refractory to it or in which constituent groups in a society lack shared and consensual definitions of what exists and how it is to be experienced and acted on (Sahlins 1981). Writing derived directly or more distally from Marx has continued to explore the dialectic of the labor process as a historical dynamic, the conflicting ideologies and interests of the differentially empowered, hegemonies and counterhegemonies, and the distorting relationship between structure and the consciousness people have of it.

Many of the thematic concerns with disorder can be assimilated to the dialectic between the cultural sign system as a socially shared (although problematically conscious) semiotic "structure" and its referential contextualization in enacted situations. Signs are experienced in or as definite situations, experiences, relationships, persons, and objects in the world. To reprise an introductory example, the meaning of any given experience with a bear is conditioned both by the conventional meaning of bear as a category in Cree culture and by the unique entity and circumstances that the category references in a particular instance. Neither referent nor context necessarily reproduce in all their specificity the character of their predecessors or of the convention itself. The witiko (Brightman 1988) exists as a structural category, defined by a complex set of oppositional, metaphoric, and metonymic associations. It exists also as an element in consciously negotiated ideologies or systems of Cree knowledge in which it is experienced not as an oppositional value but as a name for an independently existing entity in the world. Finally, the witiko acquired worldly denotata: individuals were identified as or, more rarely, identified themselves as witiko. These referential contextualizations prompted recurrent enactments of cures, ostracisms, executions, and, in at least one instance, murder and cannibalism. No one individual defined as witiko and no individual set of circumstances created by the definition would replicate others in all respects, the disparities producing a condition of unstable heterogeneity between the socially shared signs, ideology, and practices.

The site of cultural disorder is not, however, exclusively in the tension between conventional sign and novel referent or context or, more broadly, between cultural structure and the world. Structures contain within themselves instabilities that make possible the deliberate or unintentional transposition of their constituent signs to novel referents. In the case of the Cree categories *pisiskiw*, animal, and *iðdiniw*, human, this instability can be specified in terms of each sign's inability to retain consistently its oppositive value to the other. This is one instance of the more general semiotic condition that Sergej Karcevskij (1982) characterized as the asymmetric dualism of the linguistic sign. Karcevskij proposed as the precondition for both change and poetic function in language the fact that each lexical sign may exist simultaneously along axes of homonymy and synonymy. Homonymy in Karcevskij's idiom is the capacity of a single linguistic signifier to stand for different semantic values, both in the senses of polysemy and of multiple meaning. Synonymy refers to the reverse condition where multiple signs stand for a single series of analogous semantic values. Every occurrence of a sign implicates these two series: the other homonymic values of the occurring sign and the other signs in the synonymic series that might have occurred.

If. . . the same phonic sign can signify different values in different series, the reverse is equally possible: the same value can be signified by different signs in different series. . . . Homophony is the general term for this phenomenon. Homonymy is only a particular case of it, occurring in the conceptual planes of language; the opposite phenomenon, "polyvocity" or heterophony, occurs in the conceptual planes as synonymy. But these are really two sides of the same general principle which could, though rather imprecisely, be formulated as follows: every linguistic sign is potentially a homonym and a synonym at the same time. It belongs simultaneously to a series of transposed values of a single sign and to a series of analogous values expressed by different signs. (Karcevskij 1982:51)

Linguistic metaphor provides a privileged context for examining this transposition that continually occurs, although with reduced visibility, whenever linguistic and other cultural signs are referenced to the world.

By then they're medium beavers, by that second winter. That's about the time they leave. They go looking for their. . . they stay [mate] with their brother and sister. They don't look for somebody else. In Cree we sometimes call a guy "*amisk*" ['beaver'] if he turns around on his first cousin, you know? We call him "*amisk*," we call him "beaver."

This is one of a series of conventional animal metaphors used by Rock Crees, including *maskwa* 'bear'/'adolescent girl', *omiðāhcīs* 'wolverine'/

'thief', *atim* 'dog'/'worthless person', *wāpiscānis* 'marten'/'attractive woman'. It draws on the tension in Cree society between an indigenous preference for sexual encounters and marriage with *nitim* 'my opposite sex-cross-cousin' (among other denotata) and Catholic disapproval of such unions. In Karcevskij's terms, the first occurrence of the beaver metaphor to refer to an incestuous individual (by Oblate and some Cree standards) was a transposition resulting in a new homonymic series in the structure of the lexicon: the single phonic sign *amisk* now signified both "beaver" and "incestuous human." Simultaneously, the transposition creates a new synonymic series, adding "beaver" to the noun phrase "incestuous person" as synonyms that stand for analogous significations.

Karcevskij represents this structural instability as beginning with acts of reference in which signs with existing meanings are "extended" to novel referents or contexts more or less recognizably different from the conventional sense. Such is clearly the case with metaphors that immediately invite the interpreter to examine the novel context and supply the connection between the conventional and innovated values. In this respect, Karcevskij explains a structural instability as originating in the necessary disparity between sign types (*langue*, cultural structure) and their token occurrences, denotations, and contexts (*parole*, practices, action). Sahlins (1981:70) has summarized this relation in a cultural rather than exclusively linguistic context by observing, "Reference is a dialectic between the conceptual polysemy of the sign and its indexical connection to a specific context." As his remark suggests, the disorder that attends cultural creativity and transformation is as much an attribute of existing structures as of the referential relation of structure to the world. It is not, of course, that cultural categories and propositions—as elements of structure—are discrete, ordered, and systemic and "become" disorderly or dynamic only when referenced to the world. Neither is it clear that the entropic qualities of structure are exclusively to be accounted for as originating in novel acts of reference. Relations of transposability, overlap, and resemblance always exist as virtual attributes of signs in reciprocally defining oppositional sets, that is to say, in "structure."

The Crees and other boreal Algonquians have no unique claim to transposing and intermingling the culturally constructed categories of human and animal. Cartoons, the toy industry, the animal rights movement, verbal metaphor, and the status of the dog and cat as domestic pets all attest to the blurring of boundaries between these categories in

American and other modalities of contemporary Western culture. But the game animals who appear with human bodies in dreams or converse from the shaking lodge in fluent Cree are especially developed exemplifications of this "failure" of structural categories to maintain their discreteness. It would be possible to formulate an oppositional configuration between Cree "human" and "animal" categories in the following terms (listed in table 1). Of these dichotomous and continuous contrasts, all but the last are obviated in the shaking lodge, in dreams, and in the myths of animal marriages. Crees say that animals "were like people" in the age of *ācaðōhkīwin*. Perhaps one can say that they are still people. In Karcevskij's terms, the sign *pisiskiw* 'animal' is homonymic. Its quotidien reference is to the nonhuman mammals of waking experience. But a man describing his dream will use it to refer to a being with the form and behavior of a human woman.

Table 1 *Oppositive Values: Human and Animal*

Iðiniw 'human'	*Pisiskiw* 'animal'
speech	calls
clothing	fur
cooked food	raw food
camp/town	bush
eater	eaten
+fire	−fire
physically weak	physically strong
vulnerable [climate]	adapted
mortal	transmigrant

In Karcevskij's (1982:54) words, the sign *pisiskiw* "tries to have functions other than its own." Or, more precisely, it functions simultaneously to reference the overlapping categories of "nonhuman animal" and "infrahuman animal." At the same time, the meaning "infrahuman animal" "tries to be expressed by means other than its sign" (ibid.), acquiring as its de facto synonym the sign *iðiniw* 'human being'.

It is, therefore, a characteristic of Cree cultural structure that the signs "animal" and "human" are both reciprocally defining and mutually transposable. There is probably an instability of prehistoric provenience, and, as a historical accumulation, it probably reaches back to Asia and beyond. The ubiquity of the "humanized animal" in cultural time and space may suggest that both the objective resemblances and differences between human beings and other species have been a recurrent "resource" for symbolic reality (Friedrich 1979:23), much as distinctions among animals are "natural" differentiators of otherwise homogeneous social groups or literary personae. But it is only in this sense that the polysemy of these two Cree signs can be explained as the product of their referential engagement with the world. As I argue in the next chapter, both the nonhuman and the human animal are implicated in individual events of hunting, killing, eating, and commemorating. The coexistence of the two images is not the result of novel transpositions of the sign "animal" to new contexts, or of the disparate interested concerns of the differentially empowered, or even of the discontinuities between the Cree meanings and objective characteristics of the boreal fauna. The worldly contextualizations of signs are, as Sahlins (1981, 1985) has demonstrated, implicated both in their reproduction and their transformation as elements of structural design. As a category of Cree culture, "dog" acquired the feature [-edible] in the 1800s, a major change in the significance of an animal that was earlier the staple of sacred and sacrificial feasts. It is likely that this transformation was catalyzed by observation of dogs in use as draft animals and by the incorporation of this strategy into Cree society in the late 1800s. Dogs thus acquired a new referential significance, and the sign was augmented with the meaning "draft animal." But this would not account in itself for the transformation from edible to inedible. Dogs acquired a new and important use, one that now kept many from the pot, but not all were usable as draft animals. In any case, scarcity hardly dictates judgments of edibility. Before Crees ever saw dogs in sled harnesses, the category "dog" encompassed disparate meanings as the most socialized animal—and hence a logical gift to the spirits who had none—and also as a "dirty" animal who copulates in public, eats feces, and insults the bones of game animals. The potential for redefinition of dogs as polluting and inedible was already in place, as the Cree insult metaphors from the 1800s attest (Brown and Brightman 1988). In a new productive context in which dogs could regularly be eaten only at the expense of immobilization, the pollution associations became dominant, and dog meat passed categorially from human (and spirit) diets. It is not, then, that new worldly contexts do not transform the significance of signs, but the signs may themselves contain synchronic instabilities that superintend the character of the transformation. Like the polysemy of the sacred-but-polluted dog of the pretraction period, the polysemy of the nonhuman-infrahuman animal is seemingly an enduring structural attribute, not readily assignable to any historical conjunction of the sign with new referents.

One naturally wonders whether "*iθiniw*" is similarly transposed in a reversed configuration, whether Crees ever conceive themselves as beings possessing covertly the character of the nonhuman animals of waking life. On the Northwest Coast, masks with human faces open to disclose animal identities within. The Western Woods Crees used, to my knowledge, no animal masks, but one is led naturally to reflect on the mimetic character of now-vanished dances, the attributes of strength and endurance assimilated by eating animal flesh, the magically charged animal skin garments, the animal face paintings of the James Bay Swampy Crees (Skinner 1911:21–23), the many proper names derived from animal nouns, and finally the animals in dreams whose appearance anticipates worldly encounters with human friends and relatives. All of these experiences and practices may partake as much of disclosure as of simulation. There is no evidence in Cree discourse that the infrahuman animal image is paralleled by an infra-animal identity that humans covertly possess at a nonsensible level of reality. But perhaps the animals themselves perceive humans this way. Humans see in dreams their own images reflected by the animals as if by a mirror. Possibly, animals dream of mute and quadrupedal human hunters. Or perhaps animals see hunters as animals while awake and see them as human only in their dreams.

7

"Laboring Thus to Destroy Their Friends"

Introduction

Cree hunting is "spiritualized" in the sense that diverse agencies—including the individual animal quarry, the game rulers, the dream guardian, and human sorcerers—are said to make rational decisions affecting the number of animals on the landscape and their accessibility to hunters. These agencies are conceived as reactive to human conduct, and any event of hunting potentially implicates a complex skein of prior events in which the hunter has participated. Hallowell (1976:74–75) described a "personalistic theory of causation" among the Crees' southern neighbors, the Saulteaux, and I have observed that some Rock Crees accord little scope to the concepts of "accident" and "chance."

The verb *ohcitaw* predicates of all events conceived to result from the exercise of someone's deliberate will. Vandersteene, long resident with the Thickwoods Crees of Alberta, described its semantics and contextualizations.

Pour signifier qu'un phénomène est naturel, ou naturellement nécessaire, fortuit, librement voulu, permis ou délibéré, le mot clé reviendra sans cesse sur les lèvres: Otchitaw. . . . C'est même otchitaw que la gachette de votre carabine se déclenche par hasard et que la balle s'égare dans la poitrine de votre voisin; otchitaw q'un arbre tombe avec fracas sur votre tente: mais c'est tout aussi otchitaw que vous abbattiez un arbre pour allumer votre feu. . . . Otchitaw lorsqu' après des heures d'une chasse effrénée, Tchos parvienne a approcher un caribou à portée de sa carabine, mais c'est également otchitaw—comment est-

ce concevable?—s'il manque son coup. . . . Cette expression signifie une opinion profondément ancrée: en tout ce qui arrive, la volonté de quelqu'un inter-
vient toujours pour une large part: la mienne, ou celle de mon voisin, celle du
diable ou celle de Dieu. (Vandersteene 1960:94–95)

In the case of hunting, the will is typically that of an animal or another
being with control over animals.

The Grateful Prey

The most commonly expressed Rock Cree ideology of
the hunter-prey relationship postulates an endless cycle of gift exchanges between humans and animals. *Nimosōm*, 'my grandfather,' and
nōhkom 'my grandmother' are used to address game animals, connoting
a respectful and nurturing dependency relationship. Similarly, for the
Eastern Cree (Mistassini), the idea that animals are friends or lovers
of human beings is the "dominant ideology" of hunting (Tanner
1979:151). The event of killing an animal is not represented as an accident or a contest but as the result of a deliberate decision of the animal
or another being to permit the killing to occur. The dream events that
Crees say prefigure successful kills are sometimes talked about as signs
that this permission has been given. In waking experience, the decision
finds culmination when the animal enters a trap or exhibits its body to
the hunter for a killing shot. Since the soul survives the killing to be
reborn or regenerated, the animal does not fear or resent the death. The
animals' motivations for participating in these events of killing are
figured both in the idioms of love and of interest. Animals may "pity"
the hunters who have need of their flesh, and especially is their benevolence evoked when the hunter complies with the conventional objectifications of "respect," treating the carcass, meat, and bones in the correct
fashion. Conversely, ritual omission or blasphemy angers the animals,
who then withhold themselves. But the role of the hunter-eater is
not that of passive recipient only, and the animals themselves stand to
gain from the exchange. Having received the gift of the animal's body,
the hunter reciprocates. Animal souls are conceived to participate as
honored guests at feasts where food, speeches, music, tobacco, and
manufactured goods are generously given over to them. Hunter and
prey are thus successively subject and object in an endless cycle of reci-

procities. Ultimately, the roles of human and animal are complementary, for each gives life to the other. The treatment of the remains not only objectifies respect but is said to restore the animal to a living condition.

Some Crees say that hunting is possible *only* with the permission of the animals or the game rulers (cf. Skinner 1911:75; Speck 1935*a*:97, 114; Feit 1973*a*), and the concept of the dominant animal benefactor is elevated to the categorical principle of hunting. From such a perspective, the hunter is subordinate but can influence the animal's choice to give or withhold itself through offerings and prayer. Less dogmatically, some Crees say that it is *itātisiwak*, or "natural," for animals to avoid hunters, and the gestures of respect are intended to overcome this "natural" disposition and dispose them favorably to the event of their death. These postulates are still widely shared and have survived the confrontation with nonbelievers—white and Indian—who kill animals without observing the appropriate forms. Some Crees are bewildered by this, while others point out that Indians who disrespect animals may hunt and trap but do not often do so successfully.

Marx could hardly have imagined an Algonquian labor processs in which humans and animals successively participate as producers of the other, the animals willingly surrendering the "product" of their own bodies and the hunters returning it to them as cooked food, all figured in the idiom of "love." But his reflections on an authentically social labor process are evocative of the benefactive model of Cree-animal relationships.

In your enjoyment of use of my product I would have had the direct enjoyment of realizing that I had both satisfied a human need by my work and also objectified the human essence and therefore fashioned for another human being the object that met his need. I would have been for you the mediator between you and the species and thus been acknowledged and felt by you as a completion of your own essence and a necessary part of yourself and have thus realized that I am confirmed both in your thought and in your love. In my expression of my life I would have fashioned your expression of your life, and thus in my own activity have realized my own essence, my human, my communal essence. (McLellan 1978:31)

Hunter and prey successively renew each other's lives, and, indeed, each seems to realize its innate nature in the transaction, the hunter as supplicant and the animal as benefactor. The willingness to satisfy humans becomes in narrative a virtue of which animals boast and for which they compete (Russell 1898:216).

These images possess obvious affinities with those in some American food industry advertising, particularly those representing animals as eager to become food or participating actively in the cooking process. Some blocks from my home, for example, a meat storage facility displays a sign in which a bipedal steer in chef's hat and apron presides over steaks grilling on a barbecue. One thinks also of the long-running television campaign representing a humanized tuna who aspires to the honor of being caught, canned, and eaten. The "product" of animals is their bodies, and it is these that they offer freely to hunters. The anthropomorphic animals of the dream and the shaking lodge are members of an expanded human society, a cosmic "species" transcending human and animal differences, and paralleling Marx's vision in which each producer mediates with his products the relationship of men and women to themselves and one another. The "communal essence" of human and animal is realized and created in their reciprocal satisfaction of one another's needs. To the question of how many Crees believe this to be a factual description of the human-animal relationship, I would answer none or almost none.

Animal Adversaries

Reciprocity itself possesses, of course, coercive and exploitative modalities that may be inimical to the creation of friendly feelings. When Mauss (1954:1) wrote of "the force . . . in the thing given which compels the recipient to make a return," he might easily have been describing the nuances of subarctic Algonquian sacrifice. The Severn Ojibwas of Ontario, eastern neighbors of the Rock Crees, tell the following story of hunters and moose.

Back in the ancient times, when humans and creatures were living, they stayed in separate places. These humans had a ceremony with their pipe. One evening, just before they were going out hunting, they lit up their long pipe to smoke. That evening the moose were sitting in their lodging. There was a big bull moose, some old moose, cows, young ones, and a young bull moose around the fire. Suddenly, a pipe came through the doorway in their lodging. This long pipe came sailing through the doorway. No one was holding it. It floated by the big bull, the old one, the cows, the young ones. When it reached the young bull moose, he grabbed it and started to smoke on it. The old moose told him: "You have destroyed us. This is what the humans do when they are preparing for a hunt. Now, they will be able to get us." (Fiddler et al. 1985:33)

The sacrificial pipe represents an intersection between exchange and magical control since it is an offering that, once accepted, compels the recipients to make a return. Further, it attributes to the animals—or to the more sophisticated among them—knowledge of this coercive effect. Acceptance of the offering removes the events of the later hunt from voluntary control by the animals, predestining their deaths like events in a dream.

Speck's early writing on boreal Algonquian religion contains intimations of ambiguous power relationships between humans and animals.

The animals know beforehand when they are to be slain, when their spirits have been overcome by the hunter's personal power or magic. They exact also a certain respect, which is shown to them in different ways, though generally by the proper treatment of their remains after they have been killed for their flesh or skins. If this respect is not accorded to them, the animals refuse to be killed or their souls may not be reborn. (Speck 1935b:22–23)

The synthesis juxtaposes the ideas that hunters can "overcome" animals and that animals may "refuse" to be killed, the latter imposing obvious limitations on the efficacy of the hunters' "personal power and magic." The passage thus leaves indeterminate the question of who, in the last instance, exerts the decisive influence over the hunt's outcome. Hunting songs, tobacco offerings, and the eat-all feast all implicate diverse and contradictory models of the hunter-prey relationship. Just as there is no stable resolution of the question of human and animal difference, there is no consistent answer to how the events of hunting are possible.

Rock Crees sometimes talk about hunting in terms that represent animals as opponents or reluctant victims and killings as domination rather than reciprocity. This is the relationship to animals expressed without euphemization in the trickster myths. The verb sākōtiðimīw 'overcome someone' refers to the event of a person prevailing over an adversary, through physical, intellectual, or spiritual means. These images ascribe to the animals a dispositional aversion to the hunt that is either overcome by force or magically dispelled by the hunter. The lines between supplication, manipulation, and coercion are not always explicitly drawn in what Crees say about the hunt, and all these may, of course, be implicated simultaneously in the more observable social relationships that people have with one another. But standing to one side of the animal benefactor is the well-defined image of the animal adversary who seeks to avoid death and against whom physical violence and magical coercion must be exerted. When Crees use "hunting medicine," they say that they are trying to exert a seductive influence over a dispositionally reluctant quarry, and some conceive their *pawākan* as an ally in an adversarial contest with animal victims. The parallels with warfare are suggestive, and it is probable that war-related ritual once practiced against Chipewyans and Eskimos in the eighteenth century resembled the preparations for hunting. Thompson (1962 [1784–1812]:105) observed of the Rock Crees' "Nahathaway" ancestors in the eighteenth century that "they consider the hunter to be naturally a warrior."

"Hunting medicine" usually refers today to substances that are added to baits or positioned elsewhere near trap sets, although some medicines are carried in leather bags by the hunter. They are believed to exert an infatuating influence over the animal or to bewilder it so that it will not perceive the trap or the hunter. These medicines are usually compounded of plant or animal ingredients suggested in dreams. Once discovered and used, medicines or knowledge of their ingredients are sold or given to others. "Hunting medicine" refers also to operations employing imitative magic. In the 1820s, Nelson was told of a hunter who sang and drummed to a birch bark scroll upon which the figures of three moose had been drawn. The scroll began to move, prefiguring a successful kill.

Now he desired in the beginning that if his *Familiar* would have compassion on him, he would render these three moose foolish: that they might not be possessed of their usual cunning &c. The next day we went out—the old man, his son, and myself, a hunting—we were hungry—we walked till late in the day and finding no tracks I proposed our return, but he told me we ought to proceed; for in the low ground beyond a small ridge then near in sight of us, 'we may perhaps find some tracks. I am never deceived when I am answered (i.e., my bark dances).' We soon reached this low Ground and shortly after heard a noise; jumping, running, and breaking sticks. 'Ah, here they are,' said the old man: 'see how their *head* is turned! what a noise they make—how they play—they are foolish.' We killed them all. (Brown and Brightman 1988:69)

This narrative is representative of others in which human beings use the *pawākan* and other resources to overcome animals. In the extreme case, powerful dreamers dispense altogether with the technical requisites of labor and simply summon animals to their camps, as with the great Granville Lake shaman *Manicōs* 'Insect' (Brightman 1989a:152–153). Nowhere in these practices is there reference to the voluntary cooperation of the animal in the hunt. Indeed, the animals are simply "foolish" insofar as they succumb to the hunter's power.

Black (1977:150) discovered that Ojibwas classify hunting techniques of this kind together with love magic as "bad medicine" and concluded that bad medicine techniques are those that subvert the autonomy or welfare of others. The paradoxical status of the animal—that of a person who is also a use-value—creates a moral conundrum in which hunting medicines are "good" for the hunter—since they extend his effectiveness—but "bad" because they interfere with the animal-person's volition. The valuation of hunting medicines as morally ambiguous is seemingly widespread in the subarctic. Skinner (1911:75 [Westmain Swampy Cree]) writes, "In the case of hunting medicine an *evil* spirit appears and gives the hunter a magic draught which imbues him with the power to attract the beasts to his traps" (emphasis added). Like Ojibwas, Rock Crees classify both hunting and love medicines as *macimaskihkiy* 'bad medicine'. A clear correspondence exists between the lethal effects of sorcery on human victims and the use of hunting medicine to kill animals. Nelson's manuscript (Brown and Brightman 1988:180–181) makes clear that the specific techniques of hunting medicine and sorcery—drawing and then disfiguring an image of the victim—were sometimes identical. The idea that hunting medicine is morally objectionable exists explicitly among the Athapaskan-speaking Chipewyans to the north where the use of *inkoze* 'power' against animals reflexively brings bad luck or death (Smith 1982:51–52). In depriving the animal of its volition, the hunter transcends his appropriate role as the grateful recipient of the animals' voluntary gifts. I do not know if some Crees consider such medicines harmful or dangerous because of their effects on animals, but many believe that other "bad medicines" used for sexual seduction or to cause illness reflexively harm the user. Hunting medicine is said to be "bad" because it prevents others from successfully trapping animals in the same area.

Well, people have these medicines. "Fur medicine" they call it. You buy a medicine like that. They call it *ataymaskihkiy* 'fur medicine'. You buy that and you'll be the only one that's killing the fur. You'll bring this other guy bad luck. He won't catch nothing. You'll be the only one who's going to catch fur. Anything you catch, that's yours. The guy with you, he'll have nothing. That's how that medicine works.

This typification associates hunting medicine with a kind of sorcery—the paradigm case of "bad medicine"—in which one person condemns another to starvation by ruining his hunting.

The Adversarial Animal in History and Prehistory

Mythological narratives and conceptions represent the human-animal relationship as overtly competitive and hostile in the past. Both the cosmogonic myth and the trickster cycle presuppose antagonism between hunter and prey. The Plains Crees (Ahenakew 1929) represent the original relationship as one of animal predators and human prey. Rock Crees do not know this myth, although they recognize the predatory *cimiskwanak* of the Plains Cree myth as monstrous beings hostile to humans. Other boreal Algonquian groups associated antagonism between humans and animals with the transformation of the protoanimals into their modern condition. In the 1760s, Henry (1969 [1809]:204–206) was informed of an Ojibwa tradition according to which, after the primordial flood, Nenabozo the transformer deprived animals of the power of speech because their increasing numbers made them a threat to human beings and because they had entered into a conspiracy against humans led by the bear. At the same time, beavers were deprived of speech because they were growing more intelligent than human beings. In the 1790s, Thompson (1962 [1784–1812]:155) learned of a comparable tradition from two Indians in the vicinity of Swan River House. Beavers, originally a terrestrial race of great wisdom and power and immune from predation from humans and other species, were said to have been driven into the water by the transformer, reduced in power, and assigned the role of providing pelts for humans and food for other animals. Both of these accounts describe the intervention of spirit agencies to produce a situation in which animals are represented as equal—or potentially superior—to humans, and in both instances, the powers of the animal beings are materially reduced, in the one case to avert a threat to humans and in the other to provide them with clothing and food.

The Nahathaway, the ancestors of the Rock Crees described by Thompson (ibid.: 94–95, 152), represented the human-animal relationship in immediately precontact times in similarly adversarial terms. In several passages, Thompson reflects on the impact of European technology on the stability of Indian production, and it is likely that his thoughts were influenced by Cree discourse on the topic. The Crees told Thompson that they were vulnerable to attacks from bears, that beaver lodges were all but impervious to the aboriginal technology, and that beavers, themselves secure from human predation, had, in the centuries prior to contact, been steadily expanding their aquatic domain and encroaching on the terrestrial space occupied by humans beings. As a result, the Crees wondered how their ancestors could have survived with the aboriginal technology.

But when the arrival of the White People had changed all their weapons from stone to iron and steel, and added the fatal Gun, every animal fell before the Indian; the Bear was no longer dreaded, and the Beaver became a desirable animal for food and clothing, and the furr [sic] a valuable article of trade; and as the Beaver is a stationary animal, it could be attacked at any convenient time in all seasons, and thus their numbers soon became reduced. (ibid.:95)

These conceptions reproduce the mythological theme of an endangered human race, but it is now European technology that secures human ascendancy. Both Thompson and his Cree clients excessively devalued the efficacy of the indigenous technology, but what is of interest here is the belief that the introduction of European manufactures reversed a previously asymmetric power relationship in which human beings were subordinate to animals. Since the arrival of Europeans and their trade goods was widely understood by subarctic Algonquians as part of the intended design of the creator being or transformer (Brown 1977:46, Petitot 1886:462–472, Bauer 1971:32), the new technology may have been experienced retrospectively by some Crees as another divine intervention on their behalf. These traditions express hostility and fear in Algonquian thought about animals; it is difficult to see in them the benign "grandfathers" who voluntarily yield their bodies to dependent humans. It is interesting to note also that these myths presuppose a cosmic design, imposed by the creator being or the transformer, in which human beings are purposefully located above animals in a hierarchically ordered creation. The spirit agencies intercede on behalf of human beings, suggesting a more anthropocentrically oriented world view than is conventionally ascribed to subarctic Indians.

Hunting as a Game

There exist two additional representations of hunting that occupy transitional positions along a continuum between reciprocity and exploitation. Rock Crees also talk about hunting and trapping as though it is *mītawīwin* 'a game' or as though there exists *sākihitōwin*, romantic or sexual love between hunter and prey. Both images presuppose the animals' voluntary participation, but neither resolves the question of who exerts power over the outcome. Neither of these two images figures prominently in the Cree discourses I induced or overheard, but this may well be the consequence of an uneven record. The conception of trapping and hunting as a friendly game enjoyed by both human and animal is best documented in the societies of the Eastern Crees and is directly expressed in the discourses of the shaking lodge. Among Mistassini Crees, a physical contest is understood to take place in the lodge between the operator and the spirit of a bear, a victory by the operator prefiguring the successful kill of bears in the future. Tanner (1979:138) describes this as paralleling the domination of reluctant animals in the hunt. The ability of the operator to bring the souls of animals into the shaking lodge is recognized also by Rock Crees, and they mention the "contest" between operator—or his dream guardians—and animals as predestining hunting success or failure. They describe these contests, however, as amiable games rather than as coercion and say that the animals enjoy them. A similar interpretation was given at Rupert's House.

Sometimes the bear would see when he goes in the shaking tent; he would say, "If you can throw me flat, well, I'll like that; and if you can't, you won't be able to get anything." They will try it three times. The bear isn't mad, he wants to see if the Mistabeo [operator's dream guardian] is strong enough. (Preston 1975:80)

The preliminary enactment of the hunt in the shaking lodge replicates the later encounters between hunters and animals in the bush. In this respect, the shaking lodge parallels the dream, likewise a template in which the outcome of events that have yet to happen are predetermined. This image of the hunt as a game that animals play to win is, of course, more readily assimilated to the flight or fight responses of the boreal fauna than is the doctrine of their voluntary submission.

The Animal Lover

The likening of hunting and trapping to a sexual encounter is more difficult to interpret. Like the "game" model, this image is best known from Eastern Cree sources where it has been explored

in detail (Preston 1975:198–234, Tanner 1979:138). Rock Cree
metaphors (see chap. 3) clearly liken the hunter-prey relationship to a
sexual one, and there is also evidence for a literal conception of animal
lovers. Both male and female Crees interpret dreams of sex with humanoid partners as referring to and predestining successful hunts of
animals in the future. Since sexual encounters in dreams are conceived
to be factual events in which the dreaming self participates, it may be
that animals are thought to assume human form because they desire
sexual contact with humans. The myths of animal marriages are narrative expressions of such relationships, since they always involve an initiative taken by an animal. It is not clear where to situate the ideology
of the animal lover on the continuum between reciprocity and exploitation; too little is known of the symbolism of the sexual act in boreal
Algonquian cultures. Insofar as the animal is the initiator of sexual
events in dreams, the relationship is imaginably one of *sākihitōwin*, love,
with its resonances of regard and intimacy. It is possible also to infer
that the hunting enterprise places the hunter in a role analogous to that
of a person seeking to overcome and seduce a nominally or actually
reluctant potential partner. Seduction may be assimilated to the model
of domination. If the use of hunting medicines is involved, there exists
an obvious analogy to the exploitative use of love medicines to subvert
the autonomy of a human partner. There is evidence that hunting and
love medicines are conceptually associated. One trapper, who refused
to disclose to me the ingredients of his lynx medicine, readily asserted
that his medicines made him irresistible to lynxes. "It makes them love
me," he repeated with good-natured seriousness.

Killing and Domination

These contrasting benefactive and adversarial models
provide different solutions to the question of whether hunter or prey
determines the outcomes of hunts, a problem that seemingly engages
both practical and philosophical interests. In the most general terms,
Crees say that the relative power of different life forms is visibly manifested in food chains. Those who kill and eat are more powerful than
those who are killed and eaten. This axiom—the antithesis of the dominant ideology of hunting—represents death and killing as experiences
that are not voluntarily cultivated.

While killing and eating animals are represented as events of reciprocity and communion, the same actions acquire different values when human beings are the victims. To kill other humans is to exhibit and secure a "higher" power, as in sorcery.

A guy can kill you anyplace. Like a guy might ask you something. Just to try, you know? If you refuse, then he'll try and kill you. Just for the heck of it. So he gets more . . . like he's deluding himself. Like he's more *macayis*-like ['devilish']. The more people you get, the higher power you get.

The victimization of human beings by the witiko is probably the dominant symbol of evil and chaos in the Cree universe. And it is in the witiko image that killing and eating are most strongly associated with hierarchy, exploitation, and domination. Eating beings different in type from the self need not, of course, entail the same meanings. It is *itātisiw* 'natural' for humans to eat animal flesh. At the same time, there is evidence that Crees construe the predatory relationship of human to animal as similar to the relationship of witiko to human. The analogies are present both in literature and in conventional witiko imagery. In each case, predators overcome unwilling victims by cunning or through exertion of *mamāhtāwisiwin*, power. If ordinary humans beings are the game animals of the witiko, the similitude is represented as the latter's objective perception: the witiko experiences (and addresses) human beings as animals. In the Hairy Heart cannibal narrative (chap. 5), the youngest monster tells his human wife, "When I hunt with your younger brothers, they resemble animals to me." Similarly, the *wīhcikōsis*, small witiko, addresses his intended victim as 'moose' (Brightman 1989a:135). This perspectival distortion is attributed also to persons who are degenerating into a witiko condition. It figures, for example, also in speech ascribed to the Beaver Indian *Mōstōs*, executed as a potential witiko by Thickwoods Crees in Alberta; Mōstōs allegedly perceived his children as beaver and moose (Teicher 1960:100).

The witiko image clearly exhibits fundamental associations of killing and eating with domination and with differential power endowment. The ability to kill and eat indexes the superior "power" of the hunter over the prey, and the food chain becomes a pragmatic index of the relative power of different beings in an intransitive hierarchy. The witiko is known to be more powerful than (most) humans because it kills and eats them, and it is only because it is more powerful that it can do these things. As one of my Cree hosts observed,

That person [witiko] believes he's the supreme guy. He's the best guy. He can kill the other guy. He can even eat him up. It's just that evil spirit, that evil spirit in him that's conducting his mind.

One of the executioners of Mōstōs recalled in his testimony the following conversation that occurred prior to the killing while attempts at cure were in progress.

Napaysoosee told me that when they were holding Moostoos down and trying to make him better with medicine, he threw Mihkooshtikwahnis to one side, and the other men sent him out saying his medicine was not strong enough. When Mihkooshtikwahnis came into the shack where I was, *he told me that Moostoos' medicine was stronger than his, and added "He's going to eat me now."* (Teicher 1960:96, emphasis added)

Exactly the same idea is held regarding the human-animal relationship. In the 1790s, Crees told Thompson (1962 [1784–1812]:155) that in an earlier state of the world, beavers "possessed great power" and that neither man nor other animals "made war on them." Subsequently, they were driven into the water "still to be wise but without power" and to serve as food and clothing for man. Skinner's (1911:76) Swampy Cree consultants likewise explained the modern hunter-prey relationship in terms of asymmetric "power" endowments. Animals die, they said, because their "medicine" is less strong.

The Indians believe that all animals are speaking and thinking beings, in many ways not one whit less intelligent than human beings. The reason that they are less successful in life is that they are unfortunate, their "medicine" is not as strong. The reason that the Indian is able to prey upon them is that he is more fortunate, not more intelligent.

All these texts suggest that killing and eating are irreducibly political acts. The trophic relations in the boreal forest thus provide one answer to the question of differential power. Humans kill and eat animals, while animals, by and large, do not kill and eat humans, and this is the visible measure of human hegemony. When men or women kill animals, the event indexes the hunters' superior power.

But animals possess and regularly succeed in demonstrating the power to escape. When men and women work in vain to kill animals, their failure indexes the animals' superior power. Animals, the bear excepted, do not kill and eat Crees, but they can cause them to labor for little or nothing and they could, in the past, elect to make them starve.

Today, the costs of failure may be a less-preferred diet, a diminished reputation, and reduced disposable income; previously, they could include starvation and death for self and family. The question of power over the outcome of the hunt is therefore insoluble. It is posed anew and renegotiated every time a man goes into the bush with guns and traps. This is the one message of the adversarial model of the hunt in which the outcome of each event is solved by physical or spiritual force.

The benefactive model substitutes for this indeterminacy a continuously superior animal who erases through its generosity the negative significance of killing and eating. The ideology obviates, at least rhetorically, the conjunction of killing and eating with exploitation, for how can the latter exist if the animal can only be killed through its own volition? Thereafter, when the hunter kills, the event indexes the animal's love or regard. The primary symbols of human sociality—food sharing and commensality—are conceived and made to exist between human and animal. The animal's gift of its own body parallels the gifts of meat from one family to another. In return, the animal becomes the commensal of humans through sacrifices and in the eat-all feast. In such a universe, the man who fails to kill the animals he needs has erred in judgment, committed an act that suspended the animals' love and regard. And, as with another human, the damage can be repaired with gifts.

Relations between Models

Contrasts between the benefactive and adversarial models are summarized in table 2, below.

Table 2 *Benefactive and Adversarial Ideologies of Hunting*

	Benefactive Model	Adversarial Model
power over hunting	animal, game ruler	indeterminate
status of animal	benefactor	opponent
outcome of hunt	decided by animal	determined by force
successful hunt	gift/reward	hunter overcomes animal
unsuccessful hunt	punishment	animal overcomes hunter
killing and eating	reciprocity, communion	exploitation, domination

I have had occasion to mention the other areas of ambiguity that suffuse the relation. The animal may be figured as a friendly adversary or a reluctant lover. The *pawākan*, or dream spirit, that acts as the hunter's agent in overcoming animal opponents may itself be an animal. The hunter may construe the decisions that affect his outcomes as those of the game ruler beings who replace or augment the animals as adversaries or benefactors. Human sorcerers may interfere with hunting success, independently of a man's respectful treatment of the animals he kills.

The question of whether Crees believe one or the other model to possess greater validity is exceptionally difficult to address. The same individuals will say and do things suggesting that they take account of both, and I believe that some hunters opportunistically seek to act in terms of both ideologies. It remains possible, of course, that the representations of hunting as reciprocity, exploitation, love, and sport form a set of logically relatable propositions, as conceptions Crees have of their activities, and that I have failed to understand their integration. I believe, however, that the two ideologies are *not* reconciled in Cree thought and that they provide disparate solutions to the identical moral and practical questions. It would be useful to know whether one or the other model was foregrounded during times of crisis, since this would possibly index Cree conceptions of their differential effectiveness. We lack contextual accounts of how Crees and other boreal Algonquians reacted to food crises, but it is interesting that the adversarial ideology was seemingly dominant in one such case described by Thompson (1962 [1784–1812]:101–103). The Cree "Tapapahtum" related his experiences during early winter when he was unable to kill moose. Attributing his lack of success to the absence of the strong winds that facilitate stalking, Tapapahtum sang, drummed, and sacrificed tobacco and herbs to the superior deity Kicimanitōw and to the "Manitoo of the Winds." Ultimately, he traveled to the post and appealed to Thompson, having become convinced that the latter could produce a wind if he chose. Whatever details were omitted or distorted in the original discourse, and in Thompson's record of it, the man's concern focused not on supplicating moose or their deific ruler but on petitioning other spirit beings for the winds necessary to stalk a reluctant quarry.

While I was conducting research in Manitoba, Tanner published *Bringing Home Animals: Religious Ideology and Mode of Production of the Mistassini Cree Hunters* (1979), a superior and detailed study of Eastern

(Mistassini) Cree production and religion. The convergence of our interpretations suggests the centrality of paradox in boreal Algonquian ideologies of hunting. Tanner (ibid.:138) distinguishes concepts of "equivalence-friendship" and "dominance-subordination" which correspond to what I here call "benefactive" and "adversarial" ideologies. He suggests further that the different classes of hunting ritual are divided between the two and are pragmatically stratified in temporal relation to individual hunts. Rituals of control occur before the hunt, while those emphasizing reciprocity and respect occur after. This would suggest that the adversarial ideology possesses the greater facticity since it is the one invoked before the productive event; the animal is only transformed from victim to honored benefactor after the death is a *fait accompli*.

Tanner's generalization partially coincides with Rock Cree practices. Hunting medicine, for example, is used only before a hunt and is talked about as controlling rather than supplicating animals. Similarly, the mortuary depositions of skulls and bones are described in terms of respect and regeneration rather than control, and they occur after an animal is consumed, not before new ones are hunted. However, other practices occur both before and after foraging events, and some implicate both ideologies. Hunting songs, for example, whose significance may include both control and supplication, are sung before hunting, immediately after a kill, and at feasts. Wiping the blood from the snow at a kill site simultaneously objectifies respect (the animal wishes the blood to be removed) and trickery (the blood is an unwelcome mnemonic of death). The eat-all feast discussed in chapter 8 is especially rich in its aggregation of oppositive meanings. These factors make the question of differential effectiveness difficult to answer.

As representations of how hunting works, the benefactive and adversarial models—at the cost of confounding each other's premises— exhibit a certain complementarity. The adversarial model would seem superficially to engage more readily with the hunter's experiences of wounded or trapped animals. Animals that bite, struggle, and lead their hunters on exhausting chases through deep snow cannot readily be defined as voluntary benefactors. Even here, however, instances of animal behavior may be assimilated to the reciprocity model. Who is to say that an animal does not voluntarily enter the trap in which it is found dead and frozen? The Waswanipi Crees described by Feit (1973a) interpret the moment in which the fugitive moose turns to survey its pursuers as the moment of voluntary giving. But there is another point of view from which the entire question of "realism" is irrelevant to the contextual validation of either ideology. As myths, dreams, and the shaking lodge make clear, the sensory data of waking consciousness may be illusory or partial. The lynx strangling in a snare and striking at the trapper may be only a disguise, concealing the benevolent or seductive visitor whose essential nature is only to be met with in the anticipatory dream.

The adversarial model, in contrast, foregrounds human agency, representing foraging labor as a process over whose outcomes men and women exert decisive influence. The unqualified dependency postulated in the benefactive model perhaps affords too little scope to human autonomy. But animals are powerful adversaries. The obvious practical objection to a world in which hunters use their skill and power to overcome animal opponents is that animals sometimes overcome their hunters by escaping. Human superiority is perpetually qualified whenever animals exhibit their own power by eluding hunters and avoiding traps. There is a sense, then, in which hunters may conceive themselves as lacking sufficient power to regularly and predictably prevail over an opponent susceptible only to force. Neither is the power of animals limited to their ability to escape the hunter, which is in itself sufficient justification for coming to terms with them. Bears, an exceptional case, can kill and eat human victims. More broadly, animals exhibit visible signatures of impressive powers whose full scope remains undefinable: they live without clothing and fire, move beneath the water, sleep without food throughout the winter. In their infrahuman aspect, animals figure among the *pawākanak*, the beings from whom humans may derive their safety and well-being. Animal enemies are, in all these respects, potentially very dangerous to human welfare, whatever the control that men may momentarily exert over their bodies.

The animal benefactor, epitomized by the *pawākan* who blesses the hunting project, presents different solutions to the same problems. For the uncertainties posed by an implacable and too frequently elusive opponent is substituted the ambiguity of a superordinate being amenable to petition and sacrifice but omniscient and reactive to human misdeeds. At the limits of human agency, the animal benefactor evokes the surety of food predictably shared, assistance automatically given— without, of course, reliably providing it, for hunters who carefully observe all the forms of respect nonetheless experience bad luck. The adversarial model secures for the hunter autonomy and agency but at the cost of interacting with a formidable animal victim. The reciprocity model secures a benevolent animal friend with whom exchange is possible but deprives the hunter of autonomy. The animal benefactor does, however, possess, on the moral plane, a quality lacking in the animal victim: it ensures that hunting cannot be murder and cannibalism. One explanation for the co-occurrence of two ideologies of hunting is that definitions of animals as victims and enemies are morally insupportable.

The Eating of Friends

A personified animal is first of all one with whom friendship and reciprocity may be created; second, one whose affinities to the human pose a strategic and moral paradox making reciprocity indispensable. One wonders why the Crees possess two ideologies of hunting. Why not figure hunting exclusively as warfare or as love? At the level of the event, a single answer seems inadequate to the disparate outcomes. At the level of structure, the two ideologies reflect the instability of the focal signs. If *mācīwin*, hunting, has values both of love and warfare, it is because the sign *pisiskiw* 'animal' is continuous with the sign *iðiniw* 'human'. Phenomenally discrete in waking life, animals and humans converge in dreams. In consequence, the hunter may be eating the flesh of a being intrinsically different from himself or he may be killing and eating the same. If killing and eating index exploitation and if animals are beings like humans, what differentiates the hunter from the sorcerer and the witiko? Perhaps nothing, in an expanded moral society whose deities teach that "other Indians, as well as thyself, love life—it is sweet to everybody" (Brown and Brightman 1988:57). Animals are beings like the self, but they must be killed and eaten, each death jeopardizing anew the relationship on which life depends—for who is to say that the animal is really reconciled to its death—and indicting the hunter as a murderer and cannibal. The paradox is moral and, like the Judeo-Christian theodicy, ultimately beyond solution. Since the human/animal categories are themselves continuous rather than discrete, it is unsurprising that no single representation of the hunter-prey relationship can be articulated.

Crees eat meat with relish, enthusiasm, and no visible indexes of guilt or conflict. I know no Cree vegetarians. The theme of witiko cannibalism nonetheless plays along the margins of Cree dietary practice. Certain of the myths of animal-human marriages thematize the hidden affinities revealed in dreams: the marriages are fecund, happy, enduring. And when the human partner returns permanently or transiently to human society, he or she renounces the flesh of the animal spouse's species. The dietary rules are upheld also by the progeny of the unions. In, for example, the myth of the hero Maskōkosān, a woman's bear-husband impregnates her and later returns her to her family.

The bear told her she was going to have a baby boy. He instructed her not to tell the people that he was the father. He predicted that the little boy when he became a man would see many bears but he said that the boy should be in-structed not to hunt and kill them. Only if someone who desperately needed meat asked him to kill bears would it be acceptable for him to do so. (Bright-man 1989a: 113)

Those who enter the society of animals and establish family rela-tionships with them must thereafter renounce their meat.

The worldly counterparts of these mythical human spouses of animals are the Cree individuals who refuse to eat particular species of animals with whose members they conceive themselves to possess comparable relations. The possession of an animal *pawākan* does not automatically result in renunciation of the meat of animals of the same species. But such renunciations do often occur. Consider a man who was restored to life after drowning by a doctor who called on a sturgeon *pawākan* for aid.

So he pull me through. The old man [doctor] pull me through finally. Two days [after accident]. And he says to me, "Never eat a sturgeon." That's the one who pull me through [cures me], the sturgeon. "Otherwise," he say to me, "you're a dead man. Drowned."

In all these cases, a personal relationship results in a dietary renun-ciation. Contrary to the dominant ideology, there exist contexts in which *refusing* to kill and eat is the appropriate response, an act of denial that partakes of reciprocation. The implication is that the human beneficiary should renounce the exploitation of the being that has rendered him a service.

These examples from narrative and autobiography concern individu-ated relationships between humans and particular species. But the can-nibalism metaphor exists even beyond these contexts. It is developed most visibly (and not surprisingly) with respect to bear meat, which a sizable minority of Cree men and women refuse to eat. The logic of their abstention was articulated by a Rock Cree from Pelican Narrows who "when asked if he ate bear meat, replied indignantly, 'Do you think I am a cannibal?'" (Cockburn 1984:44). Those who discussed their voluntary bear meat taboo with me said matter-of-factly that bears resemble human beings too closely in appearance and behavior to be edible. It is as if the bear—by manifesting in waking perception signs of the covert infrahuman animal—attracts to itself a more profound ambivalence.

The bear is preeminent over all other species in Cree religious ideology, a status unrelated to its (relatively minor) dietary significance. Crees say that bears possess greater spiritual power than other animals, even exerting control over the availability of other species. It is the animal most consistently and lavishly honored in song, feast, butchering, address, sacrifice, and mortuary disposal. When a bear is killed, the forms become more elaborate and are excecuted more assiduously. This preeminence is doubly significant. The bear is called *āpihtawiðiniw*, half-human. Crees emphasize the intelligence of the bear, its bipedal locomotion, its facial expressions and vocalisms, its omnivorousness, and its anatomical resemblance, when skinned, to humans. The bear, of all animals, most closely approximates in waking perception the infrahuman animals whom Crees experience in dreams and in the shaking lodge. The bear poses more forcefully than other species the moral paradox of eating beings similar to the self, a dilemma reflected both by those who abstain from its meat and in the particular intensity of its religious celebration. The bear is paradoxical, however, in yet another way. Alone among the boreal fauna, the bear possesses the capacity to invert the conventional hunter-prey relationship by killing and eating Indians. In this respect, its power in the calculus of eating and domination is more nearly coordinate with that of humans than that of other animals who manifest their power only by eluding capture. Not only is the bear more human than other animals but it is also more dangerous, and hence it is especially imperative that humans come to terms with it. But as the most hominid and most powerful animal, the bear synecdochically represents all animals that the Crees kill and utilize, symbolizing the ambiguity surrounding the hunting project more generally.

All societies possess conceptions of human-animal similitude, and the humanized animal is of probably universal provenience. There is, however, nothing inevitable to the Cree infrahuman animal image, and, although seemingly paralleled across northern North America, it is not a predictable or universal element in the religious ideologies of foraging societies. Once culturally predicated and then subjectively experienced in dreams, the infrahuman animal acquires a double significance. It is more readily imagined than the nonhuman animal of waking life as rational interlocutor and benefactor. Seemingly, at the same time, it would exacerbate the dilemma of the cannibalism metaphor. But the flesh and skins of animals are represented as distinct and iteratively detachable from the humanoid essence and identity: specifically, the body is likened to clothing that the animal discards. The conceptual split of anthropomorphic soul from zoomorphic body is evidenced in the doctrine that the soul participates with the human hunters in the eat-all feast, invisibly partaking of its flesh, which has been transformed into cooked meat. This meat becomes, in turn, a vehicle of communion through which the spiritual relationship of hunter to animal is intensified and desired physical attributes of animals are appropriated. There is no cannibalism because the similitude of human and animal exists in relation to the soul that is visible only in dreams, not to the body that it transiently exhibits. Or so, at least, the doctrine would have it.

From multiple points of view—moral, aesthetic, and strategic—the animal benefactor is therefore preferable to the animal opponent. The benefactive ideology simply vacuates the postulate that killing indexes subordination and exploitation by figuring each kill as the animal's voluntary gift. But other compromise formations are attested, for who is to be sure that the doctrine is true, or that the animals can be made to believe that it is? Potentially, each hunt is an event that the defeated animal must be made to forget and forgive or to which it must become reconciled. For the animal's disposition toward future hunts is a question of practical interest, just as it is of moral concern. Consequently, the adversarial model intrudes into the mortuary speeches that are part of the reciprocation owed the animal benefactor. These speeches make clear that neither the hunters nor the prey necessarily regard the killing as the latter's voluntary action. One strategy is moral suasion. In a reversal of the usual roles—for animals are endlessly prepared to punish humans for their past misconduct—the animal can be made to believe that it had it coming. Thus, the Cree speech to a cornered bear noted by Thompson (1962 [1784–1812]:95–96) in the 1790s:

The eldest man now makes a speech to it; reproaching the Bear and all its race with being the old enemies of man, killing the children and women, when it was large and strong, but now, since the Manito has made him, small and weak to what he was before, he has all the will, though not the power to be as bad as ever, that he is treacherous and cannot be trusted, that although he has sense he makes bad use of it, and must therefore be killed.

Alternatively, the animal may be imagined as susceptible to deception. In the 1760s, Henry (1969 [1809]:193–194) overheard his classificatory Ojibwa "mother" readily displace the guilt for a bear's death from the Indian hunters and onto himself.

The bear being dead, all my assistants approached, and all, but more particularly my old mother . . . took her head in their hands, stroking and kissing it several times; begging a thousand pardons for taking away her life: calling her their relation and grandmother; and requesting her not to lay the fault upon them, since it was truly an English man that had put her to death.

The same bear was subsequently honored with the customary mortuary treatment, the head decorated, provisioned with tobacco, elevated on a scaffold, and honored with mortuary speeches. But at this stage, the speaker adopted a different strategy. This was to acknowledge candidly what the benefactive model conceals—that animals do not voluntarily choose their deaths, that hunters exploit animals to survive, and that there will either be dead animals or dead hunters.

At length the feast being ready, Wawatum commenced a speech resembling in many things his address to the manes of his relations and departed companions; but having this peculiarity, that he here deplored the necessity under which men labored thus to destroy their *friends*. He represented, however, that the misfortune was unavoidable, since without doing so, they could by no means subsist. (Ibid.)

Predation was here represented as a lamentable but necessary act into which men enter regretfully, and there was no intimation that the killing is a gift-exchange in which the animal voluntarily participates. The speech was a politic apology for an act of violence against a rational being construed by the speaker as similar to himself. To the degree that reciprocity dominates the man-animal relationship only after the kill is already a *fait accompli*, the entailments of "respect"—songs, dances, tobacco, purity, and sacrifices—appear as wergild, as compensations for a crime rather than reciprocations for a gift.

Power Indexes and Practice

The adversarial model accords more closely than its benefactive counterpart with the understanding that non-Indians have of hunting. But both ideologies exhibit from the non-Indian point of view a tautological misrecognition of the effects of foraging labor. Crees say that spiritual influences explain particular foraging outcomes, but it is only in the outcomes themselves that the character of the spiritual influences becomes known and subject to interpretation. In the benefactive model, the hunter's success in killing animals is a phenomenal sign that spiritual relationships are as they should be. The adversarial model is more complex since the issue is differential power. If killing and eating connote and index exploitation and domination, each successful hunting or trapping event is a pragmatic index of the hunter's superior power. The certainty of human superiority is always qualified, however, because each unsprung trap or every unsuccessful hunt—and all hunters have experiences of these—is a pragmatic sign of the superior power of the animal.

Individual events of hunting and trapping thus re-create and continually refigure the hunter's changing consciousness of his or her own technical and spiritual effectiveness. Cree ideologies of hunting acquire from this point of view a particularly material kind of historical efficacy and autonomy since decisions about the technical conduct of production are made on the basis of spiritual considerations. From the point of view of an ecological or sociopsychological functionalism, the "adaptiveness" of these ideologies is problematic. If doctrines of benign animal benefactors or magically efficacious medicines sometimes inspire confidence, the opposite side of the coin is a potentially tragic fatalistic resignation (Brightman 1988). In discussing the witiko complex, Bishop (1982:398) posed the interesting question of the circumstances in which a man would suspend production and resign himself to cannibalism, suggesting that such events reflect not a culturally specific "psychosis" but the fatalistic conviction that animals cannot be killed. There is historical support for Bishop's suggestion. According to Thompson,

Amongst hunters who depend wholly on the chase, there sometimes comes a strange turn of mind; they are successful and everything goes well; a change comes, they either miss or wound the Deer, without getting it; they become excited, and no better success attends them, despondency takes place, the Manito of the Deer will not allow him to kill them; the cure for this is a couple of days rest; which strengthens his mind and body. It is something like the axiom of the civilized world, that Poverty begets Poverty. (1962 [1784–1812]:301).

For consistent failure in hunting is never merely "bad luck" but indexes events over which foragers may conceive themselves to have no control. Harmon's journal (1905 [1821]:58, 66–68) from Swan

River mentions pertinent cases. In January 1802, the two Cree or Ojibwa hunters employed by the post claimed to be unable to kill animals, although Harmon's impression was that there was no scarcity of game. One of these hunters refused to leave his tent for fear that a being identified as the "Bad spirit" would devour him. In July of the same year, what may be the same hunter came to Harmon and informed him that the "Evil Spirit" was frightening animals away from him before he could kill them. Famine, death by starvation, and cannibalism could come about through such conditions as broken tools, adverse climatic conditions, injury, or a scarcity of game, but they could also be created artificially by the inactivity of fatalistic producers.

Reciprocity and Domination

Crees seemingly experience with animals two modes of relationship familiar also in human society, the satisfactions of exchanging with a benefactor-friend and of prevailing over an adversary. In "archaic" economies lacking institutionalized mechanisms for appropriating the labor of others, Bourdieu (1977:171–197) has argued that competitive and exploitative strategies are most effectively pursued through acts of reciprocity that are publicly and officially represented as voluntary and economically disinterested. Strategies of domination—for appropriating the goods and labor (or homage or respect) of others—are present but necessarily exerted through personal relationships that may be transacted with force and physical violence or, more efficiently, with "symbolic violence," of which a characteristic modality is the engendering of obligation through strategic exchange.

Gentle, hidden exploitation is the form taken by man's exploitation of man whenever overt, brutal exploitation is impossible. It is as false to identify this essentially *dual* economy with its official reality (generosity, mutual aid, etc.), i.e. the form which exploitation has to adopt in order to take place, as it is to reduce it to its objective reality, seeing mutual aid as a corvée, the *khammes* [Algerian tenant farmer] as a sort of slave, and so on. (Ibid.:192).

The Crees' benefactive ideology of hunting exhibits suggestive analogies to Bourdieu's constructions of how actors in archaic economies orient themselves in relation to those whose labor or loyalty they desire to appropriate.

In Bourdieu's "economy of practices," actors seek whatever is "rare and worthy of being sought after" (ibid.: 178), including both material goods or services and the less quantifiable commodities subsumed as "symbolic capital," the prestige and renown acquired (among other means) by engendering obligation and by visibly exemplifying the official canons of virtuous conduct. The classic puzzle posed to economism by such institutions as the kula and the potlatch—the nominally "noneconomic" character of ceremonial generosity and redistribution—is resolved in the claim that the symbolic capital accrued through lavish giving is always then reversibly interconvertible with material capital in the form of future claims on the goods and labor of others. The actors seek capital—both material and symbolic— and endlessly transmute each form to the other. From this disenchanted perspective, the irreducible axiom of generalized sharing of meat in Cree (or other foraging societies) could be read as a systemic strategy of domination and interest. Thus A gives meat to B both because to do so accrues "symbolic capital" (or at least precludes its loss) and because this capital is convertible both into future gifts of meat from B and—in the case of long-term asymmetries in quantities exchanged—into domination of B in any context of contending interests, leadership of a foraging group, for example. All this is transacted in the name of disinterested generosity rather than economic calculation, and, as Bourdieu states (ibid.:196), the two become effectively equivalent because, in such a society, generosity is the only way in which private interest can effectively be served.

If domination is read, in part, as the appropriation of material satisfactions from others, then killing and eating animals is patently an instance of it. The Cree conception of food chains as indexing the domination of the eaten by the eaters makes this clear. Between foragers and prey, as among the foragers themselves, there exist no objective and legitimized social mechanisms that automatically secure the surety of material appropriation, for the animals periodically contest it either by failing to be caught or by exacting objectionable levels of effort. Bourdieu (ibid.:192) identifies in "archaic economies" the juxtaposition of physical with symbolic violence as techniques of domination. Force is the objective technical condition of foraging, for the animals do not come voluntarily to the hunter; they must be searched for, made incautious with medicine, trapped, cornered, or surprised. But force is never consistently successful.

In a society in which overt violence, the violence of the usurer or the merciless master, meets with collective reprobation and is liable either to provoke a violent riposte from the victim or to force him to flee (that is to say, in either case, *in the absence of any other recourse,* to provoke the annihilation of the very relationship which was intended to be exploited), symbolic violence, the gentle, invisible form of violence, which is never recognized as such, and is not so much undergone as chosen, the violence of credit, confidence, obligation, personal loyalty, hospitality, gifts, gratitude, piety—in short, all the virtues honoured by the code of honour—cannot fail to be seen as the most economical mode of domination, i.e. the mode which best corresponds to the economy of the system.

The response to force by animals, as by any person in Cree society who resents another's attempts at domination, may always be withdrawal or retaliation.

Cree animal ceremonialism does not conceal the hunters' narrowly material interests, their objective need for meat and skins. Instead, it ceremonializes this need by conjoining it with a misrecognition of the ambiguous power relationships involved in the hunt. Killing and eating are recognized indexes of domination, and hunters thus the exploiters of involuntary animal victims, and it is these relations that are disguised in hunting songs, sacrifices, eat-all feasts, and reverent mortuary depositions. Most trivially, physical violence is concealed by eliminating the evidence: the animal's blood is removed from the snow, its name is not uttered, and its meat is ceremonially consumed indoors in carefully sealed dwellings. More profoundly, the event of violent appropriation is represented to the animal as its own act of disinterested and voluntary reciprocity. The dominant hunter-eater becomes, in the benefactive ideology, the dependent client of animal patrons who control both the desired material commodity (a "truth") and the terms of all transactions through which it may be secured (a "deception"). And the dependent hunters themselves reciprocate the animal's generosity with their own, rendering tobacco, meat, "respect," and all the goods and services that could imaginably evoke either obligation or disinterested friendliness in the animal patron and thus assure an uninterrupted plenitude. The question naturally arises as to the genuineness and the emotional tenor of the beliefs and sentiments implicated in these forms. The benefactive ideology of hunting probably expresses the relation that Crees desire to create with their prey, a persisting personal and moral alignment that secures material interest more reliably than force. The respect and gratitude the forms express are as real as the exploitation they conceal.

The mute, soulless, inferior, and nonhuman animals of the Oblate missionaries may have been welcomed by some Crees because they posed fewer enigmas. The exploitation of animals as food, garments, and laboratory subjects has engendered diversity in opinion and practice within Western traditions predicating biological and spiritual distance between human and animal. Today, the indigenous trapping communities of the North are subjected simultaneously to cultural critique and economic stricture by animal welfare groups seeking the dissolution of the fur industry. There is little prospect for agreement between native fur producers and those who would destroy an industry that is for its practitioners at once a means of participation in the dominant economy, a source of meat, and a traditional mode of relatedness to the land. But many trappers are not strangers to moral paradox in the hunt; they participate in religions that both celebrate and disguise it.

8

"You Got to Eat the Whole Works"

An Eat-All Feast at Watt Lake, 1977

In December 1977, together with his partner Rick, I joined Edouard C. on his trapline. We stayed for four nights in a log cabin that Edouard had built and maintained for some years. During the days, Edouard and Rick set beaver snares through the ice and a variety of snares, leg-hold and conibear traps for lynx, fox, marten, and otter. On the third day, in the early afternoon, we crossed the snowmobile trail of Edouard's relative, Marcel, whose land adjoined to the west. We followed the skiddoo trail into Marcel's camp, two cabins, a lodge, and a canvas tent on a bluff on the shores of Watt Lake.

Marcel was one of the oldest active trappers then resident at Granville. Like Edouard, he alternated residence in Granville with trips to the trapline; unlike him, he was inclined to remain out in his cabin on the line for several weeks at a time. With Marcel were his wife, Pelagie, his father, Antoine, his son, Lawrence, and his son's wife, Pauline. During the course of our visit, Marcel invited Edouard to come to the house again on the afternoon of the following day. The conversation was in Cree, and at that stage, my comprehension was minimal. I heard the now familiar *wīmistikōsiwak* 'white people' but was uncertain of the import. I later surmised that the appropriateness of Rick's and my presence was being debated. Antoine was probably instrumental in the decision that we should return with Edouard the following day. I had given the old man rabbits at Granville, an insignificant gift that nonetheless inspired an improvised "grandfather"/"grandson" relationship. That night, Edouard said, "Marcel is going to do a whole set of beavers. We'll eat good tomorrow." I subsequently learned that Marcel had experienced a dream some weeks earlier which prompted him to trap out a large beaver colony he had built up over several years and to sponsor a feast with the resulting surplus of meat. We had been invited to *wîhkôhtôwin*, a feast of game at which a large surplus is prepared and entirely consumed. I had read and written of these feasts as practiced by Eastern Crees but was unaware that they occurred in Manitoba.

The next day, we reached Marcel's camp in the growing darkness of late afternoon. Marcel's cabin faced southeast toward Watt Lake. The door was set slightly off center toward the right and was sheltered by a plywood vestibule where stove wood and equipment were stored. Considerable effort had gone into cleaning and straightening the cabin. The previous day's collection of clothing, dirty dishes, snowshoes, shell boxes, and other paraphernalia had been neatly stowed or hung on pegs along the wall. The floor had been swept, and several chairs and makeshift seats (an upended pail, an unsplit log of stove wood, the seat from a skiddoo, grub boxes) had been arranged around the walls. Like the cabin, the appearance of the participants reflected formality. Marcel and Lawrence had shaved, and Marcel wore a necktie.

Opposite the door along the back wall of the cabin was a table made of a large sheet of plywood nailed onto two sawhorses. Over this table a clean plastic tablecloth had now been laid and the surface covered with plates, knives and forks, cups, pails, and metal pans. Immediately to the left of the table along the back wall was a cast-iron wood stove that had years ago been brought into the bush, no doubt with considerable effort, from the old Hudson's Bay Company outpost at Granville. On the stove, two large kettles contained four of the beavers that were being served; these had been cut into pieces and put to boil. Another large kettle contained an enormous quantity of macaroni and cheese. Outside the cabin, two more beavers, together with the tails of the four that were boiled, were being roasted on ponasks over a fire in a small cooking tent. Antoine, rather than either of the two women present, was supervising the cooking of the beavers and macaroni. Shortly after we arrived, however, Pelagie and Pauline began mixing and baking bannocks in the oven of the stove.

There were, as usual, no greetings, but small talk about the weather began after we seated ourselves along the wall to the right of the table. Edouard helped himself to tea, and Rick and I followed his example. Antoine periodically went outside to check on the roasting meat. The roasting beavers and the tails were brought in about a half hour later and placed in pans on the table. Marcel and his father busied themselves with cutting up the beavers. Edouard suggested that if Rick or I wanted to go outside, we should do it now because it would not be good manners to leave after we started eating. When Antoine came in the second time from the cooking tipi outside, he carefully closed and secured with a wedge the outside door to the vestibule before closing the inner door. The quantity of food that finally appeared on the table was formidable. The beavers were eventually arranged in five containers. The first pan contained the heads. A second very large kettle contained the segments of the boiled beavers. The roasted beavers were cut and placed in a large metal pan. The beaver tails were cut into pieces, the largest of which was a section of the bone with meat adhering to it, and placed in a fourth tray. Another pan contained sections of beaver fat that had been either roasted separately or separated out while Marcel and his father prepared the meat at the table. The broth from the kettle in which the beavers were boiled was placed in a smaller kettle. Bannocks were piled on a plate, and the macaroni kettle remained on the stove.

When the food was ready to be served, Marcel took a chair in front of the serving table and Antoine seated himself to his right in front of the stove, both men aligning their backs to the rear wall of the cabin. Lawrence sat to their right, his back to the left wall (facing in) of the cabin, facing Edouard, Rick, and me, similarly seated with our backs to the right wall. Edouard sat farthest to the back, followed by me, with Rick closest to the door. The two women sat with their backs to the front wall of the cabin, facing Marcel and Antoine. At this point, Marcel decided that it would be better to position some of the food in the center of the room between us and sent his son outside for another sheet of plywood that was soon propped up on pails. The cloth was removed from the table and placed over the impromptu serving board, which was about two feet off the floor. The kettles containing the beaver heads and the soup were placed on the table.

Marcel rose and began speaking in Cree. As I later learned, he said some words to the effect that he was pleased to have his family present and thanked his father for preparing the feast food. He also thanked his wife for helping to prepare the cabin. He asked that we try to help him eat all the food that had been prepared. He paused and then, speaking much more quietly, expressed his thanks for or to the beavers and all the other animals that he had trapped that fall. He then cut small pieces from each of the kettles and put them into a plate with small portions of macaroni and bannock. He opened the lid of the stove and silently emptied the pan into the fire.

Marcel then took the kettle containing the "soup" in which the beavers were boiled and gave it to his father who drank from it and passed it to Lawrence; he drank, and the kettle then passed successively to Edouard, me, Rick, Pelagie, and Pauline. While it went around, Marcel prepared plates for each of us, serving successively Antoine, Edouard, Lawrence, me, Rick, Pauline, and Pelagie. Of the six beaver heads, Marcel and Lawrence each ate one, and two each went to Antoine and Edouard. Rick and I were given one or two of the disarticulated lower jaws. The women were not served meat from the head or the pieces of the anterior quarters of the beaver, including the forelegs. Otherwise, everyone received a portion of each kind of food available. Tea was served with the meal.

Conversation went on uninterruptedly throughout the meal, Edouard and Marcel switching from Cree to English for the benefit of Rick and me, translating a long and funny story told by Antoine about someone who got the shits from a *wîhkôhtôwin*. Whenever anyone emptied their plate or pan, Marcel or Antoine retrieved it, piled it high with meat, bannock, macaroni, and fat, and returned it. Periodically, pans and vessels containing lean beaver roasted and boiled, roasted fat, beaver tail, "soup," and macaroni were passed. These always went around the room in a clockwise direction, beginning with Marcel and winding up with Marcel's father. I rapidly became full but continued to eat at a measured pace while Antoine looked on approvingly. Antoine instructed me through Edouard to "eat good so you'll make them be lucky." Pauline, who managed to look both respectful and as though she would rather be somewhere else, was the least enthusiastic eater present. At several points, people went outside, carefully closing the inner door behind them before opening the vestibule. I ate five plates of beaver meat, fat, macaroni, and bannock and ended the feast feeling nauseous.

Not all of the boiled beaver meat was or seemingly could be consumed, although I believe more than three-fourths of it was. Marcel and Antoine collected all the plates and other containers and busied themselves wiping or licking them clean. The bones were collected and emptied into the fire in the metal stove together with the remaining beaver meat and the cloths used to clean the dishes and cooking vessels. The skulls and larger bones were boiled in a kettle to remove the remaining meat and then fished out with a stick and wrapped in a clean rag for later deposition on trees. The kettle in which they were boiled was then covered and set off on the back of the stove. The women stowed away the cooking gear and the remains of the macaroni and bannock and then served more tea and also jelly doughnuts, of which everyone ate at least one. After the cleanup, Marcel extracted a suitcase from under the bed and removed a single-headed drum perhaps two inches in depth and two feet in diameter. The drum was given to Antoine who held it vertically in front of him, drumming with a carved stick, and singing so softly that I could not have understood him even if the words had been English. The drum passed successively to Marcel and to Edouard, each of whom sang softly while the others smoked and talked. Although not all the food had been eaten, Marcel's *wīhkōhtōwin* was unquestionably successful in the most important of respects: except for the skulls and other bones, not a trace of the animals taken from the beaver lodge in the preceding days remained. All had gone into our stomachs or into the fire; no meat remained in the camp.

Historical Background

Every inclination of theirs is brutal; they are naturally gluttons, knowing no other beatitude in life than eating and drinking. Their brutality is remarked even in their games and diversions which are always preceded and followed by feasts. There are farewell feasts, complimentary feasts, war, peace, death, health, and marriage feasts. In their banquets they pass days and nights, especially when they make feasts they call "eat-all" for no one is permitted to leave until he has swallowed everything. (LeClercq 1881[1691]:222)

This uncharitable testimonial, set down by the Recollect missionary LeCaron in 1618, is perhaps the earliest reference to the Algonquian ceremonial game feast of the type I chanced to experience at Watt Lake in 1977. LeCaron here described the Laurentian Montagnais near Tadoussac, and it is among the groups referred to today as Montagnais and Eastern Cree that the practice has been most extensively described (Turner 1894; Speck 1935a; Henriksen 1973; Rogers 1963; Tanner 1979). There exist, however, scattered earlier references to the practice among Western Woods Crees in Manitoba and Saskatchewan. The earliest source is Bacqueville de La Potherie (1931:231–232), who described the Crees trading at York Factory between 1697 and 1713 and referred briefly to a mortuary feast at which the guests were required to consume all the prepared food. Isham (1949 [1743–1749]:76) wrote of the Crees trading into York Factory in the 1740s:

They have particular Days they make feasts of which is at a time when several tribes meets together, at such a time, one treats another tell all their provender is gone, Eating from morning to night,—and itt's to be observ'd he who Keeps the feast obliges Every one to Eat what is alotted him, and not to make waste, or to give any of his Companians any.

Graham (1969 [1767–1791]:165–166) described eat-all feasts as practiced at York Factory and Churchill in the late 1700s. Married men and women with children received invitation sticks from the sponsor, while others attended without such formalities; everyone arrived carefully groomed and dressed. The seating arrangement was circular, men, women, and the children and unmarried women successively forming three concentric circles outward from the central fire. The host provided a speech of welcome, while a younger hunter performed the office of server. "Every person must eat what he gets, none is to remain or be carried away." Overfull feasters sometimes hired others to consume the remains of their portion. The feast concluded with dancing and singing. Drage's (1968 [1748–49], 1:219–220) observations on York Factory Crees in 1746–1749 indicate that collective feasts in general were ceremonial affairs even when the leftover food could be carried away by the guests and eaten later. Like eat-all feasts, these occasions were characterized by formal invitations, serving procedures, and seating arrangements; Drage observed also a second seating for women after the men had eaten and the performance of dances and hunting songs. Daniel Harmon (1905 [1821]:313) observed the eat-all feast among Crees in the first decades of the nineteenth century, also distinguishing it from those in which the guests removed the surplus.

Richardson (Franklin 1823:122–123) provided a detailed description of a feast at Cumberland House in 1819 at which he was evidently a participant. The feast was held to celebrate the coming of spring and took place in a specially constructed oblong lodge with the door facing the west. The interior of the lodge was cleaned, supplied with three equidistant fires, and ornamented with wooden effigies of the spirit "Kepoochikawn" and other beings which were oriented to face the doorway. In contrast to some Rock Cree eat-all feasts and to earlier Eastern Cree practice, the door was intentionally left open and unobstructed. Women were categorically excluded. Guests were invited by a "slave" and attended in formal dress, the older men being seated toward the rear of the lodge and the younger toward the door. The sponsor's speech was a prayer for successful hunting and included "an invocation to all the animals in the land." The feast of marrow, pemmican, and berries was served to the guests by one of the younger men. "This was done in new dishes of birch bark and the utmost diligence was displayed in emptying them, it being considered extremely improper in a man to leave any part of that which is placed before him on such occasions" (ibid.:123). The feast concluded with smoking, singing, and dancing.

Nelson also attended feasts of this kind among the Crees with whom he traded in the early 1800s and left a synthetic description, emphasizing once again the obligations of the guest to consume all that was given to him:

Some of them [feasts] are very grand and ceremoni[o]us: the *tit* bits of the animal only, as the head, heart, and liver, tongue and paws, when of a Bear: It is only the Great men that are allowed to eat of these: others again, besides the above, the brisket, rump, and ribbs and very seldom a woman is allowed to partake of them, particularly if it is *un festin à tout manger*, i.e., to eat the whole; tho' there may be sufficient for 2 or 3 times the number of Guests, all must be eaten before day; though in certain cases the Feaster is obliged, and commonly does take part back, providing a knife, a bit of tobacco, or something else attend with the dish. (Brown and Brightman 1988:100–101)

Nelson availed himself of this expedient on at least one occasion:

The Feaster was uneasy and said he would have been proud had we eaten all, for in that case his dreamed would have been propitious: we were obliged to dance also; but when I could stan[d] no more I gave him my knife and a bit of Tobacco and walked off leaving him to settle with his God as well as he could. (ibid.:101)

The eat-all feast was and continues to be a Maussian "totality," simultaneously implicating economic, political, social, aesthetic, and religious principles. Within it are also aggregated the most disparate intentions and dispositions, both among humans and between them and animals.

A Composite *Wīhkōhtōwin*

Raconteurs at Pukatawagan and Granville Lake recalled eat-all feasts more elaborate than the one I attended and provided the information on which the composite account is based. Characteristically, there were major discrepancies between different accounts. I use the present tense below, although Crees say that few eat-all feasts are sponsored today. Some Crees consider the feast to be anti-Catholic, and it is also associated with sorcery. Several persons were visibly surprised when told that I had attended such an event.

Crees use the word *wīhkōhtōwin* to refer to the eat-all feast and to other collective meals associated with indigenous religion. The verbs *wīhkōhtōw* 'someone makes an eat-all feast' and *wīhkōhtōhīw* 'make an eat-all feast for someone' also occur, the latter with connotations of hostile competition. Eat-all feasts are distinguished from *makosīwin*, a general term for collective meals shared by two or more family units. Such events are prompted by any number of circumstances, occur both in the bush and on the reservation, and may involve two families or the entire reservation community: "*makosīwin*, that's 'party'. Like Christmas. When you feed people in a big bunch. That's what it means, *ī-makosīt* ['he/she gives a party-feast'], when you're putting on a party. Another word is *ī-yisākīt*. The real word is *ī-makosīt*, you're putting on a party. You're feeding people. Lots of food. A few drinks." Birthdays, religious holidays, reunions, and marriages are the principal contexts for *makosīwin*.

Wīhkōhtōwin, in contrast, is given in response to dreams, to express the sponsor's gratitude for some good fortune, to celebrate a boy's first kill of a moose or caribou, when an abundant kill is made, to mark the first kill of a species in the fall, often when a bear is killed, and to inaugurate the beginning of the fall and spring seasons. Edward Rogers (1963:65) and Tanner (1979:163) discuss similar prompting circumstances in Eastern Cree communities. In the past, eat-all feasts were typically initiated by the senior active man in a winter hunting group, sometimes by two or more such men. The winter group often included two or more families, in which case preparations involved cooperation between the family of the sponsor and the other co-resident families. Efforts were also made to extend invitations to other winter bands of the same *tōtīm*, or bilateral kindred, as the sponsor, or, more generally, to anyone who could attend. During the period of summer aggregation at Pukatawagan, invitations were extended selectively, but people say that few eat-all feasts were held at this time. Today, I am told, eat-all feasts occur exclusively in trapline camps or in bush hamlets.

Most feasts in living memory were held either in log cabins, in the traditional three-pole lodge, or in rectangular tents of Euro-Canadian derivation. One individual stated that during his childhood, feasts were held in the *sāpohtotawan*, an exceptionally long and narrow lodge built specifically for the purpose. This form is cognate with Eastern Cree *šāpatowan*, (Speck 1935*a*:103), which referred both to the feast and to the large lodge in which it was held and which might also be a multi-family dwelling. Prior to the feast, the vicinity of the dwelling is cleaned of refuse and dog excrement, and the feast lodge itself is cleaned and put in order.

Through rules regulating eligibility to attend, seating arrangements, priority in serving, and quality of food served, the eat-all feast sub-categorizes its participants by vectors of gender, age, and marital status. Some Crees recall eat-all feasts at which adult males were the only participants but state that both women and children are usually present. In the more recent past, no feasts are recalled from which either women or children were categorically excluded. Adolescent and menstruating women, it is said, "wouldn't go." During the Eastern Cree caribou feast described by Henriksen (1973:36–37), women and children entered to eat at two specified intervals, remaining outside for most of the meal. A more complex system was observed by LeJeune (1897*a*:217–219, 279–293) among the Laurentian Montagnais in the 1630s. Eat-all feasts and feasts in general were primarily male affairs; women and children were generally excluded, although widows attended non-eat-alls. In the case of a bear feast, widows and married women with children ate at a preliminary sitting after which the men convened to consume the rest. Adolescent, unmarried, and childless women were required to leave the camp entirely. The significance of marital and parental status is also indicated by Graham's (1969 [1767–1791]:165) description of Cree feasts near York Factory: formal invitations were extended only to couples with children, and the unmarried women and children formed a third circle around the married women who sat in turn in back of their husbands.

Preparation of the feast food normally occurs prior to the arrival of guests, contrary to the practice in a Naskapi feast where the food was prepared by the participants during the course of the ritual (Henriksen 1973). Bears, beavers, moose, caribou, lynxes, and geese are the focal foods consumed at eat-all feasts. Bannock, bread, macaroni, and sweet bakery goods figure as supplementary dishes, while tea and occasionally home brew are the customary beverages. Sometimes feasts include meat from only one species, often a single animal. Meat is served boiled or roasted. Fat is served in the form of liquid grease, hardened slabs, and roasted pieces. The tibia of moose, caribou, and bears are crushed, the marrow extracted, and the bone splinters and ends boiled to yield marrow fat. The head, legs, and some organs of the animal are served separately (cf. Tanner 1979, Henriksen 1973:36–37).

The feast formally begins with the entrance of the guests. Those attending wash and wear clean clothing if available. In some cases, they bring plates, cups, and eating utensils with them to the feast dwelling. Crees describe different seating arrangements. Seating may be in a circle or a rectangle with the participants facing inward. In one account, women and children form a second circle around the men, while in another they sit along the walls of the front of the cabin while the men occupy the rear opposite the door. The latter arrangement corresponds most closely to the Watt Lake seating where women faced the rear of the house and the two oldest men faced the door. In male-only feasts, the same correlation of the rear and front of the cabin with notional or actual higher and lower status is reproduced in a separation of senior from junior men, as in Richardson's desciption. More prosaically, most accounts describe family groups of men, women, and children seated in clusters next to one another. Some people simply say that "people sit wherever they want."

Before the food is served, the sponsor addresses the guests briefly, thanking them for coming and instructing them that all the food has to be consumed. In some instances, the sponsor also addresses a discourse to one or more *ahcāk* beings, requesting that hunting and trapping success and other benefits be forthcoming. Whether or not these beings are formally addressed, portions of each of the prepared foods are burned in the stove. The recipients are addressed as "grandfather."

The cooked foods are placed in kettles, pans, or other containers in front of the "owner" and server. Food is given to seated guests by the server or placed on plates that are then handed around the circle to the guests. In some cases, a container of food is itself handed around, each individual removing a portion and passing it on. Food travels clockwise, a direction intended to replicate movement from north to east to south to west. The order of serving sometimes interferes with the clockwise movement of food. The status distinctions regulating attendance are reproduced also in the order of serving. In cases where there is insufficient space to seat everyone simultaneously, older men eat before younger men and adult men before women and children. When all are seated together, the same distinctions organize the order in which individuals are served. Dietary rules to which women are subject reproduce those conventionally observed. Compliance with such rules is said to be more punctilious at feasts than at secular meals, and certain meats ordinarily eaten by women perhaps shift into the male-only category at feasts. At the same time that the feast subcategorizes the participants, it figuratively unites them through a kind of hypercommensality. It is said that the feast will not secure positive effects unless each guest eats part of each variety of food for which he or she is eligible.

In some eat-all feasts, including the feast at Watt Lake which I attended, the entrance to the lodge or house is closed, and after this point the lodge is ideally kept sealed. The sponsor in such cases instructs the guests not to enter or leave the lodge. In the event that a participant needs to leave to defecate or vomit, the prepared foods are covered with cloths or placed temporarily in sealed containers. This aspect of the feast is not elsewhere mentioned in connection with Western Woods Crees but is amply documented among the Eastern Crees prior to the middle of the present century. Clouston's account (Davies 1963:36–37) of an Eastern Cree eat-all feast makes clear that the food was carefully covered each time the lodge was opened. The caribou marrow and bear meat were covered with clean skins while the guests entered. "Every person was then ordered to keep in the tent and all the holes on the tent carefully closed up." Later, when pans were brought from outside, the food was again temporarily covered.

In *wīhkōhtōwin*, meat cannot be removed from the cabin or lodge. Ideally, all is consumed, but if this proves impossible, it is kept in the kettles or pans and guests can return later to eat it. If food still remains, it is then burned. Again, this practice is documented among the Quebec groups. Clouston observed, "None of the feast durst be taken out of the tent" (ibid.). A *faux pas* by Lucien Turner at an Ungava band feast in the 1880s gives additional information:

I soon departed, and attempted to take the remnant of the pemmican with me. This was instantly forbidden, and information given me that by so doing I should cause all the deer to desert the vicinity and thus make the people starve. (Turner 1894:323)

In the recent past, Eastern Crees have replaced this rule with the requirement that uneaten food be carefully wrapped before guests remove it from the feast lodge or cabin. More generally, in the Quebec-Labrador area, all cooked food carried outside dwellings is ideally covered (Rogers 1963:67, Cooper 1934:34, Tanner 1975:298). The idea that the food should remain in the lodge is strongly expressed by Rock Crees.

It's dirty to take that kind of food around [outside]. Makes it get dirty. So the old guy [the feast giver] tells them they gotta' eat all of it. Eat the whole thing up.
Q: What do they do if there's too much food to eat?
You can't take the food out of the house. Lose your luck. Maybe get nothing to eat any more. Where they make it, I suppose [?] So they can burn it. But you got . . . you're supposed to eat the whole thing.

The careful disposal of uneaten food, bones, crumbs, and other residue at the Watt Lake "eat-all" parallels Eastern Cree practice. Tanner's (1979:166) statement about the Mistassini, that "it is as if every morsel must be accounted for," is apt. Like other large bones from game animals, the bones of animals eaten in wîhkôhtôwin are either burned, placed into the water, or, especially in the case of skulls and antlers, suspended in trees. Smaller bones and even very minor residue like crumbs are burned in the stove. This concern with residue extended even to the cloths used to clean the dishes and vessels used in cooking and eating; these also were put into the fire. The singing of individual hunting songs with which the Watt Lake eat-all feast concluded is seemingly the attenuated form of more elaborate musical celebrations that formerly involved collective dances.

The Feast as Gift

Of the ceremonial meals of the Crees at Lac la Ronge in the 1820s, Nelson wrote,

We denominate these Feasts, and from their own Term it would seem they so mean; but I consider this again as a premature interpretation which I have not leisure to explain: I consider them rather as *sacrifices*—indeed they may perhaps rather be esteemed as partaking of both. (Brown and Brightman 1988:100)

Wîhkôhtôwin is first of all a sacrifice and partakes of the sacrificial logic delineated by Henri Hubert and Marcel Mauss (1964:97): "This procedure consists in establishing a means of communication between the sacred and profane worlds through the mediation of a victim, that is, of a thing that in the course of the ceremony is destroyed." The significance of the victim in this scheme derives from its successive identification both with the sacrificers and the deity to whom it is given over. Because of its attachment to both, the animal victim serves as a conduit, effecting through its ingestion a communion with the deity and simultaneously committing the latter to a delayed obligation, "for the gods who give and repay are there to give something great in exchange for something small" (ibid.:15).

Already identified with animals, the meat, as a gift from humans to nonhumans, acquires further significance through its symbolic identification with the humans who have become the owners of it. Notionally, the meat becomes the "property" of humans when the animal is killed. Since the meat is typically interpreted as a gift from the animal to its hunters, the sacrifice is directly reciprocative, a sharing of the food with the beings from which it came. The identification of the meat with the sacrificers is effected both by the cooking process that transforms it into a cultural product and by its ritual manipulation inside the feast cabin.

The cabin or other site becomes a space in which facets of human society are celebrated and reified. Specifically, the feast is a carefully orchestrated sequence of symbolic actions whose referents are drawn from different domains of Cree political, economic, and social practice. These actions symbolize human society or, more specifically, nīhiðawīwin, the particular modality of social existence in which Crees understand themselves to participate. It is in this respect surely significant that the eat-all feast and such other visible manifestations of man-itōkīwin as drumming and the shaking lodge have—like Cree marriage practices, clothing, hairstyles, and language—been the subject of a sustained cultural critique by Euro-Canadians whose effect has been the identical one of objectification. The lodge is cleaned, and the participants wear clean clothes. The feast is the site of elaborate cooking procedures and of aesthetic performance: song, drumming, and, in the past, dances. The seating arrangements, the division of the meat, and the order in which it is served symbolize and presuppose the status distinctions organizing relations between men and women, seniors and juniors, unmarried and married, parents and the childless. At the same time that the feast is a sustained diacritic of status differentials, it stands for community and for the primordial and axiomatic morality of sharing meat. The commensality and extravagant sharing (for more food is provided than can easily be eaten) of the eat-all feast are symbols that refer both to their quotidien counterparts and to the essential notions of sociality with which they are associated. The feast is a gift given by one man to others or a collective event in which multiple families cooperate. The rules effect a hypercommensality. At the Watt Lake eat-all, the kettle containing the "soup" was passed from hand to hand, each participant drinking from the same vessel. Similar sharing of a single dish is reported from Eastern Crees (Skinner 1914*a*:204–205; Speck 1935*a*:104, 107; Rogers 1963:43). Further, it is required that all participants eat each kind of prepared food for which they are eligible.

The eat-all feast is in all these respects the antithesis of liminal *rites de passage* or of reversal rituals that suspend or invert conventional practices. The meat is identified with the social condition of the sacrificers not only through cooking but metonymically as the focus of a rite in which Cree society is ceremonially enacted. The relevance of a distinction between human and animal (or more broadly nonhuman) spheres is suggested by a curious piece of exegetical testimony. Some thirty years or more before the oppositional values of nature and culture became a structuralist aria, Speck (1935*a*:234) interviewed a Montagnais who interpreted distinct designs on his pack strap as representing "animals" and what Speck interpreted as "the artificial world of man." It is the latter artificial world that is enacted in the feast lodge.

The practices of closing up the lodge or cabin from within and covering the meat indicate an obvious concern with the creation of a privileged space. Unlike the shaking lodge, which is erected in the bush, the eat-all feast typically occurs within an existing dwelling, possibly one proximate to others in a bush hamlet. The feast thus occurs *ōtīnahk*, in town, or *kapīsiwinihk* 'in camp' rather than *nōhcimihk*, in the bush. The movement of animals in production is from the bush into camp or town and then into individual dwellings. As noted earlier, the bush is considered to embody *pīkisitōwin*, cleanliness and holiness, in contrast to human spaces, which contain *wīðipisiwin* 'dirt'/'pollution'. The closure of the feast dwelling interposes a barrier between *pīhtoka-mihk* 'inside' and *waðawītamihk* 'outside' (Tanner 1979:90). One meaning of the closure is to secure a clean space for the meat and for the *ahcāk* beings to whom it is made over. "Outside" becomes, from this point of view, the polluted human space around the feast dwelling.

The dwelling is simultaneously a conduit within which transfers of food and more immaterial commodities between humans and *ahcāk* beings can be effected. From this perspective, "inside" is a sanctified human space and "outside" is the sphere associated with the sacrificial recipients. Tanner's analysis (ibid.:93) suggests that Mistassini Crees

(Quebec) situate the "spirit world" to which sacrifices are addressed in the upper air. Rock Crees do not identify or situate cosmographically a single spirit world. Rituals involving spirit-human communication almost invariably presuppose barriers or distance, but these may involve underwater, underground, and remote terrestrial domains as well as the upper air. The game rulers, for example, are somewhat vaguely said to "live in the bush, but in a particular place." The closure of the lodge may be understood to create contiguity between the interior and a more generalized domain of *ahcāk* beings which traverses and perhaps invisibly parallels and coincides with the space conventionally perceptible to humans. At the same time, the lodge must leave a passageway open, either for the entrance and departure of *ahcāk* beings or for the transmission of the sacrifice. When the structure is sealed, the only visible opening is the smokehole in the nineteenth-century lodge or the stovepipe that now replaces it in lodges, tents, cabins, and houses. There perhaps exists a parallel here with the shaking lodge that spirit beings are said to enter through apertures at the top. These openings are, of course, vertically aligned with *ispimihk* 'above', or what one Cree called in English "the top of the earth." Crees do not elucidate a theory of burning in sacrifice, beyond saying that that conversion of meat into smoke "feeds" the sacrificial recipients, allowing them to appropriate an invisible simulacrum of the meal. It is interesting to compare Richardson's account of an eat-all feast at Cumberland House, Saskatchewan, where the entrance to the lodge was kept open throughout the meal (Franklin 1823:122–123). The door opened on the west, and wooden effigies of *ahcāk* beings were positioned inside the lodge to face the same direction; the meal was arranged so that no obstructions were interposed between these images, the doorway, and the west. More needs to be known of the symbolism of doorways in boreal Algonquian cultures, but here the doorway is seemingly a transformation of the stovepipe or smokehole. It is also significant that Rock Crees are careful to avoid physical contact between the doorway and slain animals introduced into a house.

The most observable moment of sacrifice in the feast is *pakitinikīwin*, the burning of a portion of each variety of feast food in the stove. These offerings sometimes accompany other meals. The most singular aspect of this practice to me was the minuscule quantity of food made over. In *wīhkōhtowin*, however, these gifts are peripheral to another economically convenient doctrine: the *ahcāk* beings invisibly appropriate both the meat eaten by the feasters and the implements employed.

You kill a bear. And after you eat the whole bear, whatever you use on the bear—dishes, cups, whatever you use—when you're eating the bear, after you eat the whole bear, after it's gone, everything's gone, that's when he picks up the ones you were using. He's got it in his pack and he goes back living again and he's got all your junk. He goes back in his den next year and comes back to life. But he's got all your junk with him. All the food, the cups and plates, anything you use eating it. It's got everything.

I was told by one person that the *ahcāk* beings are immaterially present in the lodge, by another that they ate the food "somewhere else," and by a third that they are simultaneously near and far; most people did not know. The idea that the food eaten by the feasters is taken by spirits is probably of wide subarctic provenience. It is not specified in Eastern Cree ethnography, but Landes's (1968:34) southwestern Ojibwa teachers understood bear feasts in this way. The *wīhkōhtowin* juxtaposes in a single act two practices that W. Robertson Smith (1956) imagined as successive stages in the evolution of sacrifice: the feast in which sacrificer and deity are commensals and a separate offering is made over to the latter. And it is consistent with the logic of Algonquian economic sociality that the spirits should be represented as commensals of humans. It is not only gifts of meat between families but events of collective eating that symbolize and create friendship and reciprocal dependence. In the eat-all feast, the hunter feeds the spirits in the act of feeding himself. Indeed, the assistance of the spirit is what allows the feaster to eat excessive quantities of food:

He's [the feaster] not eating, it's not him that's eating. By the time he's done eating, he'll have nothing in the gut. Somebody else is eating it. It's disappearing as you eat. It's not in your belly after you're through eating. *ī-mamāhtāwisit*, that's a witchcraft. Well, somebody's got to be . . . you can't eat one hindquarter on the beaver. You'll be full. Never mind the rest of it. Fifty pounds of meat there. A big beaver. You got to eat the whole works.

Just as secular reciprocity subsumes both gifts of food separately consumed and shared food collectively consumed, and just as the eat-all feast is simultaneously a gift from a sponsor to others and a collective meal, the sacrificial movement encompasses both a separate gift of food placed in the fire and a collective meal with the spirits.

Crees identify four kinds of entities as the recipients of food in *wīhkōhtōwin*: the "soul" of the game animals being eaten, living game animals of the same species, game rulers such as *Mistamisk* 'Great Beaver', and the *pawākan* of the man who makes the feast. The latter two are unexceptional, since it is assumed that *ahcāk* beings desire offerings of cooked meat. The notion that the animals derive satisfaction from the meat of their own worldly bodies is more enigmatic. One naturally reflects on the logic of a system in which powerful beings superior to man can be persuaded to discharge benefits in return for a sacrificial victim over which they already exercise dominion or with which they are, indeed, identical. On this paradox, Robertson Smith (1957:393) cited Jehovah: "I will take no bullock out of thy house, nor he-goats from thy fold; for every beast of the forest is mine, and the cattle on a thousand hills." Ingold (1987:247, 253), in a discussion of sacrifice, seeks to resolve this ambiguity that is central to Cree and perhaps other boreal Algonquian sacrificial practices: "An animal, quite simply, cannot simultaneously be the focus of veneration and an object [i.e., victim] of sacrifice, for towards the former man is the subordinate party, towards the latter he is dominant." Ingold concludes that the recipients of sacrifice in forager and pastoralist societies are everywhere beings of the type of the game ruler, not the souls of the animals themselves. Crees do not conceive events of sacrifice this systematically, and neither are the power relationships unambiguous or continuous. In Cree religious thought, animals or humans endlessly exchange dominant and subordinate statuses from one foraging event to the next. The question of characterizing one or the other as "dominant" could only be approached by induction from multiple discourses in which Cree foragers articulated their subjective understanding of their spiritual control over hunting. There is every reason to assume substantial variation in these understandings between different individuals and for single individuals over time as they revalue their self-conceptions in the light of worldly successes and failures.

More paradoxical is the cannibalistic implication that animals derive gustatory satisfaction from consumption of their own flesh. But this is precisely what some Rock Crees understand to occur. "Oh, sure, they [animal souls] take all the food," I was told by a man who seemed surprised that I would ask. "It's like they're there in the house with you. But at the same time, they're way off somewhere else." Again the ethnography of the Eastern Crees is consistent, confirming this doctrine with respect to the burnt offerings: "Certain parts of the bear's flesh are burnt ('given to its soul to eat') including a small piece of its heart" (Skinner 1914a:204). At a Mistassini beaver feast, the names of different species were called out as the portions of food were placed in the fire, suggesting also that the flesh of one species may be used to feed the souls of others (Lips 1947:389). The most explicit expression of this autocannibalistic doctrine known to me occurs in a myth told by the Salishan-speaking Thompson Indians of British Columbia in which deer provision themselves by hunting each other, killing and eating the animal forms of their companions who then regenerate and participate in the meal (Thompson 1966:169–173). In *wīhkōhtōwin*, the animal is simultaneously sacrificial victim (as cooked meat) and among the sacrificial recipients. The problem of the identification of the meat with the deities is from this point of view already solved. All this suggests an implicit distinction between the infrahuman essence of the animal, which dines with the feasters, and the transient bodily form of the animal manifest in worldly experience.

Another facet of the feasters' hospitality remains to be discussed. Crees say that the eat-all feast was formerly the occasion for collective singing and dancing, a fact confirmed by the documentary sources. The hunting songs individually sung with the drum by Edouard, Antoine, and Marcel were reflexes of more substantial musical entertainments intended to honor and please the animals and other beings. Thompson (1962 [1784–1812]:81) wrote, "All their dances have a religious tendency, they are not, as with us, dances of mere pleasure, of the joyous countenance: they are grave, each dancer considers it a religious rite for some purpose; their motions are slow and graceful; yet I have sometimes seen occasional dances of a gay character." The earlier reports from Hudson Bay indicate that eat-all feasts—and feasts in general—usually concluded with collective singing and dancing (Drage 1968 [1748–49],1:219–220; Graham 1969 [1767–1791]:165–166, Franklin 1823:124). Dances might involve either all-male, all-female, or mixed participation. The animals and other *ahcāk* beings are both fed and courteously entertained.

Communion

Hubert and Mauss (1964:39–40) wrote that sacrificial victims, when eaten by the sacrificers, transferred to them "the religious qualities that the sacrificial operation had kindled within them." Likewise, Robertson Smith's (1957) reconstruction of the early stages of Semitic sacrifice, whatever its relevance to the Semites, has Algonquian resonances since it postulates a theology in which, as in *wīhkōhtōwin*, sacred animals were at once sacrificial victims and the commensals of the sacrificers. According to Robertson Smith, food was understood to be constantly refashioning the flesh and other physical substance of the eater. For him, then, the sacrificial meal unites men with sacred animal both socially as commensals and physiologically through ingestion. By eating the sacred animal, the sacrificer "creates or keeps alive a living bond or union between the worshippers and their god. . . . The notion that by eating the flesh, or particularly by drinking the blood, of another living being, a man absorbs its life or nature into his own is one which appears among primitive people in many forms" (ibid.:313). And, as he might have added, among Catholics, a parallel Crees acknowledge when reflecting on the mass.

Apart from the obvious advantage of having a good meal, the rationale for forging such consubstantial bonds with deity is rather underspecified in the classic theories of sacrifice. The Algonquian testimony is quite specific. That Crees understand food (in most circumstances) as constitutive of the eaters' flesh is clear from certain of their foraging strategies, for example, the practice of harvesting hares only after they have fattened themselves on jackpine needle bait. Eating is thus the transformation of animal flesh into human flesh. As such, it is more than a means of materially renewing life. It also facilitates communication with animal beings through dreams and allows humans to acquire characteristics of animals that, it is said, they would otherwise lack. In a happy circularity, eating meat confers aptitudes and experiences congenial to the project of hunting successfully and thus being able to eat more meat. In this respect, the eat-all feast rehearses perhaps the most compelling of reasons for eating gods: the appropriation of the gods' superior endowments. In this respect also, the feast is continuous with the logic of the dietary rules to which individuals subject themselves and with that of other eating practices in nonfeast contexts. That eaters appropriate qualities that have been imparted to the meat by the sacrificial practice of the feast itself is not clearly evident; the meat may always contain such benefits. At the same time, the special cooking methods used and the rules requiring total consumption suggest that the meat at eat-all feasts is in exceptionally sacred condition.

I have already made reference (chap. 4) to the idea that a man both amplifies his dream guardian's "knowledge" of him and facilitates "getting in touch" with it by eating meat from an animal of the same species. A more general conception was recorded from an Eastern Cree:

"To eat that which is alive [meat], is certain to bring on animal visitors in dreams" (Speck 1935a:190). At a more immediate level, there is evidence that animal flesh contains within it just those endowments that allow humans to function most effectively as hunters. I was told by one man that he drank raw moose blood from freshly killed animals in the hope that this would impart to him in reverse the "invisibility" of the stealthy moose to its stalkers. I was not explicitly told that the food consumed in eat-all feasts has such effects, but there is evidence, admittedly paraphrased, that Eastern Cree feasters hope that this is so. At Eastmain bear feasts, the heart was eaten "in order that he [hunter] may acquire the cunning and courage of his victim" (Skinner 1914a:204). Likewise, four Montagnais stated that they ate raw marrow from the metapodial bones of caribou "in order to obtain the same courage (*vaillance*), the same nerves, as this caribou had" (Harper 1964:58). These cases focus attention on particular meats, undoubtedly aligning with the intersecting male/female, older/younger, and idiosyncratic dietary classifications adumbrated earlier. The Eastern Cree literature also refers to rules proscribing the use of utensils while eating certain meats at eat-all feasts (Davies 1963:37, Skinner 1914a:204–205, Comeau 1923:87), conjecturally the inverse of the prescribed utensils that insulate pubescent women from the forces of the external world (cf. Lévi-Strauss 1969:336). It should be noted that this appropriation of animal attributes is not secured only by ingestion; charms of diverse kinds and animal hide clothing (cf. Skinner 1911:54) effect the identical goals through contiguity. Beyond the pragmatic desire to assimilate the courage, strength, endurance, stealth, and warmth of animals, these Algonquian doctrines of consubtantiation intersect with more imaginative themes—those exemplified by the trickster's animal impersonations, for example (Brightman 1988:79–80,86–87)—and perhaps with more diffuse moral and spiritual concerns.

Negative reciprocity

Wîhkôhtôwin epitomizes the dominant model of reciprocity between humans and animals, but it connotes also the relationship of adversarial conquest. If the sacrifice symbolically conjoins reciprocity between hunter and prey with a ceremonial reciprocity among hunters, it also associates the ambiguities and tensions of human food sharing with the adversarial relationship of hunter to animal victim. Meat-sharing practices, I am told, have undergone changes in the course of the present century. Prior to the 1950s, Crees spent most of the year in small multifamily groups in the bush. Older people described a system in which any large game animal was apportioned among the proximate households, either in a formal division or by casual gift.

The mode of distribution of meat following the capture of animals by Crees is today conditioned by the social context of the settlement in which it is butchered and consumed. When two or more families are co-resident in the bush, meat obtained cooperatively is divided among the producers. Other meat is usually maintained "privately," each family storing the surplus of its own kills. Notionally, each person "owns" the meat he or she hunts or traps. In fact, each person is subject to rules dictating that the meat must be shared with co-resident families. What is objectively "owned" is the right to consume meat one has produced, to give it to other families whose supplies are significantly lower (or who simply happen not to have quantities of that kind of meat on hand), and to receive meat in like circumstances. Gifts of food are readily exchanged between the commensal units, resulting in a general distribution of the surplus over time. At Granville Lake, for example, fish retrieved from Johnny Bighetty's fishnet circulated rapidly around the hamlet, whenever it was lifted. Fish were given immediately on the lake to those who helped lift the net; these, in turn, shared with other households. Feasts are another occasion during which the meat produced by one household is shared with others.

Enormous prestige accrues to kills of big game, and potentially any gift of such meat can carry the connotation that meat givers are superior to takers, the more so as the persons involved are differentially accomplished (cf. Tanner 1979:177). Recipients probably resent those who consistently hunt and trap more successfully than themselves. They are, in any case, imagined as liable to such feelings since jealousy over hunting skill is said to provoke sorcery. Resentment is also sometimes expressed toward those who consistently receive without commensurate reciprocation, often in the form of a criticism of the meat takers' lack of initiative or skill. A third conflictual aspect of meat sharing derives from the sedentism and increased density of post-1950s settlements. A hunter who brings meat either to the reserve at Pukatawagan or to a larger bush settlement such as Granville must make decisions from among multiple eligible recipients. Attempts are sometimes made to conceal both the meat and the identity of the specific recipients from among all the possible ones. These attempts at secrecy are often unsuccessful, leading sometimes to resentments that are only assuaged by later gifts of meat. Prior to the sedentism of the 1950s, this problem must have been negligible during winter when the number of co-resident families entitled to gifts of meat was limited and each family was engaged in foraging. During summer aggregation, comparable problems perhaps existed. To these ambiguities must be added the supposition that there are surely some persons in some contexts who do not wish to share what they have killed.

The social tensions provoked by sharing should not be exaggerated. I have never encountered more generous people in my life than at Puka-tawagan and Granville Lake. People visibly take satisfaction from giving, receiving, and reciprocating gifts of meat, equipment, and services. It is my impression that most Crees experience this sharing not as an onerous genuflection to official morality but as one of life's pleasures. The ambiguities nonetheless exist: the acts of giving and receiving meat that mean and create equality and community may also engender hierarchy and distance. They persist despite the presence of diverse mechanisms whose effect is to deny differentials in hunting skill: the categorical proscription of bragging and the use of mediating parties to transfer meat from one household to another. Lee (1979:244–249) documents similar measures among the !Kung. In the conventional eat-all feast, there is no apparent reference to these conflictual aspects of quotidian food sharing, unless the prestige diacritics of the dietary rules can be considered as such. The feast seeks to create between humans and *ahcāk* beings the generalized reciprocity among humans to which it refers and of which it is a ceremonious instance.

The associations of food sharing with competition and hierarchy are, however, directly expressed in a distinct kind of eat-all feast that is sym-bolically the antithesis of the one described thus far. The feast becomes not a celebration of community but a shamanistic duel between human adversaries. The significance shifts from how much meat the collectivity can cooperatively consume to which of two contending parties can eat the most. Nelson recorded a myth describing the conflict of the hero Nēhanīmis with the monstrous "Hairy Heart beings" (chap. 5). The opponents attempt to overcome one another in simultaneous competi-tive eat-all feasts.

"Now," said Nayhanimis, addressing his family, "we must take 20 beavers, one for each man of them (meaning the hairy breasts [hearts]) and make a feast. If it turns out that we be able to eat these twenty Beaver, and they not, then we shall be superior to them and have the upper hand." The Beaver were cooked accordingly: he took his rattler which he shook to the tune of his songs—performed the usual ceremonies, and they eat the whole twenty beaver with ease. . . . The Hairy Breasts on their return did the same as Nayhanimis and cooked also 20 B[eaver] thinking that his [Nēhanīmis's] band did really consist of that number. They eat but everyone was already full and yet more than 3/4 of the feast remained. (Brown and Brightman 1988:77)

Here, each beaver in the feast symbolizes a member of the opposing party, and consumption symbolizes the domination that it magically ensures. The myth illustrates the association of the eat-all feast with competition and aggression, recalling the more amiable competitive eat-all feasts of some Great Lakes Algonquians. It is interesting that the transitive verb *wīhkōhtōhīw* 'feast someone' has connotations of this murderous competition absent both from the corresponding intransitive and the noun that refer to the conventional feast.

Like a guy might cook two beavers. Two swans. He give you one swan and he have one swan. One swan apiece. You got to eat your swan, the whole thing. If you don't, well, you're not sure to see next year. You make sure you wouldn't see next year. You're going to die between . . . in no time at all. You're a dead man. If you do eat the whole thing, well . . . you're alright. The guy is trying to kill you. If he can't eat it, well he's a dead man. After about a month after, he'll die. Just because . . . who's going to be the big *okimāw* ['leader'], you know? He's trying to get you. Either you or him. If he don't eat the whole thing, it means he can't do it.

I do not know whether Crees actually participated in competitive feasts with enemies, but there is little reason to doubt that such challenges were sometimes issued and accepted. In these cases, the meat is a medium for rivalry between human beings. The symbolism, however, is consonant with the adversarial model of hunting. The meat, as in the Nēhanīmis myth, stands for the opponent, and the latter's destruction is effected by devouring it. These duels between human adversaries suggest that consuming all the food prepared at conventional eat-all feasts possesses also the significance of a collective and aggressive act of magical control over animal adversaries. For the effectiveness of the feast is clearly proportional to the quantity eaten. Each animal eaten may, from this perspective, correspond to and prefigure the successful kill of an individual animal, or the same animal, in subsequent hunting, just as each beaver represents a member of the opposed party in the Nēhanīmis myth. To eat all in the feast is thus a coercive act that prefigures domination of animals and secures in advance the event of eating well in the future. It is tempting to see also in the closure of the lodge an anticipatory capture of the animal in the future. Crees employed fences and impoundments in caribou hunting, surround techniques in stalking, and, of course, a variety of traps. Possibly the "imprisonment" of the animal in the lodge magically precludes its worldly escape from such devices and stratagems.

If the gift of meat between families sometimes connotes the superiority of the giver, this is consonant with the ideology of reciprocity in human-animal relationships that represent the hunters as the dependents of superordinate animal benefactors. The previous chapter suggested that the adversarial model provides an alternative to this self-conception of dependency. There is no indication that the prestations made over to animals in the eat-all feast connote human superiority. There is, however, reason to suppose that the closure of the lodge possesses the additional meaning of concealment. The entire complex of "respect" practices that the eat-all feast epitomizes has as its function to redefine as voluntary reciprocity events of hunting that the animals may experience as exploitation: theft of life, body, and autonomy. Speck (1935a:202–203) first raised the question of the polysemy of the closure in Eastern Cree feasts:

It is hard to see what the main religious aim of this feast may be. Whether intended to placate spirits of slain animals or whether it is a breaking forth of indulgence in carnal appetites—since we observe that measures of deceit are taken to preclude animal spirits from witnessing it—it is certainly an orgy of repletion.

In the same context, Speck cites exegetical testimony that "the openings of the lodge are kept closed lest the animal spirits who are thronging outside enter or obtain a glimpse of the proceedings inside." Three aspects of the feast—the closed lodge, the eat-all practice itself, and, in latter day Eastern Cree feasts, the covering of cooked food taken outside the lodge (cf. Tanner 1979:167)—all have the effect of concealing events in which animal flesh is eaten. When Turner (1894:323), for example, attempted to remove food from a Naskapi feast lodge at Ungava, he was told that to do so would result in the caribou deserting the vicinity. Tanner's (1975:308) first analysis of Eastern Cree feasts proposed that they implicate two discrete categories of spirits, benign beings who are the recipients of sacrifices and the hostile game rulers from whom the feast must be concealed. It is, however, clear that in other Eastern Cree groups the feasts are understood to be required by the game rulers, not objectionable to them, as in the Naskapi feast observed by Henriksen (1973:35). Tanner's later analysis (1979:173–176) of concealment strategies as expressing more general adversarial elements in human-animal relations is identical to the interpretation I offer here. The animal friend is within the cabin, partaking of the feast. The animal victim is outside where it can be kept in ignorance of its fate. They are really the same being. Rather than presupposing discrete classes of spirits, the paradoxical juxtaposition of display and concealment seems attuned to the disparate and ultimately unknowable moral evaluations that animals and their rulers bring to the hunt. In *wīhkōhtōwin*, eating is reciprocity and communion: the ingestion of meat simultaneously feeds the spirits and suffuses the human body with their essence. But eating is also domination, and the eat-all feast is concurrently a display of eating as reciprocity and a concealment of eating as exploitation. One naturally reflects on the significance of covering the blood at kill sites with moss or snow, likewise a practice that gratifies the animal friend and tricks the animal victim. Tanner (1975:306) suggested, following Jean Briggs, that the practices of eating all the food and wrapping it outside the feast dwelling parallel the tactics available to the owner of a surplus who desires not to share with others: it must be secretly consumed or concealed. The analogy is apt, but, less than concealing a surplus from animals with whom the feasters do not wish to share, the sealed tent, the empty plates, or the covered vessel conceal the transformation of the animal into food and its ingestion by humans. Eating is no less culpable than killing.

The strategy of concealment raises the question of the degree of awareness of human comportment that Crees ascribe to animals. With respect to certain other spirit beings, there is no question: Crees conceive themselves as subject to a surveillance reminiscent of the panopticon.

"How durst thou doubt anything I say—knowest thou not how clearly and distinctly objects are discovered and seen in a plain, from an eminence; and my abode is in the regions above—I see every object as distinctly as you see at your feet, doubt then no more, and never hereafter call our Power into question."

"Aye!" replied some of the other spirits. "We not only see all that you do, however secret and hid you think yourselves, but we also hear every word you utter." (Brown and Brightman 1988:41–42)

Similar omniscience on the part of animals seems to be presupposed in all the objectifications of respect: rules of address and reference, mortuary deposition, dietary practices, music, and the eat-all feast itself.

Eating and Regeneration

Beyond reciprocity and duplicity, *wīhkōhtōwin* is an instrumental involvement of humans in the reproduction of the game animals. Both the sealing of the cabin and the disposal of the inedible remains are implicated in this regeneration. Since the feast food is covered when the door is opened and uncovered only when the door is sealed, everything appears as if some immaterial or intangible property of the meat itself is intended to be immobilized or contained within the cooking vessel and the cabin. Further, the meat is carefully channeled to prescribed destinations, the entire conduct of the ritual serving to ensure that the meat is either further contained in the feasters' stomachs or disposed of in the fire. Speck (1935a:209) makes this association, whether from his own inference or Eastern Cree exegesis is not clear.

At the feast, all the holes in the covering of the lodge, whether it was of bark, skin, or canvas, were carefully closed so that the spirits of the beasts whose flesh was being consumed would not go out and in consequence, fail to return to life in the others of their kind to be reborn. Only after all the meat had been eaten would the lodge be opened.

Here the spirits conjoined with the flesh are preserved from dispersal and nonreproduction by being confined within the lodge. The most obvious analogy is with menstrual blood, which, like the meat-soul of the animals, "flows out" of an open container to the outside where it becomes a "wasted" substance that does not result in reproduction. The eat-all lodge is itself a simulated womb within which the game animals are prepared for the event spoken of as *akwanaham otoskana* 'they cover their bones' in which they regenerate as mature animals or are reborn in fetal form. Concern that the random physical dispersal of animal products may have negative consequences is expressed in other contexts. The Cree discourse at the beginning of the book inveighs against "scattering" meat, blood, and furs around a dwelling or settlement.

The attention focused in most feasts on grease, fat, and soups from water in which meat or bones have been boiled reflects Cree tastes but is also directed toward regeneration. The indigenous theory of reproduction identifies menstrual blood as the substance from which the flesh and blood of the fetus are built up. Simultaneously, the fetus feeds on and forms its bones from semen. Menstrual blood that is retained in the womb eventuates, like the flesh contained in the lodge, in reproduction.

They got this special way of eating the moose. They mix some of that [raw] marrow from the long bones with the fat from the bones. Kinda' like pemmican. They smash that bone to make fat. Boil it up in a big kettle. And then they mix it. And they say you're . . . making a little moose. You make it over again from its bones by mixing it like that.

Inferentially, the marrow fat is semen and marrow is menstrual blood in this equivalence that can be generalized to diverse fat products and soups, on the one hand, and to all boiled and roasted meat, on the other. This may explain the importance attached to the soup and to the roasted fat that were served separately from the meat at the Watt Lake *wīhkōhtōwin*. Henriksen's (1973) detailed account of an Eastern Cree eat-all feast seemingly exemplifies the same scheme: marrow from caribou metapodial bones was mixed both with boiled meat and with fat boiled from the marrow and bone splinters. Ultimately, not only hunting but also cooking and eating are metaphors of sex and reproduction.

Simulated regeneration was probably represented in an event at an Eastern Cree feast in 1820 which occurred immediately after the guests arrived and before the tent was sealed.

A painted deerskin [caribou] was then wrapped around a child who could crawl but not walk. The child thus wrapped was laid outside the door, and its mother began to call it to her. The child was so wrapped that it could only move like an earthworm and though it had only about two feet to crawl, about ten minutes elapsed before it could move that distance. The innocent cried in vain for assistance, though within reach of its mother's arm where she sat calling it to her. As soon as the child had got inside the door, the Indian began to beat the drum and sing for a little time. (Davies 1963:37)

The child's labored progression from the outside through the doorway and into the lodge symbolized both the quotidian introduction of caribou meat into the household and the ingress of animal souls invited to partake in the feast. That the child is induced to crawl into the lodge under its own power suggests perhaps a simulation of the caribou's voluntary entrance. Put another way, the child prefigures caribou that will come to hunters with the same determination with which the child seeks to rejoin its mother. The significance of moving "like an earth-

worm" is obscure, unless the actors desired to impart a similar immo-
bility to their prey. The closure of the lodge after the child's entrance
is metaphorically a capture. As a metaphor of regeneration, the child
represents an animal soul that is recovered with flesh within the lodge,
sent outside, and then brought in again. This particular theatrical
moment microcosmically represents the whole ceremony it precedes
and also the larger cycle of human-animal reciprocity in which it is embedded. *Wîhkôhtôwin* reclothes the animal with flesh. It returns to the
bush, there subsequently to be killed and once again brought into the
lodge in the capacity of honored guest.

While the symbolism of rebirth is not directly implicated in the
digestion of meat or the burning of offerings and residue in the stove,
both practices are implicitly connected with regeneration. Eating, burning, and mortuary deposition of bones are the only appropriate ways of
disposing of animals, aside from the uses made of skins and some
bones. All must be appropriately disposed of or the lethal intervention
of hunters in the animal's cycle of existence becomes permanent instead
of momentary. The life force of the animal is imagined to be as partible
as the meat in which it inheres, and everything must be concentrated,
kept together, and rechanneled.

They say that it just comes up again and again. It will die and go back to life
again. But then if you get it in your trap. Or you shoot it. Well, that's taking it
away. You've spoiled it. Like there's holes in the skin now. Or you cut it apart
for the skin. It's [animal] all ruined. So you have to be careful to put it back.
Careful how you cut it up. Because it won't come back like before. Not if you
don't treat the bones right. It'll stay dead forever.

The Auspicious Famine

The eat-all feast is simultaneously communion, reciproc-
ity, trickery, and regeneration. Any given feast is contextualized as one
moment in a perpetual series of transactions between humans and game
animals. Each eat-all feast necessarily refers to two other moments and
possesses in this sense a dual time reference to the past and to the future. The feast simultaneously reciprocates nonhuman others for the
gifts of meat already procured—especially those eaten in the ritual—
and initiates or anticipates subsequent prestations of the same order.

Like any gift of meat between humans, it simultaneously discharges an existing obligation of the giver to the recipient and re-creates a new obligation. In the dominant ideology of reciprocity, it is animals and the game rulers who are the meat givers in the two events of hunting that the eat-all feast—as a gift initiated by humans—concurrently reciprocates and anticipates. These gifts from animals to humans are themselves transactions interpreted as responses to previous gifts given by humans. In the first moment, the animals are "given" to the hunter, a prestation that may be prefigured in dreams or through other media but that is consummated when an animal is shot or taken dead from a trap. Hunters receive the animal corpses both as gifts and guests, eating the meat and employing the skins in trade or domestic manufacture.

The eat-all feast represents a reactive communicatory moment initiated by humans. The techniques that are used to induce contiguity between humans and the animal sphere are precisely those that differentiate the eat-all from secular meals: collective attendance, the sealing of the lodge, the special treatment of the food, music, and the enactment of status differentials. These operations place both the lodge and the meat—as sacrificial victim—into a sacred condition appropriate to communication with *ahcāk* beings. The eating of the feast food is a complex act in which multiple functions and influences intersect. Through the food, from the nonhuman others to the hunters flow modalities of *mamāhtāwisīwin*, or power. Eating is also regeneration, the mingling of fat and meat in cooking and consumption prefiguring conception. Eating is also giving, for the animals and spirits partake in the feast as invisible commensals.

As an instance of reciprocity, the feast is doubly significant. First, through burnt offerings and the act of consumption itself, the food and other objects are made over as gifts to *ahcāk* beings. In this respect, to eat all is to give all. But it is also to receive all. Crees say that wasting usable animal products is offensive to the animals and their rulers (cf. Strong 1929:284–285, Speck 1935a:83). In dealings with animals, total utilization is to gracious acceptance as waste is to refusal: uneaten food connotes a gift taken lightly or an unwillingness to receive. The eat-all feast thus discharges in a particularly conspicuous way the obligation to receive. Here also, relations between hunter and prey parallel relations between hunters. I never committed the error of refusing food but had occasion to observe the negative social effects of refusing alcohol. LeJeune (1897b:249) had similar experiences with the Montagnais in 1634:

It is giving a sort of insult to a savage to refuse the pieces which he offers you. A certain one, seeing that I had declined what my host had offered me to eat, said to me, "Thou dost not love him, since thou refusest him." I told him it was not our custom to eat at all hours; but nevertheless, I would take what he would give me if he did not give it to me quite so often. They all began to laugh; and an old woman said to me that, if I wished to be loved by their tribe, I must eat a great deal.

The eat-all feast is simultaneously an event of receiving and of reciprocation, relative to the gifts of animals that are consumed within it. It is in this respect that the magnitude of the feast becomes important: the more the feasters eat, the greater the magnitude both of their graciousness and of their return gift.

As one moment of reciprocity with nonhumans, *wīhkōhtōwin* should structure economic relations between camp and bush such that the animals occupy the role of meat giver in future interactions. This is, above all, the *raison d'être* of the feast, and it defines the most fundamental meaning of the act of eating everything and destroying all remains. Lévi-Strauss (1966*a*:225) summarized the significance of the sacrificial victim in the Hubert-Mauss scheme as follows:

Sacrifice seeks to establish a desired connection between two initially separate domains. . . . It claims to be able to do this by first bringing together the two domains through a sacralized victim (an ambiguous object in effect attaching to both) and then eliminating this connecting term. The sacrifice thus creates a lack of contiguity, and by the purposive nature of the prayer, it induces (or is supposed to induce) a compensating continuity to arise on the plane where the initial deficiency experienced by the sacrificer traced the path which leads to the deity, in advance, and, as it were, by a dotted line.

It is through the destruction of the victim that human sacrificer and divine recipient exchange roles. Contiguity between giver and receiver is effected through the victim, an offering made over by the sacrificers. When the victim is destroyed, the contact is severed, ideally inducing the recipient to discharge future benefactions. In *wīhkōhtōwin*, hunters initiate contiguity between human and animal domains, and the sacrificial victim is the meat. Already attached to the animal domain, the meat is identified with the sacrificers by being cooked and ceremonially eaten. The importance of bears derives from a similar logic: transitional between categories, they are especially appropriate mediators between hunters and animals. Contiguity is created both through the ingestion of animal attributes in the meat and through the commensality and sharing that the feast effects. The feast redefines the meat, originally a gift from animals to hunters, as a gift from hunters to animals. Both the contiguity and the statuses of human host and animal guest continue as long as the meat remains. When the last of the meat is destroyed, contiguity is broken, and the statuses are exchanged. The absolute destruction of the meat, primarily by ingestion, ideally provokes resumption by the animals and game rulers of the status of generous benefactors. If the quantity of food consumed is important, the fact that none must remain is essential to the logic of sacrifice.

There is another meaning to the destruction of the meat-victim in *wīhkōhtōwin*, consistent with but distinguishable from its position in the global scheme developed by Hubert and Mauss. It is a more markedly local meaning in that it implicates both the anticipated benefaction of successful hunting and the principle of generalized sharing that suffuses Algonquian economics. The feast begins with an abundant surplus of food and terminates with the absolute absence of food. The scarcity may be objectively realized since I am told that at some feasts everything edible in the camp was consumed. In other cases, only the food cooked for the feast is consumed, the people retaining other supplies. Or, as among Eastern Cree, the absence of food may be simulated by concealing the remains of the feast. In any case, the feast concludes in a genuine or simulated condition of famine. All the food is disposed of, and the hunters are thus left figuratively bankrupt. Gifts of meat between hunters occur automatically whenever disparities exist between stocks on hand. "Only a very bad man," I was told succinctly in Cree, "fails to share food with other people." Even more morally axiomatic is the obligation to share food with the destitute, those who have no food at all. In this connection, consider the formal resemblance of *kitimākisiw* 'someone is destitute' to *kitimākīðimiw* 'relieve someone's distress'. By devouring all the food on hand, hunters manufacture a condition of indigence that animals and other beings in the expanded moral society will feel themselves bound to remedy. The discrepancy between the infinitely renewable supply of animal flesh in the bush and the poverty of the hunters is ceremoniously dramatized. Further, the hunters represent themselves as hungry beings in the throes of famine. The feast premises a moral universe in which the *ahcāk* beings will not see people starve. "It is believed," Speck wrote (1935a:93), "that caribou spirits constantly visit the hunter in his dreams when food is exhausted." By fabricating a condition of scarcity, a simulated famine, *wīhkōhtōwin* seeks to evoke the moral response appropriate to the tragedy of genuine starvation.

9

"The More They Destroy, the Greater Plenty Will Succeed"

Introduction

The symbolic constitution of mythological narrative and ritual practice is readily agreed on anthropologically, and, indeed, these subjects have long enjoyed an unofficial status as the privileged topical venue of assorted semiotic, symbolic, structuralist, and hermeneutic anthropologies. Less agreed on is the pertinence of these theoretical specializations to the constitution of the labor process, traditionally the provenience of the various Marxisms, economisms, sociobiologies, and ecologies. The remaining three chapters make an affirmative argument in this respect, suggesting that the technical conduct of production—in this case hunting—is no less "symbolic" than ritual in its structure, ideology, and practice and consequently no less refractory to interpretive elucidation. The corollary, developed at greater length in the conclusion, is that the existing materialist theories are insufficient in themselves as specifications of the *letzter instanz* determinations of foraging labor. The following chapters make these arguments for harvesting strategies, resource scheduling, management, diet, and animal classification.

During the 1740s, James Isham, chief factor at York Factory on Hudson Bay, wrote, "It's a little strange the Breed of these beaver does not diminish greatly considering the many thousands that is killed of a year" (1949 [1743–1749]:143). Isham's mild puzzlement proved to be prophetic, since, by the early 1800s, both beaver and big game had been depleted in the Churchill River drainage and in others areas south and west of Hudson Bay (Ray 1974:117–124). Although other factors—disease and predation by Europeans, for example—may have been implicated, the active role of Crees and other Indian groups involved as fur producers and post provisioners in the trade is difficult to dispute. These game shortages have been interpreted, on the one hand, as the inevitable effects of technological innovation and expanding Indian consumer demand for trade goods. On the other, they have been seen as the result of the historic breakdown of indigenous religious rules with overt management effects on animal populations. Neither interpretation is sustainable except through the most selective use of the documentary evidence. Technology and demands for European manufactures had, at best, mediated influences on the game shortages. Further, there is evidence that Algonquian spiritual conceptions did indeed play a formative role in the shortages but not as specified in the existing literature on Indians as aboriginal conservators.

Since the Crees and other boreal Algonquians involved in the fur trade were the victims of these environmental tragedies, the question naturally arises as to how and why they killed caribou, moose, and beaver in quantities sufficient to initiate population declines. According to the conventional reading, Indians increased rates of predation to satisfy their desires or needs for trade goods, and these rates eventually exceeded the reproductive rates of the animals. There is no question that Crees needed and desired European goods, but it is far from certain that the additional level of hunting necessary to procure them would cause the animals to decline. First, their demand for goods remained largely unchanged from the 1700s until 1821 when the Hudson's Bay Company merged with its competitors and established a monopoly. As Ray (ibid.:68) writes, "the Indian's demands for goods during this early period, and indeed, essentially until 1821, was relatively inelastic." Second, competition kept the price of goods low. As a result, it is likely that the Crees and other Indians involved in the depletions could have satisfied their desires for trade goods without increasing rates of predation to a level that caused population declines in animal resources. The chapter addresses this paradox: the animals were depleted, presumably as a result of the Indians' fur trade involvements, but the Indians' motivation for depleting them remains obscure.

Cree Foraging before the Fur Trade

Only the most general remarks are possible regarding prehistoric foraging by Crees in the Churchill River drainage. Following French (1961), I employ here the convention of marking with an asterisk reconstructions of prehistoric and early contact conditions for which there exist no positive evidence but which can provisionally be assumed given knowledge of later conditions. The boreal forest is a type case of a specialized ecosystem, exhibiting short food chains, low species diversity with relatively large numbers of each species, and high entropy rates manifested in extreme fluctuations in animal populations. Apart from the effects of human predation, animal populations in the boreal forest are subject to both random and cyclic fluctuations of varying duration and regional extent, influenced by climatic variables, forest succession, water levels, food chains, disease, and fire (Waisberg 1975, Smith 1976). The distribution of species on the landscape also alters from one winter to the next, a factor especially relevant to caribou. *Both prehistorically and during the fur trade, Cree populations in the Churchill River drainage thus had experience with hunger, and perhaps with starvation, as a result of game scarcity, especially when important resources were in convergent decline. *They also had recourse to the characteristic hunters' strategies of movement to more abundant areas or to alternate foods. *Food resources were ordinarily abundant with intermittent and usually transient periods of scarcity in midwinter and spring. *Resource scheduling was sensitive to seasonal or climatic variables facilitating access to particular resources, but delayed consumption of preserved meat was minimal; people foraged, ate until food on hand was exhausted, and then foraged again. *No intentional management of resources through selective harvesting was practiced. *The diet breadth was wide and included most of the species later sought by the traders.

Whether human predation resulted in animal shortages prehistorically in the Churchill River drainage is unknown. *Strategies included stalking, still hunting, and drives of migratory caribou and wood bison. *The indigenous wood-stone-bone technology of bows, arrows, lances, ice chisels, and traps probably provided the potential for such events (cf. Martin 1978:16–17), but there was no motivation for the intensified labor necessary to deplete animal resources. *Rather than occupying camps for long periods and making increasingly extended logistical foraging expeditions to and from the base, Crees made frequent residential moves except in summer when abundant fisheries were exploited. Paine (1973:303) posits a "principle of least effort" for northern foragers, suggesting that they either leave an area or switch to a different subset of resources when returns in meat begin to be perceived as disproportionate to effort. *Residential moves typically occurred well before convenient resources were exhausted (see Woodburn 1972:203). Frequent residential movement may have had unintended conservation effects on animals. Movement would occur before resource populations within the foraging area were depleted. Furthermore, if beaver, moose, and caribou populations are density dependent—that is, if fecundity and growth rates decline when populations exceed "carrying capacity"—transient human predation would keep them well below the ceiling and in a condition of rapid growth (Paine 1973:303).

The Early Fur Trade

Although some Crees from the Churchill River drainage may have interacted with Indian middlemen at Lake Nipigon, direct involvement in the fur trade probably began after 1670 with the construction of the Hudson's Bay Company establishments on the coast of Hudson Bay. *Churchill River Crees traded initially at York Factory and later at Fort Churchill after its construction in 1717. There were diverse alignments with the posts. Some Crees, the "Home Guard," were employed as provisioners and remained near the posts throughout the year. Others worked as provisioners in the summer and then went inland to hunt for the winter. The majority seemingly remained inland for most of the year and only came down to the bay to trade (Drage 1968 [1748–49], 1:181). Among the latter were Cree and Assiniboine middlemen who blocked the coastal access of Blackfeet, Chipewyans, and other inland groups and exchanged with them their used trade goods for furs that they then brought down annually to the bay. Ray (1978:355) suggests that most Crees trading at York Factory before 1763 were middlemen, and this may also have been the pattern at Churchill. The proportion of Crees from the Churchill drainage who bartered rather than hunted the furs they brought to the bay is not known. Presumably, most lower Churchill River Crees themselves traded directly at the coast rather than dealing through middlemen. Involvement in the trade required some intensification of hunting since Crees had alternative uses for animals skins as material for their own garments. But most of the animals sought by the traders were eaten. Relatively more time was now allocated to hunting beavers and other smaller furbearing animals that were staples in the trade, and this may have alternated consecutively with big game hunting throughout the year. Bishop's (1984) detailed reconstruction of the early fur trade at Fort Albany undoubtedly applies in many respects to the Crees hunting inland on the Churchill River, although animal biomass was greater in the latter area.

The New Technology

The corollary of the economistic thesis is technological: the trade simultaneously provided the incentive to exterminate animals and a more lethal inventory of taking devices to do so. Innis (1962:5) argued this point in the appropriate idiom:

The heavy fixed capital of the beaver became a serious handicap with the improved technique of Indian hunting methods, incidental to the borrowing of iron from Europeans. Depreciation through obsolescence of the beaver's defense equipment was so rapid as to involve the immediate and complete destruction of the animal.

The new technology was doubly significant. First, it is clear that everyone concerned understood the situation as one in which Indians were now dependent on technological means that they could not themselves manufacture but only acquire through trade. Daniel Harmon (1905 [1821]:63) wrote of the Saskatchewan Crees in 1801,

The Indians of this quarter have been so long accustomed to use European goods, that it would be with difficulty that they could now obtain a livelihood without them. Especially do they need firearms, with which to kill their game, and axes, kettles, knives, etc. They have almost lost the use of bows and arrows; and they would find it nearly impossible to cut their wood with implements made of stone and bone.

Similarly, Crees in the Churchill River drainage told Thompson (1962 [1784–1812]:95) that "if they were deprived of the Gun, they could not live by the bow and arrow and must soon perish." There is evidence that concern over dependency was present in ceremonial contexts (Brightman 1990:114–115). Whether a return to aboriginal manufactures was objectively impossible is another question, but the Crees' conception of dependence created, in any case, the factual condition of it, regardless of its reversibility. Crees needed the new goods both to hunt for their own consumption and to obtain animals that could be exchanged for the goods. The indispensable weapons and tools were, however, only a subset of the inventory, and there is no evidence that dependence on them necessitated the increased rates of predation that later caused the beaver shortages.

More significant were effects of the new weapons on the time and energy costs of Cree foraging. The degree of increased efficiency must, of course, be evaluated in terms of individual items and the strategies in which they were deployed. The arquebus and matchlock muskets traded to the Crees in the seventeenth and eighteenth centuries often exploded, misfired, broke at low temperatures, and had limited long distance accuracy (Smith 1987). Arrows were superior to muskets in accuracy, safety, and rate of fire. Muskets, however, had greater range and were perhaps most effective when the small size of winter trapping groups precluded cooperative bow hunting (Bishop 1984:42). Possibly, guns were more efficient than the bow in stalking and killing moose and solitary caribou, allowing hunters to make lethal strikes at a greater distance. It is unlikely that guns gave any particular advantage in hunting migrating caribou, which continued to be taken with arrows or lances at fences or from canoes at river crossings. Guns probably facilitated killing waterfowl, and they were used extensively in traps set for smaller furbearers (Graham 1969 [1767–1791]:22–25). Iron ice chisels and axes were undoubtedly superior to their indigenous counterparts for cutting into beaver lodges during winter or through ice for winter fishing. We know too little of the aboriginal fishing technology to assess the impact of fishnets, but these were probably more productive than the indigenous fish traps and almost certainly more productive than angling. Knives, hatchets, and scrapers probably reduced the labor time of diverse tasks that could then be redirected to foraging. The effects of steel traps and castoreum bait are discussed below.

While the effectiveness of the indigenous technology is undervalued in the literature, it is probable that the new taking devices materially increased the efficiency of Cree foraging, substantially increasing the capture of animal biomass per unit of time spent hunting. As discussed below, Crees reduced the number of furs they brought to the posts when offered better prices since it then took fewer furs to obtain the goods they required. One can speculate by analogy that the result of increased foraging efficiency may have been a net reduction in the average time devoted to it, as compared with the precontact period, even though some additional animals now needed to be taken for commercial purposes. Another change was a reduction in time spent manufacturing the indigenous material culture. By trading, the Crees both increased the returns of their foraging labor and displaced onto the posts the tasks of providing many of the technological means. For the Crees, as for the Montagnais quoted in the 1630s by LeJeune, "The Beaver does everything perfectly well, it makes kettles, hatchets, swords, knives, bread; and, in short, it makes everything." Or, as another put it, less diplomatically, "The English have no sense; they give us twenty knives like this for one Beaver skin" (LeJeune 1897*b*:297–299). While the traders were implicating the Algonquians in the world system, the latter were reciprocally maintaining the traders as a source of cheap goods whose equivalents they would otherwise have had to manufacture themselves. Increasingly, the relationship assumed the characteristics of a rudimentary division of labor.

"Imaginary Wants" and the Leisured Trapper

Obviously, the fur trade resulted in intensified predation, since at least some Crees were killing additional numbers of animals for commercial purposes. According to Hutchinson (1972:4), for example, "the Indian" exterminated animals "because he was only human. The white man offered him material goods—iron and woolens and gewgas and alcohol—which he could not resist." Here, the Algonquians awaited only the necessary technology to exterminate boreal wildlife, their motivations to do so objectively given by human nature and the catalyst of English manufactures. To acquire trade goods, Indians labored to kill more animals, an automatic response to their encounter with the European market. In Wolf's (1982:161) representation of the fur trade, this appetite for trade goods emerges both as objectively given and as a relation of technological dependence.

[T]he demands of the Europeans for fur increased competition among the Native American groups—competition for new hunting grounds to meet the rising European demand, and competition also for access to the European goods, which soon became as much essential components of native technology as markers of differential status.

These images of the marketized Indian presuppose both the infinite wants of the Euro-American consumer and an intensification of labor geared to satisfy these needs. Supposedly, the trade inscribed the Indians in the dialectic of limited means and infinite wants.

Whatever relevance these images may possess for Cree society in the depleted landscapes over which the Hudson's Bay Company monopoly presided after 1821, there is no evidence for their significance south and west of Hudson Bay prior to that time. There is no question that Crees desired and ultimately became dependent on trade goods. New tools and weapons reduced the search and capture time of foraging and facilitated other domestic tasks. Guns were useful in terrorizing and displacing enemies. Alcohol and tobacco satisfied new appetites, European textiles transformed the aesthetics of self-adornment, and luxury goods became means of reproducing and modifying prestige distinctions, more through redistribution than consumption. But nowhere is there evidence during this period that demand for these products was sufficient to motivate a rate of predation that resulted in the game shortages.

The traders themselves, with their continual exhortation to "not be Lassy, Keep close to trapping in the winter" (Isham 1949 [1743–1749]:54), provide little evidence for unremitting Indian industry. Rather it appears that the trade and the technology may have reduced rather than intensified foraging labor. Under conditions of competition prior to 1821, the trade allowed Indians to indulge to the full their penchant for a leisurely seasonal round. This was particularly true of the middlemen who moved between Hudson Bay in the summer and the interior in the winter, bringing north the furs trapped by parklands groups, passing back to them their own used English trade goods, and, as Graham (1969 [1767–1791]:268) observed in 1768, rejecting the role of fur producer entirely in favor of "harboring and strolling among the Archithinuw [Blackfeet] and Asinepoet [Assiniboine] Indians for the sake of good living." Indians, as has been abundantly documented, desired and needed trade goods but only in fixed quantities.

This obliviousness of the Indians to scarcity raised concern during the London Parliamentary Enquiry of 1749 into conditions of the fur trade. The Indians trading at Hudson Bay were not producing furs in quantities sufficient to meet the European demand. One assumption, yet to be expounded as doctrine by Adam Smith, was that Indians would naturally increase their production if offered better prices. Veteran traders predicted that they would not.

James Isham, the most experienced trader available, an acute observer with a speculative turn of mind, and by no means uncritical of the company was forthright: "The giving Indians a larger Price would occasion the Decrease of Trade." Captain Spurrell was equally emphatic: "Would not the Natives kill more Game, if more Goods were sent to them for their Fur?" "They might, but they're too lazy to take any Extraordinary pains, suppose they have their bellyful." "Suppose there were two markets would not the Indians raise the Price of their Furs?" "Yes." "Would they kill more?" "No, less." (Rich 1960:49)

Isham and Spurrell predicted here the phenomenon of a backward-bending supply curve: the quantity of furs brought to market would decrease inversely with the price offered. Graham (1969 [1767–1791]:263) likewise wrote that raising the price of furs would diminish the trade. So far were the Crees from the condition of disproportion between scarce means and infinite wants that they might not know what to trade for:

And if the trading standard were enlarged in favour of the natives, would ruin it all; for I am certain if the natives were to get any more for their furs, they would catch fewer, which I shall make plainly appear viz. one canoe brings down yearly to the fort one hundred made beaver [furs equal in exchange value to 100 prime beaver pelts] in different kinds of furs, and trades with me seventy of the said beaver for real necessaries. The other thirty beaver shall so puzzle him to trade, that he often asks me what he shall buy, and when I make an answer, Trade some more powder, shot, tobacco, and hatchets, etc., his answer is, I have traded sufficient to serve me and my family until I see you again next summer; so he will drink one half, and trade the others with me for baubles.

These accounts contextualize the postulates of Polanyi's (1968:140) substantive rationality: "The substantive meaning [of economy] implies neither choice nor insufficiency of means; man's livelihood may or may not involve the necessity of choice and, if choice there be, it need not be induced by the limiting effect of a 'scarcity' of the means." John Hardman, a merchant, astutely identified the problem as one of finite consumer demand for European goods. The question then became how the Indians could be made to experience scarcity by expanding the domain of their material desires. Said Hardman,

but if they were once made sensible of the Conveniency of having some Property, they would then desire to carry on a trade, and supply their Neighbors . . . that this notion of Property would increase; though it would not increase their real Necessities, yet it would furnish them with imaginary Wants. The Indians necessities and Desires would increase in proportion to his Property. (Rich 1960:49)

Or, as Marx (1975:115) later wrote, "Under private property... every person speculates on creating a *new* need in another, so as to drive him to a fresh sacrifice, to place him in a new dependence, and to seduce him into a new mode of gratification and therefore economic ruin." If infinite need was not, then, innate to the Indians, it might, perhaps, deliberately be cultivated. This the Company proceeded to attempt, introducing such "imaginary wants" among the Indians as German toys, dolls, raisins, and prunes. These items proved immensely popular, but the Indians insisted on receiving them as gifts and refused to trade furs or meat for them. As Rich (1960:50) succinctly concluded, "They were hardened enough traders to exploit competition and an alternative market, but un-European in their reaction to better prices." Ray and Freeman's (1978:218–245; see Ray 1974:141–142, 1978) detailed analysis of the Hudson Bay fur trade before 1763 demonstrates quantitatively that better prices indeed reduced the volume of Cree fur production. The documentary evidence for this period thus provides an impressive contrary argument to the thesis that an expanding consumer demand motivated increased pressure on the now-marketable boreal fauna. The question concerns the increased number of animals now being killed for commercial purposes. Since consumer demand remained inelastic and prices of trade goods remained low, this number would ordinarily remain within sustainable limits.

Ray (1978) emphasizes the inelastic demand of the Indians, the role of the middleman, and the limited transport capacity of canoes in preventing environmental deterioration prior to 1763. The Hudson's Bay Company's rivalry with the Canadian traders increased Indian purchasing power, while Indian demand remained constant or expanded only slowly. Logistical impediments to trade with the coastal forts limited the quantities of animals killed for market. Much of the inland trade was in the hands of Cree and Assiniboine middlemen who lacked the disposition and capability to transport goods in sufficient quantity to motivate intensified hunting by their clients. Similarly, the capacity of the canoes used to travel to Hudson Bay for trade limited the quantities of furs that could be transported and thus the incentives to hunt or acquire furs for commercial purposes. "Hence the excessive exploitation of the environment that characterized the latter fur trade did not take place" (ibid.:356).

Cree Harvesting Strategies in the Eighteenth Century

While the traders' observations in the 1700s suggest that unrelenting productive industry was uncharacteristic of the Crees, they also indicate that Crees attempted to kill all the animals possible once hunting events were under way. There exists little information on the harvesting strategies used specifically by Crees in the Churchill River drainage. A composite picture of these strategies can be reconstructed, however, for boreal Algonquian groups in general and for the Crees trading at the coastal forts on Hudson Bay in particular. The Crees made little use of food preservation and storage, preferring to live on fresh meat. They sometimes discarded marketable pelts. After opening a beaver lodge, they killed all the animals readily accessible. They sometimes killed many caribou and retrieved only delicacies and marketable skins. They specifically rejected the appropriateness of killing only in quantities sufficient for their current domestic and commercial needs.

In the 1630s, LeJeune (1897c:57) wrote of the Quebec Montagnais, "When the Savages find a lodge of them [beavers], they kill all, great and small, male and female. There is a danger that they will finally exterminate the species in this region, as has happened among the Hurons." This was the pattern that advanced west with the fur trade, taking effect in the Churchill River drainage by the 1820s. Dobbs's (1744:39) polemic against the Hudson's Bay Company contains evidence that Crees killed beaver in excess of the number whose pelts could be brought down to the Bay in the small canoes of the period. The meat was undoubtedly eaten, but the "waste" of the skins is suggestive.

At present they leave great Numbers of Furs and Skins behind them [inland from Hudson Bay]. A good Hunter among the Indians can kill 600 Beavers in a season, and can carry down but 100; the rest he uses at home, or hangs them up in Branches of Trees, upon the Death of their Children as an offering to them, or use them for Bedding and Coverings; they sometimes burn off the Fur, and roast the Beavers like Pigs, upon any Entertainments, and they often let them rot, having no further use of them.

Beaver skins clearly had multiple use values: they could be converted to clothing, eaten, made over as offerings, or thrown away if there was no current need for them. Similar observations were made of other boreal Algonquian groups, the issue again being the effort involved in conveying the pelts to the post. Bishop (1974:291) cites trader James Sutherland on the Ojibwa to the north of Osnaburgh House in 1795: "The Beaver is in great plenty here, the Indians throwing away numbers of the half Beaver as beneath their notice, and even cuts pieces of the Whole Beaver to make them lighter carriages."

Hearne's observations pertain to the Crees and Chipewyans trading at Fort Churchill in the 1770s and 1780s. Describing the exploitation of a single beaver house, Hearne (1958 [1795]:148, 155) wrote that the hunters took twelve mature and twenty-five juvenile animals and abandoned the remainder only because the trouble entailed in securing them was judged excessive. Hearne, however, took issue with Dobbs on the "waste" of beavers already killed, stating that numbers killed in excess of those a family could manage were given to less fortunate relatives, "so that the whole of the great hunters' labours were always brought to the Factory."

The slaughter of big game animals in excess of what the hunters could consume, transport, or trade has been documented in the eighteenth century, carried on by the "Home Guard" Crees employed at the coastal forts, the groups resident inland in the boreal forest, and the probable progenitors of the Plains Crees who wintered in the parkland to the south. While Vecsey (1980:30–31) and Martin (1978:176–179) have minimized the role of Native Americans in overhunting the buffalo, Hendry (1907) on his 1754 journey from Hudson Bay into the interior parklands repeatedly observed the Crees killing more buffalo than they could consume. Similar harvesting of migrating caribou herds is noted in sources for both the eighteenth and the nineteenth centuries. Says Isham (1949 [1743–1749]:81) of the York Factory Crees,

I have found frequently Indians to Kill some scores of Deer, and take only tongues or heads, and Let the body or carcass go Adrift with the tide, therefore I think it's no wonder that godalmighty shou'd fix his judgemen't upon these Vile Reaches, and occasion their being starvd. and in want of foods when they make such havock of what the Lord sent them plenty of.

Isham was one of many traders dismayed by what he interpreted as waste and needless killing. In 1746, Drage (1968 [1748–49], 2:17) attributed the scarcity of caribou in the vicinity of York Factory to the extent of the slaughter during the migrations: "In other years, they have kill'd Numbers for the sake of their Tongues only, which is the most delicious part, leaving the Carcases to rot and for the Beast to prey on." He goes on to add that the Crees were reproved by the traders for this excess, a recurring theme in the accounts of the period. Graham (1969 [1767–1791]:16) makes clear that such practices were motivated, in part, by the desire to trade meat and hides to the posts:

I have seen at York Fort eighty carcasses in one day and in some season they have crossed the Hayes river in such numbers that many have been refused by us, having salted a sufficient stock of that kind of provisions. The natives even then keep slaying, only to get the skins to barter with us for necessaries.

Graham (ibid.:154) goes on to make the familiar observation that large numbers of caribou were killed only for especially valued cuts of meat. "Several score of deer I have known killed at one time, the natives only taking the tongues, heads, hearts and feet, according as they choose; letting the carcasses go adrift in the river." A century later, the same practices prevailed at York Factory where the migrating woodland caribou herd was hunted as it crossed the Hayes River and most of the carcasses abandoned to rot or float downstream (Dunn 1845:62).

Since most of these descriptions apply to the Home Guard Crees, it would be possible to interpret them as representing a breakdown of aboriginal patterns. Graham stated that the brandy trade was a powerful incentive for such harvesting; most caribou products in summer were traded for brandy (1969 [1767–1791]:280–281). However, the Crees in the interior were pursuing the same policies with no intention of trading the meat or hides. Hearne, who was inland in the 1770s and 1780s with Crees and Chipewyans, repeatedly mentioned the customs of killing more animals than could be consumed and of abandoning the meat rather than laying it up or transporting it (1958 [1795]:25–26, 42, 48–59, 75–76, 87, 259).

As national customs, however, are not easily overcome, my remonstrances proved ineffectual; and I was always answered, that it was certainly right to kill plenty, and live on the best, when and where it was to be got, for that it would be impossible to do it where every thing was scarce: and they insisted upon it, that killing plenty of deer and other game in one part of the country could never make them scarcer in another. Indeed, they were so accustomed to kill everything that came within their reach that few of them could pass by a small bird's nest without slaying the young ones or destroying the eggs. (Ibid.:75)

Hearne's eyewitness observations pertain to Chipewyans, but he wrote that this killing, "however wasteful it may appear . . . is a practice so common among all the Indian tribes as to be thought nothing of" (ibid.:25). These accounts need to be placed in the context of other evidence (see below) describing conscious management strategies from early in the fur trade. They suggest, however, that rates of predation were not ordinarily limited to the number of animals needed in the short term. When animals were aggregated at a site—as was often the case with caribou and beaver—Crees killed as many as possible, since doing so required little additional labor.

This practice of killing many animals and making selective rather than intensive use of the products was evidently a common characteristic of Cree hunting. Assuming that foraging labor alternated with consumption, intensive utilization of each carcass would seemingly be favored since it would provide longer intervals between foraging episodes. Since, however, Crees did not preserve or transport large quantities of meat, many situations favored selective use. Animals had multiple uses, domestically as food and clothing and commercially as exchange values; the quantities of animals desired for each purpose varied seasonally and situationally. When needs for skins and meat did not coincide, animals might be killed for one product but not the other. Crees also seemingly killed caribou in quantities greater than could be eaten before the meat became fly-blown or before the next residential movement. The motivation here was seemingly to live on preferred cuts of meat rather than to kill fewer animals and use each carcass more intensively. Therefore, any time that multiple animals were killed concurrently at the same site, there was likely to be selective use. Additionally, the effort involved in retrieving all of the meat of large game may have encouraged selective use when hunters already had adequate short-term supplies on hand or when they felt confident that other kills could easily be made. Retrieval costs were highest in summer if moose or caribou were killed at a distance from water where canoes could be used, but pulling the meat to camp on a toboggan in winter was also laborious. The weight of raw meat could be reduced by two-thirds by smoke drying (Thompson 1962 [1784–1812]:84), but processing the meat in this way required additional effort, and Crees preferred fresh (unsmoked) meat. If guns made it easier to stalk and kill animals, dispositions to hunt more, retrieve less, and live on preferred meats would have been reinforced. There may thus have occurred a historic shift from relatively more intensive use of each carcass to more frequent hunting with more selective utilization. Such utilization was clearly extended for commercial purposes. The Crees at York Factory, for example, killed large numbers of barren land caribou to trade their skins for brandy (Graham 1969 [1767–1791]:280–281).

Beaver Management in the Early Fur Trade

There exist scattered references to deliberate beaver management by Algonquian and other Indian groups from relatively early in the trade. Around 1660, Radisson (1943 [1853]:226) wrote of the "Christinos" [Crees] resident in summer on the south shore of Lake Superior, "They kill not the young castors [beavers], but leave them in the water, being that they are sure that they will take him againe, wch no other nation doth." Lahontan (1905 [1703], 2:481–483) wrote that the Ottawas in the late 1600s preserved beaver habitat and maintained breeding populations by sparing males and females at each colony. If Lahontan had the facts correct, the Ottawas were at this time using an allotment system in which delimited trapping tracts were assigned each year to different groups after collective deliberation.

In the region of Hudson Bay, I know of only one eighteenth-century mention of this practice. Speaking of Crees at York Factory in 1746, Drage (1968 [1748–49], 1:149) wrote, "When they take a house of them [beavers] they generally leave two to breed." Bacqueville de La Potherie (1931:235) and Hearne (1958 [1795]:245) described private marking of beaver lodges at York Factory and Churchill. Usufructuary rights to the lodge, if respected, would allow the nominal "owners" to benefit in successive years from any selective trapping they practiced, but neither author mentioned management, and Hearne observed Crees killing all the beavers in a house. Harmon (1905 [1821]:237–238) described both conservation and privatized hunting-trapping territories among Crees and Ojibwas in southern Manitoba during the first two decades of the nineteenth century. These references make clear that some Crees and other Algonquians were conserving beavers and recognizing usufructuary rights in lodges or in delimited trapping tracts during the seventeenth and eighteenth centuries. There are no comparable references to selective hunting of other furbearers or of big game.

Views on the aboriginality of conservation differ. Frank Speck (1915), Calvin Martin (1978), Christopher Vecsey (1980), and Charles Bishop (1984) have proposed that the practice was aboriginal, although only Bishop introduces evidence (Radisson's observation). Others have viewed beaver management as a postcontact adjustment to the fur trade. Some have suggested that the practice was invented independently by Indians in association with usufructuary rights in beaver lodges or delimited hunting-trapping tracts used in successive winters by the same hunting group (Rogers 1963:84, Morantz 1983:120). Others have viewed the strategies as deriving from the Hudson's Bay Company's conservation policies introduced after 1821 (Hickerson 1973, Ray 1975). The question is complex because the fur trade created conditions conducive both to the inception of management strategies where none may have existed and to the destruction of indigenous or historically emergent systems. The market for beavers would provide incentives for the innovation of management practices or for the perpetuation and elaboration of existing ones. However, competition for animals and shifts in populations and territorial boundaries could lead to disregard for boundaries and usufructory rights, within or between different societies. Without such boundaries, the animals spared by one group might be taken by others, obviating the incentive to harvest selectively. Further complicating the picture are the obvious possibilities that some groups may have conserved animals before or after contact while others did not, that management evolved differently in different regions, and that groups may have alternated reversibly between indiscriminate and selective hunting during successive periods, both prehistorically and after involvement in the fur trade. The early references at least make clear that in some areas, management practices antedated the Hudson's Bay Company's policies by many years. Aside from the one reference to York Factory by Drage, I have found no mention of management practices by Crees trading on Hudson Bay until the mid-1800s. If such practices were widespread, either prehistorically or in the fur trade or both, the beaver depletions strongly suggest that they were subsequently abandoned during the late eighteenth century and early nineteenth century. The cumulative weight of the evidence indicates that management developed on a limited scale in some districts as a means of rationalizing participation in the fur trade but never became general until after the game depletions had occurred.

The Inland Posts, 1783–1821

Game depletions had occurred previously in the fur trade elsewhere, and there were local depletions in the Hudson Bay lowlands near the posts in the 1700s (Bishop 1984). There exists, however, no evidence for long-term and large-scale shortages in the Canadian Shield south and west of Hudson Bay until the first quarter of the nineteenth century. Ray (1978) attributes the chronology to changed conditions in the trade after 1763. The most significant of these was the proliferation of inland posts built both by the congeries of firms later united as the Northwest Company and by the Hudson's Bay Company. These posts simultaneously eliminated the monopoly of the Cree and Assiniboine middlemen and the logistical obstacles to increased predation for commercial purposes. Previously, the limited capacity of canoes provided little incentive for Crees living in the Shield to increase predation for commercial purposes. After 1763, the traders were interacting directly with an expanded population of Indian consumers, among whom, no doubt, were most of the former middlemen, now participating in the trade as fur producers. Inland groups now had easier access at all times of year to inland posts annually stocked with goods. The culmination of this trend was a situation in which the competing traders, each seeking to preempt their rivals, visited Cree camps to collect furs and meat, a practice mentioned recurrently in the Nelson House journals in the early 1800s. The task of killing animals remained part of the Cree labor process, but transport costs were increasingly assumed by the traders. Ray's argument is that the game depletions occurred because, after 1763, there were more Indians directly involved in the trade, and they were killing more animals because trade goods were easily accessible in increased quantities. The competition between the Hudson's Bay Company and the Northwest Company began in the lower Churchill and Nelson drainages in 1783, and it is probably the case that the game depletions there were the cumulative result of Indian hunting between this date and the 1820s.

Ray suggests also (1978:356) that Indian consumer demand for trade goods may have expanded in the late 1700s. His earlier discussion of the economics of the trade during this period suggests, however, that the prices paid for furs increased while Indian demand remained constant or diminished.

Of significance to the process of material culture change, the increased importance of gift-giving [in the trade] and the extensive use of credit as an allurement to trade without an adequate system for collection meant that between 1763 and 1821 there was a continual decline of relative cost of goods to Indians. . . . However, although increasingly intensive company competition was making it easier for the Indians to obtain trade goods, their demand for utilitarian and ornamental items did not rise at the same rate as prices fell. In fact . . . it actually declined in some quarters. (Ray 1974:141–142)

It would therefore seem that increased access to the inland posts prompted increased rates of predation sufficient to deplete beavers, moose, and caribou. This suggests that there were extraeconomic motivations for participating in the trade or that desire for certain trade items did, in fact, increase.

An exceptionally interesting question is the net effect of the fur trade on the quantity of time allocated to foraging labor. The trade brought increased rates of predation by providing a market for meat and furs. At the same time, the European technology resulted in new hunting strategies, some of which increased the efficiency of hunting per unit of time allocated to it. There is no way of calculating the differences between pre- and postcontact per capita rates of Cree foraging labor, but Crees almost certainly conceived of the trade as an arrangement that increased the effectiveness of their hunting over what it previously had been. Whether the difference was defined in terms of efficiency, reliability, or other criteria is unknown, but it would otherwise be difficult to explain the degree of the Cree involvement in the trade.

The question is important because the rates of predation that cumulatively depleted moose, caribou, and beavers in the Churchill River drainage must have required greater foraging labor than had been the case when the trade was limited to the coastal forts. The Crees were thus willing to increase their labor in order to increase their volume of trade with newly accessible markets. There seems no possibility that they *needed* to do this to satisfy their requirements for those trade goods that were now indispensable to hunting. The prices of trade goods declined until 1821, and the Crees could have replaced and maintained the technology in the accustomed quantities per capita with less labor than previously. This, indeed, was what occurred in the earlier phase of the trade. The dependency hypothesis thus provides little insight into the problem. But the intensified foraging requires explanation since it would seem to run counter to a disposition toward satisfying finite needs with little labor, which is characteristic of nomadic foragers (Sahlins 1972) and well documented among the Crees.

To speculate on why Crees would increase the quantities of animals they killed for trade, an admittedly skeletal reconstruction of their conceptions of foraging labor is necessary. On the face of it, the traders painted a simple and familiar picture: the Crees were lazy. Graham (1969 [1767–1791]:275) is typical: "The natives are naturally indolent, and having food and raiment for the present, never concern themselves for the future, until all is expended." Thompson (1962 [1784–

1812]:73), who had extended experience with Crees inland, provided somewhat greater detail.

They can bear great fatigue but not hard labor, they would rather walk six hours over rough ground than work one hour with the pick axe and spade, and the labor they perform, is mostly in an erect posture as working with the ice chissel piercing holes through the ice or through a beaver house, and naturally [by nature] they are not industrious; they do not work from choice, but necessity; yet the industrious of both sexes are praised and admired.

Labor was not intrinsically ennobling or valuable, and it is significant that Crees optimistically anticipated an afterworld in which game animals were killed with little effort (Drage 1968 [1748–49], 1:42, Graham 1969 [1767–1791]:160). However, labor had positive significance since it was the means for reproducing the valued conditions of autonomy and responsibility for others. As Thompson (1962 [1784–1812]:82) wrote, Cree children "very early and readily betake themselves to fishing and hunting, from both men and women impressing on their minds, that the man truly miserable is he, who is dependent on another for his subsistence." The enormous prestige today accruing to the capture of preferred resources—and, in lesser degree, to any foraging activity—is difficult to exaggerate. The man or woman who produced much could share much, enjoying marital and political advantages unavailable to the less skilled or industrious. As it is today, hunting for many Crees in the past was unquestionably a profoundly satisfying vocation in which skills, interests (practical and philosophical), and passions were exhaustively engaged. I have heard several Cree trappers express their feelings about this with the expression "Nisākihitān nipimātisiwin" 'I love my life'. With respect to Cree foraging, the Western segmentation of "work" and "leisure" had and have little relevance. More specifically, the semantic equivalence of Cree atoskīwin ['job', 'profession', 'employment'] with English "labor" is, at best, partial. In the words of a Hudson's Bay Company shareholder in the 1750s, "They won't make a Toil of a Pleasure for any Consideration" (Rich 1960:50).

Crees subcategorized labor along diverse parameters. Some forms of work introduced by the traders—leveling foundations for inland posts, for example—were not appreciated. Labor was classified by gender, men specializing in hunting big game and most furbearers and women in martens, small game, and a formidable array of domestic tasks. Men fished with spears, but fishing with nets and angling through the ice were in the female sphere. Different resources and strategies were ranked by criteria of prestige, effort, and efficiency. An obvious concern was how long a particular resource could provision a group before further labor was necessary. One of Thompson's Cree clients characterized winter beaver hunting as "hard work, and only gives meat while we are working" (1962 [1784–1812]:102). In other words, chopping through frozen beaver lodges required more physical effort than stalking moose or caribou. Additionally, beavers were consumed as rapidly as they were acquired, while big game provided a temporary surplus that would feed a group for some period without further daily labor.

Given fluctuations in animal resources, Crees were necessarily accustomed to fluctuations in the amount of foraging labor necessary to provision winter groups at preferred levels of consumption. As I have shown, a complex system of religious thought addresses the uncertainties of hunting, but what I suggest here is the opposite side of the coin of "least effort," a cultural tolerance for occasional extremes of hard work for minimal returns. In the course of a fruitless quest in 1978 to elicit what people thought were appropriate amounts of labor to invest in particular foraging strategies, I encountered only variations on the theme of "you never know." There is no Cree conception of predictable and finite units of time allocated to foraging effort, no analog to the forty-hour workweek. The preferred pattern was clearly to forage, consume, and then forage again, but the duration of the foraging efforts themselves was not limited by a fixed temporal reference value. In consequence, the quantities of labor Crees allocated to commercial hunting had some of the elasticity of its domestic counterpart and could increase within certain limits, as it did after 1783, if there were meaningful incentives.

Two exceptionally significant incentives were alcohol and tobacco for which Crees traded in sizable quantities (Ray 1978:354), and one could probably add other easily consumable luxury goods as well. The significance of these items was not exhausted by their physical effects, although, by the traders' accounts, the latter were greatly esteemed. Both alcoholic beverages and tobacco were rapidly assimilated to an elevated status coordinate with that of the most preferred meats. Animal resources had prehistorically been the means through which good men and women routinely affirmed the doxic axiom of generalized reciprocity, just as they were the means—in larger or more continuous quantities—for eminent men to cultivate and exhibit their leadership. All this became true historically for rum and tobacco, and they were routinely shared at drinking parties with whomever was present. Richardson (Franklin 1823:103) registered the usual disapproval of Cree drinking in the 1820s but observed also that rum was always shared and that the hosts of drinking parties accrued esteem for their liberality. Also, like cooked meat, the European intoxicants acquired sacred status as sacrificial offerings. Tobacco was (and is) routinely offered to the *ahcāk* beings in bulk or as smoke, and Nelson (Brown and Brightman 1988:101) observed that Crees in the 1800s held special sacrificial "feasts" of rum, logically enough to placate specifically those beings dispositionally averse to human welfare. There were probably additional motivations for increased commercial hunting after 1783. Crees undoubtedly wanted inland posts readily at hand and, within limits, were willing to produce more furs to ensure that they remained there.

The Trade at Granville Lake, 1794–95

Post journals from the lower Churchill River drainage are available for the 1790s and thereafter, providing some information on the inland trade. Prior to 1810, the journals suggest that beaver and big game resources in the Churchill River area were ordinarily adequate or abundant. The evidence is partly negative: the subsequently ubiquitous reports of declining beaver returns and starving Indians are absent. More positively, the daily transactions at the posts indicate a seemingly inexhaustible plenitude of animal biomass. George Charles's sojourn at the Granville Lake outpost in 1794–95 (HBC B/83/a [1795]) provides some insight into the abundance of the region's animal resources prior to the depletions. On June 30, Charles departed from Fort Churchill, accompanied by an undisclosed number of Crees and nine Company servants. On July 8, the party "encountered many deer [caribou] crossing the river." On July 10, Charles noted laconically that a woman was stabbed during a drinking fracas and that an Indian killed a caribou. On July 14, caribou were again encountered crossing the Churchill, and the Crees killed "many." On July 17, another caribou was killed, on the 19th three more, on the 24th another. On the 25th, the Crees killed eight geese and one swan. On the 26th, they shot a moose. Between the 27th and the 30th, they killed four ducks and twenty additional geese. August 4 brought five more geese and seven ducks. Between August 5 and 7, the Crees killed five more geese and an undisclosed number of the ubiquitous caribou.

On August 9, the party reached Granville Lake and began building the outpost five miles from the mouth of Maskwōwikan [Laurie] River. The journal thereafter is a day-by-day enumeration of the furs and meat moving from the bush into the Crees' camps and thence to the post. Including the animals already noted, Charles received on various occasions between June 30, 1794, and July 5, 1795, six caribou (exclusive of the "many" killed at river crossings on the trip inland), 30 pounds of caribou meat, 4 moose, 40 pounds of moose meat, meat from 8 beavers, a "few lbs." of beaver meat, 71 geese, 15 swans, and 11 ducks, all this aside from 1,588 pounds of fresh meat (presumably moose, caribou, and beaver) and further unspecified quantities of dry meat (mentioned twice), fat, (mentioned twice), and fresh meat (mentioned eleven times). He also received 156 beavers (with the meat), twice traded for "summer furs" in undisclosed quantities, acquired 23 "fall skins," and traded other sundry "furs" (17 on one occasion, "a few" on another) and moose skins, all in addition to assorted other furs equivalent in value to 629 large beaver pelts (cf. Ray and Freeman 1978:54). A competing Canadian post on Granville Lake was presumably doing similar volume, and there were numerous other posts in the region. Except for the month of January when Indians did not visit the post, both meat and furs were traded continuously thoughout the year.

During the 1790s, the castoreum-steel trap technique diffused into the Churchill River drainage. Steel traps had long been used in the trade for taking terrestrial animals but seemingly were not used for beavers until castoreum bait, a glandular secretion of the beaver and an exceptionally effective attractant, was discovered. The technique came into general use in the 1790s and apparently revolutionized both summer and winter trapping.

The secret of this bait was soon spread, every Indian procured from the traders four to six steel traps, the weight of one was about six to eight pounds; all labor was now at an end, the Hunter moved about at pleasure with his traps and infallible bait of Castoreum (Thompson 1962 [1784–1812]:156).

Thompson wrote that the technique left areas farther to the south and east depleted of beavers, prompting westward movement of Ojibwa and Iroquois groups onto lands occupied by the Crees (ibid.:156–157). Steel traps and castoreum presumably had similar effects in the Churchill River drainage, even without additional pressure from immigrating groups. The account books for the Nelson River District throughout the early and mid-1800s show that castoreum was also an item of trade (HBC B.239/h/1[1821–1836]). Even before 1821, traders in the district were reluctant to give traps to Indians who requested them, perhaps because they feared that beaver populations would be exterminated (HBC B.91/e/2[1820–21]).

The Churchill River Game Shortages

The evidence for game shortages in the areas south and west of Hudson Bay is contained in the post journals and fur returns of the Hudson's Bay Company's Northern Department during the second and third decades of the nineteenth century. Ray (1974:117–124, 1975) has discussed the region generally; Bishop (1974:282–283) has documented the shortages in detail in the Osnaburgh House District of northern Ontario. The remarks that follow pertain to the Company's Nelson River District whose boundaries until 1832 encompassed most of contemporary northwestern and north-central Manitoba. Between 1792 and 1806, Thompson, a careful observer of the country and its inhabitants, spent six winters at outposts in the district including houses at Sipiwesk Lake, Reed Lake, Duck Portage (Sisipuk Lake), and Burntwood River near Granville Lake.

The animals described in this Stony Region are few in proportion to the extent of country, the Natives with all their address can only collect furs sufficient to purchase the necessaries of life; and part of their clothing is of leather in summer, very disagreeable in rainy weather, and the avidity with which the fur bearing animals is sought, almost threatens their extinction (1962 [1784–1812]:71).

Thompson's description of the furbearers as in danger of extinction is confirmed by subsequent developments, although his perceptions of scarcity in the late 1700s were perhaps informed by hindsight. He related three anecdotes involving famine situations in winter 1794, but the precipitating factors—insufficient wind for moose hunting, poor hunting skills, and a broken ice chisel—do not implicate game scarcity as the cause (ibid.:101–104).

Nelson House, the central Hudson's Bay Company post of the district, was established in 1799, probably either on Flatrock or Nelson Lake. The Nelson House account books between 1810 and 1815 indicate the species that Crees were trading during this period. Since furs from many animals were used domestically or traded with other posts, the quantities of furs brought to Nelson House were, of course, substantially fewer in number than the animals actually killed in the area during this period. The figures do, however, give some indication of how Crees prioritized the animals they trapped by interacting criteria of edibility, exchange value, availability, and foraging efficiency. Cree concentrated on species that combined edibility with exchange value.

Table 3 *Furs and Provisions Traded at Nelson House, 1810–1815*

Furs	1810–11	1811–12	1812–13	1814	1815	Total
muskrat	195	129	382	1,086	554	1,792
beaver	464	517	392	291	494	1,664
beaver coating*		91 lb.	103 lb.	45 lb.	58 lb.	297 lb.
otter	78	65	48	118	152	309
marten		10		67	18	97
bear	14	29	6	22	20	71
mink	4			20	18	42
lynx	16	3		2		21
wolverine	2	2	4	4	2	15
cross fox	1				3	4
red fox	1				2	3
fisher	2					2
arctic fox					1	1
wolf	1					1
Provisions (in lb.)						
dry meat		1,737	505	1,670		
fresh meat		1,687	1,125	1,517		
pounded meat			1,044			
fish		14,469	37,673	19,338		

* skins previously sewn into clothing
Source: HBC B.141/d/1–5 [1810–1815]

During the first three years, the beaver was the animal most often traded. After 1814, it was exceeded by muskrats, presumably reflecting the former's growing scarcity. Otters, martens, bears, minks, and lynxes were all eaten, but the remaining animals were not, except in emergencies (Graham 1969 [1767–1791]:12–33).

The post journals make occasional references to Indian hunger in the early 1800s. By 1815, the traders clearly perceived both furbearers and big game as scarce. In the Report for Nelson House of that year (HBC B.141/e/1), Charles wrote, "Natives say Beaver not to be found, its skin having been sought after by traders for many years past, nearly exhausted, is the reason they give for not killing more of them." He added that other furbearers were not plentiful and that there were some moose and caribou, "not numerous but sufficient to divert Indians from trapping." Charles perceived the situation as one in which the scarcity of large game animals required greater expenditures of search time that would previously have been allocated to fur trapping. He also perceived big game hunting as more efficient than beaver trapping in terms of food returns per unit of time. The ratio of producers to dependent consumers in the winter group influenced these factors.

There is at present a notable individual A-ki-ni-ap from whom the Company's servants have received many hundred made beaver, the fruits of his own labor, but lately several of his relatives dying and leaving their families unprovided for have so encumbered this good fellow with such a numerous Band of Dependents on his exertions that of late years he can do nothing but hunt moose, deer and the large animals to keep them from perishing of want. (Ibid.)

Individuals with fewer dependents could better combine big game hunting with the less efficient trapping of beavers. Charles also referred to nine cases of cannibalism between 1811 and 1815.

It is thought that they suffer hunger and want with much less fortitude than many other tribes of Indians & is strongly suspected resort to the abominable alternative of devouring their Tentmates to save themselves from starvation . . . for within the last four years no less than nine have been destroyed in this manner. (Ibid.)

The report ends with the macabre and offhand postscript that "Ah-ki-ni-ap" and eleven other people, both young and old, "destroyed each other," seemingly in a famine-related incident. While the numbers may be exaggerated, it appears that cases of famine-related murder were occurring during this period, or at least that the Crees believed they were happening and reported them to the traders.

The returns in beaver and other furs at the Nelson House post (not the entire district) between 1810 and 1815 do not reveal a progressive decline, although this would probably be evident if figures for the previous decade were available. Moose decline is, however, suggested by the fact that the trade in moose hides stops in 1812; thereafter, there is no record of moose hides being traded anywhere in the Nelson River District. In 1819, Charles (HBC B.91/e/1) described six Crees trading at the South Indian Lake post as "good hunters but moose and deer [caribou] are scarce so they rely on fur bearers almost for subsistence."

The district fur returns between 1821 and 1836 provide an accurate basis for identifying trends in beaver production during this period since there were no competing companies and Crees presumably traded all or almost all the skins they obtained (HBC B.239/h/1). In 1821, there were three major posts operating in the district, Nelson House, Split Lake, and South Indian Lake. The clients at the first two were primarily Crees; at the third, primarily Chipewyans. In 1822, Charles wrote,

The condition of the Indians most part of this year has been wretched, both of those trading at the Churchill [Nelson House, South Indian Lake] and Nelson River [Split Lake] forts & chiefly to this I attribute our procuring more Beaver skins than last year though the marten are at the same time considerably up, as from the first setting in of the frost to the middle of February nearly after, beaver and fish were the only support they could provide in such a time of scarcity. They cannot kill Martins, for want of victuals to convert into baits for the traps, as they were several times so much reduced that the Natives themselves would have taken a bait had it been in their way. Therefore, when they found a Beaver House, necessity obliged them to work till they killed them even 3 or 4 days and not abandon it after the first trial as before, indeed I am of the opinion had this scarcity continued the whole season we should have had more furs and the Natives would not have suffered much more than they did for toward the Spring the weather hurts them but little and they are better able to exert themselves for the support of their families. (HBC B.91/e/2[1820–21])

Thus could scarcity work to the Company's advantage. When large game animals were available, they diverted Crees from trapping; when they were unobtainable, the Crees concentrated on beavers, a less efficient resource that provided both meat and marketable furs but for greater labor. This suggests that big game animals were depleted first and that beavers followed shortly after, as the result of increased hunting for food. The passage also shows that hunger was prompting more intensive beaver hunting: all the beavers in a lodge were now killed, whereas some would have been left to repopulate the colony if it was abandoned "after the first trial." One obstacle to overkill—the effort involved—was thus removed as conditions worsened. Charles also singled out for praise the hunter "Qua-qua-cus-cow" who traded at Nelson House and who provided five beaver pelts during the season. That an annual harvest of five beavers, minimal relative to production between 1810 and 1815, was noteworthy indicates the extent of the depletion. During 1823, George Simpson passed through the district en route to the Pacific and stated that he saw no sign of beavers anywhere (Simpson 1931:14–15). The South Indian Lake post was closed that year, presumably prompting the Chipewyans to trade thereafter in other districts. The District Report of 1825–26 described local conditions more unequivocally: "fur bearing animals exhausted, larger animals almost exhausted and natives have to divert time from trapping to hunt for food . . . natives all dependent on the post & would perish in winter without it" (HBC B.141/e/2). The Crees were now paradoxically dependent on the post for emergency provisions during food crises.

For the year 1826, the Company introduced a quota of 421 beavers for the district (Ray 1975:55–57) as part of its program for allowing the species to replenish, but this does not account for the year's returns of 99 pelts. It appears likely that Crees had all but abandoned beaver trapping to pursue whatever animals could be found.

In the summer 1827, Nelson House was "abandoned to recruit beaver" (Fleming 1940:lx), leaving only the Split Lake post on Nelson River operating in the district. This suggests that the traders perceived the Nelson River country as less depleted than that of the Churchill. Closing and opening posts within districts emerged in the 1820s as a policy for shifting Indians out of depleted areas to allow the animals to recover (Ray 1975:51). Presumably, some of the Churchill River Crees began trading at Split Lake while others moved west to posts in the English River District along the upper Churchill. In 1832, the Split Lake post was transferred to the jurisdiction of the Norway House District. The following year, a new post called Nelson House was established at Three Points Lake near the site of the present Indian Reserve, and it remained the only post in the reduced Nelson River District until the latter was dissolved as an administrative unit in 1836. Presumably, it attracted some of the Churchill River Crees who traded at the earlier post of the same name. Beaver returns fluctuated throughout the period, declining from a high of 1,885 (1821) to 794 (1823), increasing to 1,033 (1824), decreasing to a low of 99 (1826), increasing to 1,608 (1830), declining again to 640 (1833), and then increasing to 1,219 (1836). The variations reflect post closings and movements as well as the availability of alternative resources. The trade in big game also declined in the 1820s and thereafter. The trade in caribou skins went from twenty-one in 1821 to five in 1826 and then simply stopped.

Table 4 *Nelson River District Beaver Returns, 1821–1836*

1821	1822	1823	1824	1825	1826	1827	1828	1829	1830	1831	1832	1833	1834	1835	1836
1,885	1,441	794	1,033	702	99	510	866	1,078	1,608	784	707	640	752	804	1,219

1821–1823: Nelson House, South Indian Lake, Split Lake posts.
1823–1827: Nelson House, Split Lake posts.
1827–1832: Split Lake only.
1832–1838: Second Nelson House only.

Similarly, eighty-eight deer skins were traded in 1823, three in 1829, and none thereafter. There is no trade in moose skins throughout the entire period. Presumably, most skins from big game killed during this period were being used for clothing rather than for trade. Declines and recoveries in returns for martens, lynxes, and muskrats are also evident, although these do not coincide with the beaver decline and were undoubtedly influenced by factors other than overtrapping.

It is possible that intensified hunting interacted with disease or other factors, causing periodic resource fluctuation to produce the shortages. Ray (1974:119), for example, has noted evidence that disease may have substantially reduced beaver populations in the early 1800s. Rates of commercially motivated predation that ordinarily did not adversely affect species production may have done so if populations were unusually low. Alternatively, the decline may have been primarily the result of intensified hunting.

Territoriality

The characteristics of boreal Algonquian land tenure and territoriality, both aboriginally and during the fur trade period, continue to be explored and debated (Scott 1988; Feit 1991a, 1991b; Bishop and Morantz 1986). Cree land tenure institutions are of clear relevance to the game depletions because of the "tragedy of the commons" phenomenon. If the same hunting groups held usufructuary rights and exclusive access to delimited tracts within the regional band territory, they could have benefited from selective hunting. Alternatively, if all land and resources were free goods, no one group would have incentives to limit kills because animals it saved might be harvested by others. Rock Crees today recognize the "overutilized commons" effect, and it was the case that common tenure precluded conservation during certain periods in the past. The evidence contained in post reports from the early 1800s suggests that individual hunting groups were associated at any given time with a vaguely delimited range but that they moved often and that no exclusive tenure was recognized. In the census of the Indians trading in the Nelson River District in 1822–23 (HBC B.91/a/8), Charles identified 297 Cree men and their families in three large divisions. The "Swampy Ground Indians" east and north of Split Lake on the lower Nelson River numbered 73 persons divided among three hunting groups; the largest of these split further into "small parties" in winter. The "Nelson River Indians" were farther up the river around Split Lake and numbered 108 persons in six hunting groups. The "Nelson House Indians, Churchill River" numbered 88 persons in five groups. The census gives the names of the adult men in each group, the number of their wives and children, and the area where the group usually wintered. Unmarried younger women were presumably enumerated as children.

The number and composition of the Churchill River hunting groups here differs from that given in two earlier district reports. The Report of 1818–19 divides twenty-three male hunters between ten groups, three consisting only of one member (HBC B91/e/1). The 1820–21 Report (HBC B.91/e/2) classifies the same men into four groups. The alignments of some families differ also among the three reports. For example, *Okimāw Acāhpiy* 'Chief Bow' and "Pe-as-ku-tis-cum," the first and second hunters in group [1] below (table 5), formed a separate group in 1818 and then were listed with the three hunters in [6] in 1820. The differences undoubtedly reflect Charles's changing conceptions of hunting group personnel but also reversible or directional realignments continuously under way from winter to winter.

In the census, Charles was evidently complying with a superior's directive to provide information on Cree hunting grounds and land tenure. Given the complexity of Algonquian land tenure systems, his report is inconclusive. He was able to present information—gained both from the Crees and from winter trips to their camps—about the region each group customarily occupied, thus suggesting some stability from winter to winter in group-region alignments. However, he was careful to emphasize the flexibility of the system and the absence of concepts of usufruct. Of the "Swampy Ground Indians," he wrote, "they do not claim any particular rights to these grounds unless being more perfectly acquainted with the different parts of it may be considered such." As for the Churchill River Crees,

To judge of the country from the furs we procure from it [i.e., quantity], this part of the [Nelson River] district must be termed the worst, as the Natives have a great extent of country to traverse and need not hunt two seasons on the same grounds, as to claiming any rights in the grounds in which they hunt they do not as one party are often on the land that may have been inhabited by others a season or two before.

Such territorial shifting does not eliminate the possibility of hunting ranges habitually used by the same groups in successive winters; it might attest changing boundaries of ranges, reciprocal visiting, and

Table 5 *Hunting Groups of the Churchill River Crees, 1822–1823*

Name: Male Hunters	Wife	Children	Territory
1] Burntwood Lake			A party that shift their quarters very often but the
Ou-ke-mow-ah-chap-py	2	5	Burntwood Lake & River with Pelican Lake and
Pe-as-ku-tis-cum			between [?] and Cumberland is the country that
Ah-chim-mo-shish	1	2	may be termed their grounds.
Qua-qua-cus-cow	2	3	
Mis-tick-ou-thin		4	
Ish-tu-pu-e-sew	1	2	
2] Pukatawagan Lake			Churchill river and the lakes bordering it such as
Ou-cha-pis-kis-tu-quon	1	2	the Puc-et-tow-wag-gan [Pukatawagan] Lake,
Mtu-as-ke-weaw	1	3	Duck Lake, Fish [?] Lake &c is more than they
Ou-tin-ah-e-kis-cum			can presently occupy.
Quis-que-e-teau	1	4	
3] Loon River			This party are generally the furthest from the
A-poo-nask	1	1	House and in furs [?] the worse, they are too
Soo-qwe-wis-cum	1	1	fond of good meat. Deer River, Pock-shtwan [?]
Mus-sin-na-cus-cum	2		Lake, and Loon river and about that country is
Wus-kitch-ou-chisk	1	3	their grounds.
4] Swan Lake			This party generally hunt in and about the
Sa-sase-quon	1	2	Crooked Paint River, Paint Lake and Swan lake.
Ag-e-new-e-thaw	1	1	For three seasons past they have traded at the
Wah-kah-itch	1	2	Indian Lake but Nelson House is the post they
Sa-se-putch	1	1	belong to.

5] Burntwood River

	polygynous marriage	single men
Was-ta-name		1
Noo-tock		1
Mus-cu-shish		
Kee-twam		

A set of useless wretches but all young men, fishing with a hook being their support but they generally resort around the Burntwood River.

6] Loon [Russell] Lake

	polygynous marriage	single men
Ou-ke-mow-e-quon		1
Pe-ah-qua-tes-cum		
na-siw-ou-ki-mow		1

This family generally hunt together, their grounds or at least the country they rove about is Grenouille Lake, Loon Lake & Trout Lake in a SSS Direction from Nelson House.

Group	Men	Women	Children	Total	polygynous marriage	single men
1]	6	6	16	28	2	2
2]	4	3	9	16	1	1
3]	4	5	5	14		0
4]	4	4	6	14		
5]	4	2	2	8		2
6]	3	3	2	8		
total	25	23	40	88	3	5

temporary exchange. If asked, Crees almost certainly would have denied owning the lands they hunted on, perhaps causing Charles to imagine the system as less stable than it was. Alternatively, the system may have been even more flexible than he suggests, with each group's range and nomadic itinerary formulated anew each winter and limited only by the need to space groups across the landscape when resources were perceived as scarce. When resources permitted, there is evidence that multiple hunting groups would occupy the same general region: Charles noted in 1795 that the ten Cree families trading at Granville House all wintered around Sisipuk Lake (HBC B.83/a).

In any case, it is clear that groups did not assert exclusive rights to particular regions, even if they tended to restrict their winter movements within them. It does not, however, follow that management of resources would have been impossible. In the hypothetical case, each hunting group (or its beaver trapping components) could have conserved beavers wherever it hunted each winter. Alternatively, areas within the band range could have been rotated. If there were consensus and general compliance with such practices, management could occur without notions of usufruct in delimited territories, each group benefiting from the selective hunting of each of the others. These adjustments to increasing scarcity would have required novel degrees of coordinated planning and cooperation between hunting groups, but they are not inconsistent with the conceptions of the collective good realized in the practice of generalized sharing. No such adjustments occurred until later in the nineteenth century, but there were no material factors that precluded their earlier inception. The closest empirical approximation to this hypothetical adjustment is the Ottawa allotment system described by Lahontan (1905 [1703], 2:481–483) in which trapping groups settled on different sectors of the village territory every winter, each group benefiting from the conservation practiced by the sector's previous occupants.

Demography

Increasing population density in the lower Churchill River drainage could explain the shortages, but there is no evidence for substantial migration into the region during this period. Thompson's estimate applies to the late 1790s; unfortunately, he does not precisely identify the location of the "muskrat country," but Morton (1973:76) states that the term referred to the area between the Nelson and Churchill rivers east of Sturgeon Weir River.

In the year 1782, the small pox from Canada extended to them, and more than one-half of them died; since which although they have no enemies, their country very healthy, yet their numbers increase very slowly. The Musk Rat country, of which I have given the area, may have ninety-two families, each of seven souls, giving to each family an area of two hundred and forty eight square miles of hunting grounds; or thirty five square miles to each soul, a very thin population. (1962 [1784–1812]:92)

Chipewyans moved south into the area in the late 1700s, hunting mostly north of the Churchill River, but their numbers never apparently exceeded 63 persons. It is not clear whether Thompson included them in his estimate, but his figure of 92 families coincides precisely with the 92 adult male hunters enumerated in the Nelson River District in 1822. The available population figures for the period are given below.

Charles's three censuses for 1818, 1820, and 1822 list male trappers by name and distinguish between the Nelson River Crees trading at Split Lake, the Churchill River Crees trading at Nelson House, and the Chipewyans (HBC B.91/e/1, B.91/e/2, B.91/a/8). The increase from 98 male trappers in 1823 to 135 in 1826 (HBC B.141/e/2) may reflect more exact censusing or inclusion of those who had traded with the Northwest Company before 1821 and only gradually found their way onto the Hudson's Bay Company account books; Charles claimed in 1825 that the figure of 135 had been constant since 1820. Taking Charles's 1825 figure of 135 as an estimate, approximately 110 Crees would have remained in the district following the northward emigration of the Chipewyans in the 1820s.

The population drop to 63 in 1838 is difficult to interpret because of uncertainty as to the extent of the area censused. By 1838, Nelson River no longer existed as an administrative district, Split Lake having been transferred to York Factory and the second Nelson House to Norway House. The 1838 census is entitled "Indian Population, Nelson River" (HBC B.239/z/10) and may include Crees trading at Split Lake (on Nelson River), those trading at the second Nelson House (in the former Nelson River District), or both. If both posts were included, the population loss between 1825 and 1838 was substantial, and this was probably the case, since there was substantial migration of Crees into the Saskatchewan prairies in the 1830s and 1840s (Ray 1975). Of the

Table 6 *Indian Population of the Nelson River District*

	CREES IN "MUSKRAT COUNTRY"		Total
	Male 92	Female and children 552	664

1790s

	CREES								CHIPEWYANS			
	Churchill River				*Nelson River*							
	Male	Female	Children	All	Male	Female	children	All	Male	Female	Children	All
1815	17	—	—	—	—	—	—	—	—	—	—	—
1818–1819	23	—	—	—	—	—	—	—	23	—	—	—
1820–1821	19	—	—	—	60	—	—	—	13	—	—	—
1822–1823	25	27	51	103	51	57	141	249	22	18	23	63

Total 415

1825–1826   male hunters [all groups for 1820–1826]   135

1838	Male	Female	Children	All
	63	74	114	251

76 Cree hunters named by Charles in his 1823 census (HBC B.91/a/8), only 21 appear among the 63 listed in the 1838 census fifteen years later (HBC B.239/z/10). Mortality, name changes, and children who grew to adulthood in the interval account for some of the discrepancy, but there was probably also movement in and out of the district. There is, in summary, no evidence for substantial population increase during the late 1700s or early 1800s in the lower Nelson and Churchill River drainages. The one exception to this generalization were the fur trade employees themselves who sometimes hunted and trapped and who may substantially have increased the pressure on animals.

Responses to Scarcity

From the perspective of Western attitudes toward game management, the most obvious question is why Crees did not react to increasing scarcity by limiting their kills and employing such strategies as rotation and selective trapping. In extreme conditions of scarcity, hunters would kill any animals possible, but it should be assumed that declining population trends were noticed before such extemes were reached. Neither was it impossible that collective consensus regarding the desirability of limiting kills could have been reached. Some insight into this problem comes from Thompson's conversation with two Ojibwa trappers in southern Manitoba where steel traps and castoreum had recently been introduced. They related to him a myth describing how beavers, originally a terrestrial race, had been transformed by the supreme being for some offense into their present condition as aquatic game animals. Thus matters had remained, until the discovery of castoreum bait.

The Great Spirit has been, and now is, very angry with them [beavers] and they are now all to be destroyed. About two winters ago Weesaukejauk [the transformer] showed to our brethren the Nipissings and Algonquins the secret of their destruction; that all of them were infatuated with the love of the Castoreum of their own species, and more fond of it than we are of firewater. We are now killing the Beaver without labor, we are now rich, but shall soon be poor, for when the Beaver are destroyed we have nothing to depend on to purchase what we want for our families, strangers now over run our country with their iron traps, and we, and they will soon be poor. (Thompson 1962 [1784–1812]:155)

Here, myth was repeating itself as contemporary event, both the technological innovation and the anticipated resource scarcity being figured
as effects of an unfolding cosmic design. Human agency is identified
only as the proximate cause of a process that is, in any case, inevitable.
Thompson's companions were seemingly aware of the effects of castoreum bait in other districts but fatalistically resigned to their future
poverty. In any case, lacking dispositions or institutions to exclude
strangers from their country, a philosophical posture was appropriate
since there was nothing they could do about it.

There is no reason to believe that this particular myth was shared by
the Churchill River Crees, and neither is it clear that they had knowledge of the effects of intensified predation in other areas. The Ojibwas'
explanation is, however, one instance of the more general subarctic
Algonquian postulate that human-animal relations are mediated by
spiritual entities. The exceptional magnitude and duration of the shortages undoubtedly prompted other explanations similar to those of the
Ojibwas, but these were not likely to be communicated to the traders.
Earlier localized and temporary shortages were conceived as changes in
the distribution of animals on the landscape. They had known explanations such as Eskimo sorcery (Drage 1968 [1748–49], 2:43) or the in-
scrutable designs of the game ruler beings (Thompson 1962 [1784–
1812]:87–88) and known solutions such as residential movement elsewhere. When asked, the Crees simply told the traders at Nelson House
in 1815 that beavers were scarce because they had been overhunted for
many years in the fur trade (HBC B.141/e/1 [1815]). I suspect that this
was "the answer best adapted to avoid other questions, and please the
enquirer," conventional Cree practice when queried about things sacred
(Thompson 1962 [1784–1812]:75), although it may also have been a
belated deduction from a novel experience. The game shortages occurred because Crees conceived the moose, caribou, and beaver as infinitely renewable resources whose numbers could neither be reduced
by overkilling nor managed by selective hunting. This was why it was
appropriate to kill large numbers of animals and retrieve only delicacies
and also to kill as many animals as possible for commercial purposes.
And when the new technology and market increased rates of predation
to levels that caused populations to decline, the Crees continued to
hunt indiscriminately because they did not initially construe the two
processes to be related. The fur trade provided the means and incentive
for what were probably unprecedented harvests, but the spiritualized

philosophy of hunting was itself distinctively Algonquian and almost certainly of prehistoric provenience.

Sacred Conservation

The representation of Indians as "ecologists" has deep roots in the European image of the Indian as *naturvolken*, uncultured beings synecdochically attuned to the wilderness. Commercial images of Indians weeping over blighted industrial landscapes or smiling benignly as white youths remove garbage from camp sites today acquire legitimacy from popular representations of Indian religion. The image of the Indian ecologist has drawn extensively on representations of human-environment relations abstracted from religious expressions in Indian societies. The basic postulate of these images is that Indian subsistence systems did not adversely affect New World ecosystems and that they did not because Indian spirituality fostered practices of sustained yield management. Indians, it is said, were and are "conservationists" of wild resources; with respect to animals, "conservation" means variously limiting kills to what is needed for survival, utilizing all products of slain animals, and deliberately managing animal populations on a sustained yield basis. These kinds of conservation efforts are purportedly of pre-Columbian antiquity, reflecting Indian awareness of the harmful effects of indiscriminate hunting.

The architect of the aboriginal conservator image in anthropology was Speck (1915), who described sustained yield beaver trapping by boreal forest Algonquians during the first quarter of the present century. Speck began with the assumption that conservation, like the institution of delimited and privatized hunting tracts, was an indigenous adaption to the uncertainties of subarctic foraging. Of the tract system in general, Speck wrote,

Despite the continued killing in the tract each year the supply is always replenished by the animals allowed to breed there. There is nothing astonishing in this to the mind of the Indian because the killing is definitely regulated so that only the increase is consumed, enough stock being left each season to ensure a supply for the succeeding year. In this manner, the game is "farmed," so to speak, and the continued killing through centuries does not affect the stock fundamentally. It can readily be seen that the thoughtless slaughter of game in one season would spoil things for the next and soon bring the proprietor to famine. (1915a:293)

The Indians represented the institution as of pre-Columbian antiquity, and Speck accepted it as such. Speck's conception of management as an indigenous practice continues to be professed (Martin 1978, Vecsey 1980) and related to a religiously motivated "aboriginal land ethic." The fact that some Algonquian management practices possess religious significance was first established in Feit's (1973a, 1973b) descriptions of Eastern Cree ethnoecology. The Waswanipi conceive the practice of limiting kills by rotational use of hunting tracts as an obligation that the human hunter owes to the prey.

It is (also) claimed that men have the skill and technology to kill many animals, too many, and it is part of the responsibility of the hunter not to kill more than he is given, not to "play" with animals by killing them for fun or self-aggrandizement. . . . Bad luck is the result of a decision on the part of *chuetenshu* [North Wind spirit] or the animals that a man should not get what he wants—usually because he has failed to fulfill one or more of his responsibilities. One of the most important responsibilities is not to kill too many animals. Thus the hunter is often confronting the consequences of his own activity when he goes hunting, and this confrontation occurs through the will of *chuetenshu* and the animals. (Feit 1973a:117)

As Feit points out, the objective consequences of these beliefs are comparable to those produced by secular game management policies that make no reference to environing spirits. Whatever the mystifications of the cognized model, the latter, at least in this case, "elicits behavior appropriate to the material situation of the actors" (Rappaport 1984:239). There is no question that some subarctic Indians today limit their kills, rotate their hunting tracts, and practice sustained yield conservation of furbearer populations. Further, it is clear that some conceive the effects of such management in terms of traditional religious postulates. In addition to Feit's pioneering work, Nelson's *Make Prayers to the Raven* (1983) is a detailed exposition of these practices among the Athapaskan Koyukons, and some Rock Crees today also understand the effects of their management in religious terms. When these practices and understandings developed is another matter.

Martin (1978) and Vecsey (1980) maintain the aboriginality not only of management but of the religiously significant management described by Feit. Vecsey, in particular, confidently generalizes an "environmental ethic" to all North American Indians, past and present.

In addition to the conservation (total utilization) of each animal killed, Lithic Indians [sic] conserved certain members of each species of animal, sparing female or pregnant deer. We find Indian admonitions not to waste animal sources for consciously economic and religious motives to the extent that it is said, "with animals they are careful, and in general their attitudes are those we would call conservation minded." (1980:9)

With respect to an Indian role in game depletions, Vecsey concludes that "overkill by Indians is unfounded in the historical period outside of the fur trade context" (ibid.:31). It is, in fact, to boreal forest Algonquians in the fur trade that the available data on both game shortages and game management primarily pertain. Vecsey acknowledges the boreal forest game shortages, representing them as the consequence of the disintegration of indigenous religious values.

But does Indian participation in the white fur trade rule out the thesis that Indians possessed an environmental ethic? Did Indian religious beliefs not have an effect on Indian actions in historical events? It is unfortunate that Indian ideals regarding environment were often vitiated by white economic and religious thrusts, but weakening does not mean that ideals were non-existent or aboriginally ineffective. They simply were not strong enough always to withstand white pressures. . . . The Indian complicity must be seen in the context of white colonial trade in which Indians often had to sacrifice their ideals to survive. (ibid.:28).

Blaming Indians for the subarctic game shortages, Vecsey goes on to say, deflects guilt from the Europeans who provided the incentives, and he proceeds, in a near-hysterical vein, to indict scholars who document such shortages as apologists for the Hudson's Bay Company monopoly (ibid.:30). Vecsey's politically correct extenuation works doubly to the Indians' disadvantage. First, the "environmental ethic" and sustained yield management practices were not elements of Algonquian culture in the first place. Subarctic Indians are portrayed as opportunists or victims, renouncing in exchange for trade goods an "environmentalism" that is a creation of the white popular imagination and its academic redactions. Second, the Algonquians are excused for practices that Vecsey calls "overkill" or "waste" of resources but that originally possessed no such meanings for the Algonquians. Rather than "sacrificing their ideals," Crees and other boreal forest Indians reproduced them with utmost fidelity in the fur trade. There existed no conception of "waste" attached to the material bodies of animals, and neither was there a conception of regional animal populations manageable by selective hunting.

The War against the Animals

Martin's controversial book, *Keepers of the Game* (1978; cf. Krech 1981), popularized the fiction of the aboriginal and religiously motivated conservation ethic that informs Vecsey's analysis. The argument I outline below is critical of Martin's interpretation but at the same time shares with it the thesis that the boreal forest game shortages need to be understood from the perspective of the Indians and the conceptions of animals that they brought to the trade. Martin begins by addressing the seemingly paradoxical behavior of Indian trappers. Aware of the ultimately destructive effects of indiscriminate killing, they persisted in it nonetheless, eventually depleting animals that were both a food resource and the basis of their purchasing power. Martin assumes that the Indians were technologically capable of producing game shortages in the precontact period. They avoided doing so because of the latent conservation effects of residential movement and seasonal resource scheduling; large surpluses of meat could not be transported and hunters focused serially on species throughout the season, diffusing the impact on any one resource. To these factors might be added the awareness that Martin ascribes to the Indians of the ensuing scarcity and famine that indiscriminate killing would produce. Martin identifies the major factor preventing overkill as the fear of punishment that it would provoke from the animals and their deific "owners." According to Martin, the obligation to limit kills was part of the indigenous respect complex focused on animals.

And here is the real crux of the issue. The single most important deterrent to successful hunting, in the Eastern Algonkian's mind at any rate, was the fear of spiritual reprisal for indiscrete slaughter. . . . The issue is that there were traditionally powerful, genuinely compelling sanctions against overkilling wildlife. We know they were vestigially operative at the time of white contact because eyewitness observers described them, and they have survived well into modern times in parts of Eastern Canada. (Martin 1978:18)

The footnote to which the reader is referred at the end of this passage contains no references at all to eyewitness observers in the early contact period. The sources cited are two articles by Harvey Feit (1973*a*, 1973*b*) describing the religious significance of moose and beaver conservation among Eastern Crees in the 1960s.

Martin's thesis is as follows. Algonquians originally refrained from excessive killing because they feared retribution by the animals. Epidemic diseases, introduced by Euro-Canadians and preceding them into the interior, were defined by Indians, within the context of native disease theory, as unprovoked assaults on them by animals. Thus, the traditional religious respect complex broke down, missionary entrepreneurship and the incentives of the fur trade delivering merely the *coup de grace*. Religious sanctions against overkill disappeared, and Algonquians enthusiastically and vengefully exterminated subarctic big game and furbearers. This retaliation was simultaneously profitable in the short run, given new roles as post provisioners and commercial trappers. Martin argues further that in the wake of the epidemics and game depletions, traditional religious attitudes and conservation practices reemerged and continued thereafter, much as Feit found them in Quebec. Martin concludes by identifying two contemporary orientations toward animal conservation, one commercial and the other spiritual.

It is my conviction that the second motive, the spiritual sense of obligation and fear of retribution, in the absence of a compelling commercial incentive in late prehistoric times, was adequate to ensure the effective conservation of game resources. What we are witnessing today, among the Waswanipi Cree, for example, is the recrudescence of a kind of aboriginal land ethic—a sentiment which has stood opposed to the excessive slaughter of wildlife for whatever purpose, whether for commercial gain or vendetta. (1978:176)

Thus, sacred management was practiced prehistorically, abandoned during the fur trade, and then belatedly resurrected. The primary ethnographic criticism of this thesis—that boreal Algonquians do not associate disease sanctions with animals—has been well argued elsewhere (Krech 1981). Other facets of the argument have received less attention. First, there is no basis for the assumption that game depletions never occurred prehistorically, since, as Martin notes, indigenous foraging strategies could have produced such events. Second, Martin introduces no evidence whatsoever that management was practiced in the seventeenth and eighteenth centuries, much less defined as a practice whose omission angers animal beings. Finally, there is indeed evidence that "religious" beliefs influenced harvesting patterns, but the effects encouraged rather than prevented unlimited hunting.

Infinite Resources

Martin's theory of the aboriginal "land ethic" assumes that hunters understood animal populations to be manageable and could anticipate the long-term effects of intensified predation.

> It is difficult to imagine how an individual whose subsistence economy was underpinned by a reliance upon fish, game, wild plant foods, and, in some cases, cultivated plants could have been so oblivious to wildlife population dynamics as not to see that his present course of hunting was far too exploitive. The fur trading Indian, whether he be a member of a hunter-gatherer society or a horticultural society, was simply too skilled a hunter to overlook the ultimate consequences of wildlife overkill. Early records confirm this skepticism. More than one fur company agent or missionary recorded in his journal the lament of some heart-sick Indian informant who plainly recognized that the reckless hunter was digging his own grave. And yet the raid on fur-bearers continued, encouraged by Jesuit missionaries and fur company agents and prosecuted by the Indian himself. (Martin 1978:3)

Martin's retaliatory "war against the animals" is introduced to explain this contradiction. In his argument, Indians are represented as continuing their "holy war" even after the consequences of indiscriminate killing, which they anticipated all along, were objectively felt as material impoverishment and famine. An alternative question is whether Crees and other Algonquians would have continued to exploit declining animal populations indiscriminately if they recognized the potential effectiveness of management in stabilizing and reversing such decline. Animal populations fluctuated in the boreal forest because of many factors unrelated to human predation. That the size of animal populations can be manipulated by limiting kills or killing selectively by age and sex is not objectively given to the consciousness of even the most practiced foragers, especially residentially mobile groups with low population densities.

Two Cree representations of the hunter-prey relationship—as benefactive and as adversarial—coexist in unstable equilibrium, and both of these were also present in the eighteenth and nineteenth centuries. Crees conceive any event of hunting as morally ambiguous and thus potentially hazardous in its consequences for later foraging. The disposition of the animals toward hunting is an unresolvable question to which the contradictory models of the human-animal relationship provide distinct answers. In the 1700s, as in the present, the dominant ideology was that of the animal benefactor who "loves" the hunter and voluntarily surrenders its body. In return, the animal exacts diverse expressions of ritual deference and respect, but there is no evidence at all that either limited killing or total utilization was included among these. Some Crees today regard unlimited killing and selective utilization of animals as lamentable or dangerous, but all of the ethnographic evidence for these dispositions dates from the present century.

It is not, then, that the number of animals killed was religiously insignificant but that the significance was precisely the opposite of what it has today become. The Crees in the 1700s believed—or told the traders they believed—that the more animals they killed, the more they would kill in the future. According to Robson, who was on Hudson Bay in 1733,

they have a maxim very prejudicial to this country which is that the more beasts they kill, the more they increase; and in consequence of this they destroy great numbers for the sake of the tongues, leaving the carcasses to rot. (1965 [1752]:41)

Ellis's observations possibly copied Robson:

They make prodigious Slaughter every Season among the Deer [caribou], from an unaccountable Notion that the more they destroy, the greater Plenty will succeed; therefore sometimes they leave three or four hundred dead on the Plain, taking out of them only their Tongues, and leaving their Carcasses either to rot, or be devoured by the wild Beasts. (1967 [1748]:85)

Graham (1969 [1767–1791]:154) wrote, "They kill animals out of wantonness, alleging the more they destroy the more plentiful they grow." He then went on to describe the practice of retrieving tongues and other delicacies and abandoning the carcasses. Finally, the same concept was described by Umfreville:

As their country abounds with innumerable herds of deers, elks, and buffaloes, they frequently make great slaughter among them; and upon these occasions they have no regard to futurity, or providing for an unsuccessful day. Whether they happen to be pining under the grasp of pinching necessity, or enjoying themselves in all the happiness of health and plenty, they kill all they can, having an incontrovertible maxim among them, which is "The more they kill, the more they have to kill" and this opinion, though diametrically opposite to reason or common sense is as pertinaciously held by them, as his tenets are by the most bigotted enthusiast. (1954 [1790]:38)

Given the enthusiastic plagiarism practiced by the early chroniclers of Hudson Bay (Pentland 1976), the passages above need not all be taken as independent attestations, but it is clear that a distinctively Algonquian conception was recorded. All the usual caveats apply here: the Cree discourse may have been misunderstood or distorted, and there may have been other undescribed conceptions of animal population dynamics. But these are the earliest sources that exist on the subject, and they exhibit a striking compatibility both with the elastic scope of Cree predation and with themes still present in Cree society. Unlike the English and Scottish traders, who incredulously observed their harvesting practices in the eighteenth century, the Crees had no conception of the boreal fauna as a finite quantity of biomass, manipulatable by selective killing or reducible through predation when harvests exceeded rates of increase. Animal flesh was infinitely renewable; animals could not be destroyed but only temporarily displaced. Thus, it was no more possible to kill too many animals than it was to waste their carcasses. Neither management nor overkill was imagined as feasible on the technical plane. Hunters could kill animals in great numbers and retrieve only delicacies, but since this behavior was not contrary to the wishes of the game rulers and the animals, it would have, in the long term, no influence on the numbers of animals in the bush or the number available to the hunter.

"Waste" and "overkill" could occur in this cosmos but only as events of ritual omission. The numbers of animals in the world, their distribution on the landscape, and their accessibility to hunters were all conceived to be determined by the wishes of the immortal animals themselves or by those of their deific "owners." The nominal death of an animal was only one moment in a cycle: animals live in the bush, are killed by hunters, persist as souls after their bodies are eaten, and return again to the world through birth or spontaneous regeneration. The fine details of this system—whether the number of animal souls in the cosmos fluctuates or remains constant—are not recoverable, if they were, indeed, ever socially agreed on. By killing, humans participate in the process, interrupting the duration of one physical manifestation. They also ensure the next by exhibiting respect and returning the bones to the bush. It was only the *ahcāk*, or "soul," of the animal that could be "wasted" by neglecting the practices that facilitated its rebirth. It was in the eat-all feast and in the mortuary deposition of bones in water and on trees that Crees and other Algonquians "managed" animals; both are described in the late 1700s and early 1800s, concurrently with the indiscriminate harvesting practices that produced the game shortages. The numbers of animals available to hunters in the future could be influenced by ceremonial regeneration; the numbers killed or the parts utilized were irrelevant. Neither, seemingly was it, necessary to ritualize each animal but only those whose entire bodies were brought out of the bush and into camp. The caribou left "either to rot, or be devoured by the wild Beasts" (Ellis 1967 [1748]:85) remained in the bush, there naturally to return to life.

All these practices are consistent with the image of the animal benefactor. The significance of unlimited killing alters if the adversarial conception is foregrounded. If the animal is an enemy, the numbers killed and the use (or nonuse) of the products are of no consequence. If all hunting has connotations of murder and cannibalism, the hunter is jeopardized whether she or he traps two beavers or the entire lodge, utilizes an entire caribou or takes only the tongue. However, an animal that the hunter confronts and does not kill, for whatever reason, may inform its cohorts. In the 1600s, Dallion wrote that the Iroquoian-speaking Neutrals

have this maxim for all kinds of animals, whether they need them or not, that they must kill all they find, for fear, as they say, that if they do not take them the beasts would go and tell the others how they had been hunted and that then, in times of want, they would not find any more. (LeClercq 1881 [1691], 1:269)

The Neutrals were also farmers, and the adversarial model of hunting may have been culturally dominant among them. But their explanation reiterates the theme of concealment dramatized in the Cree eat-all feast. Indiscriminate killing was a sacred act, but it also implicated the image of the adversarial animal. Crees in the Nelson River District in the 1790s understood the new weaponry introduced in the trade to have altered a prior hegemony in which animals were superordinate, physically attacking humans (bears) or resisting them in impregnable lodges while inundating the earth with water (beavers) (Thompson 1962 [1784–1812]:94–95). The early fur trade was a new epoch in which humans were ascendant over their animal adversaries. Thus, the conflictual themes central to Martin's thesis were very much present, but they were nothing new and had nothing to do with indigenous disease theory. These themes reiterated under new technological conditions the meaning hunting possessed prehistorically: killing and eating indexed the predators' dominance and power.

On another level entirely, the Neutral who spoke with Dallion may have been trying to say that the animal would tell its fellows that the human hunters did not need them. "Tell the others how they had been hunted" means, in such a context, "tell the others that they are rejected." This aligns with the Algonquian axiom that one must take what one is given from the *ahcāk* beings. It was *failure* to kill all the animals offered that would jeopardize future hunting in Cree ideology in the 1700s and early 1800s. To kill all the animals possible may be expedient from the point of view of commercial incentives or preferred diet. Simultaneously, on the plane of sociality, it is an act of love and gratitude. If a hunter is "offered" much, it is obligatory to take much. Indiscriminate killing, like the eat-all feast, discharges the obligation to receive, an insight for which I am indebted to Richard Preston. Ray (1975:59–60) and Bishop (1981a:55) have argued similarly that boreal forest Algonquians during the early fur trade lacked a Western conception of animal population dynamics and thus "respected" animals in religious terms while unknowingly decimating them. To this, it is necessary to add that the dominant ideology of human-animal relationships not only allowed indiscriminate hunting but enjoined it. "Respect," in other words, was not originally conjoined with technical management in the way that it is in some subarctic Indian communities today.

One can speculate that the first signs of declining animal populations were assimilated by Crees to their prior experience with short-term fluctuations. Later, when the magnitude and extent of the depletion became known, it would have been concluded that something novel was occurring and an explanation sought in the relations between hunters and *ahcāk* beings. Increased hunting was undoubtedly recognized as the proximal cause of the shortages, but it is unlikely that significance was ascribed to it since indiscriminate predation had never produced such effects in the past. If hunting was now producing such effects, it was because the game ruler beings were now causing it to do so by failing to re-create the slain animals. Limiting kills would not have been a rational response to such an enigma.

Since there are scattered references to beaver management by Crees in the seventeenth and eighteenth century, the conception of game as infinite resource seemingly coexisted in some areas with conceptions of beavers as a species whose numbers could be controlled by selective trapping. Whether this subdominant and more superficially Western doctrine was aboriginal or of historical inception remains unknown. It would be obvious to nomadic hunters that animals become progressively harder to locate the longer a single activity area is exploited, but this datum would not necessarily make the effectiveness of selective hunting obvious. When submitted to the doctrine of infinite renewal, decreasing efficiency would be interpreted not as an objective shortage of animals in the bush but as the result of decisions that animals no longer wished to be hunted in the area or that they had not yet been reborn.

The conception of animal resources as infinitely renewable was not unique to the Crees. Julius Jetté (1911:604) wrote of the Athapaskan Koyukons in the early 1900s, "No fear of killing too many is entertained, for the Ten'a hold that no animal species endowed with a *yega* [soul or game ruler being] can become extinct." More recently, it has been described also among the Crees' Chipewyan neighbors to the north: "[Since] the Chipewyan believe that the size of animal populations does not vary, only its distribution, there is always enough subsistence material to go around but not enough magical power to obtain it" (Sharp 1979:91). The conception persists among some contemporary Crees and Ojibwas (Bishop 1974:35–36), although sustained yield management of furbearers has been practiced since at least the late 1800s. Further comparative material could almost certainly be added. The idea that animals regenerate after death is widely distributed in forager societies. Less is known of how forager societies conceptualize their own impact on animal populations. Since their ethnoecological systems have been or will soon be transformed through articulation with Western management (and antimanagement) practices, their study is an important desideratum, one of great relevance to comparative study of forager modes of production.

The Resilience of Cree Foraging Strategies

It remains to indicate the relevance of these events to anthropological analyses of the forager labor process. I began the chapter by suggesting that Cree hunting practices in the years before the game shortages provide a privileged example of the symbolic organization of labor. Superficially, this is the case because Cree hunters acted on animals in terms of conceptions that we categorize as "religious": the belief that game animals magically regenerate after death and therefore need not and cannot be managed by selective hunting. Magico-religious systems, by general consensus, are integrally "symbolic," and therefore a labor process influenced by them is also "symbolic." The point, however, is not to register a novel application of the Weberian thesis that religious values influence economic dispositions to action. It is rather that the labor process itself is integrally symbolic to the degree that it is organized by categories and propositions that are not mechanically deducible from human biology, available technology, or the environing ecosystem.

The Churchill River game shortages indicate that human foraging populations do not invariably exist in conditions of equilibrium with their resources and that homeostatic mechanisms for adjusting to changing conditions are not invariably present. It remains unclear when (or whether) during the later 1800s beaver and big game populations subsequently increased to levels permitting acceptable rates of capture, but it is clear that no mechanisms existed to prevent their decline or to reverse it before the system became dysfunctional by energetic criteria. Sahlins's (1972) original formulation of "affluence" in nomadic hunter-gatherer society presupposes that resources were ordinarily sufficient to satisfy finite needs and desires. Given generalized reciprocity, effective foraging strategies, broad diet breadth, and frequent residential movement, food was procured with less per capita work than in other conditions of society. Such conditions can be assumed to have existed prehistorically and during the early fur trade in the Churchill River drainage, although the absence of botanicals for most of the year and extreme fluctuations in animal resources produced occasional scarcity. We can provisionally assume that the prehistoric and early contact Cree populations satisfied their resource needs and desires with rates of predation that did not ordinarily cause species declines. Increased human population, increased per capita predation, and decreasing animal populations are all potential perturbations to such a system. During the late 1700s and 1800s, the expansion of inland trading posts prompted intensified rates of predation by Crees which led to a long-term decline in beaver, moose, and caribou populations.

Rappaport (1984:241,341) introduced the distinction between "goal ranges"—the range of states of variables consistent with the persistence of some subsistence system—and "reference values"—states of some variable recognized or desired by human actors. The former is a property of objective ecosystems, the latter of the socially mediated consciousness people have of ecosystems in which they participate. As a measure of resources, the concept of "reference value" can be further subcategorized as quantities that people believe they need, want, expect to obtain under various circumstances, and can harvest renewably. With respect to the Crees in the early 1800s, the goal range in question was the number of moose, caribou, and beavers that could be hunted without initiating population declines and consequent human starvation. This number can be assumed to shift reversibly over time with fluctuations in these populations caused by other factors. In the late 1700s and early 1800s, the "reference value"—the number of animals Crees desired to kill for domestic and commercial purposes—increased. The factors explaining this increase were the availability of trade goods, the expanded commercial market for animals, and a technology that allowed intensified killing without exceeding another reference value: culturally tolerable levels of foraging labor. This increased reference value eventually exceeded the goal range, and the animals went progressively into decline.

Multiple responses by foragers can be postulated in a situation where animal resources are conceived to be (and are factually) declining but have not yet been reduced to the point where survival requires harvesting any individuals encountered. Since declining animal populations would require progressively increasing foraging efforts, one would predict that some adjustments consonant with "least effort" would occur to reverse the declines before hunger and starvation became relatively commonplace and adjustments obligatory. The characteristic foragers' strategy in such circumstances is movement into an area with more abundant resources, if one exists and is known. There is no evidence for emigration out of the Nelson River District, except later in the 1830s and 1840s. Movement within the district was common, but seemingly no areas were avoided for intervals sufficient to allow animal populations to increase. Thompson (1962 [1784–1812]:104) wrote of the Crees, "Notwithstanding the hardships the Natives sometimes suffer, they are strongly attached to the country of Rivers, Lakes, and Forests." Sentiments such as these, or the belief that there were no greener fields elsewhere, presumably limited emigration.

Other imaginable responses to increasing scarcity would involve altering certain variables in the system to preserve others in the face of environmental perturbation (cf. Vayda and McCay 1975), for example, adding new resources. One such adjustment could be management: manipulation of the future availability of the resource by limiting current rates of harvest. Reference values for resources may or may not be calculated in relation to some quantity beyond which people anticipate future shortages. If such a culturally recognized quantity exists and is within the goal range as objectively given, foragers may consciously manage their harvests. In such a self-equilibrating system, predation may thus be maintained continuously within the goal range or it can be adjusted downward periodically in response to perceived declines in animal populations that signal that the goal range is being exceeded. Such an adjustment requires the familiar compromise between levels of immediate desire for the resource and its long-term sustainability: the forager must be prepared to harvest less than is possible and, perhaps, desirable. These are the strategies used today by some Crees who manage the furbearers and big game populations on their traplines. Such equilibrating responses did not occur in the early 1800s because Crees at this time recognized no reference value beyond which predation could not continue without resource depletion. Human predation had no effect on animal populations and hence no quantitative significance: the numbers killed in the present bore no relation to the numbers subsequently available. The significance of the doctrine of infinite renewal is precisely that there was in Cree ideology no equivalent to a "goal range" at all.

A third response to resource decline could involve altering the values of existing variables, for example, by increasing consumption of previously underutilized species. Cree hunting for both domestic and commercial purposes was focused on moose, caribou, and beaver. To maintain acquisition of meat and furs at the desired levels, more labor could have been redirected onto other furbearing animals and onto fish and hare. Such a substitutive response might or might not be conceived to be reversible. Foragers could be motivated by the expectation that the declining resources would subsequently increase in numbers and again become harvestable at the accustomed levels. The substitution would allow declining populations of the preferred species to recover, increase the reliability with which needs could be met, and possibly reduce the energy costs entailed in hunting an increasingly scarce quarry. Since boreal animal populations fluctuate annually and seasonally in numbers and in accessibility, reversible switching between resources—or between relative amounts of time invested in different resources—must have been a short-term strategy. Transitions to economies based on fish and hare have been documented for subarctic Ojibwa groups in the 1800s but only as *a posteriori* adjustments to long-term game shortages in which preferred resources were unobtainable (Bishop 1974:245–254, Rogers and Black 1976). The Cree diet was relatively broad (see chap. 11), but the evidence suggests that throughout the period of the game shortages most male labor continued to be allocated to big game, which was originally the most efficient (and preferred) food source, and secondarily to beavers, which were both the staple of the fur trade and a good source of meat. Other furbearers such as martens and muskrats were eaten but provided substantially less meat per animal. During the game shortages, there is evidence that Crees trapped other furbearers more intensively as beavers became scarce, and the proportion of fish and small game in the diet undoubtedly increased. Switching to other resources did not occur early enough or for sufficiently long periods to allow beavers, moose, or caribou to recover. One obstacle to such change may have been the relatively inflexible character of the sexual division of labor. While big game hunting, beaver trapping, and summer fish spearing were male activities, winter fishing through the ice and marten and hare trapping were usually performed by women (Thompson 1962 [1784–1812]:67). In winter 1794, during a calm in which moose hunting was impossible, a Cree came to Thompson's post at Reed Lake to obtain fish and hooks.

He said his three wives and his children had had very little to eat for nearly a whole Moon adding you may be sure we suffer hunger when I come to beg fish and get hooks for my women to angle with. . . . I felt for him, for nothing but sad necessity can compel a Nahathaway hunter to carry away fish and angle for them, this is too mean for a hunter; meat he carries with pleasure, but fish is degradation. (Ibid.:101)

Despite worsening conditions, fish were not exploited intensively except in emergencies. In 1815, the same year in which nine cases of famine cannibalism are alluded to, the Nelson House District report stated that the Crees "think it below them to fish until so weak that all they can do is angle on the ice which they are often driven to" (HBC B.141/e/1, cf. Bishop 1974:205). As big game and beavers declined in number, women's production of fish and hare undoubtedly increased, but men seemingly did not routinely include these activities in their foraging until later in the century. In 1825, the Crees were still hunting big game whenever possible, to the relative neglect of furbearing animals (HBC B.141/e/2).

A fourth adjustment could be to seek to maintain the predation level of the most preferred resources at the desired level by progressively increasing the value of the labor variable, and this, as long as it could be sustained, was seemingly the Cree response. Cree men apparently responded to growing scarcity by increasing their labor and attempting to kill moose, caribou, and beavers in the same numbers as previously. This would have the effect of intensifying their population declines. Eventually, the resources were depleted to the point where the desired capture values could not be maintained, whatever the level of work. Proportionately greater labor was being expended for proportionately fewer animals than had been the case at the beginning of the period. At this point, tragically, the reference value became whatever animals could be found to sustain life or trade for indispensable tools and weapons. The basic variables of the foraging system itself remained unchanged throughout this period: Crees remained in the same region, sought the same animals, and did not innovate novel management strategies. The increasing scarcity of animals brought the system to a condition where it was no longer capable of providing adequate quantities of food or sufficient furs to acquire trade goods. This was especially the case after 1821, when the Hudson's Bay Company increased the price of goods. In summary, the organization of Cree foraging changed substantially in the later 1800s, but there occurred no equilibrating adjustments or homeostatic innovations during or immediately after the game shortages. People continued to hunt animals indiscriminately as they declined. The human costs in increased labor, hunger, malnutrition, and starvation are only obliquely refracted in the traders' characterization of the Crees' condition as "wretched." The combined effects of environmental depletion and technological dependency thereafter created a combined mode of subsistence and commercial foraging so unstable in the long term that it could only be perpetuated by energy subventions from outside the boreal forest (Ray 1984).

An important desideratum concerns the consequences of indiscriminate killing and selective use of carcasses under prehistoric and early fur trade conditions. In these circumstances, desired predation rates were undoubtedly lower because of the absence or relative inaccessibility of markets for furs and provisions. Additionally, the indigenous technology required greater labor investments in many kinds of foraging than was subsequently possible with guns, ice chisels, and the steel trap-castoreum complex. Given these factors, an argument could be made that the doctrine of infinite animal renewal was originally a religiously mediated representation of the factual effects of indiscriminate human predation on animal populations. If the major animal resources were density dependent, and thus subject to declining fecundity and reproductive success above certain levels, indiscriminate hunting by highly mobile bands might have functioned to enhance reproduction by keeping populations well below "carrying capacity" and in a condition of rapid expansion (cf. Paine 1973). More would need to be known of the population dynamics of the boreal fauna before indiscriminate killing is inscribed along with cow taboos, Aztec sacrifice, the potlatch, Australian circumcision, and shoulderblade divination in the roster of exotic practices with (purported) ecological silver linings. While indiscriminate hunting did not subject the Crees to biological destruction as a population, it remains unclear whether the practice was more "adaptive"—in terms of reproductive fitness, protein, caloric efficiency, reliability, or other currencies—than more limited killing. Human predation rates interact with other factors causing boreal resource fluctuations, and consequently the effects of any harvesting strategy will vary from one year to the next. It is clear, in any case, that indiscriminate killing was ultimately disadvantageous under the new technological and market circumstances of the fur trade. While the Crees' involvement in the fur trade was a causal factor in the depletions, there is no reason to believe that technological innovations, trade, conflict, human population changes, and fluctuating animal populations never had comparable effects among their prehistoric ancestors or in other forager populations. The strategies foragers use are "chosen" from within a permissible range limited but not determined by technological, demographic, and ecosystem variables. They are neither the only strategies possible nor necessarily the most appropriate, relative to these variables.

The Indigenization of the Fur Trade

A final consideration concerns the relative significance of the Crees' existing culture and their historical articulation with the world market in bringing the game shortages about. Throughout, there was no historic inevitability to the game shortages arising from exogenous market influences on a reactive Cree population. The Crees' desire for the introduced goods was finite, and the avarice of the traders could not directly be translated into increased rates of predation for commercial purposes (however often they wished that it could). Consequently, throughout the seventeenth and eighteenth centuries, the Indians, especially the Assiniboine and Cree middlemen, held the upper hand in the fur trade at York factory, and to a considerable extent they dictated the terms of the trade. Thus the [Hudson's Bay] Company was forced to make most of the adjustments during this period. (Ray 1974:61)

Woodburn (1980,1982,1988) has used the phrase "immediate return" to identify a specifiable type of foraging society of which the Tanzanian Hadza, the Dobe !Kung, the Mbuti, and most Australian Aboriginal groups were typical exemplars. Prior to the late 1800s, the Crees approximated the characteristics of this type, and there is no reason to believe that their ancestors were doing things differently. From the perspective of a historical anthropology that takes social reproduction and transformation as conjoined facets of the same process (Sahlins 1981, 1985), the most remarkable characteristic of Cree fur trade involvements is the subjection of European traders and their goods to the social designs of immediate return. This is not to discount the substantial changes in foraging strategies, rates of predation, material culture, property concepts, and seasonal cycles which accompanied the Crees' new roles as commercial fur trappers and provisioners. But these innovations were all the by-products of reproducing prehistoric intentions under novel circumstances.

Of the immediate return type, Woodburn (1980:99) writes,

All these societies are nomadic and positively value movement. They do not accumulate property but consume it, give it away, gamble it away, or throw it away. Most of them have knowledge of techniques for storing food but use them only occasionally to prevent food from going rotten rather than to save it for some future occasion. They tend to use portable, utilitarian, easily acquired, replaceable artifacts—made with real skill but without hours of labor.

Woodburn (ibid.:101) goes on to identify "what amounts to a repudiation of all measures of conservation, of all investment in fixed assets, and of all attempts at planned development of resources" and to observe that "those who consume most of their food on the day they obtain it and who are unconcerned about storage, also appear to be relatively unconcerned about conservation and about planned development of their resources." One could add, in the domain of the "economy" proper, a disposition toward generalized sharing of preferred foods and a conception of land and resources as free goods. Woodburn opposes this type to "delayed return" foragers who are sedentary, store food, invest in complex equipment, and may manage resources. The two categories partially coincide with Alain Testart's (1981) *nomades* and *stockeurs* and Louis Binford's (1980) "foragers" and "collectors." Representations of the Crees in the traders' accounts coincide very closely with Woodburn's constructions. They were mobile, stored little food, hunted primarily when food on hand was exhausted, invested in no stationary equipment (except caribou fences), did not accumulate property, and did not manage (by Western criteria) animal resources. As to food distribution, Thompson (1962[1784–1812]:74) wrote, "Those acts that pass between man and man for generous charity and kind compassion in civilized society, are no more than what is everyday practiced by these Savages; as acts of common duty." It is unlikely that these characteristics were historic transformations of qualitatively distinct prehistoric antecedents.

How does a society of foragers change when its members begin hunting for commercial as well as domestic purposes and must secure their technological means through this commerce? Prior to the game depletions, the cumulative answer was not very much. In the fur trade, Crees continued to be foragers. Trade with outsiders could not have been anything new, although the materials and magnitude of the European trade were. For the Crees who produced their own furs, the animals that acquired new significance as exchange values were, with some exceptions (wolves, wolverines, foxes), existing use values whose meat and hides figured in prehistoric consumption and manufacture. Crees were killing the same animals, although probably in different proportions than previously and with increased effort devoted to beavers and the smaller furbearers. There were certain minor adjustments in the direction of "delayed return" since Crees had to plan to kill furbearers in desired quantities and cache or transport the pelts until they could be traded. The fur trade, by and large, did not innovate novel resources, although it introduced new foraging strategies linked with guns and steel traps. The increased focus on furbearers possibly had such effects as a reduction in group size during some periods in winter, the practice of marking beaver lodges as private property, and the consecutive scheduling of beaver and big game hunting in winter. Those Crees who became professional middlemen traders continued to hunt while displacing the labor of commercial fur trapping onto their inland trading partners. The Crees rapidly became dependent on a new foraging technology, but since the goods they needed could be obtained with little effort, the dependency initially had minimal structural effect. Neither was the (sometimes?) increased labor devoted to foraging a structural change, since the reference values for appropriate quantities of labor were elastic with respect to short-term objectives. Although rates of predation increased, the weapons and tools acquired from the traders compensated by making some forms of hunting more efficient and by reducing the time spent fabricating and maintaining indigenous manufactures. The particular historical preconditions for participation in the trade without structural transformation were finite demand, low prices for trade goods, and sufficient faunal resources to purchase them. As prices for trade goods fell in the late 1700s, Crees "spent much more of the free time they gained at the local trading posts drinking and smoking and leading what the traders termed the 'indolent life'" (Ray 1974:142). It is difficult to see in the trade anything but the intensification of the "immediate return" design to which Crees assimilated it. Indeed, the inland posts themselves became like the animals an "infinite resource," or at least this was the productive relation to them Crees tried to establish. One of the institutions of the trade was "debt": the traders advanced Cree hunters goods to be repaid subsequently in furs. In 1794, George Charles at Granville Lake received from Malcolm Ross at Reed Lake a list of delinquents from whom to collect debts "as these Indians hereabouts is very guilty of going from house to house, and by that means gets off paying their debts, and is the loss of many Hundred Beaver of Goods to our Employers" (HBC B.83/a[1795]). Overall, there occurred little qualitative structural change in Cree society in the early fur trade; most change during this period entailed alterations in the values of existing variables (more winter fragmentation, more beaver hunting, less big game hunting).

There were, however, substantial changes in the ecosystem. The introduced technology and the desire for trade goods provided both the means and the incentive for rates of predation that ultimately reduced caribou, moose, and beaver populations. But these factors only acquired historical efficacy as they were integrated into the "immediate return" design. Infinitely renewable as use values, the animals were equally renewable as exchange values, and commercial hunting thereafter proceeded like the domestic foraging with which it was, in part, coextensive. Ultimately with tragic consequences, since the animal populations being hunted more intensively with a more lethal technology were not objectively the "same" in their resilience as the animal populations previously known. Contrary to Cree theology, moose, caribou, and beaver are not infinitely regenerated or reborn, or, at least, they proved not to be under the regime of intensified harvesting that followed the expansion of the inland posts. Of another encounter with the European market, Sahlins (1985:149) writes,

In action, people put their concepts and categories into ostensive relations to the world. Such referential uses bring into play other determinations of the signs, besides their received sense, namely the actual world and the people concerned. Praxis is, then, a risk to the sense of signs in the culture-as-constituted, precisely as the sense is arbitrary in its capacity as reference. Having its own properties, the world may then prove intractable. It can well defy the concepts that are indexed to it. Man's symbolic hubris becomes a great gamble with the empirical realities. The gamble is that referential action, by placing *a priori* concepts in correspondence with external objects, will imply some *unforeseen* effects that cannot be ignored.

Or, as Rappaport (1984:336) writes, "The utilities that cultures constitute and sometimes maintain for long periods of time may contradict organic and ecosystemic requirements" without anyone, initially, being the wiser. For Crees in the eighteenth century, the category "*pisiskiw*," animal, possessed as an important facet of its significance the property of inexhaustibility, at least as far as the effects of human predation were concerned. Consequently, "*māciwin*," hunting, was constituted as an activity that had nothing to do with the numbers of animals subsequently to be accessible in the world. The gun and the steel trap were new and more efficient "tokens" of known "types": weapons used to kill animals. These meanings guaranteed an obliviousness to the cumulative effects of commercial hunting. For if the animals were inexhaustible, killing twelve was no different than killing one. The prehistoric effects of this optimistic ecological principle are not known, but, after contact, its impact seemingly remained within the range of beaver, moose, and caribou productivity as long as the remoteness of the coastal forts discouraged substantial commercial hunting. Throughout this period, the Crees' practical experience with animal populations conformed to the presupposed axiom of plenitude referenced in it. Animals were usually available, and localized and temporary shortages were predictable and had known explanations and solutions. The expansion of the inland posts ultimately provided the incentive for unprecedented rates of per capita predation. This intensification simply reproduced the convention that animals were inexhaustible benefactors (or adversaries), existing in the world to be killed in whatever numbers people had uses for. But these conventions had never previously been referenced to a world in which people had uses—as commodities—for such great numbers. Under this regime, the animals themselves eventually proved refractory to the Crees' definitions of them. But the Crees' reaction to the growing scarcity appears retrospectively as a collective profession of faith in the principles of infinite game and immediate return. It exhibited a profound aversion—as much "religious" as "economic"—to long-range planning, scheduled consumption, and delayed satisfactions. The Crees neither intensified their food storage nor limited their kills nor privatized resources nor managed beaver. Treating the catastrophe like any localized food shortage, they continued to attempt to kill as many animals as possible.

10

"Let the Young Ones Go for Next Year"

Introduction

During the middle and late 1800s, management practices focused on beavers and other furbearers were adopted by some Rock Cree trappers, and they continue to be used in the 1990s. Seemingly during the same period, complete use of each animal killed became the preferred norm. Beliefs and practices regarding management and intensive use are today distributed through Rock Cree society in an exceedingly diverse manner. Not all Crees manage animals, and those who do apparently have different understandings of the causal principles involved. A whole series of cultural transformations are implicated in these practices: infinite animals resources came to be figured as finite, indiscriminate killing was replaced by scheduled capture, and rates of human predation were assigned causal significance in determining the quantities of resources available on the landscape. Rather than entirely displacing the earlier conceptions, these innovations have come to coexist with them. For some Crees, the finite animal has been indigenized and management defined as a spiritual technique. For others, management has no spiritual significance.

In the previous chapter, I discussed sources describing beaver management by boreal Algonquians in the seventeenth and eighteenth centuries and noted differences in scholarly opinion regarding the aboriginal or historic inception of the practice. The problematic character of the documentary references and probable variations within and between different Algonquian populations make any categorical solution to this question an unreflective one. There are no such references describing Crees in the Churchill River drainage, and I have suggested that conservation was absent there prior to and during the game depletions of the 1820s. I believe also that early references to conservation in other areas describe practices that arose historically in the context of the fur trade. In some areas, these appear to have been invented independently by Indian trappers. In others, they derive historically from the Hudson's Bay Company policies introduced in the 1820s and thereafter.

The Hudson's Bay Company's Management Policies

Following the merger of the competing Hudson's Bay and Northwest companies in 1821, George Simpson proposed a series of measures intended to restore depleted furbearer populations, and these may be the prototypes of the strategies later used by Rock Crees in the Churchill River and Nelson River drainages. Concern with scheduling Indian foraging to the Company's advantage was expressed even before this time, although the conditions of competition between companies prevented conservation policies. Hearne (1958 [1795]:148) wrote that the Crees sometimes ate summer beaver and otter pelts rather than trading them since their exchange value was small. The traders considered it "impolitic to encourage the natives to kill such valuable animals at a time when the skins are not in season."

George Charles's Nelson River District Report of 1820–21 suggests that some traders were trying to discourage beaver hunting in certain regions. He explained that the following year's returns in beavers from the South Indian Lake area would be less than in the past when the twenty Indians who stayed in the vicinity during summer sometimes procured over one hundred beaver pelts during the time of open water.

But this season it was with difficulty that I could prevail upon six of them to remain and they are not to molest the few that are yet in Being of the Beaver. Consequently for the present we may be short of the usual returns though it will certainly turn to our advantage hereafter, as at present this part of the Low Country is among the best for these valuable animals and it's by no means improvident to desist in time, while it is worth it, before it is reduced to that state of Poverty which some parts of the Upper Country [farther south] is in at present. (HBC B.91/e/2)

The author then discusses the effects of steel traps on beaver hunting, noting that two years earlier the Crees had requested steel traps and threatened to trade elsewhere if they were not provided "for the Beaver too difficult to be killed by Chisel Hunting." Reluctantly, Charles gave them poor quality traps that they used for two years with little success, killing fewer beavers than they had by chiseling open the lodges. He concluded that several of the "less indolently inclined" Crees had refused the traps in fall 1820 and that "traps ergo have not made much havoc." Seemingly, he was responding to directives discouraging the use of steel traps because of their potential for exterminating beaver.

Ray (1975) has summarized the policies introduced after 1821 and the different factors that initially obstructed their implementation. Recognizing the impact of the steel trap-castoreum complex on beaver populations, George Simpson prohibited trade in traps in those districts free of competition. To divert Indians from hunting beavers, premiums were placed on other animals such as martens and muskrats. In some instances, trading posts were closed or shifted to less depleted areas, as with the closing of the Nelson House and South Indian Lake posts on the Churchill River. It was proposed in 1823 that the age and breeding season of animals be taken into account.

The Indian ought to be discouraged from killing beaver and other valuable animals when young or in the breeding season, and, when practicable, considerable districts should be left unhunted for three or four years. By arrangements of this kind, the numbers will be increased. (Fleming 1940:90)

Quotas limiting the numbers of beaver pelts to be traded were devised for each district between 1826 and 1829 and again between 1841 and 1844. Simpson later proposed in 1828 that Indians be encouraged to occupy bounded tracts of country, presumably as an incentive to practice conservation whose benefits, as successive and exclusive users of the tracts, they would be able to realize:

We are endeavoring to confine the natives throughout the country now by families to separate and distinct hunting grounds. This system seems to take among them by degrees, and in a few years I hope it will become general, but it is a very difficult matter to change the habits of Indians, although they may see the ultimate benefit thereof to themselves and families. (Ibid.:229)

Since delimited hunting tracts were already in existence among some Algonquian groups in southern Ontario and Manitoba by this time (Harmon 1905 [1821], Masson 1889–90, 1:326), these proposals presumably concern areas where they had not yet emerged or, perhaps, where earlier tract systems had disintegrated because of trespass or resource depletion. It is also possible that the traders were unaware that some Indians already used strategies similar to those they were proposing.

A detailed archival study of reactions to these policies by Crees in the Churchill River drainage remains to be undertaken, but, on the basis of comparative evidence, the initial response was probably noncooperation (Ray 1975). Indians often circumvented closed seasons, closed areas, quotas, and bans on steel traps by migrating to posts where these regulations were not in effect or were loosely enforced. Where the game shortages continued, Crees adopted the characteristic expedient of migration from the depleted area. During the 1830s, Indians were retreating south from the boreal forest in such numbers that Simpson feared too few would be left to support the fur trade. With particular reference to the Crees of the Churchill River and Nelson River drainages, there were substantial migrations into the parklands of the Saskatchewan District. Although it might be supposed that experimentation with the conservation programs would have been optimally "adaptive" at this time, many Crees selected initially the traditional option of mobility.

Among Crees who remained in the boreal forest, both hunting tracts and selective trapping appear to have become conventional institutions by the 1850s (Ray 1975:64–67). By this time, for example, Crees trading at Lac la Ronge in Saskatchewan were using such a system with the country divided into "hunting portions" that were exploited every third year (Denig 1952:56). It is unclear whether individual hunting tracts or the entire band territory were partitioned in this way. Bishop (1974:214–219) demonstrates a similar time sequence for management by Ojibwas trading at Osnaburgh House, Ontario. Bishop's analyses suggest that experimentation with conservation was functionally linked to the emergence of delimited hunting territories on which hunting groups trapped in successive winters without uninvited competition. While this is not the only way conservation could have worked, it probably developed in this way for Crees in the Churchill River drainage. This transformation entailed basic changes both in consumption patterns and in property concepts, and it is unsurprising that Crees neither immediately adopted the Hudson's Bay Company's schemes nor spontaneously developed their own as an adjustment to the shortages and to the Company's monopoly. The concept that the finder possesses rights to the beavers in a lodge he discovers and marks dates from at least the early eighteenth century (Bacqueville de La Potherie 1931:233; cf. Hearne 1958 [1795]:76). There was undoubtedly formidable resistance to such claims, and the notion of exclusive access by individuals or families to whole areas of land would have developed only slowly. Even today, Crees typify the land tenure system prior to the Registered Trapline as one in which "everyone could go where they wanted," although it is clear that this was not actually what most people did. The conception of land and resources as ideally free goods to all members of the community was and is a fundamental moral principle. It persisted even among Algonquians who institutionalized hunting territories early in the 1800s. Peter Grant, for example, described in 1804 the use of hunting territories (see Rogers 1963:82–83) by the Rainy Lake Ojibwas. However, the boundaries were readily suspended in times of need since, as the Indians said, "the lands were made for the use of man, therefore everyone has an equal right to partake of the produce" (Masson 1889–90, 1:326). As long as the legitimacy of individual usufructuary rights to beaver lodges and hunting territories was contested within the community—as it undoubtedly was by many—no group could be assured of being able to harvest resources spared in the present.

But more than property concepts was in question. During the game shortages, any planning people were willing to undertake was under continual hazard from immediate needs for meat and pelts. In a depleted environment, management of preferred resources possesses objectively beneficial consequences but only at the cost of immediate privation. And this, in turn, raises the question of how much planning Crees were, in fact, disposed to make. Virtually every aspect of the Cree mode of production—the opportunistic use of carcasses, the inattention to food storage, the frequent residential mobility, and the alternating cycle of consumption and labor—would have run contrary to the practice of sparing animals in the present for use in a subsequent season. Finally, there is the question of the significance scheduled capture would have in a universe where resource quantities could not be manipulated either by killing or failing to kill. Initially, at least, quotas and closed areas must have made little sense.

Despite these obstacles, both management and de facto hunting territories developed in the Churchill River drainage, probably sometime between the 1850s and around 1900 when they were described in the region by Rossignol (1939). By 1900, a constellation of factors had led also to increased residential sedentism in winter and to more intensive food preservation. In summary, the events of the 1800s had the cumulative effect of transforming the Cree foraging praxis from an "immediate return" to a relatively "delayed return" design. The material circumstances in which Crees were now situated—a depleted environment and a monopolized market—did not *require* that management be innovated but provided a context favoring experimentation with it. Crees may have reflected on increases in beavers and other species in areas where quotas and seasons were strictly enforced. Successful experimentation would rapidly become known, stimulating imitation and the dissemination of new techniques. At the same time, usufructuary rights of groups to furbearers on hunting territories must gradually have gained legitimacy. As both cause and consequence of technical experimentation, animals were redefined as beings over whose reproduction and populations human beings could exert influences. This redefinition must have constituted a minor scandal in a theology whose dominant postulate was human dependence on animal benefactors. It is not surprising, therefore, that technical management was conceived, at least by some Crees, as yet another submission to this dependence and thus assimilated to the prevailing ideology of foraging. Specifically, what seems to have happened was a reconceptualization of limited killing and intensive utilization of animals as an obligation newly imposed on hunters by the animals and the *ahcāk* beings. This would imaginably follow as the corollary to a novel historical experience of animals as *scarce*, both ecologically as use values and economically as commodities. Killing unselectively and consuming opportunistically were thereafter for some Crees refigured as *pāstāhōwin*, acts that bring spiritual retribution.

A similar transformation among the Naskapi of northern Quebec-Labrador suggests that Crees ultimately interpreted the game shortages as a judgment inflicted on them for indiscriminate and wasteful hunting. If such an explanation became general, it would have provided an intellectual context in which conservation practices could articulate with spiritual conceptions of foraging. Unlike the Rock Crees, the Barren Grounds Band of Naskapi specialized in caribou for meat and hides, remaining peripheral to the fur trade for most of their history. Sources from the late 1800s document the pattern of unlimited killing and selective utilization of the carcasses. The animals were killed in large numbers for their hides or preferred cuts of meat, with the greater part of the remains being left to rot. Accumulations of articulated skeletons are noted in several sources (see Davies 1963, Turner 1894). It is not clear whether these practices significantly reduced the size of the herd, but in 1914, it failed to migrate south by the usual route, and widespread starvation resulted. Strong (1929:2) describes how this disaster was interpreted:

As a result of the slaughter of former days there are great heaps of deer bones around Indian House Lake, which have been commented upon by all travelers in the region. The caribou smelled these bones, the Indians say, and were offended, so that they returned to Caribou House and told the caribou god, who directed the chief of the caribou to take them into his mountain. Since then the caribou god has refused to let the herd come south, and as a result the Indians have been starved out of their interior homes. Today they are extremely careful in observing all the varied rites pertaining to the caribou and thus hope to appease the anger of the god.

A didactic text obtained from the same band makes clear that a concept of "waste"—of failing to make appropriate use of the slain animals—was now foregrounded. In the text, the caribou deity speaks in the first person:

I indeed will divide the caribou. I will give them to the people. It will be known to me. . . . He who obeys the requirements is given caribou, and he who disobeys is not given caribou. If he wastes much caribou he cannot be given them because he wastes too much of his food. (Speck 1935a:81)

Speck (ibid.:89) adds, "The obligation to use for tools the bones of each caribou killed has almost the force of command," demonstrating that the injunction against waste applied not only to the meat. Here, a famine of exceptional magnitude provoked the interpretation that killing caribou in excess of the numbers used was offensive to animals and spirits. If a similar interpretation followed the Churchill River game shortages, the new management strategies were probably defined as yet another obligation hunters owed to their prey. It can, of course, be added that the stability resulting from conservation would be interpreted as so many worldly indexes of the validity of this doctrine.

Thus, conceptions of how slain animals should be utilized were likewise revalued. In the 1970s and 1980s, I was told repeatedly by Rock Crees that hunters should kill only animals for which they have uses and that the carcasses should be thoroughly utilized. Although I am sure there are exceptions, I never saw Crees kill an animal whose skin and meat was not used. The verb *wîsakîhîw* 'waste someone' refers to such negligence, and, predictably, the agent is conceived to invite bad luck through his or her actions. This conception of utilization as a religious obligation is noted also in accounts of Eastern Cree groups (Cooper 1931:34, 1939:69; Burgesse 1945:15; Speck 1935*b*:47).

Management Strategies in the Twentieth Century

Evidence for furbearer management is obliquely present in the Hudson's Bay Company post journals during the late 1800s. In 1891, the trader at Pelican Lake anticipated uncertain beaver returns because "the Indians had to hunt hard for them and very few were left for breeding purposes" (HBC B.158/e/1). In the form of land tenure practiced by 1900, the regional band assembled at Pukatawagan to fish during the summer. In fall, the band divided into multifamily hunting groups that traveled by canoe to the loosely delimited territories they reoccupied in successive winters. Within these territories, the members had exclusive rights to trap furbearing animals, while fish and big game continued to be free goods. Beaver lodges were marked to indicate individual claims. The territories were sometimes internally segmented into tracts used by constitutent families. Visitation and temporary exchange of territories were common. Seasonal movement between points within territories was also common, but log cabin hamlets were increasingly occupied as centers from which men made logistical hunting and trapping sorties. Crees say there was always unoccupied country, groups sometimes establishing new territories and abandoning old ones to others. Groups retained usufructuary rights to their territory's resources as long as they utilized it with some continuity. Solomon Colomb, traditional chief of the Mathias Colomb Band at Pukatawagan, summarized the system this way:

The people would come to Pukatawagan in the summer. Before there were houses, they'd live in tents or *mitikīwāp*. This was the central place for them. In the winter, there's places that they moved to, different places. Burntwood Lake, Granville Lake, Russell Lake. If the house was rotten, they moved to another place, and they were all over the place. They built a house at one place and they get tired of the place, they'd move. Same lake though. Each family stayed at a particular spot. It goes by generations and generations. The old people die in one camp, well, the next family's staying there. Their children would be living in the same place.

In talking about this period, Crees emphasize both that "everyone could go where they wanted"—an affirmation of the deeply felt value that access to resources should be collective—and that groups spaced themselves in such a way as to minimize reciprocal interference. According to Pierre Bighetty,

People used to live peaceful at that time. They used to have an agreement right there: "Okay, that's your part of the land, I'll leave it alone. I'll go my part, eh?" If he wants to trap this [trap] line, then the other fellow would say, "Go ahead. You take that one and I'll take this one."

During the early 1900s, the Oblate missionary Rossignol wrote that Rock Crees sometimes spared juvenile big game like moose and caribou and deliberately managed beaver and muskrat populations on their hunting territories. Crees estimated the size of beaver colonies and left a few animals alive in each lodge. Spring trapping of muskrats ended with the birth of the young. It was Rossignol's impression that the Crees in the early part of the century deliberately resisted the traders who, under competitive conditions, were urging them to kill all the animals possible (Rossignol 1939:66–67).

My discussions with Cree elders confirm Rossignol's description, although they make clear that not everyone used these strategies. Crees refer to management practices with the verb *iskōhīw* 'leave someone there'. English glosses of inflected forms included 'I leave that animal alone', 'we let him get away', and 'he leaves them there'. The verb can denote acts as diverse as allowing a trapline or trapline sector to "rest" for a season, not firing on a large game animal, removing traps from a beaver house after a certain number have been taken, or exempting an entire house from trapping. The word usually implies the hunter's intention to spare the animal for possible future use but predicates also of situations in which the effort of killing and retrieval is disproportionate to the rewards. A fat and desired porcupine, for example, disappeared up a tree at a time when no axes were handy, and the verb was used to express a decision against further pursuit. The semantic opposite is the verb *cāhkitaw* 'someone kills them all'.

Most Crees associate the strategy of "chiseling" beaver lodges with indiscriminate rather than selective beaver trapping. This technique involves blocking the runways from the frozen beaver lodge with sticks, chopping into the lodge, and removing all the trapped occupants with dogs and hooks. Below, Solomon Françrois describes the practices of his father, Leon, during the first three decades of the 1900s on his territory at Narrows Lake.

Q: Did they ever try to save a few beaver for later?
A: In the old times they didn't bother with steel traps. That time they were chopping houses. They'd block the holes and runways. They'd use big hooks mounted on poles. They'd hook the beaver, throw it up on the shore, and hit it on the head. They'd try to kill all of the beavers. Usually they didn't bother to save any. Other times, they kill a few and leave the rest. So there will be a few for next year.
Q: How did they know how many beavers were in the lodge?
A: It's easy to know if you're a trapper. You can tell. There's two big ones, three mediums, and four small ones in a big family house. If you happen to get two mediums and one big beaver, then you pull your snares. So there will be six beavers left for next year.

Here Mr. François, when questioned about management, shifted his focus from chiseling to the technique of setting snares on vertical poles in beaver runways under the ice. In the first case, some beavers might be left after the lodge was opened, and, in the second, beavers were saved by lifting the snares after the desired number at a lodge were captured. Pierre Bighetty describes practices around the same period near the Prayer River hamlet at High Rock Lake.

Q: Did they used to do that [save beavers] when your dad was trapping?
A: Yeah, they always did that. If it's their land, they know how many beaver they got there. If they left the family alive they know there will be little ones there. Sometimes they leave a [whole] house alone. You know when they shoot beavers, the male comes up first. So they saw the male and once they shot that one they leave the female alone. That's how they knew. That's how they worked.
Q: Did they ever put the snares or traps away from the lodge?
A: Oh yeah, that's the big ones that are caught that way, away from the lodge. And they usually trap by the dam. The small ones don't go over there very much. They don't go around the dam. The vent is different too [on adult female] where the kids are born. You can tell [from placental scars] how many small ones when she breeded. Old beaver has a lot more kids, you know? If it's a young beaver, maybe it has two young ones. The largest family would have six-seven little ones in one litter.

During the 1930s, beaver and big game were again depleted in the Pukatawagan-Granville Lake region. The most plausible explanation for this event is the incursion of white trappers into the region who practiced no conservation and did not respect the boundaries of hunting territories. As a result, most Crees themselves seemingly abandoned management, and all resources within the band territory again became a free good to whomever came first. In Quebec, white invasions had the same effects on Eastern Cree and Montagnais institutions (see Rogers 1963:72, Burgesse 1945:12–13). Crees born and raised during this period sometimes lack knowledge of the management practices that formerly existed, questioning whether they could function without the provincial Registered Trapline system that was established in the mid-1940s.

Q: Were the people saving animals when you were a kid?
A: No. They [beavers] were closed [season] then [early 1940s]. Back in my dad's time or granddad's time *they didn't save them over*. That's when there was no beavers. If a guy finds beavers, he try and clean them right away 'cause there'll be another guy coming behind. You got to catch whatever you find. Because there'll be another guy behind you. Whoever find something, that's his. Even if you're trappng, there'll be someone coming in, because it's not your trapline. It's nobody's. As long as he doesn't bother your sets, he could be sitting right besides you. There was no law. That's why they clean up everything. [Emphasis added.]

During this period, which the speaker apparently conceives as extending indefinitely into the past, usufructuary rights to territories were no longer recognized, an obvious economic transition from the earlier regime described by Pierre Bighetty in which "they used to have an agreement right there: 'Okay, that's your part of the land, I'll leave it alone. I'll go to my own part.'"

Diverse explanations for the 1930s game depletions are proposed by Crees, but none of them invoke religious postulates. Disease, changing water levels, and overhunting by white trappers are mentioned. Some say that the problem of trespass caused Indian trappers to suspend their own conservation. Certain elders associate the game depletions with the passing of the entire bush-oriented way of life. Luke Dumas of Pukatawagan: "The people slaughtered all the beaver. When they killed all the beavers, they killed their own culture. You can't really blame them. They did it to survive. When the beavers disappeared, the other animals began to disappear."

Q: How were the beavers and rats cleaned out [overkilled] back in the 1930s?
A: There were white trappers come up here. And Indians were chopping the houses. I guess the white guys never know that [about chiseling the winter lodges]. It was a lot of work. They didn't even try it, I don't think. Maybe they did, but I guess they just freeze the beavers. But Indians usually catch every one. Well, mostly. Them days they didn't leave any. You try and catch all that you

can. There was nobody's trapline. But after we had those traplines, well, everybody has to watch for himself. Around 1945, that's when they gave out the traplines. And that's the time a guy is supposed to kill half of what he had. If you got seven houses, you're allowed to kill three. So you leave the rest. Till about 1950. Around '50, I think that's when there were a lot of beavers. And then from then there was no limit, you can kill all you want.

The closed season, quotas, and registered traplines were introduced in the Pukatawagan area in the mid-1940s. After boundaries between Pukatawagan and other Indian reserves were agreed on, the Pukatawagan area was divided into sectors corresponding to the old hunting territories. Thereafter, the quota system allowed the beaver populations to recover, and trappers once again could benefit from the conservation they practiced.

Q: How did they work it after Registered Trapline came in?
A: Well, you put your trap away from the lodge because the male [beaver] usually go and check the far end of his lodge . . . that's his territory where you put your trap. One or two traps and you don't get the females.
Q: You don't get the female?
A: You might get a young buck and you pull the traps out. That's what I seen my old man [father] doing that. You usually get a male and maybe a young buck. That's all he takes out, the rest, let the young ones go for next year. . . . But saving the young ones, that's what they used to do. The far end, that's where you trap. Even in the wintertime. Oh the feedpile, you might find . . . they usually make a lot of holes, you know, in the shoreline. The far end, that's where you set your snare. Sure to get a male. But around the lodge, you get the young ones. Or female. Especially in the spring you get the males away from the lodge. Down below the dam, that's where they're going to check. And the young bucks that travel, they monkey around close to the house. They're scared of the [snare] pole. Small beaver born around the end of May. About the quitting of trapping we can see some nursing the young ones. We quit around the twentieth of May. And when you shoot the beavers you can tell it's a baby. When he comes up from the water, he's way above [the body floats]. But a male, you only see his head sticking out. Female floats on top because she's carrying the little ones. That makes her float up higher in the water. You can't see the tail but you can see the back. But a male, you don't see the back. You just can hardly see the head sticking out. He's heavier, you know. The female just floats. You can see the whole back."

The same speaker made clear that for many trappers, including himself, management strategies were sensitive to perceived levels of abundance or scarcity.

That [conservation] was before. After there started to be lots of beavers, we didn't care. Puts lots of traps near his lodge. Yeah, anyplace. Got a lot of beavers one time, we got a hundred and thirty once, one spring. Yeah there were lots of beavers that time. But 1940 to 1960, there was hardly. . . I think he [father] only had four houses [in the 1940s]. I think around 1960, that's when there's a lot of beavers 'cause they start to spread. They didn't kill. . . they only catch few [before the recovery]. Once they started to spread, there was a lot of beavers.

Management could thus be suspended when beavers were abundant and then reintroduced if population declines were identified. This sensitivity of management to perceived changes in animal populations is probably of much more general provenience, and so is the contrast between managers and nonmanagers. Of Crees and Ojibwas in southern Manitoba during the early 1800s, Harmon (1905 [1821]:331) wrote that only some were conserving furbearing animals and that such scheduled capture was practiced specifically on tracts "not well stocked with animals."

Ironically, the recovery of the beavers coincided with the formation of the sedentary village community at Pukatawagan and the increasing attenuation of hunting and fur trapping that has continued from the 1960s into the present. Crees say that there are today fewer professional trappers and that many of the younger generation lack the skills to trap effectively. As a result, many men conceive existing populations of beavers as more than adequate to their needs, even though declines in population are noted. The same speaker observed,

Now again they're [beavers] feed hurt [?]. Wherever they [whites] make dams, they kill the feed. There's hardly any beavers again. Now. Water comes up. Drown. He leave the place, I guess. . . they die off somehow. There's nothing now. . . hardly. They starve, I guess. But nowadays I don't think we care about saving some. Cause most of those guys now they don't know how to trap. Lucky if he gets one.

This final observation is characteristic of many older trappers today. Although the speaker perceives beavers as on the decline, conservation is superfluous because the incompetence of most younger trappers ensures that sufficient animals will be available. In the bush settlements at Granville, High Rock, and Burntwood lakes, trapping continues to provide substantial proportions of food and cash income, and there some trappers continue to make use of conservation techniques. Some speak proudly of the colonies of furbearing animals they have "built up" and maintained on their traplines.

As the interviews quoted above make clear, conservation is focused on beavers, long the *sine qua non* of the fur trade and a species whose sedentary colonies facilitate its scheduled capture. Cree trappers say they know the locations of most beaver colonies on their traplines. Some practice a form of conservation in which particular colonies are killed out while others are left unhunted, saying that the former will be colonized by the latter. More typically, trappers attempt to maintain continuous colonies by killing only a certain number of the animals resident there. This approach requires knowledge of the numbers of animals present and their age and sex composition. Observations of the colony in summer when the animals are visible, the size of the lodge, the size of incisor marks on tree stumps, and the age and sex of animals previously killed all enter into these calculations. To conserve the colony, Crees simply stop hunting or setting traps and snares after the desired number of animals has been killed. To spare juveniles and pregnant females, trappers set traps and snares away from the lodge or hold fire when shooting the animals during open water. Observation of seasons also protects pregnant females and young.

Some trappers also manage other furbearing species. Muskrats, like beavers, occupy colonies and are susceptible to similar conservation techniques. At the present time, Crees perceive muskrats as nearly inexhaustible in their abundance, but older trappers recall periods of shortage that prompted conservation of pregnant females. Muskrats breed three times a year between April and August; trappers would stop killing the animals in May when the spring litters were anticipated. Crees say that martens are relatively territorial, and they may stop setting traps for them after a certain number have been killed. Other furbearing animals such as foxes, otters, minks, lynxes, and weasels are conserved by suspending trapping operations for them when population declines are noted. The trapper may alternate in successive winters between different sectors of the trapline or arrange to trap on someone else's to allow populations to increase. "Rotation" of this kind has been described also among the Eastern Crees in the 1960s (Feit 1973*a*, 1973*b*).

With regard to moose and caribou, *iskōhīw-* refers simply to the act of holding fire on an animal that might easily be killed. Some Crees say that they specifically spare pregnant or juvenile moose and caribou. The mobility of these animals makes it uncertain that a hunter will encounter them again, although the general whereabouts of a moose or caribou may be monitored for several days before hunters go out to try to kill it. Crees say that there was and is variation with respect to this kind of forbearance. Older men, for instance, sometimes ascribed to younger men the inclination to shoot any game animal that was encountered. One reason for sparing such animals is the logistical problem of transporting the carcass or meat, especially in summer if the animal is far from a lake or river connected to the camp or village. If the hunter is well provisioned with meat, the tasks of butchering and transport may outweigh the advantages. This kind of selectivity is not, however, conditioned only by practical considerations. I observed two instances during the same week in which woodland caribou encountered on a lakeshore near a camp were unmolested. The explanation was that the hunter already had plenty of caribou meat and would have "bad luck" in the future if he killed the caribou without needing them.

How Conservation Works

Cree society is exceptionally tolerant of internal diversity in many spheres of practice and belief. It is not surprising, therefore, that today and apparently in the past some trappers practice conservation while others do not. It has been possible since the mid-1800s for some hunters to acquire desired quantities of meat and fur without using—or admitting to using—any management strategies whatsoever. Increasingly, this may have become the case because there are alternate sources of cash and food and fewer full-time trappers using the land. As long as usufructuary rights of managers were respected, the productive system from the mid-1800s until the interwar period could probably sustain both managers and nonmanagers. At least some of those who reject conservation explain themselves in terms that would have made sense to their eighteenth-century ancestors. I was told by one man that conservation was unnecessary because a good hunter can always find enough animals as long as he treats them with the appropriate modes of ritual respect. Another, a staunch Catholic but also a practitioner of animal ceremonialism, told me simply that it was God who determined how many animals people caught and that maintaining breeding colonies of furbearers had nothing to do with it. Exactly the same diversity existed among the Osnaburgh House Ojibwas in Ontario in the 1960s:

Views held on the conservation of beaver vary. Some men said that two beaver should be left in each house, while others said that since the animals were given to them by God whenever they were needed, conservation methods were unnecessary. (Bishop 1974:35–36)

The postulate that game is infinite—or at least that present rates of predation have nothing to do with the numbers to be caught in the future—is therefore still present in the Algonquian subarctic.

The large majority of Granville Lake trappers who discussed the subject with me either practiced conservation or had done so in the past. There is, however, seemingly no single explanation for the effectiveness of conservation that is socially shared among them. The practitioners express very diverse (and unaligned) conceptions of the causal principles involved. First, most trappers categorically reject the relevance of *manitōkīwin* to animal conservation. These individuals do not necessarily question the effect of spiritual influences on trapping success, but they deny that selective killing had any religious significance. They explain beaver management simply as a strategy for maintaining a breeding stock of animals in each lodge. An apparently Western conception of game management has clearly been independently invented or borrowed, although I do not know when this happened.

Second, there are individuals who say that limiting kills through management is—like killing animals quickly or using the entire carcass—part of the respect that the hunter owes to the prey. It is this second interpretation that in all probability derives from the mid-nineteenth century when Crees in the Churchill River drainage first began experimenting with conservation. As I understand this conception, human predation exerts determinate effects on animal populations but does so only in the short term and to the degree that the game ruler deities or the animals themselves allow it to do so. The latter desire that hunters forage selectively, letting part of their lands "rest" at intervals and maintaining populations of *living* animals on the land. As with the diverse other requirements to which some hunters understand themselves subject, compliance is sanctioned with successful hunting and violation is punished by "bad luck." When a trapper kills too many animals, the deific game ruler responds by failing to restore the animals to life or by suspending rates of animal reproduction. The beings associated with management today are Mistamisk, Great Beaver, and Misiwacask, Great Muskrat. Some Crees say that Mistamisk determines the number of young beavers that are born, causes slain beavers to return to life underwater, directs the movements of beavers over the landscape, and controls the availability of beavers to trappers by directing them to avoid or enter traps. In response to overhunting, Mistamisk may create an objective *scarcity* of animals on the trapline. It may, as one individual put it, "stop all the little ones from being born." In these conceptions, the influence of human predation on the sizes of animal populations subsequently available is recognized but figured as mediate. Feit (1973*a*, 1973*b*) describes a comparable hunting theology among Eastern Crees at Waswanipi, Quebec. There, the number of animals a hunter conceives himself to be "given" voluntarily by spirits is the number that can be killed without causing population declines on the hunting territory. Feit indicates that Waswanipi Cree hunters monitor the size of animal populations on their territories, estimating the numbers they can kill each winter without initiating a decline. These reference values, which alter from winter to winter, are calculated by integrating knowledge of past hunts with current evidence of population trends. Declines are interpreted as signs that a hunter has exceeded the number he has been "given" and that the "Master of the Moose" and other deities are responding by causing animals not to be born. Hypothetically, both "secular" and "spiritualized" interpretations would have much the same consequence. From an ecological perspective, the consequences of human agency are here misrecognized as the result of decisions by *ahcāk* beings reacting to the hunters' conduct.

There exists (at least) a third conception of the articulation of management with the traditional conception of hunters' dependence. Some Crees who conserve animals deny that human predation has any effect whatsoever on animal populations, even in the short term. They say that there are always more or less the same numbers of animals on the landscape, their numbers determined by the decisions of the game ruler beings. This explanation was difficult for me to understand because the men who professed it used trapping techniques that selectively spared juvenile and female animals. They said that the Great Beaver and the Great Muskrat considered hunters to be "playing" with the animals if they killed all the females and juveniles without saving any. But killing the latter makes no difference in terms of the numbers of animals regenerated or reborn. Overhunting does not result in decreased animal population but only in decreased availability to the trapper. As one man explained this,

Suppose then that some young man kills all the young beavers and depletes his trapline. This *Mistamisk* will be extremely angry about it. Then that young man will be accursed. The-one-who-owns-beavers [the Great Beaver] will see him playing with the yearling beaver.
Q: He kills all the yearling beavers?

The beavers will come back again. They have to come back always [be reborn]. But that young man is accursed. Everywhere in the bush he will see signs of beaver. But he will be unable to kill anything.

This representation of the consequences of overkill presupposes a more or less continuous supply of animals in the bush. Overkill operates not on the population of animals but on their accessibility. Of all the explanations for conservation, it is this that is most dominated by the conception that animal populations are unaffected by the existence or intensity of human predation. The animals are still infinite, and only the hunters' access to them can become scarce.

Efficiency and Management

I have noted the happy ecological, principle that those foraging strategies entailing the least labor may possess latent (and unrecognized) management effects. The marginal value theorem (Winterhalder and Smith 1981) is an example of a model borrowed from evolutionary ecology into ecological anthropology and applied to the foraging strategies of human hunters. Charnov's theorem predicts the foragers' withdrawal from an area when continued predation has reduced resources to below their average density and thus before continued predation will entail increased energy costs. In any foraging site, returns in biomass for foraging labor will progressively decline over time as the most proximal and least aversive prey are captured. The relative ease with which "immediate return" foragers provision themselves is predicated in part on frequent residential mobility (Sahlins 1972). Charnov's theorem thus plausibly identifies limits to the duration of foraging (and residence) within an area, although, as among the Tanzanian Hadza (Woodburn 1972:203), movement may usually occur well before declines in resource capture are experienced. In addition to maximizing efficiency, frequent residential mobility may have conservation effects if resource populations are density dependent (Paine 1973). Mobility itself may thus combine the manifest function of efficiency (among other values) with latent management effects.

Eric Alden Smith has suggested that strategies understood to maximize long-term reliability—the boreal Algonquian management practices—are better understood as maximizing caloric efficiency.

The marginal value theorem demonstrates that certain phenomena that have the effect of conserving resources may well rise from simple self-interest (efficiency maximization) even when there is no territoriality or other guarantee of exclusive us. . . . Hunting territory rotation may well have the effect of managing prey populations and preventing overhunting, but is it designed to do so? . . . I suggest that it is more reasonable to view the Waswanipi [Cree, cf. Feit 1973a] rotational system and similar practices in other foraging societies as primarily devices to increase foraging efficiency and optimize time allocation, only incidentally having the effect of "managing" prey populations. (1983:633)

Smith's argument takes energetic efficiency as the institution's evolutionary raison d'être and management as a secondary—and perhaps unintended—by-product. "Rotation" between hunting territory sectors, which is a scheduled and calculated mode of residential movement between foraging sites, may, indeed, be more efficient than recurrently hunting the same territory in successive winters. Winterhalder's (1981) excellent analysis of the energetics of Cree foraging in Ontario suggests that the same may be true for conservation of beaver colonies. Just as it is efficient to move residentially between regions, it may be efficient to apportion traps among different colonies. The marginal value theorem thus predicts the Cree practice of positioning snares at only a subset of the underwater chutes in each beaver lodge.

Although a beaver house may have 3–5 underwater shoots (openings), snares are set at only two or three of these, suggesting that the return is greater on two snares at the next beaver house than on the additional snares at a house which already has some. (Ibid.:92)

Assuming, as Rock Crees claim, that some beavers are more aversive to snare poles than others, it is possible that dividing the same number of snares between two houses would catch more beavers more rapidly than using them all at one site. However, positioning snares at each point of egress from a single house would also seem to be an efficient strategy. Since separate holes must be cut through the ice for each snare pole, the labor costs of the two strategies are the same, excluding the additional time needed to check the multiple house(s).

Winterhalder considers the question dichotomously, seemingly rejecting the possibility that efficiency and reliability could be simultaneously relevant to the existence of the practice. His analysis suggests either that the Crees were never asked why they utilize the strategy or that their answers were deemed irrelevant to deciding which theory is correct. It would be consistent with much ecological, specifically, sociobiological, writing to conclude that management is misrecognized optimal foraging: the false consciousness Crees have of their energetically efficient strategies. However, Winterhalder and Smith make no such explicit suggestion, and neither is all optimal foraging theory sociobiological in conception. The question remains as to the position of the foragers' self-conception of their activity in optimal foraging theory. As the Rock Cree trappers quoted above make clear, these strategies are *said* to be practiced because they secure long-term reliability. They say that wire snares and traps involve less effort than the old technique of chiseling open the winter lodge, but they also say that the latter produced more beavers. Decisions about how many traps or snares to set, where to position them, and when to remove them all intentionally seek to limit the number of beavers killed and to selectively trap mature males. Since trapping only a subset of the chutes at each lodge minimizes the likelihood that all the occupants will be killed, I suspect that these were also the intentions of the Crees described by Winterhalder. Management strategies of certain kinds may, indeed, possess greater efficiency than intensive forms of foraging labor intended to capture every animal at a site. But the explanation of what these strategies are "designed to do," in Smith's terms, must surely incorporate the foragers' current intentions, even if, in "evolutionary time," strategies adopted for one purpose may be retained because they serve another. The Cree trapper Luke Dumas described the well-managed trapline as "like the white man's bank," and I believe he meant by this a renewable resource that could reliably supply in predictable quantities the animals Crees transform into food, clothing, and cash. Winterhalder and Smith establish the important point that a single strategy may have multiple advantageous consequences. To assume, however, that short-term caloric efficiency possesses more explanatory value than long-term energetic reliability—in terms either of the actors' knowledge or of evolutionary success—is simply an act of faith in the more measurable of the two currencies. Under conditions of extreme scarcity, for example, foragers may practice strategies that maximize not efficiency but gross energy capture. Such was the case with beaver chiseling, which usually allowed Crees "to catch every one"—at the cost of "hard work." But many Crees continued to use this strategy well after animal populations had stabilized. Similarly, in a situation of market dependence, long-term sustainability of furbearers may be factored into the foragers' decisions, whether or not the techniques are more or less efficient than their alternatives.

There is, indeed, no reason to assume that caloric efficiency, any single other currency, or any configuration of multiple currencies will predict the strategies ethnographically attested for boreal forest Algonquians or other hunter-gatherer societies. The strategies are not objectively given by human wants, and neither are they deducible from particular ecosystem variables. The indiscriminate hunting and selective utilization described during the eighteenth century were not the only harvesting and consumption practices possible in the boreal forest. Neither was management the inevitable consequence of resource depletion. Crees initially reacted to the game shortages by intensifying their labor, and many of them simply abandoned the region. Among those who remained, management was institutionalized only slowly, and the practice remained elective rather than categorial. Finally, if foragers elect to manage resources, the strategies they use to do so constitute a subset of the feasible practices. The Eastern Crees described by Tanner (1979), for example, conserve beavers by rotating their traplines, not by selectively trapping beaver colonies. More generally, some foraging strategies may effectively maximize multiple ecological currencies while others maximize a subset only at the expense of others. What one would expect would be strategies that simultaneously procure multiple currencies—efficiency, gross energy capture, nutrition, and reliability—within parameters set by cultural conceptions of labor, human needs and wants, and appropriate material satisfactions.

11

"No Notion of Frugality"

Introduction

Anthropology's purported "exhaustion with a paradigmatic style of discourse" (Marcus and Fisher 1986:x) is little in evidence in contemporary hunter-gatherer research. Most theoretical writing on foragers is explicitly materialist in orientation. The term "materialist," of course, underdifferentiates the internal diversity of this writing, but I use it very schematically to refer to the congeries of theories that identify human biology, technoenvironmental factors, and the production process as exerting the decisive influences on social forms and systems. Among the most influential recent approaches to hunter-gatherer societies, optimal foraging theory represents mobility, resource management, the division of labor, group size, settlement pattern, and diet as strategies that, within the parameters of relevant ecosystem variables, maximize caloric efficiency or other biological currencies and thus reproductive fitness (Winterhalder and Smith 1981; E. A. Smith 1983, 1991). Others, writing in a Marxian tradition, have emphasized the determining effect of the foraging labor process on other aspects of social practice (Godelier 1977; Meillassoux 1973; Lee 1980; Hindness and Hirst 1975; Southall 1988). The debates of the 1970s and 1980s between materialist and nonmaterialist theories of society continue to possess, in this respect, an impressive topicality in forager studies, regardless of their diminishing value as currency in other contemporary theoretical markets. Not everyone, of course, construes the issues identically or accords them a focal position in their research agenda, but the question of whether material or symbolic influences are dominant continues to be engaged—explicitly or implicitly—as a theoretical problem. Since the significance of material influences on foraging societies has been enormously exaggerated, I attempt here to characterize what a nonmaterialist analysis of a foraging society—specifically, of foraging itself—might contribute. Having argued in the preceding chapters that neither indiscriminate nor scheduled foraging were necessary or even probable effects of material causes, I extend the demonstration here to zoological taxonomy, diet, and food storage, suggesting that the social forms directly implicated in material production and reproduction are not at all materially determined but relatively arbitrary with respect to their technoenvironmental and biological coordinates. While these forces impose constraints on possible social forms and on the functional compatibility between them, the limits are sufficiently broad that the finalities of explanation are not material. Given any set of material coordinates, multiple arrangements of society are possible. It is in this variance between existing social forms and the multiple alternatives that could exist in their place that a semiotics of human ecology and production can be situated.

Some materialist theories have attempted to understand not just production and reproduction but the entire configuration of society in terms of material influences. Writing that defines itself variously as semiotic, symbolic, or hermeneutic has been, in the aggregate, less enterprising in its delimitation of topics, less explicit as to the scope of its theoretical project. Since materialist and nonmaterialist theories provide, in certain respects, alternative rather than complementary explanations of the same social phenomena, the value of the semiotic perspective can best be assessed when it is extended beyond its conventional venues of ritual, performance, and the carnivalesque and into the spheres of ecology and the labor process. The effectiveness, for example, of Sahlins's (1976:166–204) theoretical critique of Marxist, ecological, and utilitarian themes in social theory is amplified by his examination of the symbolic organization of American production and consumption.

Folk Dichotomies: The "Material" and the "Symbolic"

The hegemony of materialist perspectives in forager studies has persisted despite the demise of the stereotype of ecological marginality (Sahlins 1972), raising the question of why biology and ecology should be so consistently invoked as the explanatory finalities. Materialist discourse is not, of course, limited to forager studies, but its prevalence there suggests that Western academics conceive hunters as uniquely susceptible to biological and biophysical imperatives. Foragers are believed to effect relatively little anthropogenic modification of ecosystems in which they participate, seemingly conductive to the view that they are themselves inversely and proportionately modified. Foragers may thus appear maximally constrained in contrast to agricultural, pastoral, and industrial societies whose technological routines seemingly afford greater autonomy from "natural" determinations. Then again, foraging is observable in nonhuman species, whereas agriculture and industrial manufacture are less readily identified among them.

Within anthropology, a dichotomous classification of the sectors of the sociocultural object as differentially "material" and "symbolic" organizes both theoretical discussion and the topical division of labor. Social forms are implicitly apportioned between two sectors on the basis of their distinct determinations or imputed essential properties. Ecologists and Marxists characteristically focus on labor, politics, demography, and economics, while language and religion are franchised to the various symbolisms and semiotics. Thus, in the conventional ethnological division of labor, diet and fertility regulation are "material" topics, while mortuary practices and trickster myths are "symbolic topics." Kinship studies appear, at this writing, to be common property, and there exist, of course, numerous other areas of overlap. One set of institutions may be represented as material and the other as symbolic, or, more subtly, the analysis may distinguish discree material and symbolic aspects of the same institution. The diverse references of "symbolic" in anthropology are beyond my compass here, but the oppositions of "symbolic" culture to "nonsymbolic" social action and "symbolic" animal ritual to "nonsymbolic" animal trapping encompass many of them. In folk-anthropological usage, social forms are "symbolic" if they pertain to ideation or consciousness, if they stand for other things, and especially, as Sperber (1975:3) noted, if they are nonfactual in a Western epistemology. "Religion" and "symbolism" are thus near-synonyms in the anthropological lexicon.[1] "Material" practices, in contrast, are those with immediate consequences for the production and reproduction of society and population and are thus maximally conditioned by human biology and the ecosystem. It is sufficient to point out the anthropological separation of such departments as "production" or "economy" or "ecology" from "art," "magic," and "religion," domains whose symbolic constitution is readily agreed on. Objectively distinct in their characteristics, these different domains would call forth distinct methods and theoretical perspectives. In practice, it is typically a question of two classes of institutions addressed by two congeries of theory.

In most anthropological writing, no judgment need be (or usually is) entered as to which sphere includes the explanatory finalities. Institutions grouped in one sphere are commonly understood to exert influences over those in the other, and institutions seen as predominantly material or as predominantly symbolic may be represented as subject to secondary influences from the opposite mode. One can, for example, represent rabbit snaring as predominantly material and rabbit rituals as predominantly symbolic, while believing that each is respectively subject to secondary symbolic and material influences. Single institutions or whole social systems can be represented as simultaneously material and symbolic in equal or unspecified degree. Social forms could, from this point of view, be segmented into subsets defined by the material or symbolic qualities they embody: all material, dominantly material, mixed material-symbolic, and so on. All of these phrasings are congenial to the conclusion, frequently to be met in summary paragraphs of journal articles, that multiple theoretical perspectives provide complementary explanations and that their synthesis is a desirable (and usually deferrable) objective. In addition to such eclecticism, diverse other compromise formations have been proposed: that some societies are materially constituted while others are not, or that the same society may transit between the two conditions in different stages of its evolutionary trajectory. Whatever the difficulties—and they are, of course, formidable—of identifying logical or empirical criteria to address the question, it is exceedingly improbable that foraging societies respond to different finalities than capitalized states or that the finalities of any society are simultaneously material and symbolic in equal degree.

Biology and Production

Theories that explicitly identify material forces as dominant may also exhibit this dichotomous conception of "material" and "symbolic" (or "ideological," "historical," "superstructural," etc.) spheres, as in the conventional Marxian articulation of a determining mode of production with the subdominant ("symbolic") superstructure. For such a theory to be totalizing, it must represent material forms as regulating symbolic forms or identify symbolic forms as themselves ultimately material in their inception or conditions of existence. Thus, in a Marxian reading of the play of consciousness in history, ideas are neither inert nor the mechanical reflexes of the labor process but nonetheless ultimately engendered in and constrained by it. Concern with the *letzter instanz* determinations of society is most evident in Marxian writing. Much ecological anthropology does not explicitly commit itself with respect to these issues or limit the scope of material determination to the labor process.

In the terms of the "material"/"nonmaterial" dichotomy, otherwise diverse materialist theories of foraging societies converge in addressing three distinguishable sets of relations. The first set articulates properties of human biology and the ecosystem with all those social practices conceived as factually implicated in the material provisioning and biological reproduction of society. For foraging societies, these would minimally include technology, diet, the division and organization of labor, anthropogenic modifications of the environment, food storage, settlement pattern, mobility, foraging techniques, demographic structure, fertility regulation, trade, property concepts, and patterns of distribution and consumption. Joseph Birdsell's (1953) study of rainfall and Australian Aboriginal population density, many of Julian Steward's (1955) foundation articles in cultural ecology, and Binford's (1980) correlation of climatic variables with different rates of logistical and residential mobility are all examples. These practices are typically understood as the functional entailments—variously necessary, optimal, or merely possible—of the satisfaction of human biological requirements in a given ecosystem. Theories identifying these ecological consequences as *explanations*, in one or another sense, of social forms need to be distinguished from those addressing them from descriptive and nonteleonomic perspectives (cf. Rappaport 1984:334). The second set of relations concerns the determinations or functional alignments that exist between two or more of these productively implicated practices themselves, holding their articulation with biology or ecosystem constant.

The third set of relations, often but not exclusively a Marxian franchise, is that holding between the material "base" and the other concurrent social, political, legal, and religious forms not directly implicated in production, or at least not conventionally regarded as so implicated by prevailing anthropological convention. Steward's (1955) writing on "family," "composite," and "patrilineal" bands and Maurice Godelier's (1977) Marxian analysis of Mbuti social structure and religion exemplify these concerns. Since the effects of material social forms on each other or on other institutions often implicate their articulation with biology and environment, much ecological and Marxist writing is simultaneously concerned—either tacitly or explicitly—with two or all three of the sets of relations distinguished here. Post-Stewardian ecological writing has directed attention to the productive and biological consequences of religious or other "symbolic" forms of culture previously regarded as peripheral to production. Rappaport's (1984) classic analysis of the ecosystem consequences of the Tsembaga *kaiko* and, with particular reference to foragers, Megan Biesele's (1986) examination of the functions of !Kung oral literature exemplify these concerns. Such studies have had the salutary effect of redefining the scope of the institutions identified as directly implicated in material and biological production and reproduction. Whether the ecological consequences of such practices "explain" in any sense their existence, properties, and distribution remains, of course, an issue closely tied to debates on the sufficiency of functional accounts.

Signs in the Material World

The term "semiotic" possesses diverse resonances in anthropology, signaling, variously, inspirational affiliation with its coiner, Charles Sanders Peirce, analysis of social practices as signs, and, most vaguely, alignment with hermeneutic, structuralist, symbolic, and interpretive theories of society. I use it here with liberal generality as a rubric for the congeries of theories that identify socially constructed significance as logically prior to material forces in the constitution of society. Whereas Marxian and some ecological writing postulate that material forces exert the dominating influence over the content and articulation of social forms, global "semiotic" theories locate this influence in social meanings as historical constructs, in the relatively arbitrary definitions, distinctions, equations, and proportions that everywhere organize social life according to schemas that are irreducible to biology, environment, and labor.

The distinction thus drawn is uselessly vague without more specific definition of the "meaningful" in relation to the "material" and of the articulation of these properties in and between social forms. In one sense, the claim that all social forms are meaningful is a noncontroversial truism since humans necessarily act on and react to persons, objects, and events as these are socially discriminated and defined. The "symbolic" then subsumes human consciousness and action since it predicates of any entity, condition, or event to which meanings are attached. In this sense, such phenomena as diet and settlement pattern are as "symbolic" as Balinese performance or Ndembu rituals. All social forms, whether examined as unconscious structures, socially shared ideologies, or recurrent classes of practices (including the emergent properties of these), are necessarily "meaningful" in this sense, and there is no antithesis here to a Marxian or ecological naturalism that would interpret any society's meanings as the products of labor, environment, and biology, as the relatively determined cultural "doubles" of whatever the locally relevant material realities happen to be.

The issue is not, then, recognition of the necessity of signs but rather the position taken on the relationship between social meanings—in structure, ideation, and practice—and their material coordinates. The position invoked here takes all social forms as irreducibly "symbolic" precisely to the degree that they are *unnecessary* given any configuration of technoenvironmental forces with human biology (Sebag 1964, Sahlins 1976). Such a point of view need not dispute that some social forms—trapping beavers versus ritualizing them, for example—are more directly implicated in social production and reproduction than others and thus more intensively regimented by biological viability and functional compatibility. But this is not "determination" or "domination," either teleologically as functional consequence or historically as antecedent. Even the social forms that immediately satisfy biological requirements and articulate with the biophysical environment— subsistence techniques and technology, for example—are symbolic because they are commutable with functionally equivalent forms.

Social significance and symbolism are, then, as much a matter of birth-spacing decisions and diet as of narratives and performances. And the significance that infuses social production and reproduction is demonstrably autonomous and relatively arbitrary with respect to material forces and constraints. Societies are, in this sense, symbolic entities not because they embody meanings—a conclusion that no one would dispute—but because these meanings are creatively independent of the material contexts and coordinates. The conception that societies are *arbitrary* with respect to these coordinates represents the extension into social theory of the much-debated semiological arbitrariness delineated by Saussure. For him, the lexical and grammatical categories that exist in a language at a given time are not the only ones possible, since alternatives are attested in other languages and in earlier conditions of the same language. Generalizing from lexicon to cultural forms more generally, Sebag wrote in this regard that

chaque société apparait comme soumettant à un principe d'organisation qui n'est jamais le seul concevable, une réalité qui se prête à une multiplicité de transformations. On comprend de ce fait pourquoi l'explication naturaliste est toujours insuffisante; car l'être du besoin dévoile en deçà de diverses modulations culturelles ne peut jamais nous donner que l'esquisse de la forme même de la culture, jamais de son contenu; or c'est ce dernier qui doit être compris. (1964:166–167)

It is precisely in this commutability, in the variance between what is materially possible and what is historically present, that the dominant position of significance in society is specifiable.

If diets and subsistence strategies—much less deities and kinship designs—are always, in large measure, substitutable, the relationship of social forms to material coordinates is representable through the metaphor of selection (Sahlins 1976:206). Given multiple possible designs for production and reproduction, social orders "select," for example, lizards and not rodents as a resource, or maternal carrying but not alternate care as a means of managing children while foraging. These selections may then have functional entailments and determinate effects once instituted, but they remain "unnecessary" because they are commutable with other functionally equivalent forms or complexes of forms. The corollary assumption is that the biological and environmental constraints to which cultural systems are subject are limiting but not prescriptive, a theoretical elaboration of the "possibilist" perspective on culture-ecosystem relations. Within specifiable material limits, a diverse range of institutions is possible, including productive and economic institutions (ibid.:168, 208–209).

An industrial technology in itself does not dictate whether it will be run by men or women, in the day or at night, by wage laborers or by collective owners, on Tuesday or on Sunday, for a profit or for a livelihood; in the service of national security or private gluttony, to produce hand-fed dogs or stall-fed cattle, blue collars or white dresses; to pollute the rivers or infect the atmosphere. (Ibid.: 208)

Neither, as Damas (1968) demonstrated in his classic comparative analysis of Iglulingmiut, Netsilik, and Copper Eskimo groups, do exploitative strategies and settlement pattern dictate whether leadership is vested in a regional band chief or in family headmen, whether the typical co-residential unit shall be an "extended" or a "nuclear family," or whether seal meat shall be pooled and redistributed or circulated through dyadic exchange partnerships focused on particular body parts.

This diversity did not always conform to a concomitant variation in subsistence and ecology. Although strong arguments can be advanced for a close harmony existing between the pattern of exploitation and certain features of the settlement pattern in the Eskimo area and probably in the world of hunters as a whole, the relationships that exist between these settlement patterns and variable community patterns [leadership, food distribution, co-resident group composition] appear to be less rigid and perhaps will allow alternatives in every conceivable case. (117)

Damas, not averse to ecological explanation, found no microecological variations among the three groups with which these contrasting practices could be placed in correspondence. The variability he documents can be conceptualized analogically in terms of paradigmatic and syntagmatic relations between social forms in the three Eskimo divisions he compares. Netsilik reciprocity is paradigmatically related to Copper and Iglulik reciprocity, which could substitute for it as its competential equivalents: any of the three designs for sharing meat accomplish the socially necessary objective of leveling disparities in energy capture between different hunters. Simultaneously, Netsilik reciprocity is syntagmatically related by adjacency with the other Netsilik forms with which it is concurrent. This commutability of the forms of leadership, commensal group structure, and reciprocity demonstrates arbitrariness at two distinguishable levels: syntagmatically between each form and the others with which it coexists in each group and paradigmatically between each of the three functionally equivalent forms in the three different groups. More generally, any practices that directly provision and reproduce society can be represented as unnecessary (1) in relation to "natural" biological requirements and environmental variables, (2) in relation to each other, and (3) in relation to other coexisting social forms. It is, of course, possible to argue that the three sets of relations are differentially arbitrary or that some are arbitrary while others are not. Hypothetically, for example, the limits of functional compatibility between component practices in the labor process [2] might be viewed as extremely high (or relatively nonarbitrary) but the process itself nonetheless arbitrary [1] relative to other processes that could exist, given the same biological and environmental context. If one takes "determine" to mean "uniquely specifies one outcome," it is clear that production in Damas's examples is not determining the institutions that coexist with it. His analysis raises the question of whether even the most learnedly qualified conceptions of material determinism can be upheld within the comparative context of variations between foraging societies. No two foraging societies interact with the same environment, even in the event that their geographic territories are coextensive. This being the case, microecological variation can always potentially be invoked to explain variations. But such explanations are mere professions of faith that social variation indexes ecological difference, not demonstrations that such is in fact the case.

Some of the ambiguities surrounding materialist and semiotic theories and their respective takes on the cultural object are evident in Stephen Mosko's (1987) conclusion to his excellent structural reanalysis of Mbuti band organization, kinship, and religion. He argues,

Finally, I suggest that structural analyses of hunter-gatherer cultures are as potentially fruitful as the more common materialist-empiricist interpretations. The ethnographic materials upon which this [Mosko's] ideational exercise rest were all collected by materialist or empiricist-inclined researchers, and doubtless their insights have possessed considerable insight. However, they have not necessarily gotten the whole of it; indeed, they have tended to leave aside or unexplained precisely those dimensions of the culture and social organization (i.e., the patterns *for* behavior) that here comprise the very essence of the analysis. The value and necessity of retaining both perspectives in some kind of complementary relationship have been widely recognized for quite a while now in anthropology, but with hunter-gatherers the decided imbalance persists nonetheless . . . the cultures of hunter-gatherers, along with the rest of us, are as much products of logically ordered symbolic expression as they are of material, ecological, demographic, economic, historical, or even social forces. (909)

Leaving aside the Geertzian allusion, Mosko asserts that there is an object of study—"culture and social organization"—that possesses multiple dimensions. Certain of these dimensions are better explained by structural than by materialist theories. Materialist theories possess, nonetheless, "considerable insight," suggesting that there exists a second set of dimensions that they *can* successfully address. These two dimensions of culture derive from the fact that culture results *both* from "logically ordered symbolic expression" and from "material, ecological, demographic, economic, historical, or even social forces." Since culture possesses these two dimensions, materialist and symbolic theories have a complementary rather than conflicting relationship: each addresses "dimensions" (aspects of the same cultural forms or perhaps discrete classes of cultural forms) that the other cannot. The two dimensions of the cultural object thus require two theoretical orientations whose joint application will produce more knowledge than will either deployed individually.

Mosko's conclusions about the excessive prevalence of materialist theories in hunter-gatherer studies are unquestionably true, and his analysis cogently demonstrates the value of structuralist interpretation. But from the perspective of a more encompassing semiotic theory, both his dichotomous conception of discrete material and symbolic "dimensions" and his conclusion that materialist and symbolic theories are complementary are unacceptable. This is the case because "logically ordered symbolic expression" is not something *other than* ecological, demographic, or economic forces—much less historical or social forces—with which it then becomes coordinate as a cause or determinant of society. In any society, "logically ordered [and disordered] symbolic expression" *constitutes* all of these domains as significant practices that exist in place of others equally compatible with the existing material forces.

Responding in part to Sahlins's (1976) critique of ecological anthropology, Rappaport wrote,

What seems to me distinctive of humanity is that it lives in terms of meanings it itself must construct but it is not fully constituted by those meanings, nor is the world in which it lives. Humanity no whit less than any other species is a product of organic evolution. The makers of meaning are organisms living in and absolutely dependent upon ecological processes, processes constituted not by meanings but by natural law. We are a species that lives in terms of meanings in a physical world devoid of intrinsic meaning but subject to causal law. (1984:336)

Rappaport eloquently characterizes the duplex identity of social forms as phenomena symbolically constituted but implicated in production and reproduction and subject to material constraints and influences. He also makes anthropology's most reasoned and persuasive argument for the significance of the physical in the finalities of social life. But it does not automatically follow that the ecological processes in which foragers, or anyone else, participate are constituted not by meanings but by natural law. The ecological processes are themselves decisively constituted by the cultural designs of the ecosystem's human participants. No one would claim that these meanings must not submit to some articulation with physical law, but articulation is not determination or dependency.

Symbolic Efficiencies

The existing state of affairs in hunter-gatherer studies suggests forcefully that much could be gained by reversing the inattention to cultural significance and to ecological process exhibited respectively by materialist and nonmaterialist camps in anthropology. An attractive but reprehensible relativism might be invoked to advance the thesis that, say, symbolic and ecological anthropologies are embarked on entirely different and complementary projects, the usual conception of the humanistic and (social) scientific disciplinary blend. It is, however, inadequate to propose an intradisciplinary division of labor within which each perspective separately labors with nominally distinct problems. Insofar, for example, as the two each attempt to identify factors engendering resemblances and differences in the subsistence practices of hunting-gathering peoples, they invoke the same underlying question of the determinants of social life. Consider, for example, Lévi-Strauss's alignment of conceptual structure and material life:

Ethnographical observation does not confront us with the alternative of either a plastic mind passively reflecting the ecology outside, or universal psychic laws unfolding everywhere the same inborn properties mindless of the ongoing history of each group and of the concrete features of its natural and social surroundings. Rather, we witness and should try to describe, ever-changing attempts to compromise between *given historical trends and special characteristics of the environment* on the one hand, and on the other hand, *fundamental psychic requirements which, at each stage, are the outcome of previous ones*. As a result, human history and natural ecology become articulated so as to make up a meaningful whole. (1972:7, emphasis added)

Presumably, the forager labor process, as much as mythology, is the product of this compromise. Compare William H. Durham's summary of optimal foraging strategy:

Drawing upon the work of animal ecologists and economists, the authors attempt to explain hunter-gatherer subsistence activities as part of the general "strategies" for optimal resource procurement. This approach assumes that hunter-gatherer survival and reproduction are maximized when the techniques of resource harvest optimize the returns per unit of time and/or energy expended. If this is true, then *much of the variability in hunter-gatherer food preferences, settlement patterns, spatial and temporal organization of foraging, and social organization of subsistence should be interpretable as the product of ecological adaptation to different environments and different resources.* (1981:219, emphasis added)

The positions expressed here are not complementary, despite the fact that neither author situates himself within an exclusively symbolic or ecological framework. For Lévi-Strauss, the regularities derive from "fundamental psychic requirements," the diversity from a process in which "each ideological construct becomes inflected by techno-economic conditions and is, so to speak, first attracted and then warped by it" (1972:7). For Durham, on the contrary, parallels between societies are specified outside the symbolic faculty of mind or culture in a universal currency of caloric efficiency and survival. The prospects for theoretical "synthesis" either within or between these divisions are, of course, no greater than they are elsewhere in anthropology, which is to say, exceptionally slight. There seems, nonetheless, to exist potential for a more constructive dialogue across the existing lines drawn by topical and theoretical proclivities. Such a dialogue could seek to identify logical and perhaps even empirical criteria relevant to distinguishing semiotic process from material constraint and assessing their relative influence as *letzter instanz* determinations of particular social practices. From the perspective of a semiotically oriented perspective on hunting and gathering societies and on hunting-gathering itself, optimal foraging theory (see Winterhalder and Smith 1981; Smith 1983, 1991; Hill et al. 1987) provides an exceptionally interesting occasion for such dialogue, both because of the theoretical and methodological sophistication of its practitioners and because of their seeming inattention to foragers' conceptions of their own activities. Assuming the operation of neo-Darwinian evolutionary selection on human foragers and their practices, optimal foraging theory introduces into cultural anthropology and archaeology models developed in evolutionary ecology to predict the foraging behavior of nonhuman organisms. The models propose that reproductive fitness is maximized by those strategies (diet breadth, time allocation, group size, mobility) that produce the highest rates of net energy gain ("foraging efficiency") within the given ecosystem coordinates and that there occurs evolutionary selection for such strategies and for their practitioners. Net energy capture is the currency most commonly measured, but other biologically relevant currencies—gross energy capture, nonfood yields, nutrition, reliability—have been examined, either as alternative measures of fitness or as ancillary factors explaining deviations from the postulated caloric optima. This brief discussion is excessively skeletal in content, and the reader is referred to E. A. Smith (1991:1–63) for an articulate exposition and defense of the theory. In contrast to writing in the "cultural materialist" mode, and to other varieties of materialist writing in anthropology more broadly, optimal foraging theory is distinguished by its commitments to hypothesis testing, long-term ethnographic fieldwork, attention to measurement of biological currencies, and concern with disparities between predictions and findings. The principle of caloric maximization is not, in optimal foraging theory, extended beyond the labor process itself to explain other facets of society, and the practitioners are well aware that influences other than energy enter into foraging strategies and choices, dealing with these "local" or "cultural" effects (prestige, taboos, etc.) as factors that deflect practice from the calorically optimal.

Critiques of caloric reductionism have long been institutionalized within and outside ecological anthropology (Vayda and McCay 1975, Ellen 1982), and nonconverts to optimal foraging theory may well remain skeptical regarding its currency of choice, its neo-Darwinian evolutionary assumptions, and its methodological individualism. In particular, there exist in optimal foraging theory (as elsewhere in the social sciences) unresolved ambiguities regarding the interplay of individual conscious choice, received cultural form, and evolution. The relationship of the foragers' conceptions and consciousness of their own activities to the evolutionary selection of the calorically most efficient practices remains underspecified. Smith (1991:22–23), for example, argues reasonably enough that the incorporation of historical and cultural factors directly into optimal foraging models would deprive them of generality and that the actors' ideational repertoires are irrelevant to the primary objective, that of examining empirically the predictive value of models based on a culture-neutral evolutionary trajectory of caloric maximization. But if it were to be determined that caloric efficiency does, in fact, predict the qualitative and quantitative characteristics of foraging strategies in diverse settings, any principled theoretical explanation of how evolutionary selection produces these effects would need to incorporate both agency and cultural form into the theory.

The effects on hunter-gatherers of their own strategies are among the most interesting things we can seek to know about them, and it is not, of course, that energy and other currencies measured in optimal foraging theory are irrelevant to their labor. But the question of whether there are processes other than evolutionary selection that cause these currencies to become significant needs to be posed. Foragers themselves make decisions in terms of (ethnographically) local conceptions of efficiency, reliability, and nutrition, and the articulation of these with the culturally neutral currencies examined by optimal foraging theory remains an exceptionally interesting and important desideratum. For example, I encountered at Granville Lake a strategy for killing snowshoe hares that employed a Cree conception of food chain efficiency, the ratio between the energy consumption of the prey and the energy yielded to the predator at the next trophic level (see Ricklefs 1973:784). In Slobodkin's (1972) celebrated example, mice, from the point of view of cats, are devices for turning mouse food into cat food. In this case, Crees hung snares for hares only after the hares had nearly devoured the jackpine needles on the trees cut down to attract them to the snaring area. With this strategy, as Johnny Bighetty didactically pointed out, one caught not only many hares but many *fat* hares. One could consider also the following short narrative that a Manitoba Swampy Cree told to Frank Russell (1898:216).

A hare accosted a passing moose one day with the remark, "You are proud."
"I am no prouder than you are," was the reply.
"Yes, you are, for I go into any snare; even a woman's garter will catch me. I serve as food for a great many."
"I am more benevolent than that, for when a man kills me he has a great deal of meat."

In the idiom of the benefactive ideology of hunting, the two species here proclaim the different currencies they respectively maximize. The hare, after fish the most reliable item in the Cree bush diet, boasts of its easy accessibility, while the moose, far from reliable but maximally efficient in net energy return, brags of its dressed weight. Crees have, to my knowledge, no consciousness of their practices as the products of evolutionary selection, but they articulate conceptions partially translatable into such ecological currencies as efficiency, nutrition, and reliability. In particular, the attributes of prey types that determine their caloric efficiency ranking—weight, mobility, density, aggregation, aversiveness—are, of course, well known to foragers. These "proxies," in Smith's (1991:47) idiom, would seem to open a perspective on questions crucial for both ecological and semiotic perspectives on foraging.

The alternative perspective on foraging with which I experiment here is explicitly skeptical with regard to the prediction of diets, group size, mobility, and other strategies from technoenvironmental coordinates or biological currencies. It is self-consciously "possibilist" in the sense of French geographic and Boasian critiques of environmentalism. It begins with the postulate that the ecosystem and the available technological forces impose limits on the possible set of foraging strategies but that these limits are quite broad and that multiple strategies are possible. The optimistic ecological creed of the 1960s, tacit or implicit, was not that multiple strategies were not possible but that selective forces or other functional mechanisms, often of relentlessly vague character, were such as to produce and thereafter maintain in place that strategy (or congeries of strategies) most congenial to the maximization of the kilicalory, protein, dollars, reliability, or another ecological currency of choice. Optimal foraging theory has introduced into the shadow realm between functional effect and social form an explicit conception of neo-Darwinian evolutionary selection: the strategies producing the highest net energy gain confer reproductive success on families that practice them and so are disseminated and perpetuated. The strategies in place should then be or should tend toward the most efficient possible, given the technoenvironmental coordinates. This postulate can be disputed on both logical and empirical grounds. In some societies, or sectors thereof, the minimum viable rates of procurement of biologically indispensable currencies may be frighteningly minimal indeed. Whole societies have endured for decades—and perhaps centuries—with per capita rates of energetic and nutritional intake just sufficient to allow people to drag themselves around—and to reproduce new generations to do the same. While the economic structures producing these effects are not present in the foraging societies that we have knowledge of, foraging (and other nonindustrial) populations likewise can reproduce themselves biologically and socially through time with strategies that are *not* the most calorically efficient, relative to the technologically and environmentally possible alternatives. It is, I believe, the case that foragers stay and have stayed in the existential game with group sizes, patterns of residential mobility, divisions of labor, diets, child-rearing practices, and food storage customs that are nonoptimal with respect to ecological efficiency, gross energy capture, reliability, nutrition, and provisioning of nonfood materials. Biological needs, of course, impose certain limits. Practices that recurrently cause provisioning of energy and nutrients to fall below the minimum rates necessary for survival and reproduction are not, of course, likely to be transgenerationally perpetuated. Crees could not, for example, have institutionalized a diet breadth limited exclusively to blueberries and weasels. Neither is it likely that arctic or subarctic foragers could reproduce themselves with diets lacking hare, fish, or some comparably reliable resource type. But this tells us nothing about the system as instituted and historically transformed. Foraging practices are arbitrary—and proportionately "symbolic"—precisely to the degree that they are unnecessary, undetermined, and—one can add—nonoptimal with respect to human biology and the ecosystem. Even in the boreal forest, an ecosystem in which energy is periodically limited, there exist multiple alternative strategies, each of which can reconcile and satisfy needs for efficiency (and for gross energy capture, reliability, nutrition, and nonfood yields) at rates permitting biological and social reproduction. Given the multiple possible designs for satisfying the needs, the needs themselves cannot possibly dictate the logic of the designs.

It is, from this point of view, not biological needs that cull and select foraging strategies but the foraging strategies that regulate, above the minimum rates consistent with reproduction, how and at what rates biologically needful currencies are procured. And what conditions the foraging strategies? They derive from earlier foraging strategies, none of which were necessarily any more (or less) determined or biologically optimal than their successors, together with a historical accumulation of experimentation and external influence. And the production process is, throughout, dominated by conceptions of edibility, gender, prestige, and labor that are themselves irreducible to it or to the technological and environmental context. The fact, for example, that the Rock Crees' eighteenth-century ancestors defined summer fishing with spears as male labor and other fishing strategies as female labor was no more necessary—or calorically efficient—than the fact that fish ranked low in the preference hierarchy (Thompson 1962 [1784–1812]:101, 128). It would then follow that the rates at which biological currencies are procured above the minimum levels of viability are conditioned by a diverse set of structures, ideologies, and practices, none of which are deducible from reproductive benefit. Further, in foraging societies, net energetic efficiency, gross energy capture, nutrition, reliability, and nonfood yields may sometimes constitute competing currencies in the sense that, with respect to certain resource types and techniques, one currency is satisfied only at the expense of others (Hill et al. 1987). Some resources satisfy multiple currencies. Fish, for example, are nutritious, reliable, and (with certain techniques) very efficient, and they could also, in the early fur trade, be converted into nonfood yields through trade. Moose hunting, in contrast, ranks high in efficiency but low in reliability. If the maximization of any single currency causes rates of procurement of the others to drop, we should expect a mix of strategies addressing these objectives, insofar as they require different resource types in different proportions. The character of this reconciliation—specifically, how certain currencies are prioritized and satisfied at the expense of others—is likewise, in the last instance, unrelated to biology. It may prove to be the case that different foraging societies institute very different prioritizations. Sedentary and food storing foragers, for example, may rank reliability and gross energy capture over efficiency, collecting more energy but working harder for each unit of it. Conversely, some nomadic foragers seemingly value efficiency over reliability or gross energy capture.

Hunter-gatherers, then, do not necessarily prioritize efficiency, in the sense that the strategies in place are the most efficient possible, given technology and ecosystem parameters. But efficiency *may* indeed be "selected"—by structural design or deliberate intention or both—in the sense that the foragers prefer to use those strategies that they understand to produce relatively great quantities of food for relatively small investments of time and labor. Such strategies may be chosen in conscious preference to others that are known to procure greater reliability or gross energy capture but at the expense of greater labor costs. Foragers do not calculate efficiency ratios, but they recognize differences between more or less productive and laborious categories of foraging labor. The quantitative indexes of forager "affluence" (Sahlins 1972)— the low rates of per capita labor in some societies—would appear to be effects of practices that are objectively efficient. It is, for example, usually (not invariably) more efficient to have a broad diet breadth than a narrow one, to move frequently to new foraging areas rather than staying put, and to distribute food through generalized sharing rather than privatizing it. In a different context, I cited earlier Friedrich's (1979:23) observation that "material reality may be seen as in part a sort of resource for symbolic reality." Foraging strategies are symbolic realities, cultural things of this world that may model themselves on the objective potentialities for net energetic efficiency in given technoenvironmental contexts. And there are reasons other than evolutionary selection that this should be the case. Energy was periodically limited in the boreal forest, but it is reliability rather than efficiency that most directly addresses this hazard, and the Crees' cavalier unconcern with reliability dumbfounded the traders. And it is by no means "natural" for productive modes to evolve toward the maximally efficient; much of the human productive career has seemingly been a journey in the opposite direction. Foragers may prefer, experiment with, and institutionalize calorically efficient strategies because they are easier and because they permit longer and uninterrupted periods of sociality. Moose and caribou stalking are probably the strategies with the highest net efficiency return, and Crees in the early 1800s clearly preferred to hunt such big game rather than trap beavers and other furbearers. As Thompson's Cree client observed, winter beaver hunting was "hard work, and only gives meat while we are working" (1962 [1784–1812]:102). Not surprisingly, complaints that Crees were neglecting fur trapping to hunt big game were a recurring aria in the post journals of the period. Of a group hunting to the west of Nelson House, for example, George Charles wrote that they were good moose hunters, occupied an area well supplied with them, and were thus "less serviceable as trappers" (HBC B.91/e/1[1818–1819]). In societies lacking any conception of the ennobling character of labor—and this probably describes most nomadic forager groups—one can postulate a penchant for making a virtue out of the line of least resistance, experimenting with different strategies and retaining those most congenial to the objective of obtaining food with little labor. Foragers may use efficiency, as locally recognized, as a model for their productive regimes, insofar as the efficient strategies are compatible with other values. There are, for example, group sizes above and below which per capita rates of labor begin to increase. Nothing requires that group size remain within these values: ceremonial events or sheer love of sociality may operate routinely to maintain group size at levels well above the calorically most efficient. But insofar as it is compatible with other objectives, a group size that maximizes per capita consumption while minimizing per capita labor is consistent with conceptions of the good life professed in many nomadic forager groups. Similarly, with respect to diet breadth, a generalist diet including some of the most efficient resource types is likelier than a specialist diet focused on less efficient resources. In the long term, then, one might observe the transformation of dietary choices—the experimental addition and subtraction of particular resources—as a result of their submission to local conceptions of "efficiency." In this way, foragers' own conceptions of the efficient may produce strategies whose energetic consequences align with those predicted by optimal foraging theory models, an interesting mimicry effect. One would then be in danger of misrecognizing cultural preference and its effects as the long arm of evolutionary selection.

The postulate that the characteristics of forager and other labor processes are ecologically arbitrary can, of course, always be challenged as a rhetorical presupposition, but it is, at worst, no more of one than the presupposed economism and evolutionism of optimal foraging theory and, at best, equally or more subject to logical and empirical clarification. In this respect, the impressive methodological repertoire of optimal foraging theory may permit investigation of the degree to which the practices in place are *not* optimal, relative to net efficiency and other currencies. The strategy of optimal foraging theorists has been to compare the observable indexes of strategies—group sizes or animals harvested, for example—with the estimated caloric optima. As Winterhalder (1981:95) cogently observes, it is not possible directly to measure the efficiency (or other biological effects) of alternative possible strategies that the foragers do not practice. For example, no subarctic foragers, to my knowledge, eat small rodents. If these rodents rank low in efficiency, this would support the theoretical project of optimal foraging theory. If, however, small rodents could be shown to be among the most efficient (and reliable) resources in the boreal forest, this would discredit the assumption that the diets in place are the product of evolutionary selection. Simulating or experimenting with such alternative strategies remains an attractive possibility. In the interim, it is possible to proceed with the argument on logical grounds. The decisions Crees and other foragers sometimes make are, in fact, exceptionally surprising, if we assume their strategies are so many instrumental techniques—"selected" over the centuries—for maximizing efficiency (or other currencies). We need approaches that examine the foragers' own conceptions of the optimal, strange as these may sometimes be.

Diet

Optimal foraging theories of diet predict that foragers will pursue and eat the most energetically efficient prey species. More specifically, the optimal diet breadth model distinguishes the search costs entailed in locating resources (either the animal or its signs) from the pursuit costs entailed by deciding to hunt or trap a particular resource. The model predicts that hunters will pursue resource types in a rank order of caloric efficiency until the last "added" resource imposes pursuit costs that are not offset by average savings in search costs (Winterhalder 1981:68). Since resources and strategies may be more or less efficient at different times of year, the model potentially predicts both the species included in the diet and decisions as to whether or not edible resources will be pursued when encountered. In the model, resource types have essential or "natural" use values, measurable as differential caloric efficiency.

In opposition to the naturalized use values represented in certain of Marx's writings, Jean Baudrillard (1975) described the domination of the production process by the things produced and the constitution of the latter as arbitrary signs rather than biological givens. From this point of view, nothing in the Cree labor process requires that Crees eat porcupines, but the latter, once instituted as food, have determinate consequences for the character of the labor process. The assumptions of the optimal diet model, and the entire notion of net efficiency as an essentialist use value, are called into question by the exclusion of efficient resources from the Cree diet, by "waste" of the meat of species hunted for their exchange value, and by use of resources in proportions unrelated to their efficiency ranking.

Table 8 compares the modern Cree diet of animal foods (excluding birds and fish) with a diet reconstructed from documentary sources for the mid- and late eighteenth century (Graham 1969 [1767–1791], Isham 1949 [1743–1749], Thompson 1962 [1784–1812], Hearne 1958 [1795]). The two diets coincide rather closely, although there has occurred a shift in the direction of specialization with the subtraction of several furbearing carnivores. Crees talk about animals as being either *pīkisiw* 'clean' or *wīðipisiw* 'dirty', and these categories align almost exactly with the edible/inedible distinction. The attributes of cleanliness and impurity are transmitted upwardly through the food chain. Botanicals and most fish are "clean" and so, in consequence, are all herbivores and those carnivores (otters, lynxes) said to live on fish or on herbivores. Summer carrion and all very small animals (insects, small rodents, frogs) are inherently "dirty" and so, in consequence, are the carnivores that eat them. Human dietary choices are almost invariably explained with reference to trophic exchanges: lynxes are "clean" because they eat hare; martens are "dirty" because they eat mice; and so on. Dogs are "dirty" because they eat garbage, feces, and carrion. The classification leaks in certain respects. Bears, like wolverines, scavenge dead animals and are said to consume virtually anything,

Table 7 *Edible and Inedible Animals*

	1700s	1990s
Big Game		
moose	+	+
bears	+	+
polar bears	+	not in range
barren land caribous	+	+
woodland caribous	+	+
musk-oxes	+	not in range
buffalo	+	not in range
elk	+	not in range
mule deer	not in range	−
Small Carnivores		
lynxes	+	+
otters	+	+
dogs	+	−
martens	+	−
mink	+	−
wolverines	+	−
arctic foxes	+	−
skunks	+	−
weasels	?	−
least weasels	?	−
red foxes	−	−
fishers	−	−
wolves	−	−
Small Herbivores		
beavers	+	+
muskrats	+	+
hares	+	+
porcupines	+	+
woodchucks	+	not in range
red squirrels	+	+
"Bad Little Animals"		
flying squirrels	−	−
small rodents (10 species)	−	−
bats	−	−
garter snakes	−	−
frogs (3 species)	−	−
Manicos		
insects, worms, lampreys	−	−

but most people eat them anyway. Some individuals reject bears not because they are "dirty" but because they say they resemble human beings too closely in appearance. Lynxes eat mice as well as hares, and carnivorous birds like the arctic owl are eaten despite their rodent diet. The attributes of being "clean" and "dirty" are said to be concretely objectified in the taste and smell of meat. "Bad little animals" taste and smell badly and thus pollute the flesh of carnivores that eat them. The flesh of omnivores and of their predators preserves the purity of the vegetable diet, with its medicinal associations, and transmits it to humans who eat it.

The optimal diet model predicts that diet breadth will contract if technological factors operate to reduce search time, and it is clear that the introduction of dog traction in the 1890s and snow machines in the 1950s materially increased the Crees' access to preferred resources. The present century has also seen a steady increase in the quantity and variety of foods available from the traders. It is unclear why such resources as martens, arctic foxes, wolverines, and minks were acceptable during the early fur trade (and, presumably, prehistorically) and became "dirty" in the twentieth century. It is probable that these carnivores, because of their rodent diet, were always marginal as foods and that their reclassification as categorically inedible represents the rationalization of tendencies previously present in the dietary design; the same argument is developed with respect to dogs in chapter 6. In any case, the subtraction of small carnivores from the diet had nothing to do with caloric efficiency. All of these animals were and are exchange values in the fur trade. Each winter, red foxes, arctic foxes, wolves, wolverines, martens, fishers, skunks, and weasels are killed and cased for their fur, sometimes in sizable numbers. No additional labor would be involved in eating them beyond throwing them into a kettle, but the carcasses with their many kilograms of edible muscle and organ meat are instead reverently deposited in trees.

If caloric efficiency governs diet, we should expect that the relative proportions of different resources harvested should reflect their efficiency ranking. In net caloric efficiency, two fish nets observed by Winterhalder (1981:87) exceeded all other strategies except the spring and fall moose hunts, a fact reflected in the actual harvests: the Crees caught more fish than any other resource except moose. Further, fish are the most reliable resource in the boreal forest. Fish were presumably no less efficient and reliable in the eighteenth century, but there is evidence that these factors were not reflected in the Crees' harvests. Fish were eaten—but seemingly only as a supplement to better things—and the low harvests were an effect of the fine points of the gender division of labor. Cree males killed fish with spears during spawning runs in summer, but all other strategies—traps and weirs, nets, and angling—were in the domain of female labor. Comparing the Crees to the Chipewyans, Thompson (1962 [1784–1812]:128) wrote,

These people [Chipewyans] though subject to great vicissitudes yet suffer less from extreme hunger than the Nahathaways [Crees]. The latter pride themselves with living by hunting animals, look on fish as an inferior food, and the catching of them beneath a Hunter.

The proportion of fish eaten by Crees reflected not efficiency but the social fact—hardly given by the material coordinates—that men could appropriately forage only for high prestige meats while such pedestrian fare as fish, martens, and hares was secured by women. Only with the fish spear (an icon of the long caribou spear), a suitably masculine weapon, could men address themselves with dignity to fishing. As a result, most fish were caught by women with nets—when they were not hunting other small game, building lodges, making and repairing clothing, cutting firewood, retrieving game, hauling toboggans during residential moves, and superintending most aspects of child care. As a result, harvests could hardly have reflected the resource's efficiency ranking.

Small rodents appear as staple meats in the diets of South American, African, Australian, and Southeast Asian foraging societies, some Parisians, and those virtuosos of dietary generalism, the Great Basin Shoshoneans. Ten species of such rodents, none eaten by Crees, flourish (literally) in the Churchill River drainage, some of them active throughout the year. The individual animals have very low values for weight and fat content, but, as Winterhalder (1981:96) notes, small animals may be more efficient than larger ones. Thompson (1962 [1784–1812]:66) underreported species diversity in the late 1700s, but his observations otherwise coincide with my own: "There are two species of the Mouse, the common and the field Mouse with a short tail; they appear to be numerous, and build a house where we will, as soon as it is inhabited, they make their appearance." Although the efficiency ranking of a resource cannot be predicted directly from its density (see Winterhalder 1981), the density of small rodents in northwestern Manitoba suggests, at the very least, a potentially efficient resource. Winterhalder writes that "while the biomass of very small mammals in the boreal forest is quite high (109 kg/km² for 4 species—squirrel, shrew, and two voles—in the Alaskan boreal forest) . . . presumably they cannot be captured with sufficient efficiency for the Cree forager to pursue them" (ibid.:95). In other words, the animals are abundant, but no strategies exist for taking them efficiently, and nothing else will explain why they are excluded from the diet. At Granville Lake, the red squirrel is, in fact, eaten by some people. Mice, shrews, lemmings, and voles, however, are not. The high density of these rodents in and near human domestic space raises doubts as to the obstacle of search and pursuit costs. At least in summer, the animals could be captured easily. Isham (1949 [1743–1749]:150), for example, noted that the Crees killed "bushels" of mice and brought them home, not as food but as toys for children. It is difficult to believe that the inventors of the "rabbit village" could not develop efficient strategies for hunting or trapping mice, shews, lemmings, and voles. If a mad trader appeared and began offering substantial prices for rodent skins, the strategies would develop and disseminate. The path to efficiency is and was, however, obstructed by more than the lack of a better mousetrap. All animals classified as *āpikosīs* 'mouse' are categorically defined as inedible by Rock Crees because they are *wiðipisiw* 'dirty' or 'polluted', and I suspect that this is also why the Ontario Crees described by Winterhalder do not hunt and eat them.

The mule deer, a game animal extravagantly valued by sports hunters, began entering the southern areas of Rock Cree territory in the early twentieth century. As well it might have, since the Crees, for the most part, did nothing to molest it. Resembling the paradigmatically edible moose and caribou, the mule deer is eagerly sought by northern whites and, farther to the west and south, by Swampy and Plains Cree hunters. A few Rock Crees, today as in the past, hunt and eat it, but the great majority do not. The aversion is predictable but not from caloric criteria. The problem is that Crees think that the mule deer looks like a large dog. As Cornelius Colomb observed,

Really in Cree they call him *atimostikwān* ['dog head']. They didn't even eat them [for] long time. Because it seems like a dog head that jumps. So people didn't ever eat them. They look more like a dog. But later years, some people started to. After they seen Swampy people [Swampy Crees] in the south who were eating them.

The two specimens I encountered while with Cree hunters were allowed to bound away, unpursued and unfired upon. Even if the mule deer's low density values make it inefficient to search for in many areas, it does not follow that Crees should categorize it as inedible or ignore specimens encountered by chance. The "dog-headed deer" exemplifies a Cree dietary scruple relevant also to wolves and foxes: if an animal resembles another that is paradigmatically polluted, people will avoid eating it.

In all these cases, dietary choices are superintending the degree to which efficiency figures in the diet, not the other way around. Further, this arbitrary organization of diet existed in an ecosystem where food energy sometimes became a "limiting factor" in a literal sense, one evoking Malthus as well as Liebig. Taken more broadly, the dog-headed deer substantiates a point developed at some length by Baudrillard (1981): what is consumed regulates the process of production, but the categories of consumable object are given by schemes of symbolic differentiation that create the needs these objects satisfy.

Taxonomy

The question of diet leads to considerations of taxonomy. Eugene Hunn (1982) has advanced the claim that "folk" (non-Western) taxonomic systems name and subcategorize natural objects according to their usefulness in the productive process. The "activity signature" of a resource is the set of strategies for its acquisition, processing, and utilization. The argument is that languages will lexically discriminate resources with distinct activity signatures. The theory possesses the exceptional virtue of situating problems of lexicon and hyponymic classification in a pragmatic context, relative to the communicative intentions of speakers (Silverstein 1976). It predicts that useful natural entities will be lexicalized while nonresources will not or will be included in a residual category such as English "weed."

Such an argument initially seems to make sense of Cree animal names and their taxonomic ordering (see the Appendix). No animal species used by Crees have identical activity signatures; each resource is distinguished from each of the others by the techniques used to appropriate it and by physical and behavioral properties relevant to its utilization. All Cree resources are distinguished lexically at the "generic" level, and some, for example, "fox," are further segmented at the "specific" level along utilitarian parameters (see Berlin et al. 1973). For

Table 8 *Subcategorization of the Generic Taxon* Mahkīsiw *'Fox'*

osāwahkīsiw	yellow fox	Vulpes fulva, red phase
māsināsowahkīsiw	cross fox	V. fulva, cross phase
sōniyāwahkīsiw	silver fox	V. fulva, silver phase
kaskikwahkīsiw	black fox	V. fulva, black phase
kīnimīhcakanwahkīsiw	bastard fox	V. fulva, mixed phase
paskwāwahkīsiw	plains/swift fox	Vulpes relox
sipihkwahkīsiw	blue fox	Alopex legopus, blue phase
wāpiskahkīsiw [wāpahkīsiw]	white fox	A. legopus, white phase

example, as the theory would predict, the Cree classification of foxes is arbitrary with respect to the biological denotata but motivated in relation to their differences as exchange values.

In the 1700s, Crees trading at York Factory distinguished only triadically between *mahkīsiw* or the red fox (*Vulpes fulva*), *mahkīsiš* 'small fox' (*Vulpes relox?*), and *wāpahkīsiw* or the arctic fox (*Alopex legopus*), all presumably included within a generic category also labeled by "*mahkīsiw*" (Graham 1969 [1767–1791]:24–25). This generic taxon *mahkīsiw*, fox, today subsumes seven specific taxa (Berlin et al. 1973). Crees define the five color phases of the red fox as a single interbreeding species, but most regard the two phases of the arctic fox as different animals, and everyone distinguishes the red and the arctic foxes as different animals. As a "generic" taxon, *mahkīsiw* therefore subsumes animals that Crees identify as "unrelated" but that share physical resemblance and such traits as inedibility and commercial value. Further, the segmentation of the taxon on the specific level corresponds precisely to the color discriminations recognized by the Hudson's Bay Company and the Dominion-Soudack fur auction. It is neither biology nor domestic consumption but differential exchange value that has subcategorized the generic taxon in the Cree lexicon. The Cree categories are consistent with the uses they make of foxes, and these uses are, in turn, motivated by the changing markets in which they have participated since the seventeenth century.

It is not, of course, that taxonomic classification is arbitrary with respect to the labor process. One would expect naming and subcategorization of resources. The point is that the subset of possible resources "selected" and thus produced in a society is itself unnecessary. Cree trapping labor has, in this respect, long been conditioned by the moral and aesthetic schemes of European and Euro-Canadian consumers. To recoup a materialist argument, one would need only to identify the "necessity" that discriminates fox furs from other animal pelts, endows black, red, crossed, silver, and mixed fox furs with differential value, and, more generally, accords fur garments unique virtues for wealth display and for the expression of masculine regard within the conjugal union and its facsimiles. Unlike the ancestors of the Cree fur providers, the participants in these markets possess other options with which to address the need for warmth. Cree decisions about which animals to trap are conditioned by their own dietary preferences and by the currents of Euro-American fashion, both arbitrary.

A second difficulty with "utility" is that Cree and probably all other languages (Lévi-Strauss 1966a) lexicalize nonresources at both generic and specific levels of taxonomy. The utilitarian approach to taxonomy needs to be incorporated (see Hays 1982) as one component within a more general theory of lexical pragmatics that takes account of the full range of interactions with natural objects in which the taxonomists understand themselves to be engaged. Since nonresources deemed inedible by Crees and worthless by white fur buyers are nonetheless named and subcategorized by Cree nouns, there exist no grounds for assuming that utilitarian parameters are the only relevant ones, even in the case of resources. At the very least, we need to operate with a distinctively Cree conception of "utility." Frogs, for example, are not eaten and have no "utilitarian" activity signatures at all. Nonetheless, each of the three species present on the Churchill River is named and distinguished, and the juvenile phase of the leopard frog is even recognized as a fourth species by some Crees.

As I discovered after introducing specimens into my host's home on one occasion, some Crees are frightened by frogs, reactions that derive from practical considerations as they construe them. It would be possible, from this point of view, to motivate the four terms from the frog's status as a sign or agency of sorcery. Frogs are potentially powerful and dangerous animals, attributes indicated by the "bear" morphemes that

Table 9 *Subcategorization of the Generic Taxon Aðīkis 'Frog'*

aðīkis	'frog'		
osāwaskwaðīk	'yellow bear frog'	northern leopard frog	*Rana p. pipiens*
ocīpwīwaðīkis	'cheeping frog'	same, juvenile	
okistōtīw	'large bear frog'	wood frog	*Rana sylvatica*
iðinicawaðīkis	'human frog'	boreal chorus frog	*Pseudacris triseriata maculata*

occur as initials in the names for the leopard and wood frogs. The taxon *aðīkis* is further partitioned by other considerations. The leopard frog can be relied on to stay around water, whereas the wood frog may turn up where it is not wanted in tents. More emphatically, Johnny Bighetty glossed *iðinicawaðīkis* 'boreal chorus frog' as "goddamn noisy little frogs in the muskeg." In the spring, the calls of these animals are sufficiently loud to prevent sleep.

The subcategorization of *āpikosīs* 'mouse' also falls beyond utility, unless the propensity of some species to get into and defecate in stored food motivates discrimination of six specific taxa. The *āpikosīs* category provided an especially favorable opportunity to elicit relevant aspects of meaning. Because my teachers knew no word beyond English 'mouse' into which they could gloss the different Cree names, they spontaneously described the distinctive attributes of the different species.

The features described include physical attributes but also habitat, propensity for invading human space, metaphoric resemblance to human beings, a mythological prototype, locomotion, and proclivities for

---

Table 10 *Subcategorization of the Generic Taxon* Āpikosīs *'Mouse'*

---

wāskahikanāpikosīs 'house-mouse'. Deer mouse, *Peromyscus maniculatus*.
Found in houses where it scares some people. Gets into gear and stored food.
Has big ears and long tail.

iðinicahāpikosīs 'human-mouse'. Meadow vole, *Microtus pennsylvanicus*.
Lives in fields in refuse like old tin cans. Cans are its "house." Can observe
mother feeding infants.

kwāskwāskocāpikosīs 'jumping-mouse'. Meadow jumping mouse. *Zapus hudsonius*.
Jumps conspicuously instead of running along ground like other mice. Big hind
feet. Long tail.

kīnikiscowīyāpikosīs 'pointed nose mouse.' Arctic shrew, *Sorex arctiucus*; masked
shrew, *S. cinereus*; pygmy shrew, *Microsorex hoyi*.
Possesses a long pointed nose. Runs very fast.

amiskwāpikosīs 'beaver mouse'. Northern water shrew, *Sorex palusatris*.
Lives near water and in beaver dams. Runs up canoe paddles and scares people.

mihkwāpikosīs 'red mouse'. Boreal red-backed vole, *Clethrionomys gapperi*.
Reddish or brownish fur on back. Looks like it has been burned. Descendants
of the mouse employed by the hero Cahkāpīs to release the sun from a snare.
Gets trapped on winter trails and freezes.

āpikosīs [residual species]: northern bog lemming, *Synaptomys borealis*; mountain phenacomys, *Phenacomys intermedius*; meadow vole *Microtus pennsylvanicus*.

startling people. Most of these traits articulate with contexts in which rodents elect to interact with humans. Again, these animals have no significance as resources. From a utilitarian perspective, there is no reason for the generic taxon 'mouse' to be recognized at all, much less internally categorized.

The Determinations of Food Storage

I conclude the book not with a schematic recapitulation but with a problem. Discussions of food storage and sedentism have occupied a central position in materialist approaches to the foraging praxis. Most authorities distinguish typologically between mobile foragers who practice little or no storage and relatively more sedentary groups that preserve food and practice logistical mobility to and from more continuously occupied settlements. Binford's (1980) "foragers" and "collectors," Testart's (1981) "storers" and "nonstorers" (among other types), and James Woodburn's (1980, 1982, 1988) "immediate return" and "delayed return" foragers all subsume these differences, although with different emphases.

In both Woodburn's (ibid.) and Claude Meillassoux's (1973) analyses, the variable of food storage is identified as the aspect of the labor process most influential over cooccurring social forms. In Meillassoux's Marxist reanalysis of Mbuti (Ituri Pygmy) society, social structure equals the relations created in and by production, generalized, seemingly, to all other foraging societies. Specifically, the nature of foraging itself, as given by environmental and technical factors, is represented as determining *instantaneous* production and consumption without storage. Although cooperation in foraging is necessary, the self-contained character of each foraging project does not require enduring relations between particular individuals. There are no delayed returns on labor and hence no enduring cohesiveness. From these conditions, Meillassoux derives positively the existence and flexibility of hunting bands and, negatively, the (purported) absence of kinship institutions, sexual inequality, and enduring political authority. Meillassoux's discussion totally neglects the existence of "complex" foraging societies with intensive food preservation, relative sedentism, and delayed returns for labor investment. Instead, he contrasts a single foraging mode of production with an agricultural mode.

Woodburn (1980) has proposed broader and subtler conclusions about the positive and negative social entailments of both immediate (nonstoring) and delayed (storing) return foraging types. With respect to the elaboration of transgenerational kinship structures, Woodburn's distinction between "immediate" and "delayed return" forms of forager society resembles Meillassoux's distinction between foragers and agriculturalists. In delayed return foraging societies, kinship institutions develop as the concomitant of recurring labor cooperation between the same individuals, transcending the relatively ephemeral and transient character of immediate return sociality. We thus obtain correlations between two types of labor and two social configurations. There remains the question of factors influencing whether a group practices delayed or immediate return labor, or, more realistically, where along a continuum between these orientations it will be situated. While arguing for a decisive influence of the delayed or immediate character of labor on forager social organization, Woodburn shows that the "selection" of one or the other mode is not deducible from environmental or technological forces.

The available data on these societies demonstrate quite clearly that we cannot attribute the distinction I am making to simple environmental factors. It is easy to assume from our own sedentary ethnocentric standpoint that people who have the means to be sedentary, who have the means to store food, will store food, and who have the knowledge and skill to make and accumulate property (for themselves or for their group), will do so. None of these groups [Hadza, !Kung, Mbuti] live in a harsh environment in which, given the skills and knowledge available to them, they have to live in the way they do. None are excluded by the difficulties of their environment from having a system with the stress on delayed return. . . . I am not arguing [that] environmental factors are totally irrelevant. (1980:100)

Further, even the correspondences between the two types of labor and correlative social institutions are not predictable. The obvious counterexample to Meillassoux's and Woodburn's relatively "kinship-less" nomadic foragers are the Australian Aboriginal groups, most of whom used immediate return labor practices without any inhibiting effect—to say the least—on transgenerational kinship structures. Woodburn (1980) addresses the problem by extending the concept of delayed return to include the long-term labor obligations engendered through marriage, but neither is this development the result of the productive forces.

The evolutionary problem of the transition from nomadic to sedentary regimes is comparable in some respects to that posed by the Neolithic revolution (Testart 1988). The theoretical question is again the relative weight of "determination" and (cultural) "selection." The Mbuti, until relatively recently a type case of the "immediate return" society, did, in fact, produce and preserve a meat surplus for exchange while "selecting" against the greater sedentism that the same surpluses could have provisioned among themselves. Woodburn's conclusion—that "systems of immediate return and systems of delayed return can both occur in any environment" (1980:111)—disposes of simplistic environmentalism but fails to establish the fact that no other productive or ecological factor can be identified which determines the existence of one or the other mode. From a Marxist perspective, delayed and immediate return are two modes of property relations, two types of relations of production. But the question still remains how such disparate relations are engendered. Marx proposed reciprocal determination and potential contradiction between such relations and the labor, resources, and technology comprising the productive forces of a society. Certainly, environmental constraints and incentives can be identified with respect to storage and sedentism. Intensive food storage, for example, is facilitated by localized and abundant resources and by transport technology. Tropical climates and insects limit the duration within which preserved foods will remain edible (although, here, local judgments of edibility are critical). However, no recurrent set of productive forces has been identified which explains why the Andaman Islanders, some Australian Aborigines, some !Kung, and some subarctic Athapaskans lived on stored food in villages for extended periods, whereas the Mbuti, the Hadza, some subarctic Athapaskans, most Australians, and most subarctic Algonquians stored little and moved often.

Arctic and subarctic ecosystems are excellent venues for examining the play of "determination" and "selection" in food storage practices, especially as landscapes in which the absence of botanicals for much of the year exacerbates the uncertainty of production. The documentary references to Cree and other boreal Algonquian storage practices suggest, however, that, even here, material necessity had little enough to do with what people did. In the arctic and subarctic, there probably existed certain contexts in which some attention to food storage was objectively necessary to prevent winter starvation. There exist other ecosystems, that of the Hadza, for example, where resource abundance seemingly makes storage superfluous. These extremes give little insight into other points along the continuum at which food storage would possess both positive and negative consequences. Probably all foraging societies practice some form of food storage, so the question is not the presence or knowledge of the custom but the different values it takes as a variable and the situational factors that condition these values. The question of whether storage is more energetically efficient than nonstorage is exceptionally complex, but it is clear that the practice can significantly enhance the *reliability* of subsistence by permitting scheduled consumption of a surplus. One could thus predict increasing values for storage in foraging societies whose members recurrently faced possibilities of hunger and death by starvation. There exist, however, other conceptions of reliability that may deflect the storage variable in directions that seemingly deny all reason, at least to participants in delayed return economies.

The "Origin" of Cree Food Storage

There exist today no "nomadic" Cree Indians in Manitoba or elsewhere. There continue to be Crees who undertake much foraging-related mobility today, but it is, in Binford's (1980) terms, logistical rather than residential, hunters moving not from bush camp to bush camp but between bush camps and a residential base on the reserve or in a bush village. The creation of the reserve town at Pukatawagan in the 1950s signaled not so much increased sedentism as increased aggregation; relatively sedentary occupation of bush hamlets in winter began around 1900. At that time, the elders say, the formerly nomadic winter hunting groups of the Pukatawagan band began building log cabin hamlets on their hunting territories. Thereafter, mobility became increasingly logistical between hamlet and bush camp rather than residential between transient winter camps. There were thus multiple residential bases, and it is from these that the few remaining bush hamlets and the reserve town itself derive. It is of some interest that the Cree tradition of how this came about not only exemplifies the "great man" theory of history but also the functional compatibility between food storage and sedentism recognized by anthropologists (see Testart 1981:181). This is Sidney Castel's translation of Solomon Colomb's account.

People used to come to Pukatawagan to fish in the summer at the narrows by the [present] church. That's a good fishing place. They'd fish and then they'd pass on. One old man named *Wāpos Ocisk* 'Rabbit Ass' was the first man to camp at Pukatawagan during the winter. That was the first old man who made people settle down in one place instead of always traveling around. Because he was the one who always used to have lots of food. People who were traveling around making camps and trying to catch animals, they couldn't make their living because they're always traveling. This guy settled down in this place and he had lots of fish. He used to pick lots of berries and stock his fish and everything he gets. And those people who were traveling, they didn't have time to fish. They just had to keep on to try and get something. That's the way they first settled down. That was the first guy who settled down and stocked stuff for winter. When people got hungry, they'd come to him and he'd feed them.

Unable to accumulate a surplus, the people were unable to be sedentary, and if they were not sedentary, they could not remain long enough to store a surplus. But the history represents the potential as being there all along: Rabbit Ass's summer surplus of fish and berries could be stored to provision a winter of relative sedentism. Such had also very occasionally been the case with a large barren land caribou kill in winter. Absent from Mr. Colomb's account but probably significant were the availability at this time of food as a trade good and the inception of dog traction, which greatly increased the scope of logistical movement. Crees today enthusiastically preserve bush food, using a complex set of smoking and drying techniques, racks, recipes, and caches. My notes contain twenty-seven lexical entries referring to different varieties of preserved food and techniques used to produce them. Around the turn of the century, then, the Crees began to undertake a transition from immediate to delayed return designs: they became relatively sedentary, stored food, and managed resources. Documentary references from before Rabbit Ass's innovation suggest a strikingly different picture, however.

Cree Food Storage in the Eighteenth Century

They eat as much flesh at a time as will serve three or four Europeans; but then they can fast three or four times as long and these habits of abstinence and voraciousness seem to be determined by their natural temper and taste of life, for they are lazy and improvident, lying in their tents and feasting upon their stock until they have not a day's provision left; and if they are unfortunate enough to fail of a supply before their power of fasting is gone, they perish with hunger. (Robson 1965 [1752]:51)

Robson's comments on the Crees trading on Hudson Bay in the 1730s are typical. For European observers of the eighteenth century, Cree consumption patterns were both logically and morally objectionable. Europeans perceived the subsistence base of the Crees as precarious but as one in which hardship could be minimized by industry and rational management of food supplies. The Crees were neither industrious nor rational by these criteria. Two of their practices were especially inexplicable to English and French observers. First, the Crees ate up all their stores on hand before resuming hunting. What this means in practical terms is that any kind of surplus—meat in quantities greater than those consumable at a single meal—was the occasion for the suspension of further productive effort. *After* the surplus had been consumed, the men would again go hunting. Second, Crees threw meat away instead of preserving it. In either case, the Crees were criticized for not preserving sufficient meat as an insurance against future want. Rationally unaccountable, these dispositions were also sinful to men who thought of meat as scarce. Consequently, overtones of sanctimonious satisfaction sometimes intrude upon the traders' accounts of Indians in the throes of famine.

It is of considerable interest that the traders ascribed the precariousness of Cree production neither to the uncertainties of hunting nor to a scarcity of game but rather directly to the Cree organization of work and consumption. Some observers contrasted the resources available in the inland plains to those in the Canadian Shield and Hudson Bay lowlands on the coast. Graham, for example, distinguished between the two areas but identified the same consumption patterns in both:

The country beyond the lakes is so well stocked with various kinds of animals that the Indians can indulge their indolence and never be in want of food; but those who inhabit lower down towards the sea shore are frequently in great distress. For while they have a sufficiency or abundance, they never have any thought to provide for the future; but lie in the tent and indulge their enormous appetites. (1969 [1767–1791]:154)

Crees during this period knew and used various techniques for preserving meat by freezing or smoking and drying (Drage 1968 [1748–49], 1:216). It was not the case, as Steward (1955) argued for Great Basin Shoshonean foragers, that the techniques were unknown. The traders wrote not that Crees preserved no food at all for the future but that they preserved too little to provide effective insurance against hardship:

These Natives are ofte'n starv'd and in Want of food. Especially in the winter season that Keeps by the Sea side, but upland [inland] Indians are Seldom put to these shifts,—having plentier of Beast of all sortts, than what is to be gott by the sea shore,—I have oft'n observ'd these Natives need not, or wou'd not be in want of provender if they would be at the pains to cure itt, or all the meat they Kill which they do not, Curing a small Quantity only for to serve them for the present by Drying itt in the smoak then pounding itt small, which they Style (Ruhiggan). (Isham 1949 [1743–1749]:80–81)

Isham here distinguishes the coastal Crees from those inland but ascribes the same prodigality to both. Ellis (1967 [1748]:90) wrote similarly that the Crees "dry only a little venison and fish."

This optimistic inattention to food storage would be comprehensible enough in certain tropical ecosystems; in the boreal forest, it is perplexing. Bishop (1975:245) initiated a controversy by representing the boreal forest, exclusive of the Hudson Bay lowlands, as posing little resource uncertainty: "In aboriginal times and for a considerable period after contact, the threat of starvation for most Ojibwas was nonexistent." Smith (1976) and Waisberg (1975) responded by arguing that long-term and short-term fluctuations in resource populations sometimes produced both local and regional game shortages independently of and prior to the fur trade. During the eighteenth century, resources were probably ordinarily reliable on the Canadian Shield and less so in the lowlands but subject in both areas to periodic shortage. Other factors could also threaten starvation. The famine cannibal described by Isham (1949 [1743–1749]:226–227) had elected to hunt and trap alone with his family, and the crisis developed when he became lame and could not hunt. They successfully reached a food cache that they had prepared which was three days journey away but found that the stores had been removed by others. In another context, Isham (ibid.:141) observed that wolverines posed a serious threat to Indian winter survival by getting into caches and eating or removing the stored provisions. Graham (1969 [1767–1791]:154–155) observed,

Depending, as the Indians generally do, upon each day to procure them food, it may easily be supposed they are often in great distress. I have known instances when they have been driven to that extremity that they have eaten one another. A few years ago a man came to the Factory [York] almost naked; and had eaten all the skins he had procured, and afterwards the wife and children were devoured, and he himself was almost dead with hunger. The cause of this misfortune is frequently the breaking of a gun, or the sickness or death of the men when at a great distance from the English settlements.

Starvation and cannibal tragedies were not limited to the coastal area but occurred also inland in the full boreal forest in the eighteenth century. Thompson (1962 [1784–1812]:101–104) described three famine incidents caused by poor hunting skills, lack of winds for moose hunting, and broken beaver chiseling tools. These cases suggest not that starvation was a continuous threat but that shortages or accidents sometimes interrupted food acquisition, making a continuously renewed supply of emergency food a potentially useful adjustment.

Intensive food storage is not intrinsically incompatible with frequent residential mobility but imposes limits on it. Graham was the only European to consider nonstorage in this light:

They have a method of drying meat in the smoke; would they thus preserve the venison they throw away, hunger would less frequently assail them. But frugality and prudence in this respect are not among the virtues of these natives. Though, to be impartial, it is just to mention that the reason of a conduct, so unaccountable to Englishmen, may proceed from the difficulty that would arise from conveying a stock of provisions from place to place in their migratory way of life. We ought therefore not to be rash in our censures. The natives about the Factory, indeed have taken our advice; but then they lay it up in places they intend to visit in the winter. (1969 [1767–1791]:154)

By storing and living on the meat they threw away, Crees could, of course, have been less migratory than they were, decreasing the number of residential moves necessary during the winter round. Desire for fresh meat or the demands of fur trapping might promote movement sooner than the surplus could be consumed. Even if the meat was substantially reduced in weight by drying, the energy costs to women entailed in drawing it by toboggan through the series of residential movements in winter would presumably be formidable. The obvious alternative is the cache that Graham represented, perhaps correctly, as an English innovation for some of the coastal Crees. Drage (1968 [1748–49], 1:216) registers similar variation, noting that certain individuals, perhaps also those most subject to English influence, hunted consistently to maintain an existing stock of food on hand.

Caches, too, are subject to material constraints. First, they are vulnerable to predation by animals and free goods to anyone with critical need of them. Second, the cache imposes limitations not on nomadism but on unplanned nomadism. To be useful, food surpluses must be positioned across the landscape in such a way that they are available in times of scarcity. If the objective is risk aversion, food caches must be accessible when emergency conditions dictate their use.

If sizable territories were traversed in winter, the effort of building and traveling to caches could be considerable, especially prior to dog traction. Caches do not require that the same territory be hunted each year, but they necessitate seasonal or annual planning, which compromises the foraging group's flexibility and spontaneity. Crees hunting in the Churchill River drainage during the 1820s seemingly returned to the same general territories each winter, so a system of caches would have been technically possible, at the cost of additional planning and labor.

By the 1820s, the game shortages in the Churchill River country and elsewhere had created a state of uncertainty in which the reliability afforded by storage would presumably be welcomed. In 1815, for example, nine cases of famine cannibalism are mentioned at Nelson House (HBC B.141/e/1), and by 1825, the Crees were described as starving every winter (B.141/e/2 [1825–26]). In this context, the traders reported the same behavior recorded in the preceding century near Hudson Bay.

In their habits they are indolent at least in the summer or during the season the deer [caribou] are crossing the Rivers, and they are remarkably improvident or else they might make themselves comfortable comparatively to what they generally are. For while they have anything, they feast and enjoy themselves as long as it lasts and let tomorrow provide for itself. Some seasons, when the deer happen to cross the Rivers late in the Season, that the meat can be preserved with little trouble, they lay up stores for the winter but it's but seldom. (HBC B.91/a/8 [1822–23])

The traders, in short, reported the same prodigality both prior to and in the midst of the game shortages. On the coast and inland, in the 1700s and during the shortages of the 1820s, the Crees were disposed to "let tomorrow provide for itself."

LeJeune in the Bush

The Jesuit Paul LeJeune passed the winter of 1633–34 south of the Saint Lawrence River with a nomadic band of Montagnais. His *Relation* (1897*b*) remains a unique firsthand account of the day-by-day experiences of a boreal Algonquian hunting group during the winter. In justifying this excursion from Rupert's Land to New France, I emphasize both the cultural resemblances of the Montagnais to the Crees and the lack of any comparable document describing the latter.

LeJeune's Montagnais companions were not entirely inattentive to food storage but were, to say the least, seemingly ambivalent about it. By the 1630s, the fur trade activities near Tadoussac had produced game shortages comparable to those that would follow two centuries later on Hudson Bay (Waisberg 1975, Gadacz 1975). As a result, Le-Jeune's hosts made concessions to food storage while simultaneously celebrating the logic of immediate return.

LeJeune qualified his remarks on Montagnais prodigality by describing in his ethnographic sketch what sounds like an intensive program of food storage and scheduled consumption. Moose meat obtained in winter was dried and eaten until September, and the Indians went into the bush in autumn with packages each containing one hundred dried eels (1897b:277, 313) that were used as staples until January. However, the members of LeJeune's group, at least, did not utilize their preserved food in this way. The band left Tadoussac and went inland in September with what appears to have been ample stores of eels and flour, some donated by LeJeune himself. At their first camp, they devoured all of it over the course of a few days, not sparing LeJeune's contributions.

Our Savages had feasts every day, so that in a very short time we found ourselves without bread, without flour, without eels, and without any means of helping ourselves (Ibid.:47)

The behavior was significant since it left the band at the beginning of the fall hunting season with no food on hand. This pattern is reproduced in subsequent contexts: the Montagnais would accumulate and preserve a surplus of food but then eat through the existing stock given the appropriate circumstances. For example, LeJeune writes of a feast given during the autumn when two bands encountered each other and amalgamated:

As soon as he came, there was nothing but feasting in our cabins; we had only a little food left, but these Barbarians ate it with as much calmness and confidence as if the game they were to hunt was shut up in a stable. (Ibid.:93)

Subsequent events make clear that considerable effort *was* invested in smoking meat and either transporting it or storing it in caches. Given the band's experiences, it seems likely that its leaders anticipated starvation and death as probable consequences if no storage at all were practiced. All the members of two other bands in the vicinity starved to death that winter. Consequently, what were probably formidable quantities of dry meat were sometimes prepared and conveyed from camp to camp by the women.

> When there are a number of things to be carried, as often happens when they have killed a great many Elk, the women go ahead, and carry a part of them to the place where they are to camp the following day. (Ibid.:109)

In December 1633, after a period of famine, the hunters successfully killed several caribou; most of the meat was brought to camp, but some was buried in the snow near the kill site and retrieved a few days later (ibid.:161–163). On January 29, 1634, the hunters succeeded in killing sufficient caribou to provide the basis for a long-term surplus. Predictably, the first reaction was a round of feasts and dancing, but what appears to have been the greater part of the meat was preserved by smoking and transported laboriously from camp to camp thereafter. The transport problem explains why the meat was smoked rather than frozen, smoked meat being substantially lighter in weight. Seemingly, the band chose not to restrict its movements by setting up caches. The objective need for such reserves during this winter is confirmed by LeJeune's observation that the smoked meat, "hard and dirty and in small quantities," was the staple on which the band subsisted through February, March, and April. The Montagnais regarded smoked meat as emergency food and thus classified this period as continuous with the earlier famine (ibid.:179). Finally, between March 6 and March 13, the hunters succeeded in killing beavers in quantities sufficient to provide another surplus. Here, decisions about what to preserve were conditioned by the desire to provision the collective eat-all feast in spring. Consequently, some beavers were eaten immediately, others smoked for scheduled consumption in the interval, and the "best ones" were reserved, presumably frozen, for the anticipated feast.

LeJeune's observations have multiple relevance to the Crees trading into Hudson Bay in the eighteenth century. First, food storage was clearly a subsistence option in the boreal forest, probably necessary for survival in the depleted landscapes of the Laurentian Montagnais and logistically *possible* anywhere despite undesirable labor costs. Second, the Montagnais seemingly preserved food only as a response to extreme privation. The preferred strategy was to live on fresh meat, preserving only what was necessary to ensure against death by starvation and eating the rest at once. As a result, the Montagnais' behavior appears as a series of extemporized compromises between immediate consumption and risk aversion. Even preserved foods were vulnerable to the eat-all feast under some circumstances, as the fate of the eels and LeJeune's supplies attests. These were not "affluent" hunters by any objective criteria. They passed the winter in a state of nearly continuous famine punctuated by feasts; other groups died of starvation. Finally, food storage might be undertaken not as a survival measure but instead to provision an anticipated feast in spring. Willingness to forgo a feast in the present depended on the prospect of a future feast in which all could be eaten at once. Throughout, one discerns the tension between smoking meat as survival insurance and eating everything on hand.

The Cultural Logic of Hunger and Scarcity

Food storage, whether practiced in the short term or the long term, levels the temporal fluctuations in resource availability, introducing thereby an assured constancy in rates of consumption over time. In delayed return foraging societies, those of the Northwest Coast and California, for example, localized and seasonally abundant resources were intensively harvested and preserved (cf. Testart 1982). From the perspective of optimal foraging theory, food preservation and storage is "adaptive" behavior, allowing the energy from seasonally aggregated resources to be appropriated throughout the year (Yesner 1981:164–165). This would explain the Montagnais' practice of storing eels—an abundant and seasonal resource—but not their decision to consume the entire surplus at the first winter camp. In ecosystems that contained either the possibility or the assurance of protracted hunger during winter, why did boreal forest Agonquians not preserve and transport or cache more food than they did? There were no technological or ecosystem conditions that would have made more intensive preservation impossible. For the Crees of the Churchill River, there was even a proximal model of a foraging society with delayed return orientations: the Chipewyans hunting north of the river in the late 1700s practiced, according to Thompson (1962 [1784–1812]:106), a "steady frugality," preventing the starvation crises to which the Crees were subject. In the boreal forest, the variable of storage could assume diverse values. In terms of Rappaport's (1984) distinction, there existed a "goal range" for storage below which Crees were at objective risk of hunger and starvation and also a Cree "reference value" that determined how much storage was actually practiced. From a Western perspective valuing continuity and predictability in subsistence, the two measures appear seriously discrepant: the Montagnais and the Crees were storing little food in ecosystems and during periods in which many of them were starving to death.

The disparity can be explained in part as the product of historical changes in resource strategies. Prehistorically and during the early food trade, resources were probably obtained with sufficient predictability to make intensive food storage unnecessary to group survival. As Sahlins observed, the characteristic prodigality of hunters must be predicated on at least a usually reliable food supply: "if hunters and gatherers really favored gluttony over economic good sense, they would never have lived to become the prophets of this new religion" (1972:31). At the same time, greater use of food storage could have prevented hardships and occasional tragedies caused by fluctuating resource populations and accidents. The levels of resource uncertainty reported for Crees and Montagnais in these sources were probably not typical of the aboriginal situation. The Hudson Bay lowlands may not have been permanently occupied before the fur trade because of scarcity, and the Montagnais of the 1630s and the Churchill River Crees of the 1820s were occupying depleted environments. One would expect experimentation with food storage in such circumstances. That certain Crees were adopting European cache strategies in these circumstances is readily understandable, although the majority who did not pose the more interesting ecological issue. These latter groups were seemingly living out foraging contradictions, reproducing immediate return strategies predicated on the more reliable resources of earlier periods.

From the perspective of a delayed return economy, the reliability introduced by more intensive food storage would have been "adaptive" both prehistorically and in the fur trade, the more so as resource uncertainty increased. It is clear that French and English observers thought the Algonquians desperately in need of it. Equally clearly, the Indians usually thought it not worth the trouble. Restricted mobility (the cache system) and a diet of smoked meat were high prices to pay for reliability. Not to mention the additional labor. The author of the 1822–23 Indian Lake journal (HBC B.91/a/8) observed that the Crees stored food only when "the meat can be preserved with little trouble," and this provides some insight into the values organizing their prodigality. The effort, or, in the ecological idiom, the energy costs entailed by drying meat and then pulling it through the snow on toboggans or positioning it in caches, would appear excessive if the hunters hoped to kill additional animals in the near future. If meat "wasted" by nonstorage was ordinarily recouped by fresh kills, storage would maximize reliability only at the expense of additional labor.

The corollary of such optimism is a tolerant resignation to transient hardship. Ellis (1967 [1748]:90), after observing that the Crees possessed "no notion of frugality or of providing against privation" to which they were "sure to be exposed every winter," allowed that they underwent hunger with patience. Drage (1968 [1748–49], 1:216), noting the Crees did not go hunting until all supplies on hand were exhausted, wrote that "they sometimes fast for a time which they bear with patience." Robson (1965 [1752]:51) wrote that Crees could fast three or four times as long as the English. Boreal Algonquians *expected* intermittent periods of hunger during the winter, and these fasts—and even the possible threat of death—were preferable to the planning and labor entailed by food storage. The definition of the resource situation was one in which animals were ordinarily available and hunger a predictable, endurable, and usually transient aspect of the winter round. It is precisely in this arbitrary weighting of risk aversion and optimism that the operation of the cultural logic of Cree labor is specifiable. The costs of the labor, always potentially superfluous, entailed in storage was reckoned disproportionate to the reliability ensured by the surplus. Before approximately 1900, boreal forest Algonquians often fasted and sometimes perished for lack of food. These tragedies would have occurred less frequently if more intensive food storage had been practiced. Experiencing long-term game shortages as though they were new instances of transient scarcity, the Algonquians continued, with some concessions, "to let tomorrow provide for itself." The decision to store less and starve more (or, among Chipewyans, to store more and starve less) was not objectively determined by the Canadian Shield ecosystem, the limits of the technology, or caloric efficiency. The paradox of the starving Montagnais consuming all their preserved eels in autumn feasts is a particularly forceful example of the meaningful construction of utility, efficiency, and the entire structure of foraging labor and consumption. This skepticism toward advanced planning and reliability is not limited exclusively to foragers. Audrey Richards's (1932) classic monograph on the Bemba is a detailed exposition of an agricultural society whose members preferred transient hunger to what they deemed excessive labor.

One additional facet of this logic remains to be explored. We are disposed to think of storage as securing reliability, but for the Algonquians it could possess precisely the opposite significance, ensuring present stability only at the cost of future privation. One of my Cree acquaintances always left the village for his trapline unencumbered by food supplies. He took tea, bannock, and sometimes candy bars but never meat or fish. Since he was an expert beaver and lynx trapper, there was usually meat available after he lifted his traps. His father had told him that only an unskilled trapper need take food onto his line, that the experience of hunger is educationally effective, and, finally, that it is "bad luck" to carry meat into the bush. It is not surprising to find other evidence that, in boreal Algonquian thought, the beings who regulate hunting punish those who store food by withholding food in the future. In 1887, a Naskapi hunter responded to the exhortations of a Catholic priest in northern Labrador:

Nos pères mangeaient tout ce que leur envoyait le Grand-Esprit, et nos pères étaient *fins*, nous faisons comme nos pères. . . . Je tue dix caribous; *c'est le Grand-Esprit qui me les envoie parce qu'il voit que j'ai faim*; il a un gros coeur pour moi, le Grand-Esprit, et *il veut que je mange. . .je mange tout*. Le Grand-Esprit rit, et m'engraisse encore mille caribous là-bas, dans les terres des Naskapis. Tu voudrais . . . que je cache le pemmican que le Grand-Esprit m'envoie? Mais cela insulte le Grand-Esprit. Si je meurs cette nuit, après l'avoir fait, je paraîtrai devant la face du Grand-Esprit, son oeil sera fâché, et il me dira: tu es un mauvais fils, tu n'as pas eu d'esprit. Tu me traites comme un matshimanitou [evil spirit]. . . . Tu fait pitié à ton père d'en haut. . . . *Il n'enverra plus ses caribous dans ton chemin de chasse.* (Cooper 1933:55, emphasis added)[2]

The speaker, as reported or in fact, referenced scriptural conceptions of deity, but the deity's disposition toward food storage was identifiably nonscriptural and Algonquian. Why is the *Grand-Esprit*—presumably, the Naskapi caribou god—angered and insulted by preserved food? Why would the speaker imagine himself as a "bad son" in the Catholic idiom, and why is storing pemmican from caribou meat spoken about as treating the caribou god like an evil spirit?

Testart (1982), following Sahlins (1972), has suggested that storage constitutes in the social life of foragers a "transgression of the rule of sharing." This depends, of course, on the degree of consensus as to storage. Given generalized sharing, the family that stores cannot long coexist with the family that consumes immediately. But if all co-residential commensal groups store, the preserved food can either be pooled or apportioned and thereafter shared to level ensuing disparities in the same fashion as fresh meat. The Algonquian concept turns, I believe, on a different denial of reciprocity. As between human beings, so between human beings and animals: meat is routinely "given" when the recipient is in need. To store food may therefore be to question the willingness of others to give. The emotion imputed to the *Grand-Esprit* is that of resentment for a sacrilegious skepticism: only a *macimanitōw* would withhold food. Stored food usurps the authority of the entities who provision human beings. By using it, foragers acknowledge and anticipate that the generosity of these entities can be unreliable and secure for themselves an artificial substitute through technical means. But in doing so, they disinvite the others' generosity, which is best assured by objectively *needing* the gift of meat. Animals will not give themselves to hunters who do not need them, and hunters do not need them if they have a surplus already on hand.

Feasting and devouring everything on hand was thus the opposite value of food storage, and the nominally secular scheduling of production and consumption was organized throughout the Algonquian subarctic as a day-to-day replication of the logic of the eat-all feast. I am not suggesting a theological determinism that imposed the design of ritual meals on secular labor. It was not only in sacred feasts that Crees ate their way through all the available food on hand. In both good times and bad, sacred and (relatively) secular, decisions about when to hunt and how much food to consume were organized by the postulate that successful production presupposes an existing shortage that humans must create by eliminating surpluses and maintaining a condition of scarcity. This logic was dominant even at the extremities of survival and explains why the Montagnais described by LeJeune embarked on their winter hunt only after consuming all their preserved food. In the eat-all feast, the surplus was entirely destroyed. In the quotidian round, men went hunting only when the food on hand was nearly or entirely consumed. In a cultural universe so skeptical of the sufficiency of human agency, this disposition for "feasting upon their stock until they have not a day's provision left" (Robson 1965 [1752]:51) appears as a reasonable—if not, indeed, rational—mode of production.[3]

Appendix

A polythetic taxonomy of Cree animal categories [*not in present range]

OWĪYĀSĪSAK 'ANIMALS WITH MEAT'

atik	caribou	
apiscacīhkos 'small caribou'	barren land caribou	*Rangifer arcticu*
mistatīhk 'big caribou'	woodland caribou	*Rangifer caribou*
askiwatīhk 'earth caribou'	woodland caribou	
mōswa	moose	*Alces alces*
paskwāwatik* 'plains caribou'	buffalo	*Bison bison*
apiscimōswas 'small moose'	mule deer	*Odocoileus hemionus*
atimostikwān 'dog head'	mule deer	
wīpaðōs*	whitetail deer	*Odocoileus virginianus*
wāpiti*	elk	*Cervus canadensis*
asinīwimāðatik* 'ugly rock caribou'	pronghorn antelope [?]	*Antilocapra americana*
māðimōswa* 'ugly moose'	musk ox	*Ovibos moschatus*

maskwa	bear	
maskwa	brown/black bear	*Ursus americanus*
osāwask 'yellow bear'	brown/black bear	*Ursus americanus*
iðinitomaska 'human bear'	brown/black bear	
mistahaya*	grizzly bear	*Ursus horribilis*
wāpask* 'white bear'	polar bear	*Thalarctos maritimus*

mistasoy* 'great tail'	cougar	*Felis concolor*
pisiw	lynx	*Lynx canadensis*
misipos* 'great cat'	wildcat	*Lynx rufus*
mistacākanis	coyote	*Canis latrans*
omiðāhcīs	wolverine	*Gulo luscus*

mahīhkan	gray wolf	*Canis lupus*
paskwāwahīhkan 'plains wolf'		
mistahīhkan 'great wolf'		
apiscahīhkanis 'little wolf'		

mahkīsiw 'fox' or mahkīsis		
osāwahkīsiw 'yellow fox'	red fox	*Vulpes fulva*, red phase
māsināsowahkīsiw 'marked fox'	cross fox	*Vulpes fulva*, cross phase
sōniyāwahkīsiw 'silver fox'	silver fox	*Vulpes fulva*, silver phase
kaskikwahkīsiw 'black fox'	black fox	*Vulpes fulva*, black phase
kīnimīhcakanwahkīsiw 'bastard fox'	bastard fox	*Vulpes fulva*, mixed phase
paskwāwahkīsiw* 'plains fox'	swift fox	*Vulpes relox*

sīpihkwahkīsiw 'blue fox'	blue fox	*Alopex legopus*, blue phase
wāpiskahkīsiw	white fox	*Alopex legopus*, white phase
wāpahkīsiw 'white fox'	white fox	

amisk	beaver	*Castor castor*
wacask	muskrat	*Ondatra zibethica*
nīkik	river otter	*Lutra canadensis*
sīhkos	weasel	*Mustela rixola, M. erminea*
sākwīsiw	mink	*Mustela vison*
wāpiscānis	marten	*Martes americana*
ocīk	fisher	*Martes pennanti*
sikāk	skunk	*Mephitis mephitis*
wīhask*	woodchuck	*Marmota monas*
kākwa	porcupine	*Erethizon dorsitum*
mistanask*	badger	*Taxidea taxus*
wāpos	snowshoe hare	*Lepus americanus*

anikwacas	squirrel	
anikwacās	red squirrel	*Tamiasciurus hudsonicus*
cāswikanikwacās	flying squirrel	*Glaucomys sabrinus*

sāsākawāpiskos	chipmunk	*Eutamias minimus*

MACI-PISISKISĪSAK 'BAD LITTLE ANIMALS'

apahkwācīs	bat	*Lasiurus* sp.

āpakosīs	mouse	
wāskahikanāpakosīs 'house-mouse'	deer mouse	*Peromyscus maniculatus*
iðinicahāpakosīs 'human-mouse'	meadow vole	*Microtus pennsylvanicus*
kwāskwāskocāpakosīs 'jumping-mouse'	meadow jumping mouse	*Zapus hudsonius*
kīnikiscowīyāpakosīs or cīpōscowīyāpakosīs 'pointed-nose mouse'	arctic shrew masked shrew pygmy shrew	*Sorex arcticus* *Sorex cinereus* *Microsorex hoyi*

amiskwāpakosīs 'beaver mouse'	northern water shrew	*Sorex palustris*
mihkwāpakosīs 'red mouse'	boreal red-backed vole	*Clethrionomys gapperi*
āpakosīs	northern bog lemming mountain phenacomys	*Synaptomys borealis* *Phenacomys intermedius*

kinīpik*	snake	
kinīpik	garter snake	*Thamnophis sirtalis parietalis*
sīsīkwan-kinīpik 'rattle-snake'	rattlesnake	*Crotalus* sp.

aðīkis	frog	
osāwaskwaðīk 'yellow bear frog'	northern leopard frog	*Rana p. pipiens*
ocīpwīwaðīkis 'cheeping frog'	same, juvenile	
okistōtīw 'large bear frog'	wood frog	*Rana sylvatica*
iðinicawaðīkis 'human frog'	boreal chorus frog	*Pseudacris triseriata masculata*

Notes

1: "You Got to Keep It Holy"

1. Linguists today use the term "Cree" to refer to a complex of Algonquian dialects spoken from Quebec-Labrador to British Columbia. The assignment of dialects to Western and Eastern divisions reflects both phonological criteria and a break in mutual intelligibility at the Quebec-Ontario border. Eastern Cree comprises three dialects spoken in Quebec: East Cree, Montagnais, and Naskapi. The five dialects of Western Cree are conventionally distinguished by their different reflexes of Proto-Algonquian *l; the degree to which this criterion coincides with other dialect differences remains to be established. "Moose Cree" retains l as the reflex of *l, while, in corresponding positions, "Woods Cree" shows ð, "Plains Cree" shows y, and Swampy Cree shows n. The Atikamek dialect of southeastern Quebec shows r. Another r dialect was spoken in the eighteenth century west of Hudson Bay, but its present locations, if any, are unknown. The contemporary distribution of these dialects only problematically reflects their aboriginal provenience. Anthropologists have used the terms "Woods," "Swampy," and "Plains" in a different sense to label Cree social and geographic divisions; these coincide only partially with the dialect distributions. "Cree" has also been applied as a social designation to some Ojibwa-speaking groups in northern Ontario and Manitoba. The term has thus been extended both in the past and in the present to groups speaking other than Cree dialects as these are presently defined.

2. People in Pukatawagan, Manitoba, also identify as Rock Cree bands those of Nelson House, South Indian Lake, Hughes Lake, Granville Lake, Southern Indian Lake, and Churchill in Manitoba and Lac la Ronge, Lac Wollaston, Sandy Narrows, Sandy Bay, Sturgeon Landing, Island Falls, Pelican Narrows, and Southend in Saskatchewan.

3. In Manitoba, Canadian posts were located at Kississing Lake in 1785, Pukatawagan Lake in 1786, and Granville Lake in 1794. The Hudson's Bay Company's inland establishments in the area were operated initially as outposts of Churchill. Malcolm Ross was at Reed Lake in 1789–90, thereafter at Pukatawagan, and again at Reed Lake in 1794–95. George Charles established Granville House on Granville Lake, wintering there in 1794–95 and 1795–96. A post operated at Pelican Narrows, Saskatchewan, between 1793 and 1799. In 1795, Thomas Linklater maintained a post at "the Forks" of the Churchill and Kississing rivers near Flatrock Lake. In 1799, Nelson House was established on Nelson Lake with two outposts at Reindeer Lake and Duck or Sisipuk Lake and operated as the major post of the district until 1827. The Indian Lake post on Southern Indian Lake was established as an outpost of Nelson House in 1805 and operated until 1823. David Thompson (1962 [1784–1812]:72) maintained Hudson's Bay Company posts during this period at Sipiwesk Lake in 1792–93, Reed Lake in 1794–95, Sisipuk Lake in 1795–96, Reindeer Lake in 1796–97, and at Granville Lake in 1804–05 and Reed Lake in 1805–06 for the Northwest Company.

3: "Dreaming All the Bottom of the Water"

1. *Pawākan* beings may serve as agents of more powerful and remote entities and transmit information from them to humans. Some eighteenth-century sources on the Crees trading into coastal forts on Hudson Bay refer to beings understood as servants of the benign creator entity. Isham (1949 [1743–1749]:171) translates as "angels" the plural noun "Paw kus ko cun nuc." Graham (1969 [1767–1791]:160) describes beings called "Pawkuskumuck" who live in the upper air. Neither of these words is familiar to Rock Crees, although the root/*pawā*/'dream' is recognized as a probable constituent. If these words are Old Woods Cree synonyms of *pawākan*, they suggest the idea of the latter as mediating between humans and the remote creator being Kicimanitōw. Such an idea is also suggested by Thompson (1962 [1784–1812]:81) who describes a Cree religious specialist petitioning the creator being "to give to his poowoggin where to find the deer."

2. The Oxford House Cree Tom Boulanger provides a similarly diverse list in his memoir: "When they dream of something they believe it. They sometime dream of animals and dream of different kinds of roots, lakes, rivers, rocks, muskegs, mud and grounds, leaves, water, snow, ice, winter birds, summer birds, kinds of flies, summer, winter, fall, spring, north wind, south wind, west wind, east wind, kinds of prayers, creatures and etc." (Boulanger 1971:49).

3. These remarks contrast with the belief of the Mistassini Cree (Quebec) that a man should never kill his individual animal "friend" (Tanner 1979:139).

4. Both Rossignol (1939:69) and Boulanger (1971:50) state that the vision fast occurred between the ages of fourteen and sixteen. Rock Cree consultants denied that prepubescent children were encouraged to fast and undertake

preparatory vigils as is noted for some Siouan and Algonquian Woodlands groups. However, Honigmann (1956:71 [Westmain Swampy Cree]) states that males and females might begin the fast as early as the age of ten.

5. Godsell (1938:134) apparently attended such an event among Swampy Crees which included burnt offerings, a proscription of eating utensils, singing, drumming, and prayers for the boy's success.

6. The Moose Factory Crees described by Skinner (1911:61) permitted the novice to return to his family during the day, but this appears to be exceptional; Skinner adds that the Albany Crees did not permit this. The vision site was always at at least a symbolic remove from areas of human settlement. "The dreamer's camp might be only 200 feet from the house, but the point was to live there without fire and to eat only lightly" (Honigmann 1956:71 [Westmain Swampy Cree]).

7. The duration of the vision fast varies in the published typifications. Godsell (1938:135), for example, describes a vigil that lasted one night while Honigmann (1956:71) states that the fast might last two weeks to a month; other estimates are from five to six days (Semmens 1884:109), a week (Boulanger 1971:50), seven to ten days (Skinner 1911:61), three to four days (Rossignol 1939:69), and one to twenty days (Mason 1967:49).

8. An account from Moose or Albany Crees suggests a symbolic role for the novice's father in reestablishing social contact or effecting aggregation. The latter was supposed to visit the faster with food after the end of seven days; if he failed to do so, his son became a sturgeon. In general, persons who "fasted too long" might die or become animals (Skinner 1911:61).

9. This classification exemplifies what is probably a near-universal: the identification of *terra incognita* with spirit entities. Western speculation, for example, places God and the Devil, respectively, above and below the earth, peoples large lakes with cognates of the Loch Ness monster, and locates the Sasquatch in the wilderness hinterland.

10. Skinner (1911:61) refers to a Swampy Cree platform made entirely from poles and probably resembling a cache rack in appearance. Rossignol (1939:69) refers simply to a vigil conducted while straddling a large tree limb. Rock Crees assented to this but pointed out that the dreamer would probably fall off unless secured to the trunk in some way.

4: "The Same Respect You Give Yourself"

1. On Hudson Bay in the 1700s, Bacqueville de La Potherie (1931:230–231) wrote that the girl occupied a separate lodge for four weeks, received food from her mother, painted her face black, and was careful to mark the ice hole from which she drew water so others would avoid it. They repeated the separation during successive periods. Isham (1949 [1743–1749]:98) wrote nothing about seclusion at puberty but stated that women during their periods wore their hair over their faces, avoided sexual relations, and ate separately. Graham

(1969 [1767–1791]:177) says that the isolation persisted only as long as the first flow, after which the girl rejoined her family but signaled her condition for one or two months by wearing a cap that concealed her face. For more than two months, she ate only from her own vessels. The use of hair or caps to cover the face suggests both a sign of the girl's condition and a hood preventing eye contact with others. Hearne (1958 [1795]:66) wrote that the isolation lasted five days, after which the girls returned but wore the veil or cap. They slept separately from others during subsequent periods but, unlike Chipewyan women, did not have to leave the lodge. Robson (1965[1752]:52) stated that the girl lived separately for three weeks and that those who brought food to her did not speak to her. According to Cameron (Masson 1889–90, 2:250–251), the girl isolated herself when the flow began and had to be located by her female relatives; thereafter, she stayed at some distance from the lodge for two or three weeks, receiving food and utensils from her mother. The utensils she employed in eating, poisonous to "all but herself," were kept by her and used during subsequent periods. The isolation was repeated every month until an indeterminate time after marriage, but even then women were required to cook and eat outside.

6: "They Come to Be Like Human"

1. McClellan (1970) has compared versions of the "bear husband" myth from the Northwest Coast and western subarctic; Cree texts of what are substantially the same narrative were obtained by Petitot (1886:46–63) from Thickwoods Crees and by me from Angelique Linklater of Brochet, Manitoba (Brightman 1989a). The myth of the "beaver wife" was also obtained from Mrs. Linklater (ibid.); other versions have been collected from Swampy Crees at Fort Albany (Skinner 1911:104–107) and from Eastern Crees at Ungava (Turner 1894:339–340), St. Augustin (Savard 1979:24–26), Fort George (Bauer 1971:36–49), and Rupert's House (Steager 1976:175–196, Bell 1897:1–8). The Ojibwas of Bois Fort, Ontario, have a related story in which the human spouse is female (Jones 1919:251–257). The myth of the "caribou husband" appears to be limited to the Eastern Crees (Speck 1935b:87–89, Tanner 1979:136–137).

11: "No Notion of Frugality"

1. Consider the following extract from Yehudi Cohen's introduction to an article by Mary Douglas:

The lives of people at the lowest level of socio-technological development (such as the Lele) seem extraordinarily rich in symbolism. Everywhere are spirits, magical influences, nuances of meaning, unseen dangers, and unappreciated potential benefits. (Cohen 1974:221)

A little farther on, Cohen distinguishes more explicitly the "symbolic" complexes of belief and ritual from productive activity.

At several points in this selection, Douglas suggests that symbolism and ritual determine people's behavior in respect to the habitat. . . . My own view is the opposite, that these beliefs serve to justify and give meaning to activities made necessary by an adaptive strategy. In either event, it is clear that people seem to need ideologies and rituals in maintaining their relationships with the environment; without them, these relationships may become meaningless. (Ibid.)

2. Our fathers ate all that the Great Spirit sent to them, and our fathers were clever, we do like our fathers. . . . I kill ten caribou; it is the Great Spirit that sends them to me because he sees that I am hungry; he has great love for me, the Great Spirit, and he desires that I eat . . . I eat everything. The Great Spirit laughs, and he again enriches me with a thousand caribous there in the Naskapi country. You would wish . . . that I cache the pemmican that the Great Spirit sends me? But that insults the Great Spirit. If I die tonight, after having done this, I will appear before the face of the Great Spirit, his eye will be angry and he will say to me: you are a bad son, you have had no sense. You treat me like an evil being. . . . You take pity on your father on high. He will send no more of his caribou to your hunting road.

3. To broaden the areal focus, comparable practices existed even in a "delayed return" foraging society like the Alaskan Koyukons who occupied sedentary winter villages provisioned by preserved fish and caribou meat. According to Sullivan (1942), the Koyukons sometimes disposed of their stored foods during lavish feasts in late summer, midwinter, and early spring. The midwinter feasts, in particular, sometimes occasioned hardship if hunting was unsuccessful, but they continued into the present century. The Koyukon feasts pose the same paradox as the Montagnais: the surplus was accumulated and preserved but then consumed, precluding its use to level fluctuations in the long term. Murphy (1970:153) described among the Brazilian Munduruçu "the hunter's glut, an abundance of meat that had to be consumed before it spoiled, and the men stayed at home because further hunting would have been a crime against the game and because they had to apply themselves steadily to the serious business of eating."

References

Ahenakew, Edward. 1929. Cree trickster tales. *Journal of American Folklore* 42:309–353.

Ahenakew, Beth, and Sam Hardlotte. 1977. *Nehiyaw A-tayoka-we-na (Cree Legends): Stories of Wesukechak*. Saskatoon: Saskatchewan Indian Cultural College.

Bacqueville de La Potherie. 1931. Letters of La Potherie. *In* J. B. Tyrrell, ed., *Documents Relating to the Early History of Hudson Bay*. Toronto: Champlain Society.

Barthes, Roland. 1972. *Mythologies*. New York: Hill and Wang.

Baudrillard, Jean. 1975. *The Mirror of Production*. St. Louis: Telos.

———. 1981. *For a Critique of the Political Economy of the Sign*. St. Louis: Telos.

Bauer, George. 1971. Cree tales and beliefs. *Northeast Folklore* 12:1–70.

Bell, Robert. 1897. The history of the Che-che-puy-ew-tis. *Journal of American Folklore* 10:1–8.

Benveniste, Émile. 1971. *Principles of General Linguistics*. Miami: University of Miami Press.

Berlin, Brent, Dennis Breedlove, and Peter Raven. 1973. General principles of classification and nomenclature in folk biology. *American Anthropologist* 75(1):214–242.

Biesele, Megan. 1986. How hunter-gatherers' stories "make sense." *Cultural Anthropology* 1(2):157–170.

Bighetty, Marie, and B. Senyk, eds. 1986. *Missinippi Ethiniwuk*. Winnipeg: Pukatawagan Language Program.

Binford, Louis. 1980. Willow smoke and dogs' tails: Hunter-gatherer settlement systems and archaeological site formation. *American Antiquity* 43:4–20.

Birdsell, Joseph. 1953. Some environmental and cultural factors influencing the structuring of Australian Aboriginal populations. *Natural History* 87:171–207.

Bishop, Charles. 1974. *The Northern Ojibwa and the Fur Trade.* Toronto: Holt, Rinehart and Winston.

———. 1975. Northern Algonkian cannibalism and windigo psychosis. *In* T. R. Williams, ed., *Psychological Anthropology.* The Hague: Mouton.

———. 1981*a.* Northeastern Indian concepts of conservation and the fur trade: A critique of Calvin Martin's thesis. *In* S. Krech, ed., *Indians, Animals, and the Fur Trade.* Athens: University of Georgia Press.

———. 1981*b.* Territorial groups before 1821. *In* J. Helm, ed., *Handbook of North American Indians,* Vol. 6, Subarctic. Washington, D.C.: Smithsonian Institution.

———. 1982. Comment on "Windigo Psychosis: The Anatomy of an Emic-Etic Confusion" by Lou Marano. *Current Anthropology* 23:398.

———. 1984. The first century: Adaptive changes among the Western James Bay Cree between the early seventeenth and early eighteenth centuries. *In* S. Krech, ed., *The Subarctic Fur Trade: Native Social and Economic Adaptations,* 21–53. Vancouver: University of British Columbia Press.

Bishop, Charles, and Toby Morantz, eds. 1986. Who owns the beaver? Northern Algonquian land tenure reconsidered. *Anthropologica* 28(1–2).

Black, Mary. 1977. Ojibwa power-belief system. *In* R. D. Fogelson and R. N. Adams, eds., *The Anthropology of Power.* New York: Academic Press.

Bloomfield, Leonard. 1930. *Sacred Texts of the Sweet Grass Cree.* National Museum of Canada Bulletin 60, Anthropological Series 11.

———. 1934. *Plains Cree Texts.* Publications of the American Ethnological Society 16. New York: G. E. Stechert.

———. 1957. *Eastern Ojibwa: Grammatical Sketch, Texts, and Word List.* Ann Arbor: University of Michigan Press.

Boas, Franz. 1940. *Race, Language and Culture.* New York: Free Press.

Boon, James. 1982. *Other Tribes, Other Scribes: Symbolic Anthropology in the Comparative Study of Cultures, Histories, Religions, and Texts.* Cambridge: Cambridge University Press.

———. 1986. Symbols, sylphs, and Siwa: Allegorical machineries in the text of Balinese culture. *In* V. Turner and E. Bruner, eds., *The Anthropology of Experience.* Urbana: University of Illnois Press.

Boulanger, Tom. 1971. *An Indian Remembers.* Winnipeg: Peguis.

Bourdieu, Pierre. 1977. *Outline of a Theory of Practice.* London: Cambridge University Press.

Brightman, Robert. 1983. *Animal and Human in Rock Cree Religion and Subsistence.* Ph.D. dissertation, Department of Anthropology, University of Chicago.

———. 1988. The windigo in the material world. *Ethnohistory* 35(4):337–379.

———. 1989*a. Acimowina and Ācaðōhkīwina: Traditional Narratives of the Rock Cree Indians.* Ottawa: Canadian Museum of Civilization Mercury Series.

———. 1989*b.* Tricksters and ethnopoetics. *International Journal of American Linguistics* 55(2):179–203.

———. 1990. Primitivism in Missinippi Cree historical consciousness. *Man:*

Journal of the Royal Anthropological Institute 25:399–418.

Brown, Jennifer. 1971. The cure and feeding of windigos: A critique. *American Anthropologist* 73:20–22.

———. 1977. James Settee and his Cree tradition: An Indian camp at the mouth of Nelson River, Hudson Bay. *In* W. Cowan, ed., *Actes du Huitième Congrès des Algonquianistes*. Ottawa: Carleton University.

———. 1982. Comment on "Windigo Psychosis: Anatomy of an Emic-Etic Confusion" by Lou Marano. *Current Anthropology* 23:399–400.

Brown, Jennifer, and Robert Brightman. 1988. *The Orders of the Dreamed: George Nelson on Cree and Northern Ojibwa Religion and Myth*. Winnipeg: University of Manitoba Press.

Burgesse, J. Allen. 1945. Property concepts of the Lac St. Jean Montagnais. *Primitive Man* 16:44–48.

Cameron, M. D. 1926. *The War Trail of Big Bear*. Toronto: Ryerson.

Canada, Department of Indian Affairs. 1889. Annual Report of the Department of Indian Affairs for the Year ended June 30, 1889. Ottawa: S. E. Dawson.

———. 1900. Annual Report of the Department of Indian Affairs for the Year ended June 30, 1900. Ottawa: S. E. Dawson.

———. 1901. Annual Report of the Department of Indian Affairs for the Year ended June 30, 1901. Ottawa: S. E. Dawson.

———. 1906. Annual Report of the Department of Indian Affairs for the Year ended June 30, 1906. Ottawa: S. E. Dawson.

———. 1907. Annual Report of the Department of Indian Affairs for the Year ended March 31, 1907. Ottawa: S. E. Dawson.

———. 1908. Annual Report of the Department of Indian Affairs for the Year ended March 31, 1908. Ottawa: S. E. Dawson.

Clay, Charles. 1938. *Swampy Cree Legends*. Toronto: Macmillan.

Cockburn, R. H., ed. 1985. "Like words of fire": Lore of the Woodland Cree from the journals of R. H. Downes. *The Beaver* 315:37–45.

Cohen, Yehudi, ed. 1974. *Man in Adaptation: The Cultural Present*. Chicago: Aldine.

Comeau, Napoleon. 1923. *Life and Sport on the North Shore of the Lower St. Lawrence and Gulf*. Québec: Étoile.

Cooper, John M. 1931. The relations between religion and morality in primitive culture. *Primitive Man* 4:33–48.

———. 1933. The Cree witiko psychosis. *Primitive Man* 6:20–24.

———. 1934. The Northern Algonquian supreme being. *Catholic University of America Anthropological Series* 2:1–78.

———. 1939. Is the Algonquian family hunting ground system pre-Columbian? *American Anthropologist* 41:66–90.

———. 1946. The culture of the northeastern Indian hunters: A reconstructive interpretation. *In* F. Johnson, ed., *Man in the Northeast*. Papers of the Robert S. Peabody Foundation for Archaeology 3. Andover: Smith.

Coues, Elliot, ed. 1897. *New Light on the Early History of the Northwest: The Manuscript Journals of Alexander Henry and of David Thompson*. 3 vols. New York: Francis P. Harper.

Craik, Brian. 1979. We are divided by the light: Experience and belief in a Cree society. *In* W. Cowan, ed., *Papers of the 10th Algonquian Conference*. Ottawa: Carleton University.

Curtis, Edward. 1928. *The North American Indian*. Vol. 18. New York: Johnson Reprint Company.

Damas, David. 1968. The diversity of Eskimo societies. *In* R. Lee and I. DeVore, eds., *Man the Hunter*. Chicago: Aldine.

Davidson, D. S. 1926. The family hunting territories of the Grand Lake Victoria Indians. *Proceedings of the International Congress of Americanists* 22:69–95.

Davies, K. G., ed. 1963. *Northern Quebec and Labrador Journals and Correspondence 1819–1835*. London: Hudson's Bay Record Society.

Denig, Edwin T. 1952. Of the Crees or Knisteneau. *Bulletin of the Missouri Historical Society* 9(1):37–69.

Dobbs, Arthur. 1744. *An Account of the Countries Adjoining to Hudson's Bay*. London: J. Robinson.

Douglas, Mary. 1963. The Lele of Kasai. *In* Daryll Forde, ed., *African Wilds*. London: Oxford University Press.

Downes, P. G. 1943. *Sleeping Island*. New York: Coward-McCann.

Drage, Theodore Swaine. 1968 [1748–49]. *An Account of a Voyage for the Discovery of a Northwest Passage . . .* 2 vols. New York: S and R Publishers.

Duchaussois, Pierre. 1923. *Mid Snow and Ice: The Apostles of the Northwest*. London: Burns, Oates and Washbourne.

Dunn, John. 1845. *The Oregon Territory*. Philidelphia: G. B. Zieber.

Dunning, R. W. 1959. *Social and Economic Change among the Northern Ojibwa*. Toronto: University of Toronto Press.

Durham, William H. 1981. Overview: Optimal foraging analysis in human ecology. *In* B. Winterhalder and E. A. Smith, eds., *Hunter-Gatherer Foraging Strategies: Ethnographic and Archaeological Analyses*. Chicago: University of Chicago Press.

Dusenberry, Verne. 1962. *The Montana Cree: A Study in Religious Persistence*. Uppsala: Almqvist and Wiksells.

Ellen, Roy. 1982. *Environment, Subsistence and System*. Cambridge: Cambridge University Press.

Ellis, Henry. 1967 [1748]. *A Voyage to Hudson's Bay, by the Dobbs Galley and California, in the Years 1746 and 1747*. New York: Johnson Reprint Company.

Faries, R., ed. 1938. *A Dictionary of the Cree Language*. Toronto: Church of England.

Feit, Harvey. 1973a. The ethnoecology of the Waswanipi Cree. *In* B. Cox, ed., *Cultural Ecology*. Toronto: Carleton Library.

———. 1973b. Twilight of the Cree hunting nation. *Natural History* 82(7):48–72.

———. 1991a. The construction of Algonquian hunting territories. *In* G. Stocking, ed., *Colonial Situations: Essays on the Contextualization of Ethnographic Knowledge*. Madison: University of Wisconsin Press.

———. 1991b. Gifts of the land: Hunting territories, guaranteed incomes, and the construction of social relations in James Bay Cree society. *In* N. Peterson and T. Matsuyama, eds., *Cash, commoditisation and changing foragers. Senri Ethnological Studies* 30. Osaka, Japan: National Museum of Ethnology.

Fiddler, Thomas, et al. 1985. *Legends from the Forest*. Edited by James Stevens. Moonbeam, Ont.: Penumbra Press.

Fienup-Riordan, Ann. 1990. *Eskimo Essays*. New Brunswick: Rutgers University Press.

Fleming, R. Harvey, ed. 1940. *Minutes of Council, Northern Department of Rupert's Land, 1821–1831*. London: Hudson's Bay Record Society.

Fogelson, Raymond. 1980. Windigo goes south: Stoneclad among the Cherokees. *In* M. Halpin and M. Ames, eds., *Manlike Monsters on Trial*. Vancouver: University of British Columbia Press.

Foucault, Michel. 1972. *The Archaeology of Knowledge*. New York: Pantheon.

Franklin, Sir John. 1823. *Narrative of a Journey to the Shores of the Polar Sea in the Years 1819, 1820, 1821, and 1822*. London: J. Murray.

French, David. 1961. Wasco-Wishram. *In* E. Spicer, ed., *Perspectives on American Indian Cultural Change*. Chicago: University of Chicago Press.

Friedrich, Paul. 1979. *Language, Context, and the Imagination*. Edited by A. S. Dil. Stanford: Stanford University Press.

——. 1986. *The Language Parallax*. Austin: University of Texas Press.

Gadacz, Rene. 1975. Montagnais hunting dynamics in historicoecological perspective. *Anthropologica* 17:149–168.

Godelier, Maurice. 1977. *Perspectives in Marxist Anthropology*. Cambridge: Cambridge University Press.

Godsell, Phillip. 1938. *Red Hunters of the Snows*. Toronto: Ryerson Press.

Graham, Andrew. 1969 [1767–1791]. *Andrew Graham's Observations on Hudson's Bay*. Edited by G. Williams. London: Hudson's Bay Record Society.

Graham, Janice. 1988. Knowing the cycle: Cognitive control and Cree death. *In* W. Cowan, ed., *Papers of the 19th Algonquian Conference*. Ottawa: Carleton University.

Hallowell, A. Irving. 1955. *Culture and Experience*. New York: Schocken Books.

——. 1976. *Contributions to anthropology: Selected papers of A. Irving Hallowell*. Edited by R. Fogelson. Chicago: University of Chicago Press.

Harmon, Daniel. 1905 [1821]. *A Journal of Voyages and Travels in the Interior of North America*. New York: Allerton.

Harper, Francis. 1964. *The Friendly Montagnais*. Lawrence, Kans.: Allen Press.

Hays, Terence. 1982. Utilitarian/adaptationist explanations of folk biological classification: Some cautionary notes. *Journal of Ethnobiology* 2(1):89–94.

Hearne, Samuel. 1958 [1795]. *A Journey from Prince of Wales Fort in Hudson's Bay to the Northern Ocean in the Years 1769, 1770, 1771, and 1772*. Edited by R. Glover. Toronto: Macmillan.

Helm, June, ed. 1981. *Handbook of North American Indians*. Vol. 6, Subarctic. Washington, D.C.: Smithsonian Institution.

Hendry, Anthony. 1907. *York Factory to the Blackfeet Country: The Journal of Anthony Hendry, 1754–1755*. Edited by L. J. Burpee. Transactions of the Royal Society of Canada Series 3, vol. 1:307–354.

Henriksen, Georg. 1973. *Hunters in the Barrens*. Newfoundland Social and

Economic Studies 12. Toronto: University of Toronto Press.

Henry, Alexander. 1969 [1809]. *Travels and Adventures in Canada and the Indian Territories between the Years 1760 and 1776.* Edited by J. Bain. Edmonton: M. G. Hurtig.

Hickerson, Harold. 1973. Fur trade colonialism and the North American Indian. *Journal of Ethnic Studies* 1:15–44.

Hill, Kim, Hillard Kaplan, Kristen Hawkes, and A. Magdalena Hurtado. 1987. Foraging decisions among Ache hunter-gatherers: New data and implications for optimal foraging models. *Ethology and Sociobiology* 8:1–36.

Hindness, B., and P. Hirst. 1975. *Precapitalist Modes of Production.* London: Routledge and Kegan Paul.

Honigmann, John J. 1956. *The Attawapiskat Swampy Cree: An Ethnographic Reconstruction.* Anthropological Papers on the University of Alaska 5(1):23–82.

Hubert, Henri, and Marcel Mauss. 1964. *Sacrifice: Its Nature and Function.* Chicago: University of Chicago Press.

Hudson's Bay Company Archives, Public Archives of Canada. 1795. Remarks Going Up the Churchill River during the Winter of 1795. B.83/a.

———. 1802–03. Nelson House Post Journal. B.141/a/1.

———. 1805–06. Indian Lake Post Journal. B.91/a/1.

———. 1808–1809. Nelson House Post Journal. B.141/a/2.

———. 1810–1815. Nelson House Accounts. B.141/d/1–5.

———. 1815. District Report, Nelson House and Deer Lake Districts. B.141/e/1.

———. 1818–19. District Report, Indian Lake. B.91/e/1.

———. 1820–21. Nelson and Churchill River District Report B.91/e/2.

———. 1821–1836. Nelson River District Returns. B.239/h/1.

———. 1822–23. District Report, Indian Lake. B.91/a/8.

———. 1825–26. District Report, Nelson House. B.141/e/2.

———. 1838. Indian Populations of Sundry Districts. B. 239/z/10.

———. 1889. District Report, Nelson House. D.25/6.

———. 1891. District Report, Pelican Lake. B.158/e/1.

———. 1893. District Report, Pelican Lake. D.25/17.

———. 1898–99. Pelican Lake Accounts. B.158/d/11.

Hunn, Eugene. 1982. The utilitarian factor in folk biological classification. *American Anthropologist* 84(4):830–847.

Hutchinson, W. H. 1972. The remaking of the Amerind. *Westways* (October):88–103.

Ingold, Tim. 1987. *The Appropriation of Nature.* Iowa City: University of Iowa Press.

———. 1988. Notes on the foraging mode of producton. *In* T. Ingold et al., eds. *Hunters and Gatherers.* Vol. 2. New York: Berg.

Innis, Harold A. 1962. *The Fur Trade in Canada.* New Haven: Yale University Press.

Isham, James. 1949 [1743–1749]. *James Isham's Observations on Hudson's Bay, 1743–1749.* Edited by E. E. Rich. London: Hudson's Bay Record Society.

Jakobson, Roman. 1978. *Six Lectures on Sound and Meaning*. Cambridge: MIT Press.

———. 1980. *The Framework of Language*. Ann Arbor: Graduate School of the University of Michigan.

Jenkins, William J. 1939. Notes on the hunting economy of the Abitibi Indians. *Catholic University of America Anthropological Series* 9:1–31.

Jenness, Diamond. 1932. *The Indians of Canada*. Ottawa: E. Cloutier.

———. 1935. *The Ojibwa Indians of Parry Island: Their Social and Religious Life*. National Museums of Canada Bulletin 78, Anthropological Series 17. Ottawa: Canadian Department of Mines.

Jérémie, Nicolas. 1926. *Twenty Years of York Factory, 1694–1714*. Ottawa: Thorburn and Abbott.

Jetté, Julius. 1911. On the superstitions of the Ten'a Indians. *Anthropos* 6:95–108, 241–259, 602–615, 699–723.

Jochim, Michael. 1976. *Hunter-Gatherer Subsistence and Settlement*. New York: Academic Press.

Jones, William. 1919. *Ojibwa Texts*. Edited by T. Michelson. Vol. 2. Publications of the American Ethnological Society 7.

Karcevskij, Sergej. 1982. The asymmetric dualism of the linguistic sign. *In* P. Steiner, ed., *The Prague School. Selected Writings, 1929–1946*. Austin: University of Texas Press.

Kelsey, Henry. 1929 [1683–1722]. *The Kelsey Papers*. Edited by A. Doughty and C. Martin. Ottawa: Public Archives of Canada.

Kinietz, W. Vernon. 1965. *The Indians of the Western Great Lakes, 1615–1760*. Ann Arbor: University of Michigan Press.

Knight, James. 1932. *The Founding of Churchill*. Toronto: J. M. Dent.

Kohl, Johann G. 1985. *Kitchi-gami: Life among the Lake Superior Ojbway*. Edited by R. Bieder. Minneapolis: Minnesota Historical Society Press.

Krech, Shephard. 1981. *Indians, Animals, and the Fur Trade*. Athens: University of Georgia Press.

Lahontan, Louis Armand. 1905 [1703]. *New Voyages to North America*. Edited by R. G. Thwaites. Chicago: A. C. McClurg.

Landes, Ruth. 1938. *The Ojibwa Woman*. New York: Norton.

———. 1968. *Ojibwa Religion and the Midewiwin*. Madison: University of Wisconsin Press.

Leacock, Eleanor. 1954. *The Montagnais "Hunting Territory" and the Fur Trade*. American Anthropological Association Memoir 78.

LeClercq, Christien. 1881 [1691]. *First Establishment of the Faith in New France*. 2 vols. New York: John G. Shea.

Lee, Richard B. 1979. *The !Kung San: Men, Women and Work in a Foraging Society*. Cambridge: Cambridge University Press.

———. 1980. Existe-t-il un mode de production "fourrageur"? *Anthropologie et Société* 4:59–74.

LeJeune, Paul. 1897a. Relation of what occurred in New France in the year 1634. *In* R. G. Thwaites, ed., *The Jesuit Relations and Allied Documents*. Vol. 6. Cleveland: Burrows.

———. 1897b. Relation of what occurred in New France in the year 1634, cont. *In* R. G. Thwaites, ed., *The Jesuit Relations and Allied Documents.* Vol. 7. Cleveland: Burrows.

———. 1897*c*. Relation of what occurred in New France in the year 1635, cont. *In* R. G. Thwaites, ed., *The Jesuit Relations and Allied Documents*, vol. 8. Cleveland: Burrows.

Lévi-Strauss, Claude. 1966*a*. *The Savage Mind.* Chicago: University of Chicago Press.

———. 1966*b*. The culinary triangle. *Partisan Review* 33:586–595.

———. 1969. *The Raw and the Cooked.* New York: Harper Torchbooks.

———. 1972. Structuralism and ecology. *Barnard Alumnae* (Spring 1972): 63–74.

———. 1978. *The Origin of Table Manners.* New York: Harper and Row.

———. 1988. *The Jealous Potter.* Chicago: University of Chicago Press.

Lips, Julius. 1947. *Naskapi Law (Lake St. John and Lake Mistassini Bands): Law and Order in a Hunting Society.* Transactions of the American Philosophical Society 37(4):379–492.

Lowie, Robert. 1954. *Indians of the Plains.* New York: McGraw Hill.

McClellan, Catharine, 1970. *The Girl Who Married the Bear: A Masterpiece of Indian Oral Tradition.* National Museum of Man Publications in Ethnology 2. Ottawa: National Museums of Canada.

Mackenzie, Alexander. 1927 [1801]. *Voyages from Montreal, on the River St. Lawrence, Through the Continent of North America to the Frozen and Pacific Oceans.* Toronto: Radisson Society.

McLellan, David. 1978. *Karl Marx.* New York: Penguin.

Malinowski, Bronislaw. 1923. The problem of meaning in primitive language. *In* C. K. Ogden and I. A. Richards, eds., *The Meaning of Meaning.* New York: Harcourt, Brace.

———. 1954. *Magic, Science and Religion.* New York: Doubleday.

———. 1961. *Argonauts of the Western Pacific.* New York: Dutton.

———. 1965. *Coral Gardens and Their Magic.* Bloomington: Indiana University Press.

Mandelbaum, David. 1940. The Plains Cree. *Anthropological Papers of the American Museum of Natural History* 37(2):155–316.

Marano, Lou. 1982. Windigo psychosis: The anatomy of an emic-etic confusion. *Current Anthropology* 23(4):385–412.

Marcus, George, and Michael Fisher. 1986. *Anthropology as Cultural Critique.* Chicago: University of Chicago Press.

Margry, Pierre, ed. 1879–1888. *Découvertes et établissements des francais dans l'ouest et le sud de l'Amérique Septentrionale (1614–1754).* Paris: Maisonneuve.

Martin, Calvin. 1978. *Keepers of the Game.* Los Angeles: University of California Press.

Marx, Karl. 1975. *Economic and Philosophic Manuscripts of 1844.* Moscow: Foreign Languages Publishing House.

Mason, Leonard. 1967. *The Swampy Cree: A Study of Acculturation.* National Museums of Canada Anthropology Papers 13.

Masson, L. R., ed. 1889–90. *Les Bourgeois de la Compagnie du Nord-Ouest.* 2

vols. Québec: Impr. Générale.

Mauss, Marcel. 1954 [1925]. *The Gift: Forms and Functions of Exchange in Archaic Societies*. London: Cohen and West.

Meillassoux, Claude. 1973. On the mode of production of the hunting band. *In* P. Alexandre, ed., *French Perspectives in African Studies*. London: Oxford University Press.

Merasty, Marie. 1974. *The World of Wetiko: Tales From the Woodland Cree*. Edited by C. Savage. Saskatoon: Saskatchewan Indian Cultural College.

Mertz, Elizabeth, and Richard Parmentier, eds. 1985. *Semiotic Mediation: Sociocultural and Psychological Perspectives*. Orlando: Academic Press.

Meyer, David. 1987. Time depth of the Western Wood Cree occupation of Northern Ontario, Manitoba, and Saskatchewan. *In* W. Cowen, ed., *Papers of the 18th Algonquian Conference*. Ottawa: Carleton University.

Morantz, Toby. 1983. *An Ethnohistorical Study of Eastern James Bay Cree Social Organization, 1700–1850*. Ottawa: National Museums of Canada.

Morton, Arthur S. 1973. *A History of the Canadian West to 1870*. Toronto: University of Toronto Press.

Mosko, Stephen. 1987. The symbols of "forest": A structural analysis of Mbuti culture and social organization. *American Anthropologist* 89(4):896–913.

Murphy, Robert. 1970. Basin ethnography and ethnological theory. *In* E. H. Swanson, ed., *Languages and Cultures of Western North America*. Pocatello: Idaho State University Press.

Nelson, Richard. 1983. *Make Prayers to the Raven*. Chicago: University of Chicago Press.

Ortner, Sherry. 1984. Theory in anthropology since the sixties. *Comparative Studies in Society and History* 26(1):126–166.

Paget, Amelia M. 1909. *The People of the Plains*. Toronto: Ryerson.

Paine, Robert. 1973. Animals as capital. *In* B. Cox, ed., *Cultural Ecology*. Toronto: Carleton Library.

Peirce, Charles Sanders. 1960–1966. *Collected Papers of Charles Sanders Peirce*. Vols. 1–6. Edited by C. Hartshorne and P. Weiss. Cambridge: Harvard University Press.

Pentland, David. 1976. In defense of Edward Umfreville. *In* W. Cowan, ed., *Papers of the 7th Algonquian Conference, 1975*. Ottawa: Carleton University.

———. 1978. An historical overview of Cree dialects. *In* W. Cowan, ed., *Papers of the 9th Algonquian Conference, 1977*. Ottawa: Carleton University.

———. 1981a. Synonymy, West Main Cree. *In* J. Helm, ed., *Handbook of North American Indians*. Vol. 6, Subarctic. Washington, D.C.: Smithsonian Institution.

———. 1981b. Synonymy, Western Woods Cree. *In* J. Helm, ed., *Handbook of North American Indians*. Vol. 6, Subarctic. Washington, D.C.: Smithsonian Institution.

Petitot, Émile. 1886. *Traditions Indiennes du Canada Nord-Ouest: Legendes et Traditions des Cris*. Paris: Maisonheure Freres et Ch. Leclerc.

Polanyi, Michael. 1968. *Primitive, Archaic, and Modern Economies*. Edited by G. Dalton. Garden City: Anchor Books.

Preston, Richard. 1975. *Cree Narrative: Expressing the Personal Meaning of*

Events. National Museum of Man Mercury Series, Canadian Ethnology Service Paper 30.

———. 1976. Reticence and self-expression: A study of style in social relationships. *In* W. Cowan, ed., *Papers of the 7th Algonquian Conference, 1975.* Ottawa: Carleton University.

———. 1978. Ethnographic reconstruction of witigo. *In* W. Cowan, ed., *Papers of the 9th Algonquian Conference, 1977.* Ottawa: Carleton University.

Radcliffe-Brown, A. R. 1933. *The Andaman Islanders.* Cambridge: Cambridge University Press.

Radisson, Pierre Esprit. 1943 [1853]. *Voyages of Peter Esprit Radisson.* Edited by G. Scull. New York: Peter Smith.

Rappaport, Roy. 1984. *Pigs for the Ancestors.* New Haven: Yale University Press.

Ray, Arthur J. 1974. *Indians in the Fur Trade.* Toronto: University of Toronto Press.

———. 1975. Some conservation schemes of the Hudson's Bay Company, 1821–50. *Journal of Historical Geography* 1(1):49–68.

———. 1978. Competition and conservation in the early subarctic fur trade. *Ethnohistory* 25(4):347–357.

———. 1984. Periodic shortages, native welfare, and the Hudson's Bay Company, 1670–1930. *In* S. Krech, ed., *The Subarctic Fur Trade: Native Social and Economic Adaptations.* Vancouver: University of British Columbia Press.

Ray, Arthur J., and Donald Freeman. 1978. *Give Us Good Measure: An Economic Analysis of Relations between the Indians and the Hudson's Bay Company before 1763.* Toronto: University of Toronto Press.

Rich, E. E. 1960. Trade habits and economic motivation among the Indians of North America. *Canadian Journal of Economics and Political Science* 26:35–53.

Richards, Audrey. 1932. *Hunger and Work in a Savage Tribe: A Functional Study of Nutrition among the Southern Bantu.* London: Routledge.

Ricklefs, Robert. 1973. *Ecology.* Newton, Mass.: Chiron.

Robertson Smith, W. 1957. *The Religion of the Semites.* New York: Meridian.

Robson, Joseph. 1965 [1752]. *An Account of Six Years Residence in Hudson's Bay from 1733 to 1736 and 1744 to 1747.* Toronto: Johnson Reprint Company.

Rogers, Edward S. 1963. *The Hunting Group–Hunting Territory Complex among the Mistassini Indians.* National Museums of Canada Bulletin 195, Anthropological Series 63. Ottawa: National Museums of Canada.

———. 1973. *The Quest for Food and Furs: The Mistassini Cree, 1953–1954.* National Museum of Man Publications in Ethnology 8. Ottawa: National Museums of Canada.

Rogers, Edward S., and Mary Black. 1976. Subsistence strategy in the fish and hare period, northern Ontario: The Weagamow Ojibwa, 1880–1920. *Journal of Anthropological Research* 32(1):1–43.

Rohrl, Vivian. 1970. A nutritional factor in windigo psychosis. *American Anthropologist* 72(1):97–101.

Rosaldo, Michelle, and Jane Atkinson. 1975. Man the hunter and woman:

Metaphors for the sexes in Ilongot magical spells. *In* R. Willis, ed., *The Interpretation of Symbolism*. New York: John Wiley.

Rossignol, Marius. 1938. Religion of the Saskatchewan and Western Manitoba Cree. *Primitive Man* 11(3–4):67–71.

———. 1939. Property Concepts among the Cree of the Rocks. *Primitive Man* 12(3):61–70.

Rousseau, Jacques. 1952. Le Dualisme religieux des peuplades de la forêt boréale. *Proceedings of the 29th International Congress of Americanists*. Vol. 2. New York.

Russell, Frank. 1898. *Explorations in the Far North*. Iowa City: University of Iowa Press.

Sahlins, Marshall. 1972. *Stone Age Economics*. Chicago: Aldine.

———. 1976. *Culture and Practical Reason*. Chicago: University of Chicago Press.

———. 1981. *Historical Metaphors and Mythical Realities*. Ann Arbor: University of Michigan Press.

———. 1985. *Islands of History*. Chicago: University of Chicago Press.

Saussure, Ferdinand de. 1966 [1915]. *Course in General Linguistics*. New York: McGraw Hill.

Savard, Remi. 1974. *Carcajou et le Sens du Monde*. Québec: Série Culture Amérindiennes.

———. 1979. *Contes Indiens de la Basse Cote Nord du Saint Laurent*. National Museum of Man Mercury Series, Canadian Ethnology Service Paper 51. Ottawa: National Museums of Canada.

Scott, Colin. 1988. Property, practice and aboriginal rights among Quebec Cree hunters. *In* T. Ingold et al., eds., *Hunters and Gatherers 2: Property, Power, and Ideology*. Oxford: Oxford University Press.

Searle, John. 1976. A classification of illocutionary acts. *Language in Society* 5(1):1023.

Sebag, Lucien. 1964. *Structuralisme et Marxisme*. Paris: Payot.

Semmens, John. 1884. *Mission Life in the Northwest*. Toronto: Methodist Mission Rooms.

Sharp, Henry S. 1979. *Chipewyan Marriage*. National Museum of Man Mercury Series, Canadian Ethnology Service Paper 58. Ottawa: National Museums of Canada.

Silverstein, Michael. 1976. Shifters, linguistic categories, and cultural description. *In* K. Basso and H. Selby, eds., *Meaning in Anthropology*. Albuquerque: University of New Mexico Press.

Simms, S. C. 1906. Myths of the Bungees or Swampy Indians. *Journal of American Folklore* 19:334–340.

Simpson, George. 1931. *Fur Trade and Empire: George Simpson's Journal*. Edited by F. Merk. Cambridge: Harvard University Press.

Singer, Milton. 1984. *Man's Glassy Essence: Explorations in Semiotic Anthropology*. Bloomington: Indiana University Press.

Skinner, Alanson. 1911. Notes on the Eastern Cree and Northern Salteaux. *Anthropological Papers of the American Museum of Natural History* 9(1):1–177.

———. 1914a. Bear customs of the Cree and other Algonkian Indians of Northern Ontario. *Papers of the Ontario Historical Society* 12:203–209.

———. 1914b. Political organization, cults and ceremonies of the Plains Cree. *Anthropological Papers of the American Museum of Natural History* 11:513–542.

———. 1916. Plains Cree tales. *Journal of American Folklore* 29:341–367.

Slobodkin, L. B. 1972. On the inconstancy of ecological efficiency and the form of ecological theories. *Transactions of the Connecticut Academy of Sciences* 44:293–365.

Smith, David M. 1982. *Moose Deer Island House People*. National Museum of Man Mercury Series, Canadian Ethnology Service Paper 81. Ottawa: National Museums of Canada.

Smith, Eric Alden. 1983. Anthropological applications of optimal foraging theory: A critical review. *Current Anthropology* 24(5):625–651.

———. 1991. *Inujjuamiut Foraging Strategies: Evolutionary Ecology of an Arctic Hunting Economy*. New York: Aldine de Gruyter.

Smith, James G. E. 1975. Preliminary notes on the Rocky Cree of Reindeer Lake. *In* D. B. Carlisle, ed., *Contributions to Canadian Ethnology, 1975*. National Museum of Man Mercury Series, Canadian Ethnology Service Paper 31. Ottawa: National Museums of Canada.

———. 1976. Notes on the wittiko. *In* W. Cowan. ed., *Papers of the 7th Algonquian Conference*. Ottawa: Carleton University.

———. 1981. Western Woods Cree. *In* J. Helm, ed., *Handbook of North American Indians*. Vol. 6, Subarctic. Washington, D. C.: Smithsonian Institution.

———. 1987. The Western Woods Cree: Anthropological myth and historical reality. *American Ethnologist* 14(3):434–488.

Southall, Aidan. 1988. On mode of production theory: The foraging mode of production and the kinship mode of production. *Dialectical Anthropology* 12:165–192.

Speck, Frank G. 1915. The family hunting band as the basis of Algonkian social organization. *American Anthropologist* 17(2):289–305.

———. 1935a. *Naskapi: Savage Hunters of the Labrador Peninsula*. Norman: University of Oklahoma Press.

———. 1935b. Penobscot tales and religious beliefs. *Journal of American Folklore* 48:1–107.

———. 1938. Aboriginal conservators. *Audubon Magazine* 40:258–261.

Speck, Frank G., and Loren Eiseley. 1939. The significance of hunting territory systems of the Algonkian in social theory. *American Anthropologist* 41(2):269–280.

Sperber, Dan. 1975. *Rethinking Symbolism*. Cambridge University Press.

Steager, Peter. 1976. The child who was not born naturally. *In* W. Cowan, ed., *Papers of the 7th Algonquian Conference, 1975*. Ottawa: Carleton University.

Stevens, James, ed. 1971. *Sacred Legends of the Sandy Lake Cree*. Toronto: McClelland and Stewart.

Steward, Julian. 1955. *Theory of Culture Change*. Urbana: University of Illinois Press.

Strathern, Marilyn. 1980. No nature, no culture: The Hagen case. *In* C. Mac-

Cormack and M. Strathern, eds., *Nature, Culture and Gender*. Cambridge: Cambridge University Press.

Strong, William D. 1929. Cross cousin marriage and the culture of the northeastern Algonkians. *American Anthropologist* 31:277–288.

Sullivan, Robert J. 1942. The Ten'a Food Quest. Catholic University Publications in Anthropology 11. Washington, D.C.

Swindlehurst, Fred. 1905. Folk-lore of the Cree Indians. *Journal of American Folklore* 18:139–143.

Tambiah, Stanley. 1968. The magical power of words. *Man* 3:175–208.

Tanner, Adrian. 1975. The hidden feast. *Papers of the 6th Algonquian Conference, 1974*. Ottawa: Carleton University.

———. 1979. *Bringing Home Animals: Religious Ideology and Mode of Production of the Mistassini Cree Hunters*. New York: St. Martin's Press.

Tedlock, Dennis. 1983. *The Spoken Word and the Work of Interpretation*. Philadelphia: University of Pennsylvania Press.

Teicher, Bruce. 1960. *Windigo psychosis*. Proceedings of the 1960 Annual Spring Meeting of the American Ethnological Society. Seattle: University of Washington Press.

Testart, Alain. 1981. Pour une typologie des chasseurs-cueilleurs. *Anthropologie et Société* 5(2):177–221.

———. 1982. The significance of food storage among hunter-gatherers: Residence patterns, population densities, and social inequalities. *Current Anthropology* 23(5):523–537.

———. 1988. Some major problems in the social anthropology of hunter-gatherers. *Current Anthropology* 29(1):1–31.

Thompson, David. 1962 [1784–1812]. *David Thompson's Narrative*. Edited by R. Glover. Toronto: Champlain Society.

Thompson, Stith. 1966. *Tales of the North American Indians*. Bloomington: Indiana University Press.

Turner, Lucien M. 1894. Ethnology of the Ungava District. *Annual Reports of the Bureau of American Ethnology 11, 1889–1890*.

Turner, Victor. 1982. *From Ritual to Theatre: The Human Seriousness of Play*. New York: Performing Arts Journal Publications.

Tyrrell, J. B., ed. 1931. *Documents Relating to the Early History of Hudson Bay*. Toronto: Champlain Society.

Umfreville, Edward. 1954 [1790]. *The Present State of Hudson's Bay*. Edited by W. S. Wallace. Toronto: Ryerson Press.

Vandersteene, Roger. 1960. *Wabasca*. Gemmenich, Beligium: Editions O. M. I.

———. 1969. Some Woodland Cree traditions and legends. *Western Canadian Journal of Anthropology* 1(1):40–64.

Vayda, Andrew, and Bonnie McCay. 1975. New directions in ecological anthropology. *In* B. Siegal et al., eds., *Annual Review of Anthropology*. Palo Alto: Annual Reviews.

Vecsey, Christopher. 1980. American Indian environmental religions. *In* C. Vecsey, ed., *American Indian Environments*. Syracuse: Syracuse University Press.

———. 1983. *Traditional Ojibwa Religion and Its Historical Changes*.

392   REFERENCES

Philadelphia: American Philosophical Society.

Voorhis, Paul. 1977. *A Cree Phrase Book Based on the Dialects of Manitoba.* Brandon, Manitoba: Brandon University.

Wagner, Roy. 1977. Scientific and indigenous Papuan conceptualizations of the innate: A semiotic critique of the ecological perspective. *In* T. Bayliss-Smith and R. G. Feachem, eds., *Subsistence and Survival: Rural Ecology in the Pacific.* London: Academic Press.

Waisberg, Leo G. 1975. Boreal forest subsistence and the windigo: Fluctuation of animal populations. *Anthropologica* 17(2):169–186.

Wallace, Anthony F. C. 1958. Dreams and wishes of the soul: A type of psychoanalytic theory among the seventeenth-century Iroquois. *American Anthropologist* 60(2):234–248.

Waterman, T. T. 1914. The explanatory element in the folktales of the North American Indians. *Journal of American Folklore* 27:1–54.

Watkins, E. A., et al. 1938. *A Dictionary of the Cree Language.* Toronto: Church of England.

Wax, Rosalie, and Murray Wax. 1962. The magical world view. *Journal for the Scientific Study of Religion* 1(2):179–188.

Weber, Max. 1978. *Economy and Society.* 2 vols. Berkeley, Los Angeles, and London: University of California Press.

Winterhalder, Bruce. 1981. Foraging strategies in the boreal forest: An analysis of Cree hunting and gathering. *In* B. Winterhalder and E. A. Smith, eds., *Hunter-Gatherer Foraging Strategies: Ethnographic and Archaeological Analyses.* Chicago: University of Chicago Press.

Winterhalder, Bruce, and Eric Alden Smith, eds. 1981. *Hunter-Gatherer Foraging Strategies: Ethnographic and Archaeological Analyses.* Chicago: University of Chicago Press.

Wolf, Eric. 1982. *Europe and the People without History.* Berkeley, Los Angeles, and London: University of California Press.

Wolfart, H. Christoph. 1973. *Plains Cree: A grammatical study.* Transactions of the American Philosophical Society 63(5).

Woodburn, James. 1972. Ecology, nomadic movement, and the composition of the local group among hunters and gatherers: An East African example. *In* P. J. Ucko et al., eds., *Man, Settlement, and Urbanism.* London: Duckworth.

———. 1980. Hunters and gatherers today and reconstruction of the past. *In* E. Gellner, ed., *Soviet and Western Anthropology.* London: Duckworth.

———. 1982. Egalitarian societies. *Man* 17:431–457.

———. 1988. African hunter-gatherer social organization: Is it best understood as a product of encapsulation? *In* T. Ingold et al., eds., *Hunters and Gatherers: History, Evolution and Social Change.* Vol. 1. New York: Berg.

Yesner, David. 1981. Archaeological applications of optimal foraging theory: Harvest strategies of Aleut hunter-gatherers. *In* B. Winterhalder and E. A. Smith, eds., *Hunter-Gatherer Foraging Strategies: Ethnographic and Archaeological Analyses.* Chicago: University of Chicago Press.

Index